PROFESSIONAL
MOBILE APPLICATION DEVELOPMENT

PROFESSIONAL

Mobile Application Development

PROFESSIONAL

Mobile Application Development

Jeff McWherter
Scott Gowell
David Smith
Lauren Colton
Ameila Marschall-Miller
Adam Ryder

WILEY

John Wiley & Sons, Inc.

Professional Mobile Application Development

Published by
John Wiley & Sons, Inc.
10475 Crosspoint Boulevard
Indianapolis, IN 46256
www.wiley.com

Copyright © 2012 by John Wiley & Sons, Inc., Indianapolis, Indiana

Published simultaneously in Canada

ISBN: 978-1-118-20390-3
ISBN: 978-1-118-22842-5 (ebk)
ISBN: 978-1-118-24068-7 (ebk)
ISBN: 978-1-118-26551-2 (ebk)

Manufactured in the United States of America

10 9 8 7 6 5 4 3 2 1

For general information on our other products and services please contact our Customer Care Department within the United States at (877) 762-2974, outside the United States at (317) 572-3993 or fax (317) 572-4002.

Wiley publishes in a variety of print and electronic formats and by print-on-demand. Some material included with standard print versions of this book may not be included in e-books or in print-on-demand. If this book refers to media such as a CD or DVD that is not included in the version you purchased, you may download this material at http://booksupport.wiley.com. For more information about Wiley products, visit www.wiley.com.

Library of Congress Control Number: 2012940037

To my daughter Abigail Grace: I will help you to
succeed in anything you choose to do in life.
—JEFF MCWHERTER

For Barbara and Charlotte, I couldn't have done it
without you.
—SCOTT GOWELL

ABOUT THE AUTHORS

JEFF MCWHERTER wrote Chapters 2, 7, 9 and 12. He is a partner at Gravity Works Design and Development and manages the day-to-day activities of the development staff. Jeff graduated from Michigan State University with a degree in Telecommunications, and has 15 years of professional experience in software development. He is a founding member of the Greater Lansing Users for .NET (GLUG.net). He enjoys profiling code, applying design patterns, finding obscure namespaces, and long walks in the park. His lifelong interest in programming began with a *Home Computing Magazine* in 1983, which included an article about writing a game called Boa Alley in BASIC. Jeff currently lives in a farming community near Lansing, MI. When he is not in front of the computer he enjoys Lego, Snowboarding, board games, salt-water fish and spending time with his beautiful wife Carla and daughter Abigail Grace.

SCOTT GOWELL wrote Chapters 1, 6 and 10. He is Senior Developer at Gravity Works Design and Development. Scott graduated from Northern Michigan University with a degree in Network Computing, and has been working as a professional in software development since Spring of 2003. Scott lives with his wife Barbara and their daughter Charlotte. When not working he loves spending time with his family, playing with Duplo and dinosaurs or snuggling up on the couch to watch a movie.

DAVID SILVA SMITH wrote Chapter 3. Dave is Director of Business Development at Gravity Works Design and Development. Dave has been creating websites and writing code since he was in 7th grade. Dave is happy he can use his technology skills to work with customers proposing solutions to their problems and proposing ways for them to capitalize on business opportunities. Dave graduated from Michigan State University and serves as a board member on a number of professional organizations in the Lansing area. When Dave is not working he enjoys spending time with his son Colin. Dave also enjoys playing football, basketball, and volleyball.

LAUREN THERESE GRACE COLTON wrote Chapter 4. Lauren is a geek fascinated by how people interact with technology to find and use information. A graduate of James Madison College at Michigan State University, her editorial work includes the *International Encyclopedia of the Social Sciences* and the *Encyclopedia of Modern China*. During much of her time spent working on this book, her husband Adam was cooking homemade pizza, while her lovely pit bulls Maggie and Beatrice cuddled at her feet.

AMELIA MARSCHALL-MILLER wrote Chapter 5. Amelia is Partner and Creative Director at Gravity Works Design and Development. She holds a Bachelors degree from Northern Michigan University in Graphic Design and Marketing. Amelia has over five years of graphic and web design experience and is continually exploring the latest techniques in website design. She has spoken at regional and national conferences about front end web technologies, including HTML5, CSS3, and the mobile web. She is one of the rare designers who likes to code. (Or, one of the rare coders who likes to design!) When she is not designing or building websites, Amelia enjoys swimming and competing in triathlons, and going on camping and ski trips with her husband John.

ADAM RYDER wrote Chapter 11. He is a developer at Gravity Works Design and Development. He has a Bachelors of Science from Lake Superior State University in Computer Science. When Adam is not working he enjoys spending time with his family. He fishes regularly and spends time camping in Michigan's State Park system with his fiancée, Alicia, and yellow lab, Jasper.

CREDITS

EXECUTIVE EDITOR
Carol Long

PROJECT EDITOR
Brian Herrmann

TECHNICAL EDITOR
Al Scherer

PRODUCTION EDITOR
Christine Mugnolo

COPY EDITOR
Kimberly A. Cofer

EDITORIAL MANAGER
Mary Beth Wakefield

FREELANCER EDITORIAL MANAGER
Rosemarie Graham

ASSOCIATE DIRECTOR OF MARKETING
David Mayhew

MARKETING MANAGER
Ashley Zurcher

BUSINESS MANAGER
Amy Knies

PRODUCTION MANAGER
Tim Tate

VICE PRESIDENT AND EXECUTIVE GROUP PUBLISHER
Richard Swadley

VICE PRESIDENT AND EXECUTIVE PUBLISHER
Neil Edde

ASSOCIATE PUBLISHER
Jim Minatel

PROJECT COORDINATOR, COVER
Katie Crocker

PROOFREADER
Mark Steven Long

INDEXER
Robert Swanson

COVER DESIGNER
LeAndra Young

COVER IMAGE
© iStock / kokouu

ACKNOWLEDGMENTS

THE SUCCESS OF THIS BOOK came from the dedication of the entire team at Gravity Works Design and Development. With Jeff and Scott acting as lead authors and co-conductors, an orchestra of highly passionate individuals — Amelia, Lauren, Dave, and Adam — spent countless hours researching and working on portions of this book to ensure it maintained high standards and contained expertise on topics from those who know them best. Professional Mobile Application Development provides the collective knowledge from all of us at Gravity Works.

Throughout the years, the whole Gravity Works team has had the opportunity to attend hundreds of conferences and user groups targeted at developers, designers, and user interface experts. It is at these events that we meet other passionate people and learn new things. We would like to thank the organizers of these events, and encourage others to host more events on emerging technologies.

Finally, a huge thank you to our families. Your patience while we worked late nights and weekends at Gravity Works, in local coffee shops, and on our kitchen tables will not be forgotten!

CONTENTS

INTRODUCTION

IN RECENT YEARS, MOBILE DEVICES have gained popularity due to lower costs, small and sleek sizes, and the capability to act as a computer with you at all times. The increased use of mobile devices has created new issues for developers and network administrators, such as how to secure the devices, how to deal with increases in bandwidth, and how to make existing codebases usable on a device ten times smaller than it was designed for.

This book discusses these problems and many more, with a detailed overview of how to get started developing for a variety of mobile devices. If you are reading this, you are interested in learning about mobile development; we hope to give you the information and tools to start down the best path to develop a mobile application.

Who This Book Is For

This book is targeted at anyone interested in mobile development. We assume the reader is a technical professional with some type of development experience during their career.

Whether you are a developer or a manager, this book explains key concepts and basic platform requirements for creating mobile applications.

What This Book Covers

Professional Mobile Application Development covers the key concepts needed to develop mobile apps and mobile websites, using a variety of platforms and technologies:

➤ Whether to develop an app or a mobile website

➤ Why a mobile presence is important

➤ Mobile user interfaces design concepts

➤ Creating mobile web apps using responsive techniques

➤ Creating web services on the Microsoft stack for mobile consumption

➤ Creating web services on the Linux stack for mobile consumption

➤ Basics of Objective C

➤ Developing an iOS app from start to finish

➤ Basics of the Android SDK

➤ Developing a BlackBerry Java app

➤ Developing a BlackBerry WebWorks app

➤ Windows Phone 7 development

➤ Basic Java Script development

➤ Creating an app with PhoneGap

➤ Working with the Titanium framework to create an app

Each chapter discusses the tools, techniques, best practices, advantages, and disadvantages of each mobile development platform.

How This Book Is Structured

Many readers of *Professional Mobile Application Development* will not have any experience with creating any type of mobile application, whereas others may have experience with some types of mobile platforms presented in this book. After the first few chapters, which are aimed at high-level design and platform decisions, this book is intended to allow a reader to "flip around" and read about mobile development for the platforms that are relevant to them, independent of other chapters.

Chapter 1: Preliminary Considerations

This chapter starts with an introduction to what it takes to develop mobile apps. Mobile development is a hot trend right now, and many companies are jumping in, spending time developing a mobile strategy. With so many options available to develop mobile apps, this chapter discusses these options, weighing advantages and disadvantages.

Chapter 2: Diving into Mobile: App or Website?

One of the most heated topics in the mobile world today is whether to design a mobile app or a mobile website, and this chapter is devoted entirely to this topic. After reading this chapter, you will have a good understanding of when you should develop a mobile app, and when a mobile website is sufficient.

Chapter 3: Creating Consumable Web Services for Mobile Devices

Most mobile apps share data and need a way to persist this data to a server. In recent years, the bandwidth that mobile apps use has increased drastically. This chapter discusses how to create services that your mobile app can consume. It discusses various options on both Windows and UNIX platform stacks.

Chapter 4: Mobile User Interface Design

Mobile interfaces are a young medium, and difficult: designers work with a telescoped view of almost limitless information. The constraints of this rapidly growing context give teams the opportunity to focus and innovate as devices and best practices evolve. This chapter gives an in-depth look at mobile design patterns and usability practices.

Chapter 5: Mobile Websites

With the growing use of mobile devices for everyday web browsing, it's important to provide website interfaces that are easy to use on these devices. From mobilizing an existing website to designing a completely new one, this chapter discusses tools and techniques to create mobile websites.

Chapter 6: Getting Started with Android

Currently Android holds the top spot in mobile device market share. Android development should be at the forefront of your mobile app strategy. This chapter discusses what it takes to get started developing apps on the Android platform. From start to finish, it provides all the resources for a developer who has never developed on the Android platform to deploy an app.

Chapter 7: Getting Started with iOS

iPhones and iPads have become the devices that many people compare other mobile devices to. Apple devices helped launch the mobile trend, but many developers are hesitant to start developing for iOS because of the tools that Apple provides. This chapter will help alleviate your worries, and provide clear examples of what it takes to develop an iOS app from start to finish and deploy to iTunes.

Chapter 8: Getting Started with Windows Phone 7

Windows Phone 7 is considered the new kid on the block when it comes to mobile platforms. Even though the market share is low, it is climbing fast, and is important to include within your mobile app strategy. This chapter covers everything you need to create a Windows Phone 7 app from start to finish and deploy to the market.

Chapter 9: Getting Started with BlackBerry

This chapter provides the reader with the knowledge of the necessary tools required to develop mobile apps for the BlackBerry platform. Even though BlackBerry has lost market share in recent years, it's still important to understand where BlackBerry fits within your mobile strategy.

Chapter 10: Getting Started with Appcelerator Titanium

This chapter is the first chapter in which mobile apps are created using a framework instead of the native tools. Appcelerator Titanium enables developers to create cross-platform mobile apps using JavaScript. This chapter explores tools and best practices that will enable you to start developing with Titanium in no time.

Chapter 11: Getting Started with PhoneGap

PhoneGap enables developers to create cross-platform mobile apps using HTML and JavaScript. Because of this, PhoneGap is an excellent solution for developers with HTML and JavaScript experience. This chapter explores this platform in depth and what it takes to get started developing with PhoneGap.

Chapter 12: Getting Started with MonoTouch and Mono for Android

The final chapter of this book looks at developing iOS and Android apps using the Mono development stack. Using Mono enables developers to create mobile apps using C#, which is an appealing option for cross-platform mobile development, especially in environments where developers are proficient in C#.

CONVENTIONS

To help you get the most from the text and keep track of what's happening, we've used a number of conventions throughout the book.

 Warnings hold important, not-to-be-forgotten information that is directly relevant to the surrounding text.

 Notes indicates notes, tips, hints, tricks, and asides to the current discussion.

As for styles in the text:

> ➤ We *highlight* new terms and important words when we introduce them.
> ➤ We show keyboard strokes like this: Ctrl+A.
> ➤ We show filenames, URLs, and code within the text like so: `persistence.properties`.
> ➤ We present code in two different ways:

```
We use a monofont type with no highlighting for most code examples.
```

```
We use bold to emphasize code that is particularly important in the present context
or to show changes from a previous code snippet.
```

SOURCE CODE

As you work through the examples in this book, you may choose either to type in all the code manually, or to use the source code files that accompany the book. All the source code used in this book is available for download at `www.wrox.com`.

And a complete list of code downloads for all current Wrox books is available at www.wrox.com/dynamic/books/download.aspx.

 Because many books have similar titles, you may find it easiest to search by ISBN; this book's ISBN is 978-1-118-20390-3.

Most of the code on www.wrox.com is compressed in a .ZIP, .RAR archive, or similar archive format appropriate to the platform. Once you download the code, just decompress it with an appropriate compression tool.

ERRATA

We make every effort to ensure that there are no errors in the text or in the code. However, no one is perfect, and mistakes do occur. If you find an error in one of our books, like a spelling mistake or faulty piece of code, we would be very grateful for your feedback. By sending in errata, you may save another reader hours of frustration, and at the same time, you will be helping us provide even higher quality information.

To find the errata page for this book, go to www.wrox.com and locate the title using the Search box or one of the title lists. Then, on the book details page, click the Book Errata link. On this page, you can view all errata that has been submitted for this book and posted by Wrox editors. A complete book list, including links to each book's errata, is also available at www.wrox.com/misc-pages/booklist.shtml.

 A complete book list including links to errata is also available at www.wrox.com/misc-pages/booklist.shtml.

If you don't spot "your" error on the Book Errata page, go to www.wrox.com/contact/techsupport.shtml and complete the form there to send us the error you have found. We'll check the information and, if appropriate, post a message to the book's errata page and fix the problem in subsequent editions of the book.

P2P.WROX.COM

For author and peer discussion, join the P2P forums at http://p2p.wrox.com. The forums are a web-based system for you to post messages relating to Wrox books and related technologies and interact with other readers and technology users. The forums offer a subscription feature to email you topics of interest of your choosing when new posts are made to the forums. Wrox authors, editors, other industry experts, and your fellow readers are present on these forums.

At http://p2p.wrox.com, you will find a number of different forums that will help you, not only as you read this book, but also as you develop your own applications. To join the forums, just follow these steps:

1. Go to http://p2p.wrox.com and click the Register link.

2. Read the terms of use and click Agree.

3. Complete the required information to join, as well as any optional information you wish to provide, and click Submit.

4. You will receive an email with information describing how to verify your account and complete the joining process.

 You can read messages in the forums without joining P2P, but in order to post your own messages, you must join.

Once you join, you can post new messages and respond to messages other users post. You can read messages at any time on the web. If you would like to have new messages from a particular forum emailed to you, click the Subscribe to this Forum icon by the forum name in the forum listing.

For more information about how to use the Wrox P2P, be sure to read the P2P FAQs for answers to questions about how the forum software works, as well as many common questions specific to P2P and Wrox books. To read the FAQs, click the FAQ link on any P2P page.

Preliminary Considerations

WHAT'S IN THIS CHAPTER?

➤ Reasons to Build a Mobile App

➤ Costs of Developing a Mobile App

➤ Importance of Developing a Mobile Strategy

➤ Difficulties in Mobile App Development

➤ Mobile Application Development Today

➤ Myths of Mobile Application Design

➤ Explanation of Third-Party Mobile Frameworks

This book is for any developer or team that needs to create, refine, or strengthen their mobile development strategy.

From a development team of one to two people to an enterprise-level team with multiple divisions, the topic of mobile development will eventually come up.

The problem is that mobile development is an animal all its own. There is a wide array of platforms, languages, features, and dimensions, and each has its own idiosyncrasies. This book will highlight those issues, and give examples for approaching and working with them. Specifically this book shows you how to develop an application that connects to a remote service and implements device-specific functionality. The book also explains the how and the whys and wherefores of mobile application development.

But first, this book assumes you're here for one of several reasons.

WHY YOU MIGHT BE HERE

As a developer in a competitive market, the following thoughts have almost surely crossed your mind, or they may have been brought to your attention by your managers:

➤ Your competitors have mobile apps, but you don't.

➤ Mobile apps make good business sense.

➤ Your services would add value to a user's mobile experience but your website isn't mobile friendly.

➤ Do you need a mobile application or a mobile website?

The following sections elaborate on these assumptions.

Competition

Do your competitors offer products or services that you do not? Is that why they have an app? Is that a market you want to expand into? If you are already in that market, can you add any features to an app that will have more draw than your competitors? Differentiate yourself by leveraging the technology your customers have available without making it a gimmick. For instance, you could offer location-based incentives: when a customer enters your premises you can have your application display a coupon, discount, or any current promotions. This leverages the device GPS, which isn't something you can get with just a mobile website.

Alternatively, you could offer an augmented reality experience: process the camera input, coupled with GPS, for a layer of information overlaying your products. Taking advantage of all device features requires a mobile application.

Quality vs. Time to Market

Sometimes, a bad mobile application or website can be worse than no mobile app or website. The iTunes App Store is littered with cookie-cutter applications that wrap RSS feed data. Often these cookie-cutter apps lose all branding of a given company, and such applications can negatively impact your reach. Things to consider when looking at developing an app is that in the Android Market, users are given a grace period during which they can request a refund for the full purchase amount. You need to know what you want to deliver, and understand that the way you deliver it makes your customers — and potential customers — know that you are serious.

Legacy System Integration

This gets into enterprise-level development, which is discussed in Chapters 3, 6, and 7. Chapter 3 explains how to use a newer technology, OData, to expose data in a very mobile-consumable fashion. Chapters 6 and 7 explain the pitfalls and caveats to mobile application deployment (as opposed to "development"), and the limitations to overcome when developing inside the company intranet bubble.

Mobile Web vs. Mobile App

You may not need a mobile application; you may need a mobile website. Chapter 2 discusses how to determine whether you need a mobile website or a mobile app more in depth.

Now that the major reasons for looking into mobile app development have been covered, the next section discusses the costs you can expect to incur when taking on mobile application development.

COST OF DEVELOPMENT

There are many costs associated with mobile application development. Each developer will need hardware and software to develop the applications on. The team will need devices to test the software on. And if you want to deploy your application to any public market, then your company will need accounts on the various markets (these often renew annually).

Hardware

To develop good mobile apps, you'll need an Intel-based Mac because, simply put, you won't be able to physically build the iOS implementation of your application without one. The nice thing about the Intel versions of Mac is that you can run Windows on them either virtually (using something like Parallels, or VMWare Fusion) or on the bare metal (using Apple's BootCamp). Expect to spend between $800 (for a refurbished machine) and $1600 (for a brand-new machine).

> *When I started at my current employer, I was given a MacBook Pro that was purchased from the Apple Refurb shop, so it wasn't as expensive as buying a brand-new one. I can say, hands down, it has been the best Windows machine I have ever used. I have developed many mobile applications on it, and am writing this book on it as well.*

In addition to the Mac, you'll also need multiple monitors. When debugging any application, it is invaluable to step through your source while interacting with the running application. When developing, I have the emulator/simulator running in one monitor, My Dev Tool (IDE) running on another, and a web browser on another with the documentation for the platform for which I am developing. Having access to all of this information at once prevents context switching for a developer, and helps maintain focus.

If you are seriously considering mobile development, you need to know that the emulator and simulators are great, but not perfect, so you'll need one of each of the types of devices you want to develop for. I can speak from personal experience: when developing an application, application behavior is not exact from the emulator to the device being emulated. This has happened to me on multiple platforms, so I cannot say that this is more prone to happen on one versus another. Here are some examples of devices you can use to test the various platforms as well as specific versions.

➤ BlackBerry (6 or 7): BlackBerry Bold 9900

➤ Android 2.2 (Froyo): Motorola Droid 2

➤ Android 3.0 Tablet: Samsung Galaxy Tablet

➤ Apple iPod Touch: iPod Touch 3rd Generation

➤ Apple iPhone (versions 3.x and 4.x) (cell service): iPhone 3GS

➤ Apple iPhone (versions 4 and greater) (cell service): iPhone 4

➤ Apple iPad (WiFi or 3G for cell service testing): iPad 1

➤ Apple iPad (with camera): iPad 2 or iPad 3

➤ Windows Phone 7: Samsung Focus

Software

When developing mobile applications there are few overlaps when it comes to software. To develop for iOS you need a Mac, to develop for BlackBerry you need Windows, for Java-based frameworks use Eclipse. Building HTML for PhoneGap can be done in your text editor of choice. Table 1-1 and the following sections present an outline for what you will need for all of the platforms.

TABLE 1-1: Software Needed for Development

TARGETED FRAMEWORK	SOFTWARE REQUIRED
Window Phone 7	Windows Phone SDK Visual Studio Express Expression Blend for Windows Phone (Windows only)
iOS	xCode 4, iOS SDK xCode 4.1, iOS SDK (on Mac OS X 107) (Mac Only)
Android	Eclipse, Android SDK
BlackBerry	Eclipse, BlackBerry Plugin, BlackBerry Simulator (only works on Windows)
Titanium	Titanium Studio, Titanium Mobile SDK + Android software + iOS software
PhoneGap	PhoneGap Plugin + iOS software (Mac only) + Android software + Windows Phone 7 software (Windows only)
Any Framework Text Editors	TextMate (Mac) Notepad++ (Windows)

Licenses and Developer Accounts

The following table contains information regarding all of the various accounts necessary to develop for each platform and costs associated with such. In most cases you can expect to pay roughly $100 per platform annually for developer accounts.

PLATFORM	URL	CAVEATS
BlackBerry	`http://us.blackberry.com/developers/appworld/distribution.jsp`	
Titanium	`https://my.appcelerator.com/auth/signup/offer/community`	
Windows Dev Marketplace	`http://create.msdn.com/en-US/home/membership`	Can submit unlimited paid apps, can submit only 100 free apps. Cut of Market Price to Store: 30%
Apple iOS Developer	`http://developer.apple.com/programs/start/standard/create.php`	Can only develop ad-hoc applications on up to 100 devices. Developers who publish their applications on the App Store will receive 70% of sales revenue, and will not have to pay any distribution costs for the application.
Android Developer	`https://market.android.com/publish/signup`	Application developers receive 70% of the application price, with the remaining 30% distributed among carriers and payment processors.

Documentation and APIs

What follows are links to the respective technologies' online documentation and APIs. This will be the location for the latest information in the respective technology. Later chapters reference specific code elements. Resources for these code elements can be found at the following websites:

- **MSDN Library:** `http://msdn.microsoft.com/en-us/library/ff402535(v=vs.92).aspx`

- **iOS Documentation:** `http://developer.apple.com/devcenter/ios/index.action`

- **BlackBerry Documentation:** `http://docs.blackberry.com/en/developers/?userType=21`

- **Android SDK Documentation:** `http://developer.android.com/reference/packages.html` and `http://developer.android.com/guide/index.html`

- **PhoneGap Documentation:** `http://docs.phonegap.com/`

- **Titanium API Documentation:** `http://developer.appcelerator.com/apidoc/mobile/latest`

The Bottom Line

Total cost per developer to create, maintain, and distribute mobile applications for all the platforms you can expect to pay a few thousand dollars just for the minimum infrastructure. And this is really the bare minimum for development. Given the opportunity to expand this more I would upgrade the laptop to a MacBook Pro, with plenty of RAM, and upgrade the hard disk drive (HDD) to a solid-state drive (SSD). By making these upgrades you will incur a higher initial cost, but the speed increase compared to the bare bones will recoup that cost, if only in peace of mind. It is difficult to quantify the savings from these upgrades, but developers without them are at a distinct disadvantage.

IMPORTANCE OF MOBILE STRATEGIES IN THE BUSINESS WORLD

If potential customers cannot reach your services, they are lost potential customers. Smartphones, tablets, and other nontraditional devices are pervasive in the market. The onus of responsibility is on developers to help customers get a product anywhere. Whether you're a content provider, product company, or service company, expanding product reach is necessary. And one of the most effective ways to reach farther is to simplify a message so that it can be delivered to a wider audience. As of September 2011, Nielsen reports that 40 percent of all mobile consumers in the United States over the age of 18 have smartphones: `http://blog.nielsen.com/nielsenwire/online_mobile/40-percent-of-u-s-mobile-users-own-smartphones-40-percent-are-android/`.

Wired states as of November 2011 that global smartphone usage has reached 30 percent: `www.wired.com/gadgetlab/2011/11/smartphones-feature-phones/`.

WHY IS MOBILE DEVELOPMENT DIFFICULT?

The simple answer to this question is the same that plagues application developers for Mac and Windows, web developers, and mobile developers as seen from the public eye. So-called killer apps are not defined solely by what they do or how they look, but rather by how they fulfill a need and codify it for the user.

Couple that with the more intimate nature of a mobile application (I touch this and it does what I told it to do), and the more rigid (fixed size) UI design patterns of the mobile device and you get a perfect storm of potential problems.

The good news is that with proper planning and research, you target your potential clients and start imposing your own parameters on the problem at hand, and the rest can be accounted for within that scope.

Some may scoff at the limitations when looking at the resolution offerings made by Apple iOS devices, but these strict requirements afford developers dimensions they can take for granted. In Android development, there are eleven standard potential configurations. Not all potential resolutions are actively being developed and produced, and the Android Development site tracks the progress and adoption of standard screen resolutions by device providers. Unfortunately, this makes finding the lowest common denominator more difficult, which you can see in Figures 1-1 and 1-2.

I have called out Android specifically in the following figures as it has the largest amount of different screen sizes. Additionally, the folks at Android mine this data regularly to provide exactly this type of information to developers. They understand the difficulty of accounting for all the different sizes when creating quality applications. Figure 1-1 is a pie chart that accounts for the different resource and resolution types as perceived on the Android Market. Figure 1-2 simply enumerates all the possible resolutions and pixel densities afforded for Android.

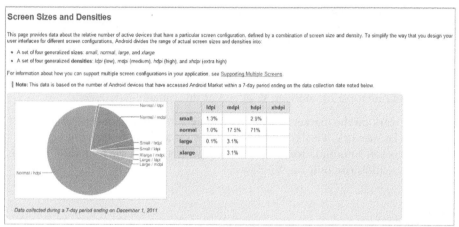

HTTP://DEVELOPER.ANDROID.COM/RESOURCES/DASHBOARD/SCREENS.HTML

FIGURE 1-1: Screen sizes and densities per Google research

	Low density (120), *ldpi*	Medium density (160), *mdpi*	High density (240), *hdpi*	Extra high density (320), *xhdpi*
Small screen	QVGA (240x320)		480x640	
Normal screen	WQVGA400 (240x400) WQVGA432 (240x432)	HVGA (320x480)	WVGA800 (480x800) WVGA854 (480x854) 600x1024	640x960
Large screen	WVGA800** (480x800) WVGA854** (480x854)	WVGA800* (480x800) WVGA854* (480x854) 600x1024		
Extra Large screen	1024x600	WXGA (1280x800)† 1024x768 1280x768	1536x1152 1920x1152 1920x1200	2048x1536 2560x1536 2560x1600

* To emulate this configuration, specify a custom density of 160 when creating an AVD that uses a WVGA800 or WVGA854 skin.
** To emulate this configuration, specify a custom density of 120 when creating an AVD that uses a WVGA800 or WVGA854 skin.
† This skin is available with the Android 3.0 platform

HTTP://DEVELOPER.ANDROID.COM/GUIDE/PRACTICES/SCREENS _ SUPPORT.HTML

FIGURE 1-2: Resolutions available to Android

Mobile development is difficult because the paradigms of design and functionality differ between it and types of development that have existed for decades. It is still new, the technologies change rapidly, and not all of the answers are known. What makes a great app different from a good app? Design? Utility? These are all things to be mindful of while developing your app.

MOBILE DEVELOPMENT TODAY

As it stands, there are really four major development targets. Each of the native frameworks comes with certain expectations and a user base. BlackBerry is often used in education and government, whereas the iPhone and Android user base is far more widespread. Windows Phone 7 being the newcomer is used primarily by developers and hasn't necessarily hit its stride yet.

iOS, the technology that is run on Apple mobile devices, has benefits and limitations specific to its development cycle. The base language is Objective-C, with Cocoa Touch as the interface layer. At this time iOS can be developed only using Apple's XCode, which can run only on a Macintosh.

The Android framework, on the other hand, is written in Java, and can be developed using any Java tools. The specific tooling recommended by Google and the Android community is Eclipse with the Android toolkit, and that is what the examples in Chapter 6 use. Unlike iOS, it can be developed on PC, Mac, or Linux.

Like Android, the BlackBerry device framework is also written in Java; however, it is limited in that the Emulator and Distribution tools run only on Windows at this time.

The newest native framework on the market is Windows Phone 7 and its framework sits on top of the Microsoft's .NET Framework. The language of choice is C# and the framework lies in a subset of Silverlight, Microsoft's multiplatform web technology. It also has the limitation that the Microsoft Windows Phone tools run only on Windows.

MOBILE MYTHS

There are many myths associated with mobile application development. It's cheap, it's easy, it's unnecessary, you can't do it without a large team, and you shouldn't have to pay for it.

Myth #1: It is inexpensive to develop a mobile solution.

As previously mentioned, mobile development is not cheap. This does not include any development time, design time, and deployment time, or any potential money lost by taking too long to get to market. Iterative design and development can be expensive. Finding a happy medium is necessary to be successful when developing a mobile solution.

Myth #2: It's easy to develop a mobile solution.

Future chapters discuss how to leverage existing data, use new technologies to expose that data, interpret the nuances of the native development platforms, and use the newer third-party platforms for mobile application development. In addition, later chapters attempt to make learning these topics easier than just hitting your favorite search engine and looking for tutorials. Each chapter explains each topic; this book hopefully makes the process of developing a mobile application easier. It is in no way easy.

Myth #3: We don't need a mobile presence.

With the smartphone market growing at such a large rate, and the ease with which mobile applications become available (through the market applications on the device and the markets' respective websites) there is a large set of potential customers to reach.

Not everyone needs to become a mobile developer. My urge to learn mobile development came from wanting to track my newborn daughter's sleeping schedule. As new parents, my wife and I needed a solution. Two years later, I do mobile development every day, as my company's clients' needs have expanded into that market.

Myth #4: You need a large development team.

Many single-developer companies are successfully releasing quality applications on the different platform markets. Certainly, a jack-of-all-trades can take an idea from wireframe to market. That being said, without a serious QA resource, development resource, and design resource it can be difficult to break away from the cookie-cutter style of applications very prevalent in the market.

Myth #5: Sweat equity can pay for the application.

Not to disparage the act of creating a startup, and not to fly in the face of innovation, but potential and dreams do not always a fortune make. Working with a partner to develop a product or solution with no capital is not easy.

You've already seen the examples of what expenses to account for and resources to acquire when starting the development process. If you already have these resources, you are probably already an application developer, most likely with a 9-to-5 job or working as a contractor. There are 24 hours in the day, but they are not all billable. Eventually, something has to give; when bills come in it is generally the "side project" that falls by the wayside. Think about that before you get started. Good luck if you start on the road to becoming a contractor — it is not an easy path to travel.

Now that you know what mobile technologies are out there, and that you understand the various myths surrounding mobile development, the next section explains the other options developers have for creating apps and elaborates on the "build one, deploy everywhere" development case.

THIRD-PARTY FRAMEWORKS

There are a number of third-party frameworks for mobile development. The idea of the "write once and deploy to many languages" is the key force driving these frameworks. There are a few different types: interpreted, translated, and web. *Translated* frameworks take a single language and use a one-for-one replacement to develop a binary in the native language. *Web* frameworks use the native language's control for displaying web content, and stick developer-generated HTML web applications in it. They also use plugins to afford native device functionality inside the web application. Lastly are the *interpreted* frameworks: Right now the Mono products are the only ones that fall into this category. They use a rewrite of the .NET Framework to interpret the code in a native application.

Appcelerator Titanium Mobile Framework

Released in December 2008, with support for iOS 5 and Android 4.0, Appcelerator is also looking to release a version that will build and deploy to BlackBerry. The framework heavily utilizes a JavaScript API, and the build process creates source code in the languages you build to. iOS gets an Objective-C source and project binary, and Android gets a compressed Java source and project binary. Titanium effectively translates its specific JavaScript objects into native objects (where possible). Specific implementations are explained in Chapter 10.

Nitobi PhoneGap

Released in March 2009, Nitobi was acquired by Adobe in late 2011. It's now up to version 1.2, with support for iOS, Android, BlackBerry, WebOS, Symbian, and Windows Phone 7. This framework uses standard HTML5 and CSS3 elements wrapped in the native web browser controls to simulate a native application, which is discussed in Chapter 11.

MonoDroid and MonoTouch

This newly formed company is made up of the original Ximian Team — after being acquired by Novell. Later discontinued by Attachmate, Xamarin is now the developers and maintainers of the MonoTouch and MonoDroid products. The Mono project itself is an open source implementation of the .NET Framework so that C#-based .NET applications can be developed on systems other than Windows.

MonoTouch

Initially developed by the Mono Team, MonoTouch was their way of developing iOS apps using .NET and specifically the Mono Framework. First released in Q3 2009, the Mono Team has been actively maintaining the project, and version 5 released Q3 2011 includes iOS 5 support.

MonoDroid

Compared to MonoTouch, this project is in its relative infancy, with the first major release in Q2 2011. MonoDroid enables users to develop and distribute Android applications using Windows and the Visual Studio environment.

SUMMARY

Upon finishing this chapter, you should feel comfortable with your knowledge of what technologies exist to develop mobile applications, and what resources you need to develop for the platform or platforms of your choosing. You should be familiar with the myths that surround developing for mobile apps, and the difficulties generally associated with mobile app development. You should know about the seven frameworks that will be covered in later chapters. You may also be asking yourself after all this if you even need a mobile application. Chapter 2 illustrates reasons that require creating an app, and what you can do with a well-crafted mobile website.

2

Diving into Mobile: App or Website?

Unless you have been living under a rock for the past three years, you know that mobile applications are the hottest technology since websites became popular in the dot-com boom of the late 1990s. Both of these technology explosions have similar traits, mainly revolving around people, companies, and developers trying to adapt to new technology and learning only enough to get the project done. Many developers read comics that poke fun of upper management learning buzzwords, from virtualization to cloud computing. If you are reading this book someone probably approached you with an idea to create a mobile application.

The parallels of the dot-com boom to the mobile boom start with nontechnical upper management and toys. In the late 1990s the toy was the Internet, and today it's the iDevice. iDevices like the iPad and iPhone are making their way into upper-management hands; they like the ease of use, and feel that every application should be developed with a user interface that is as easy to use as the iDevices. Whether it's a web app or desktop app, in most situations, entire user interfaces must be rewritten to get this type of user experience. I have worked with a few companies where the decision makers have completely replaced desktop computers with tablet computers. This creates a great number of issues for the IT staff. In many situations, these companies have a good point about the interfaces and applications that newer mobile devices contain, but dumping the trusty laptop for an iPad as a primary work machine may not pan out: try working on complex spreadsheets with a tablet.

With increasing pressure from management for mobile-device support, does it make sense to build a native application, or can you get away with a mobile website? Many times it does not make sense to spend the time and money it takes to create a mobile application if a mobile website will fulfill the needs of the user. It's just a matter of convincing upper management that they really don't need that new shiny app.

Before dismissing the brilliant idea of the person who signs your paychecks, the following sections compare when it makes sense to create a mobile application, and when a mobile website will suffice.

MOBILE WEB PRESENCE

It's not a matter of *if* you need a mobile web presence, it's a matter of how fast can you get it done. In 2010, more than 63 million people in the United States accessed the Internet from a mobile device, as shown in Figure 2-1. Technology research firm Gartner states there will be more than 1.7 billion mobile Internet users worldwide by 2013. Without a mobile web presence, you are missing out on customers; if you do not have a mobile web presence, your competitors will. Establishing a mobile presence early could get you an important head start in a fast-growing technology.

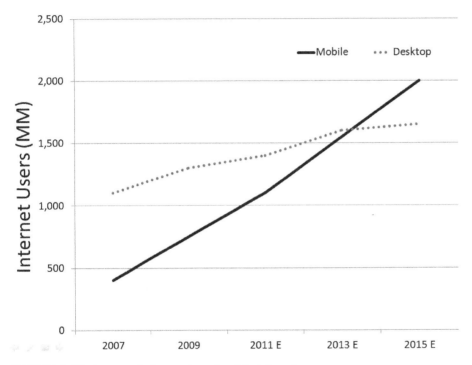

FIGURE 2-1: The increase in the number of mobile Internet users

Looking through the Google Analytics of more than 60 websites that we work with, the percentage of mobile traffic was about 19 percent in 2011. Across the Internet, this tends to be on the high end, with most others reporting between 10 and 15 percent. With mobile traffic as high as it is, and growing more popular, it is time to have a mobile website.

Most reputable companies have a website, but many do not translate very well to a mobile device. A mobile web presence takes the desktop site content and renders the information to be easily consumed on a mobile device. In recent years, Internet users and customers have begun to relate the look of a company website to how reputable a business is. Although not always the case, a well-developed and maintained website with fresh content informs the user or customer that the company cares about them, and wants to make sure they have the tools needed to comfortably do business.

Mobile Content

A mobile website experience is significantly different from the desktop view. With a limited screen size, new usability techniques have been developed to help people view and navigate data. Mobile web browsers do the best job they can, providing rich tools for panning and zooming through a website, but commonly used, complex drop-down menus make mobile navigation troublesome.

Navigation is one of the most important, and often most difficult, areas of mobile website design. It's common to present users with thinned-down content they can access on a mobile device. When in the planning stages of your mobile website project, plan for time to develop a content strategy. Chapter 4 discusses mobile content in greater detail. Figure 2-2 is an example of a company with a great deal of content on its normal website. A drop-down menu with multiple levels would not provide the best interaction on a mobile device. Figure 2-3 is the mobile rendering.

FIGURE 2-2: Desktop website of a commercial site

FIGURE 2-3: Mobile version of site shown in Figure 2-2

Mobile Browsers

Let's give credit where credit is due: to the developers of mobile web browsers. Mobile browsers have been built to render websites not intended to be displayed on small devices; tools to zoom, pan, scroll, and highlight links help make browsing normal websites more tolerable. Figure 2-4 shows the top five mobile browsers. In 2011 notice the increase of usage from the Android browser and the decrease of usage from the BlackBerry browser, which coincides with the Android bumping BlackBerry off the top spot for market share for mobile devices in 2011.

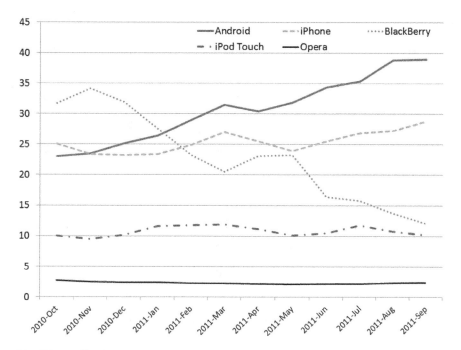

FIGURE 2-4: Top five mobile browsers

Symbian OS has not been discussed thus far, and it won't be discussed in much detail. Symbian is a mobile device OS owned by Accenture. It is found on many devices, and does have quite a large market share, but the development experience for the device is difficult. The Opera Mini browser shows up in numerous builds of the Symbian OS.

Table 2-1 shows the mobile browser share throughout the world. It's important to know this share as well. Different countries favor different devices. For example, if most of your customers are in the South America, you may want to ensure your mobile website renders well on Symbian devices.

TABLE 2-1: Mobile OS Market Share by Country as of February 2012

COUNTRY	APPLE	BLACKBERRY	ANDROID	OTHER	SYMBIAN
USA	43	7	40	10	
Brazil			18	42	40
Russia	11		19	29	41
UK	41	33	21	5	

continues

TABLE 2-1 *(continued)*

COUNTRY	APPLE	BLACKBERRY	ANDROID	OTHER	SYMBIAN
Germany	47		39	9	5
Peru	12		45	20	23
Japan	48		46	6	
Argentina	12		44	12	32
France	56		31	9	4
Mexico	25		24	26	25
South Korea	9		90	1	
Spain	38		48	6	8
Australia	73		20	3	4
China	12		33	26	40

HTTP://CONNECT.ICROSSING.CO.UK/WP-CONTENT/UPLOADS/2012/02/ICROSSING _ MOBILE-MARKETING _ 2012 _ V2.GIF

Mobile User Browsing Behavior

Not all mobile web presences should be created equally. In order to create a great mobile interface, you should spend time identifying behaviors of mobile users. Even if this phase is just asking a few internal employees, it's important to research how the mobile version of the existing website will differ, and design for that behavior. Chapter 5 discusses strategies to cater to behavior type on a mobile web page in more depth, but an introduction to mobile browsing behavior is necessary here. The following list gives a few reasons why users might need access to your mobile content:

➤ **Repetition:** Users are coming back to your site constantly. It's possible they are sitting on the page and hitting refresh to see new content. The question is, is site content changing frequently enough that users would come back and check for updates? Sports scores, weather reports, and stock quotes are types of content that need to be available, and fast, on mobile devices.

➤ **Boredom:** Maybe users are trying to pass time in the lobby of a doctor's office. They are surfing the web like they do in the comfort of their own home, but in public. They could have heard a radio announcement about a cleaning service and are interested, so they navigate to the company's page to learn more information about the offer while they are passing the time.

➤ **Urgency:** Users are out and about and suddenly have the urge for a hamburger. They need to find the nearest open burger joint.

MOBILE APPLICATIONS

The decision to create a mobile application can be difficult. It's not a decision to rush into, and it requires a great deal of thought. A mobile application can be an opportunity to improve interaction with customers, create brand awareness, and even create additional revenue. But if the objectives of the app are unclear, customers can be upset, and money can be lost.

In a June 2011 study, mobile analytics company Flurry found that time spent using mobile applications surpassed time spent using the mobile browser only in the United States; other countries have not become as "app crazed" as the United States. Figure 2-5 shows these figures. With users spending this much time in mobile applications, it's worthwhile looking into creating a mobile app if your business domain has a good fit.

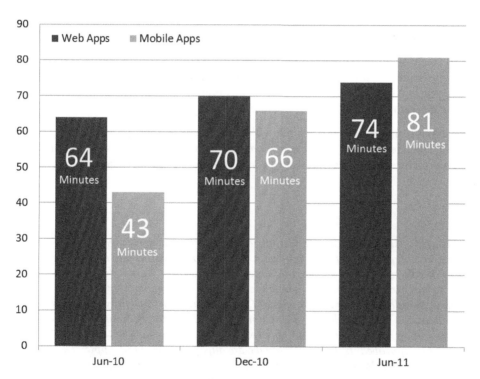

FIGURE 2-5: Mobile browsing behavior in the U.S.

You're a Mobile App If . . .

Developers like to find a definite answer to all of the world's problems, but the world is not as black-and-white as we all may like. This chapter will help provide guidelines for deciding whether to build a native app or mobile web app. The following list provides some scenarios where a native app would be the best solution:

➤ If you require graphics and processing power

➤ If you require the use of the device's camera

➤ If you need to use the device's microphone

➤ If you require access to the device's address book

➤ If you require access to the device's media library

➤ If you will be using the market for payment

➤ If you require use of push notifications

➤ If you need to run as a background service

➤ If you want to design a game

When to Create an App

Deciding when to create an app is difficult. Throughout this chapter, we are working to provide you with facts (and some opinions) to help you make your own decisions. Mobile apps can offer a way for customers to connect with a brand, if done correctly. A pretty UI that offers no value will be rated poorly in the market or iTunes (or, even worse, Apple will reject the app).

Just because you develop an app does not mean it will be successful: it must provide value. We have heard stories of silly app ideas that have made the developer thousands of dollars with minimal effort. Those days are over: for every successful silly app, hundreds more just like it are available for users to choose.

The Apple approval process for mobile applications can be a scary thing. Apple has the power to reject the app that you spent time and money to create if the app does not adhere to Apple's strict guidelines. We have spent a great deal of time reading through the Human Guideline Interface document (a lengthy specification that defines how the UI of an iOS app should work) to fully understand exactly what Apple will and will not allow. Prior to beginning development of an app, we will let our client know if we are concerned that the app may not be approved, but will also say we are always unsure until Apple has approved the app. Most questions arise with membership or subscription-based applications. We also ask that customers plan for three weeks after submission to wait for approval.

Regardless of whether you are just starting to develop a mobile strategy or have been working on it for some time, do not let the allure of a mobile app trap you into making a decision. Figure 2-6 represents a study performed by the Info-tech research group in 2010 (www.transformyx .com/s3web/1002043/docs/mktg-infotech-developmobileapp.pdf) that asked companies, across various industries include health care, manufacturing, and education, about what their plans were in regards to developing a mobile app. The numbers are still quite low, with many organizations still on the fence.

New Revenue Sources

Monetizing your hard work is something all mobile app developers want, whether it's to increase your job security or for personal gain. The mobile trend has opened up new ways for developers/companies to make money off their apps.

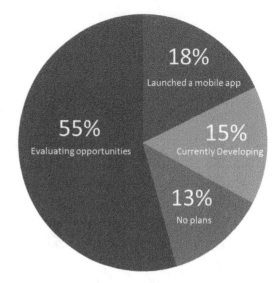

FIGURE 2-6: Plans to develop an app

➤ In-app purchasing for mobile applications has revolutionized digital commerce. People are looking for convenience, and can purchase tangible and digital goods with one click, reducing buyer hesitation. Adobe reports that 62 percent (www.scene7.com/registration/ s7datasheets.asp?id=70130000000kRTrAAM) of consumers with mobile devices are purchasing goods through those mobile devices, which equates to billions in revenue.

A much debated use of in-app purchasing/micropayments was developed within the Smurfs Village app for iOS. The Smurf Village app is a time-elapsed game, targeted at children. To speed up the game, you can purchase Smurf Berries at varying rates from $5 to $99. Think of the amount of damage a small child could do on a Sunday afternoon to your credit card.

➤ With print media on the decline, many traditional media companies have seen the trend that people are purchasing digital content. This has been popular with subscription-based services, such as magazines or newsletters. New tools within both iOS and Android provide APIs to sell content. In some cases, this technology has brought new life to a dying industry.

Types of Mobile Apps

When development of your mobile app is finished and the app is being deployed to the market, you are required to put it into a category within the market to allow users to discover your app more easily. Within all markets, apps are divided into categories, and some categories are more popular than others. It's common across all of the markets to see games being a large percentage of the types of apps available for the platform. Figure 2-7 shows a distribution of apps among the Android Market provided by AndroidZoom.

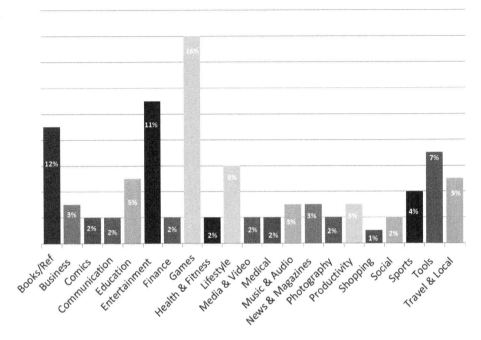

FIGURE 2-7: Types of apps in the markets

Do People Really Want to Put Your App on Their Mobile Device?

A study from Nielsen (http://blog.nielsen.com/nielsenwire/online_mobile/games-dominate-americas-growing-appetite-for-mobile-apps/) across a wide range of phone users have found that iPhone users install the most applications, coming in at 40 apps, as shown in Figure 2-8.

Although users will visit hundreds of websites in a day, they will install only a few apps. Does your app provide enough value that the user is going to take the time to download it and keep it in their list of installed apps? The only way to determine if you app has value is user research. This research can be a simple question/answer session among peers, or could be a formal user research study. User research is discussed more in Chapter 4.

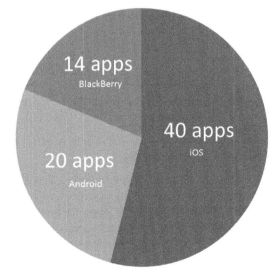

FIGURE 2-8: Average number of apps installed per platform

In case you were wondering, the average creeps up when the target of the study is mobile developers. The iOS users at Gravity Works have an average of 91 apps installed on their iOS devices.

Resources

Do you have the developers on staff to develop the app? If you do not have the staff, are you able to gauge a mobile developer's talent? Are you willing to do what it takes to support the app or should you consider outsourcing the development to a qualified firm? These are some of the questions you need to ask yourself before jumping into creating a mobile app.

Support and Maintenance

Mobile apps are software projects, just like any other. They take care and feeding; a little more than a standard website, in some cases. Mobile development is similar to desktop development in many ways. Once you deploy it, it's deployed and there is not a good way to update the app. You can't force users to get updates to the app, and when they find a bug you fixed two versions ago, they will give you poor feedback in the market. Sure, when you publish an update of your app to the market, it shows up in the available downloads, but most users do not update their apps.

The developer accounts for iOS, Android, and BlackBerry all contain tools that show the stack traces of runtime errors that are uploaded from your app on the customer's phone. Be proactive, and go through the logs and look for errors before someone lets you know about them.

Development of Your Mobile Solution

If you are planning on creating a mobile app, you will more than likely support iOS and Android. Depending on the industry, you may even take on BlackBerry; schools and government agencies are big BlackBerry users. When it comes to the initial development of the app, you have many different choices and development platforms to choose from (native vs. nonnative). Chapters 6–12 discuss these platforms, but from our experience most developers without a C backend will cringe when they hear Objective-C, the language in which native iOS apps are developed. Some platforms allow iOS apps to be created without using Objective-C, but do you have the in-house staff to make these decisions? If you decide that creating mobile apps is part of your strategy, we highly recommend that you spend time with someone who has worked in mobile environments before. Not just a few web videos — actually take the time to sit down with a mobile developer to see the tricks of the trade. Many issues arise with emulators, SDK versions, and small things that are difficult to find in the documentation, that pair programming with someone who has created an app on that platform could point out.

FRAGMENTATION

Because iOS is the hot platform to develop on, many startups and established companies are putting money and resources into creating iOS applications that will be installed on an iDevice. Android is starting to obtain majority market share, and developers are scrambling to port their newly developed apps.

What about Windows Phone 7 and BlackBerry? Do they hold enough market to go through the hassle of more app submission processes? Who is going to write the app and then maintain it when updates to the OS are pushed?

Fragmentation is costly and should be planned for when creating a mobile strategy.

Benefits of a Mobile App

Not only will your marketing department get to brag about your newly developed mobile application using the latest technology, but numerous other reasons exist why it may make sense to develop a mobile app as opposed to a mobile web app.

Make Use of the Native Devices Features

It will always be easier to stretch the hardware boundaries of a mobile app. Great features such as in-app purchasing do not have the same tight integration with the UI and operating system unless you are creating a native app. Even if you decide to go with a nonnative solution such as Titanium, PhoneGap, or MonoTouch, these solutions are slow to adapt new features in a platform's operating system.

Sometimes it's not about being on the bleeding edge of technology; it's just delivering value to your customer.

Offline Content

You may have heard that content is king; it is absolutely true in mobile apps. Many business apps need to display changing data to the user. Depending on the business domain, a mobile web app may not be a good idea. For example, a mobile application that lists all of the state legislators requires the data of the app to come from someplace. The state capital in Michigan does not get reliable cellular coverage, so for this app to function properly, an offline caching strategy should be used. When having the data stored locally, you should also define a strategy on how that offline data is going to be updated. Is it updated when the app is updated through the market or perhaps there a background service that checks to see if the device has access to the Internet, and prompts the user if they would like to obtain a refreshed set of data.

A mobile web app can serve offline content, but these features are new to the HTML5 spec. The offline content features of HTML 5 are discussed in more depth in Chapter 5.

Mobile apps have a long history, and rich set of tools for developers to anticipate the app working without Internet connectivity. Storing settings as user preferences or a more complex solution such as SQLite database will be discussed in depth for each mobile platform in Chapters 6–9.

> *If an app requires an Internet connection, the user must be informed the app will not function properly without it, or the application risks Apple App Store rejection. Features like this help make a better user experience, but make developers upset that they have to do the extra work.*

Richer User Experience

Users generally provide higher ratings for apps that have the native interface. No matter how nice the iOS interface is, if you create an Android app and provide UI elements from iOS, users are more likely to rate your app lower.

Users look for apps that have a UI that is consistent with the rest of the apps on their device. It is possible to create HTML and CSS that provide these interfaces on a mobile web app, but it can get difficult. Many developers opt for creating interfaces that do not resemble iOS, Android, Windows Phone 7, or BlackBerry. It's a design the developer created on their own. Such a design strategy can work, as long as the correct amount of user interface research has been performed. In most cases, however, it's best to just stick with the UI you should be working with, which is the native UI for the platform.

Ease of Discovery

Markets provide a place to present your app to the world. Most users are not using a search engine to find apps for their mobile devices; they are using the built-in search tools within the installed market tool.

Push Notifications

In recent years, text messages (simple message service [SMS]) have become the preferred communication over instant messaging among young people. An instant notification on your mobile device means an immediate response is expected. Push notifications simulate the same behavior of text messages, but are app based. Push notifications alert users of something that they should be aware of instantly: a new e-mail, a new tweet, or some other bit of information that may be important to the app that was downloaded.

Increased Customer Feedback

Businesses often hope to build brand loyalty through apps. When loyalty has been achieved, you can capitalize on this loyalty within the app, asking for feedback about your company. Quick polls, short forms, and rich integration with social media services such as Facebook and Twitter can provide a level of feedback that is not seen with mobile web apps.

MARKETING

After your app is created, you can't just throw it up on a market and expect users to find it. The success of your app may depend on how much marketing you put into it. Rushing an app to the market without a marketing plan could take away from your app performing to its full potential. Although you may have heard success stories where an app was an overnight success, this is not normal. Using advertisements on your existing website, press releases, and mailings to existing customers are all ways to drive interest in your app for potential users. The market is just one tool for mobile marketing; expect to use many tools to make your app a success.

When talking about enterprise apps — apps that are intended for internal employee use — strategies exist to skip the market altogether. They are discussed in Chapters 6–9.

The underlying concepts that drive mobile markets are not new. Amazon and Netflix offer similar concepts in different industries, providing hundreds of thousands of products but perhaps selling only a few copies of certain titles a month. This concept is called *the long tail*, the statistical property that a larger share of a given data set rests within the tail: a good deal of money is made from many products that are purchased only once a month. Figure 2-9 shows that the majority of the total can be calculated not from the items that had the most revenue, but rather from the combination of all the smaller sales.

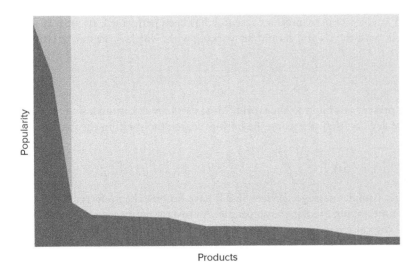

FIGURE 2-9: The long tail

It's important to understand this concept because the long tail statistical property is starting to emerge within mobile markets, meaning not all of the markets' revenue is coming from the most popular titles such as Angry Birds; it's coming from the combined income of the thousands of apps with a smaller following.

DIFFERENTIATING MARKETING AND ADVERTISING

Depending on why you are developing mobile apps, you may need to perform multiple roles. When it comes to marketing, most developers do not even know where to begin.

Advertising is not personal and directed toward the general public. Paid communications such as radio, direct mail, and TV placements are considered advertising.

Marketing is a process. Part of this process contains strategies to find out what products or services will provide value to clients, how to sell to clients, and how to communicate. Advertising is part of the marketing strategy.

Quick Response Codes

Getting the word out about your app is important, and it's important to provide the user with a very simple way to download your app while you have their interest. Typing a long URL in a web browser or remembering the name of your app can be problematic for some users. Quick response (QR) codes provide a means for users to scan an image with their mobile device, and then a web browser will open automatically to the URL embedded within the image.

QR codes were originally created for use in the automobile industry in the early 1990s, but have gained popularity in other industry use. QR codes are a type of matrix barcode, which is a machine-readable representation of data. QR codes can hold a great deal more data than the barcodes most people are accustomed to seeing. Figure 2-10 shows a QR code, with contact information for Gravity Works that could contain a product coupon code.

Another popular alternative to QR codes are Microsoft Tags. A Microsoft Tag is a high capacity color barcode (HCCB), developed by Microsoft. A Tag is web URL encoded as a color image, that when scanned using the Microsoft Tag application sends a request to a Microsoft server, then a redirect to the URL encoded in the image. Figure 2-11 represents an encoded link to the Gravity Works web page.

FIGURE 2-10: QR code

FIGURE 2-11: Microsoft Tag

Not only are QR codes and Microsoft Tags useful for marketing your app, a study from Microsoft (http://blogs.technet.com/b/next/archive/2011/03/22/tag-infographic-shares-revealing-stats-on-mobile-usage.aspx) indicates that 29 percent of smartphone users are open to scanning a mobile tag to get coupon codes. Have you thought about how this feature can help drive business on a mobile website? Have you seen these tags around?

The Advertising You Get from the App Market

iOS users tend to install apps from within iTunes or the App Store directly on their devices. Android users tend to install apps either directly from their device or from the web interface. The App Store (iOS), Market (Android), Market Place (Windows Phone), and App World (BlackBerry) give apps discoverability, and a place where users can search for keywords your app may contain, or possibly stumble on it while browsing through categories. Even in markets with more than 250,000 apps to choose from, users will find apps that are relevant to them.

Unless you are planning an enterprise deployment, these markets are often the only public locations where an app can be downloaded. The markets for the different mobile platforms are all very similar, and this section only briefly examines the marketing tools provided.

iTunes has the clean, functional App Store interface you would expect from Apple. Featured apps appear on the top of the screen, and people browse categories as shown in Figure 2-12. You can download apps in this interface, and they appear on your device the next time synchronization occurs.

FIGURE 2-12: iTunes App Store

The greatest benefit to having your app in the Android Market is discoverability, and the Android Market offers great tools for potential users to find your app; apps are sorted by category and then subcategory so potential users can browse for apps very easily, as shown in Figure 2-13.

FIGURE 2-13: Android Market

Featured Apps

New and Noteworthy, Featured, and Editor's Choice are all market sections that are maintained by the Android Market staff to promote apps. One of the most important differences between the popular apps and the ones you have never heard of before are these sections. Featured sections are the first areas users see when they access the market, and people are inclined to download what other people are downloading. No hard-and-fast rules exist on how to get on one of the featured apps lists, so plan to build the best app you can and create buzz. The staff that selects the apps are advocates for the platform, and are looking for apps that have a great user experience and provide value. Download volume, positive ratings, and artwork are all metrics many speculate are taken strongly into consideration by the market staff who select these apps

Figure 2-14 shows the Featured section of the Android Market on the web. Given the screen shot was taken in late October, you can understand why so many apps relate to Halloween. Some apps have a great deal of downloads, others do not. The one thing all these apps have in common is that they are all well written and perform well because they have been selected as a featured app.

FIGURE 2-14: Android Market Featured section

Having an app featured within the market is something every mobile developer hopes to accomplish. It is somewhat of a mystery how apps magically appear in these lists. Just because your app is well designed, attractive, and provides value does not guarantee it a featured spot.

Description

Your app description may arguably be the most important marketing tool within the market. If users are on the fence about downloading an app, your app description should push them over the fence to download. Figure 2-15 shows the description of the Michigan High School Athletic Association (MHSAA) iOS application. The MHSAA has a huge market: anyone who is interested in high school sports in Michigan. The app description is tailored to that market, providing them with a list of features, and hoping to drum up excitement with catchy text like "MHSAA Mobile lets you pick the lineup." This text is based on the feature that drives the app — the ability to follow a school and receive updates for only that school.

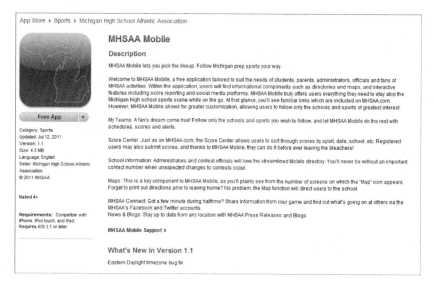

FIGURE 2-15: iOS app description

User Reviews

User reviews can make or break an app; in the mobile world, users are very harsh over all platforms. Having a good rating with positive feedback is what a potential user needs to see to download an app. If you rush to market with your app without thoroughly testing, users will give it poor feedback, and that is a permanent record. Figure 2-16 shows a set of user reviews for the MHSAA mobile application within the iOS App Store.

Customer Ratings

We have not received enough ratings to display an average for the current version of this application.

Rate this application: ★ ★ ★ ★ ★

▼ Average rating for all versions: ★ ★ ★ ★ ☆ 7 Ratings

★★★★★	5
★★★★	0
★★★	1
★★	0
★	1

Customer Reviews

[Current Version (2)] [All Versions (4)]

Sort By: [Most Helpful ▲▼]

[Write a Review ›]

Need people to update scores ★ ☆ ☆ ☆ ☆
by Scott Silberhorn - Version 1.1 - Aug 23, 2011

Report a Concern ›

I want to see real time scores. The announcers should be inputting scores to the app. Good start though.

Was this review helpful? Yes | No

Its a start ★★★ ☆ ☆
by Abletonbuttonmasher - Version 1.1 - Sep 5, 2011

Report a Concern ›

Thank you for getting this app up and running. Is there a way to get this app iPad compatable. As an announcer I would love to input scores as the game is going, similar to what maxprep has. Thanks

Was this review helpful? Yes | No

FIGURE 2-16: User reviews of the MHSAA app in the iOS App Store

With more than 9,000 downloads, the app in Figure 2-16 only has seven reviews. If the app does the job users are looking for, oftentimes they do not rate the app. If the app goes above and beyond, they tend to give positive ratings, and if it does not do everything they hoped it would, negative feedback is given. Negative feedback is often given for features that are not included. The 1-star rating in Figure 2-18 was from a user who wanted real-time score reporting. Based on business knowledge, coordinating every announcer at contests between more than 2,000 schools was too large of an undertaking for this version of the app. Because of this rating, other users may be turned off — not because it does not function, but because of a feature that one user wanted.

User reviews are often subjective, and companies or developers take them personally. It's very common for negative user reviews to be based off functionality the user expects in the app and not how the current app performs.

TRIAGE FROM POOR FEEDBACK

How to handle feedback of an app that has been poorly rated in the market is something that we discuss often. The only way to address poor feedback is with good feedback. When we first release an app to the market, we encourage the client to inform employees, friends, and family to download the application and rate the app with legitimate feedback. It's important to stress legitimate feedback: do not ask for good ratings, just ask for reviews.

We have had situations where apps have been rated poorly because users did not perform updates, or did not understand how the app was supposed to work. Not having to deal with poor feedback is the best option, so test thoroughly and get feedback from friends, family, clients, and colleagues before submitting an app.

Track Your App Sales

Tracking app sales can help provide insight as to where your app should be priced. If you are selling your app, see what the market feels is a reasonable price, and adjust the price of your app. App sales metrics are useful to free apps as well, helping to identify trends based on advertising campaigns and other app marketing Figure 2-17 shows an eight-month period of a 99-cent app, distributed only in the Android Market.

All of the mobile markets provide sales tools similar to the Android tools shown in Figure 2-17. Tracking information, such as which OS version, may help you focus on future development efforts. Meaning if you notice the majority of your Android user base is using Android 2.3, you may want to implement a new feature only included in Android 2.3 or above.

Being able to track sales down to the day will also help with marketing and advertising efforts, comparing sales trends to campaigns.

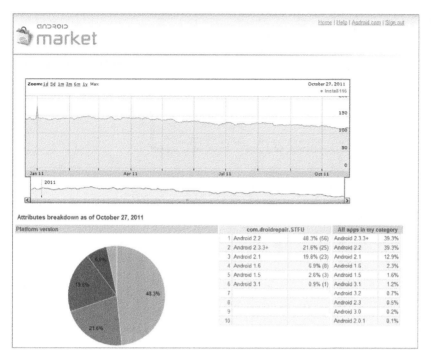

FIGURE 2-17: Android app sales

Knowing Where Your Users Are

Knowing where in the world your app is being used can help advertising and product decisions. If you find that your app is performing well in a specific region, you may decide to make adjustments, such as language localization. Advanced analytics that users may need to opt into will provide a valuable look at where users are, and how they are using your app. Determining which features are being used, when the app is being run, and how often are all valuable tools in a marketer's tool belt.

The platform markets provide some tools, but some apps may require detailed analytics. To get this level of detail, you can use advanced analytics within third-party tools like Flurry (www.flurry.com).

Flurry can be integrated into iOS, Android, Windows Phone 7, and BlackBerry apps via an SDK that is downloaded once you have created a Flurry account. Once you have added the Flurry references to your project, your app will then send detailed data — such as how long the user was using your app, geographic information, and errors — to the Flurry service. From the data that is collected, detailed reports can be generated that contain information such as frequency of app usage. Having detailed information can help you develop your app to fit your customers' needs.

Figure 2-18 shows the Analytics dashboard with a sampling of data you will have access to.

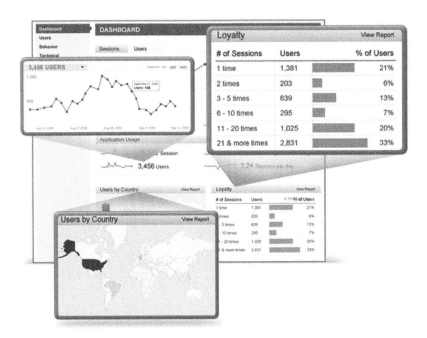

FIGURE 2-18: Flurry analytics

Discoverability

It may be difficult to think that users are sitting around browsing thousands of apps, but it's true. Although one of the lesser value marketing tools, the capability for users to stumble upon your app is important when the app is first released. As mentioned previously, crafting a description with valuable keywords about your app and placing the app in the correct market category will aid in users discovering your app.

Third-Party Markets

Depending on the mobile platform, there may be more than one market to deploy your app to. Third-party markets provide another place for your app to live, in the hopes that someone will discover it. When it comes to the Android platform, some device manufacturers (such as Archos) decide not to integrate with the Google Android Market, and have created their own market. This allows the manufacturers to restrict which apps are allowed into their market, providing users with a limited selection of apps to download.

Although the recommended market may be the easiest way to get apps, third-party markets, two of which are discussed in the following sections, offer benefits as well.

One of the best-known third-party markets is the Amazon App Store for Android. The Amazon App Store provides an online and mobile interface for users to purchase apps. Apps on the Amazon App Store are often cheaper than the same app in the Google Android Market. Amazon also offers a free download of a selected paid app each day, which has helped make this market popular among Android users who know about it.

Another great feature of the Amazon App Store for Android is the Test Drive feature shown in Figure 2-19. Test Drive allows people to try the app out before they buy. The Amazon App Store imposes a 30-minute time limit, but the app functions exactly as if it was installed on your phone.

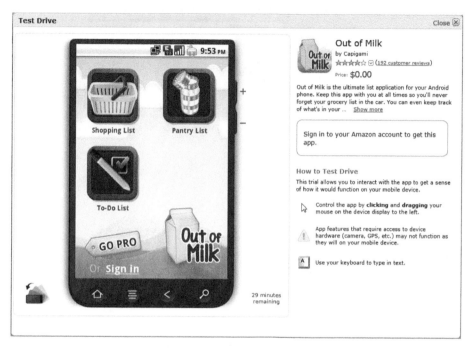

FIGURE 2-19: Amazon Test Drive

To deploy apps to the Amazon App Store, sign up for an Amazon App Store Developer account. Subscription fees similar to the Google Market may apply. Since the Amazon App Store for Android is still fairly new, Amazon is currently waving the costs for new developers.

YOUR APP AS A MOBILE WEB APP

Mobile web apps are an extremely popular solution to the "mobile app versus mobile website" problem, because they are relatively easy to create and maintain. The popularity of mobile web apps has grown proportionately to the popularity of smartphones. In 2001 alone, an estimated 1.5 million mobile web apps were downloaded.

Mobile web apps, in a nutshell, are mobile apps created using HTML and CSS, viewed in mobile web browsers. Mobile web apps differ from mobile websites by having a focused application purpose, like native mobile apps do.

Figure 2-20 shows an example of a mobile web app that has been designed with the platform UI in mind, in this case different interfaces for the iPhone and iPad. A good mobile web app will have business logic abstracted into a common library. This will allow for platform-specific UI code to be created that calls into this common library, keeping the app easily maintainable.

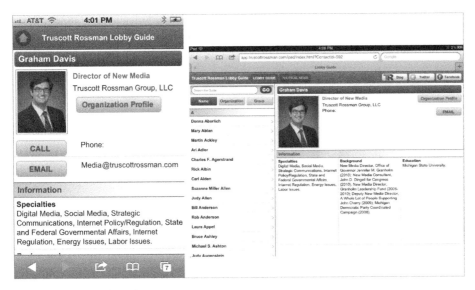

FIGURE 2-20: Mobile web apps

Mobile web apps span across many categories of apps. In some cases, such as shopping, mobile web apps are more popular choices. Figure 2-21 shows a comparison of mobile web apps versus native apps.

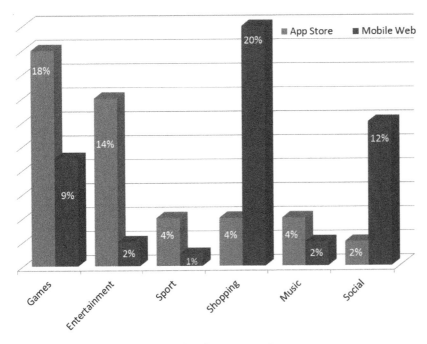

FIGURE 2-21: Mobile web app vs. App Store categories

Mobile web apps have a wonderful development story. Designers, front-end web developers, and even back-end web developers can create an app using HTML and JavaScript with familiar tools, to rival even the slickest native app. With the introduction of HTML5, many features have been added to mobile browsers that help achieve this functionality. Table 2-2 is list of mobile capabilities between the various mobile platforms.

TABLE 2-2: Native vs. HTML5 Device Features

	HTML5	ANDROID	IOS	BLACKBERRY	WP7
Location/GPS	Yes	Yes	Yes	Yes	Yes
Camera	No	Yes	Yes	Yes	Yes
Accelerometer	Limited	Yes	Yes	Yes	Yes
Video	Yes	Yes	Yes	Yes	Yes
Audio	Yes	Yes	Yes	Yes	Yes
Local Storage	Limited	Yes	Yes	Yes	Yes
Push Notifications	Yes	Yes	Yes	Yes	Yes
In-App Purchase	No	Yes	Yes	Yes	No
App Market	No	Yes	Yes	Yes	Yes

If you are looking for a fast solution that can be developed with resources you may already have access to, a mobile web app may be the better solution. The following benefits may sway your decision in favor of creating a mobile web app:

➤ **Easier to get started:** HTML is a popular technology, so there is a good chance that the developers on the team will already have experience with the language. Besides the ease of use of the language, there are no startup costs, licenses, or large SDKs to download as there is with native app development. Most developers are willing to learn something new, but are overworked. When they want to get into something, they want to do it now, not have to wait for two weeks before they can get going.

➤ **Easier cross-platform development:** Creating a mobile web app will make it easier for you to create a codebase where parts of it can be shared. Depending on the app type, be prepared to create a new UI for each platform deployment.

➤ **HTML5 offers rich features:** We have all heard that HTML5 makes it easy to create mobile web apps. HTML5 offers great new features that make mobile web apps a viable solution instead of developing a mobile app. The truth is that HTML5 is just a tool in a mobile developer's belt, and with it, developers and designers can provide apps to users that are usable and compete with native mobile apps.

➤ **Easier updates:** Not all users will update your mobile app. But if you have control over what the user sees, app updates can be made at any time. This is one of our favorite features about mobile web apps. With a mobile web app, there is no complicated process for publishing — it is just like launching any regular website.

➤ **No approval process:** With a mobile web app, there are no constraints as to if your app can be published or not. When the Google Voice app was not approved in the iTunes store, Google released a mobile web app that provided the same functionality without the iTunes hassle.

SUMMARY

When creating a mobile strategy, it's important that companies spend the time to find out exactly which model fits best for their business domain. Starting down the wrong path can be costly, and be detrimental to a company's reputation. This chapter has stressed the importance and necessity of a mobile web presence, and that app development should not be taken lightly nor rushed into because it is trendy.

Creating a mobile web app can be the better solution if it fits your business domain. The ease of updates and use of existing resources are very compelling reasons to build a mobile web app.

When you are creating a truly great app that provides user value, there are no shortcuts to build once and run everywhere. Developing an app for mobile platforms is expensive and time-consuming, but if your business domain calls for it, it's in investment that needs to be made.

At this point, you should have a really good idea of what a mobile application is, and what platforms you will look into developing for. Chapter 3 discusses Web Services as they pertain to mobile apps.

3

Creating Consumable Web Services for Mobile Devices

WHAT'S IN THIS CHAPTER?

➤ Understanding web services

➤ Using web service languages (formats)

➤ Creating an example service

➤ Debugging web services

Many of today's mobile applications are personalized, and are not useful if they can only access the data on the phone. For a user to get, for example, sports scores, retrieve stock quotes, or perform accounting work, the mobile device needs to communicate with one or more servers. The best way to achieve this communication is through web services.

This chapter covers what a web service is, the technologies involved in web services, and how to create web services on the Windows platform and the Linux platform. Four different walkthroughs show you how to create web services with four different technologies.

WHAT IS A WEB SERVICE?

A *web service* enables two electronic devices to communicate over the Internet. The World Wide Web Consortium (W3C) defines web service as "a software system designed to support interoperable machine-to-machine interaction over a network." In practice this means a server communicating over port 80 or port 443 in plain text to the client.

Other methods of communication are remote procedure calls (RPC), the distributed component object model (DCOM), and the common object request broker architecture (CORBA). These methods of communication don't work well through the Internet due to firewalls and the data formats they use. Typically their data formats are specific to whatever tool created the service, and it becomes a significant challenge to have a Java application read data from a .NET or C++ application. They generally also use a specific port, which requires IT departments or, even worse, home users, to troubleshoot and configure their firewalls to allow the application to communicate. Finally those technologies don't work well through the Internet because they aren't designed to work with the Hypertext Transfer Protocol.

WHAT IS A PORT?

A *port* is similar to a TV channel. News comes in on the news channel, sports on ESPN, and so on. Instead of watching the channels, computer applications are listening on port numbers. The information coming to the computer on that port number is routed to the application listening on that port number. For example, when your computer requests a web page from a web server, it issues the request through port 80. That traffic is delivered by the server's operating system to a HyperText Transfer Protocol (HTTP) server application such as Microsoft's Internet Information Services (IIS) or the Apache Web Server. Connecting with a file transfer protocol (FTP) client to the same server, the FTP software uses port 21. Both FTP and HTTP traffic are going to the same computer with the same address, so having different ports enables the server to route the traffic to the correct application.

Examples of Web Services

Because you are reading this book, I'm assuming you are a developer or have some type of development background, so I'll use the StackOverflow web service as an example. You can view my StackOverflow profile by using a nice user interface StackOverflow has created to access their web service by going to `http://data.stackexchange.com/stackoverflow/query/66263/find-david-silva-smith` in a web browser. That URL is a query which shows the data from my StackOverflow profile. To view my profile data in its raw form to compare it to the pretty formatted data just shown, enter this URL in a browser: `http://data.stackexchange.com/stackoverflow/atom/Users(46076)`.

Think how easily an application can be written using that data. This is the power of web services. By making your data easily consumable through web services, others can use the data you have created in ways you never imagined.

Not convinced yet? What if you wanted to display the weather for Lansing, Michigan, on your web page? How hard would that be to program? For starters, you would have to purchase equipment to measure the temperature, wind speed, and humidity, which could be expensive. Then you would have to program that equipment to report the information to a web server, which would then display that information on your web page. Wow, this is sounding difficult, and there are many issues that haven't been addressed yet, such as reliability. Instead of doing all that work, leveraging a web service will be much faster. Simply type this URL into a web browser: `http://www.google` `.com/ig/api?weather=Lansing,MI`. No equipment required, no risk of schedule overruns, and if requirements change and the software needs to display the weather for Lake Odessa instead of Lansing, you just replace the `Lansing,MI` on the end of the URL with `Lake%20Odessa,MI`.

WHAT IS THAT UGLY %20?

Not all characters are valid in uniform resource locators (URLs). A space is one such character — it is represented as `%20`. The percent sign indicates that the following two hexadecimal characters represent a single character — 20 in hexadecimal is 32 in decimal, which is the ASCII code for space. If that isn't confusing enough, different characters are valid in different parts of a URL. To encode a URL, use the JavaScript `encodeURI()` method or the equivalent function in your programming language. For parts of a URL, use the JavaScript `encodeURIComponent()` method or the equivalent function in your programming language. This JavaScript code shows an example of when this difference is important:

```
<script type="text/javascript">
    var url = 'http://www.gravityworksdesign.com/
    large images.aspx?folder=2012/April';
    document.write(encodeURI(url));
    document.write('<br />');
    document.write(encodeURIComponent(url));
    var urlCorrect =  'http://www.gravityworksdesign.com/
    large images.aspx?folder='
    var queryCorrect = '2012/April';
    document.write('<br />');
    document.write(encodeURI(urlCorrect) +
    encodeURIComponent(queryCorrect));
</script>
```

It outputs:

```
    http://www.gravityworksdesign.com/large%20images.
aspx?folder=2012/April
```

```
    http%3A%2F%2Fwww.gravityworksdesign.com%2Flarge%20images.aspx
    %3Ffolder%3D2012%2FApril
```

```
    http://www.gravityworksdesign.com/large%20images.aspx?
    folder=2012%2FApril
```

The first two URLs are invalid because the URL wasn't encoded correctly. The third URL is correctly encoded.

Advantages of Web Services

The primary advantages web services provide are ease of access and ease of consumption. Web services advantages stem from simplicity. Usage of web services for data exchange has exploded due to these advantages.

Web services are easy to access because they use the same World Wide Web technologies such as web browsers and web servers that power the Internet. These technologies have proven to be robust and work great for web services just as they work great for delivering web pages. They have no firewall issues with special ports like other communication technologies, and all modern programming languages provide a way to get web pages and, therefore, to consume web services.

The second advantage of web services over other technologies is the consumability, which is the ability to understand what the server is communicating. Web services use plain text for this. Other technologies like RPC, DCOM, and CORBA typically use the in-memory representation of their objects for transmission or use a custom data exchange format. These complexities make it expensive for languages to interoperate with the information. The memory representations don't have friendly text like `<zipcode>48906</zipcode>`, which most people can guess contains ZIP code information; the server might send something like `1011111100001010`, which could represent many pieces of information. This discussion leads us into the next section, which discusses web service languages.

WEB SERVICES LANGUAGES (FORMATS)

For communication to occur between two people they need to speak the same language. Computer systems work the same way — they also need to use the same language. Most computer languages that are widely known, such as C++, enable humans to talk to computers. But those computer languages are hard for both computers and humans to understand because computers only understand zeros and ones, and represent all data as zeros and ones. For example, the number 5 is represented as `00000101` in a computer. A lowercase *h* is represented as `01101000`, and `01001000` represents an uppercase *H*. Binary representations are the most efficient way for two computer systems to exchange data.

One of the reasons web services have been so successful is because of their self-describing nature. Instead of giving a number like 5 and hoping the user of the web service knows that 5 is a weight, an age, or dollars, the 5 is described in a service like this: `<length measurement="inches">5 </length>`. This states clearly the measurement is for length and is 5 inches.

Format choice is an important decision — it impacts the ease of accessing the web service and the performance of your application. When designing a web service, consider how the service will be accessed. For example, mobile devices have less processing power than their desktop counterparts, and the different platforms (BlackBerry, Windows Phone, Android, and iOS) have different programming APIs available for accessing and consuming the data. The two self-describing formats that have taken off for web services are XML and JSON. I recommend sticking with one of these two formats to maximize the ease of consuming the services and maximize developer productivity.

eXtensible Markup Language (XML)

XML was designed as a way to describe documents, but it took off as a data interchange format after it was introduced. XML was envisioned to be a simple human-readable language; for example, a person object can be represented like this in XML:

```
<person>
    <firstname>David</firstname>
    <lastname>Smith</lastname>
</person>
```

And the same person can also be represented like this:

```
<person firstname="David" lastname="Smith" />
```

Both XML fragments are easy for a person to understand, but different representations make it harder for programmers to write correct software. Having a single agreed-upon representation of the data will speed up your development effort.

XML enables you to define the language systems used to communicate by creating an XML Schema Document (XSD). This enables software to verify an XML document conforms to a predefined contract. For example, the XSD can specify that the cost of a movie must be a number. XSD also provides the benefit of enabling tools to generate code based on the XSD. Programmers can increase productivity by feeding their programming tool an XSD file and getting back code they can immediately use to interact with the data. Without the XSD file programmers have to write code to understand the XML.

One of the reasons for choosing XML is the maturity of the platform. It has been around since February 1998. It has many tools around it — XPath, XQuery, XSLT, and XSD. Since it is a mature language, many systems work well with XML. These advantages make XML a good choice for data interchange and it may even be required for some projects to work with existing systems.

eXtensible Stylesheet Language Transformations (XSLT)

XSLT is used to transform a document into another representation. Initially it was envisioned as primarily changing XML data documents into representations for human consumption, such as XHTML. Another common use is applying an XSLT transformation to one application's XML output to be used by another application that doesn't understand the original representation.

The following example shows how XSLT can transform an XML data fragment for display on a web page.

This fragment: `<person><age>30</age></person>` would better be displayed on a web page like this: `<span>Age:30</span>`.

The following XSLT will loop through each element in the XML with the name of person. Within each person node, the XSLT will then output the span tag with the value of the age element included within the span tag.

```
<xsl:template match="/">
    <xsl:for-each select="person">
      <span>Age:<xsl:value-of select="age"/></span>
    </xsl:for-each>
</xsl:template>
```

XQuery

XQuery is used to retrieve a subset of data from a full XML document, like a SQL query is used to retrieve a subset of data from a database.

This example shows how to get the total amount paid for this sample order:

```
<order>
    <item price="50" currency="USD" name="metal gear" />
    <item price="25" currency="USD" name="plastic gear" />
</order>
```

The following XQuery returns the sum:

```
sum(doc('orders.xml')/order/item/@price)
```

For testing or learning XQuery, a handy online sandbox is: `http://basex.org/products/live-demo/`.

JavaScript Object Notation (JSON)

JSON was created in 2001 and came into use by Yahoo in 2005. JSON has few rules, few base types, and is human readable. JSON schema enables document validation, but this is rarely used. JSON is a great format for transmitting data between systems because it is simple, text based, and self-describing.

A person can be represented in JSON like this:

```
{
    firstName : "David",
    lastName : "Smith"
}
```

One thing to watch out for is how dates are represented in JSON. There is no base type of date and there is no standard way to represent dates. It is recommended to represent dates using the International Standards Organization 8601 format. In ISO-8601 dates look like this: 1997-07-16T19:20:30.45+01:00. Representing dates in ISO-8601 keeps them human readable, ensures programming languages can parse them, and keeps time zone information.

Choosing ISO-8601 as the default data interchange format for projects is a good idea. Using JSON will reduce the amount of time spent dealing with serialization issues.

Transferring Nontextual Data

Both JSON and XML create human-readable text documents. What happens if a service needs to transmit or receive an image, a video, or a PDF document, such as a check image for a financial service or a video clip for a public safety service? This type of nontextual data is called binary data. When transmitting binary data as text, it needs to be Base64 encoded so it can be represented with the rest of the data. Base64 encoding comes with two downsides. First, the size of the text representation increases by 33 percent. Second, there is additional processing overhead by both the sender and receiver for encoding or decoding the Base64 data to binary and vice versa.

CREATING AN EXAMPLE WEB SERVICE

Having talked about the technologies behind creating a consumable web service, this section shows how to create a consumable web service in a Linux Apache PHP environment, and three different service delivery technologies on the Microsoft .NET stack: WCF, OData, and ASP.NET MVC.

Using the Microsoft Stack

The .NET platform has a variety of technologies enabling the easy creation of consumable web services. This section walks through creating a database and sample data for the services to operate on. The rest of the section shows how to create the service in three .NET technologies: WCF, OData, and MVC.

Creating the Datastore

The WCF, OData, and MVC walkthroughs later in this section all assume the database script from this section has been executed.

The example services will expose a simple data model consisting of two tables: Leagues and DerbyNames. Some of the Gravity Works staff are Roller Derby fans. They noticed the players had interesting names and decided their information (which is publicly available) would make a good example service.

Figure 3-1 shows a database diagram of the tables the script will create.

Open SQL Server Management Studio 2008 and connect to the local SQL Server instance running on the machine. Open a new query window and run the SQL-Server-Create-Derby-Database script (full SQL script can

FIGURE 3-1: Database diagram

be found within the download section for this book at http://www.wrox.com) to create the tables and insert the data used for the rest of the walkthroughs:

After running the script, SQL Server Management Studio will display "Query Executed Successfully." The walkthroughs in this section use this database to retrieve data.

Using Windows Communication Foundation

Windows Communication Foundation (WCF) is a .NET Framework library designed for developers to create communication endpoints for software. Web services are software communication endpoints, so on the surface WCF seems like an ideal choice for creating consumable web services. Unfortunately, WCF is designed for a broad number of communication scenarios, and this broad set of capabilities introduces a lot of complexity that is not necessary for web services. For example, WCF supports reliable sessions, transactions, TCP, named pipes, Microsoft Message Queuing, activity tracing, and Windows Management Instrumentation.

This walkthrough assumes the following software is installed:

➤ ASP.NET 4.0

➤ Visual Studio 2010

➤ IIS 7.5

➤ Microsoft SQL Server 2008 R2

1. Open Visual Studio and select File ⇨ New Project to create a new project.

2. In the New Project template selection screen, open the Visual C# node and select the WCF node.

3. From the WCF project types that display, select WCF Service Application. If that project type does not display, ensure the filter at the top of the dialog box is set to .NET Framework 4.

4. Set the project name to **DerbyNamesService** and click OK, as shown in Figure 3-2.

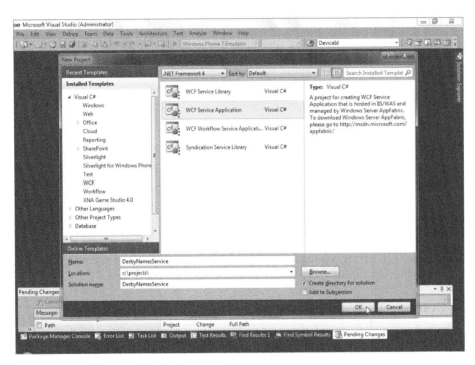

FIGURE 3-2: New WCF Service Application

For ease of database access this walkthrough uses LINQ to SQL. LINQ to SQL is an Object Relational Mapper technology that ships with the .NET Framework. Using LINQ requires an additional project reference to `System.Data.Linq`.

To add the reference, right-click the References node of the DerbyNamesService project and select Add Reference.

In the Add Reference dialog box, find `System.Data.Linq` and click the Add button as shown in Figure 3-3.

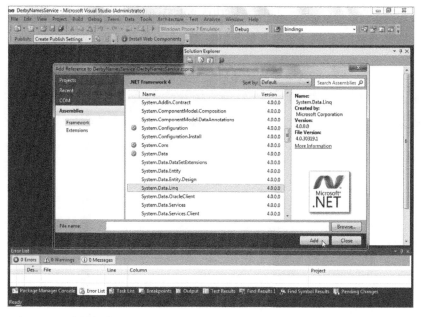

FIGURE 3-3: Add Reference dialog box

After adding the `System.Data.Linq` reference, you need to create a class to access the data. To do this, right-click the DerbyNamesService project and choose Add ⇨ New Item as shown in Figure 3-4.

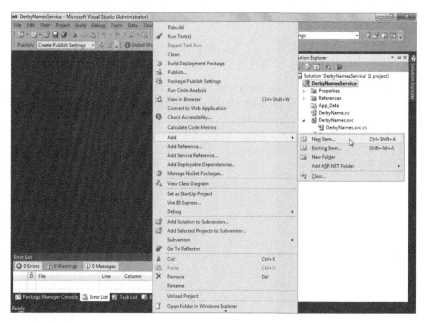

FIGURE 3-4: Add New Item

In the Add New Item dialog box, select Class, name it **DerbyContext,** and click the Add button as shown in Figure 3-5.

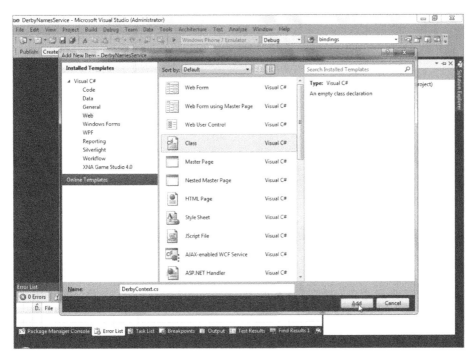

FIGURE 3-5: Add New Class

The DerbyContext class will provide the data. To represent the data as .NET objects, add two more code files: DerbyNames and Leagues. The DerbyNames class will contain the information on a derby player. Make the DerbyNames.cs file contain this code:

```
using System;
using System.Data.Linq.Mapping;

namespace DerbyNamesService
{
    [Table]
    public class DerbyNames
    {
        [Column(IsPrimaryKey = true)]
        public int DerbyNameId;
        [Column]
        public string Name;
        [Column]
```

```
        public string Number;
        [Column]
        public DateTime? DateAdded;
        [Column]
        public string League;
    }
}
```

The Leagues class will contain information about the derby leagues, such as the league name. Make the Leagues.cs file contain this code:

```
using System.Data.Linq.Mapping;

namespace DerbyNamesService
{
    [Table]
    public class Leagues
    {
        [Column(IsPrimaryKey=true)]
        public int LeagueId;
        [Column]
        public string LeagueName;
        [Column]
        public string URL;
        [Column]
        public string StateProvince;
        [Column]
        public string CountryCode;
    }
}
```

The DerbyContext will be the class providing access to the database from the DerbyService class. Modify the DerbyContext.cs code to contain this code:

```
using System.Data.Linq;
using DerbyNamesService;

namespace DerbyNamesService
{
    public class DerbyContext : DataContext
    {
        public Table<DerbyNames> DerbyNames;
        public Table<Leagues> Leagues;
        public DerbyContext()
            : base("Data Source=.;Initial Catalog=DerbyNames;
            User Id=webUser;Password=webuser;")
        {

        }
    }
}
```

In the Visual Studio Solution Explorer, rename `Service1.svc` to `DerbyService.svc` and then rename `IService1.cs` to `IDerbyService.cs`. If Visual Studio prompts if you would like to rename all project references, click Yes. This step is just a cleanup step to rename the default files Visual Studio creates for you. The `IDerbyService` interface defines the contract for the service — in other words, this interface will expose the operations the service provides. Change the `IDerbyService.cs` file to contain the following code:

```
using System.Collections.Generic;
using System.ServiceModel;

namespace DerbyNamesService
{
    [ServiceContract]
    public interface IDerbyService
    {
        [OperationContract]
        public IEnumerable<DerbyNames> PlayerNames();

        [OperationContract]
        public IEnumerable<Leagues> Leagues();
    }
}
```

With the service contract defined, a class to implement the operations defined by the `IDerbyService` contract needs to be created. The `DerbyService.svc.cs` file will implement the contract. In other words, the contract states what the service will do and the `DerbyService` actually does the work. Open the `DerbyService.svc.cs` file and replace the existing code with the following code:

```
using System.Collections.Generic;
using System.Linq;
using System.ServiceModel.Web;

namespace DerbyNamesService
{
    public class DerbyNames : IDerbyNames
    {
        [WebGet(UriTemplate="/PlayerNames")]
        public DerbyName GetNames()
        {
            //get all the names from the database.
            var names = new DerbyContext().DerbyNames.ToList();
            return names;
        }

        [WebGet(UriTemplate="/Leagues")]
        public IEnumerable<Leagues> Leagues()
        {
            //Get all the leagues from the database.
            var leagues = new DerbyContext().Leagues.ToList();
            return leagues;
        }
    }
}
```

Previously when Visual Studio asked to rename project references, it was only referring to C# code. The `DerbyService.svc` markup contains text that needs to be updated. To make the change Visual Studio missed, right-click the `DerbyService.svc` file and select View Markup as shown in Figure 3-6.

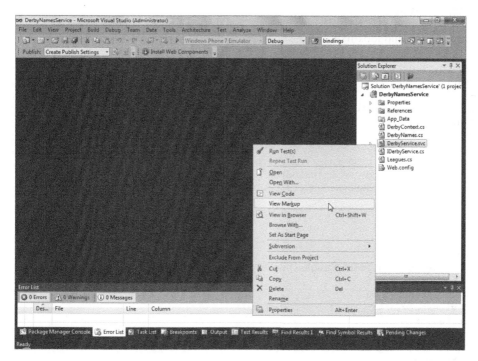

FIGURE 3-6: View Markup

Change the text `Service="DerbyNamesService.Service1"` to `Service="DerbyNamesService.DerbyService"` to match the class renaming you performed earlier. To make the service accessible it needs to be specified in the `web.config`. In this context, the service endpoint is effectively a website to which you connect your client code. This site will receive communications from your client over HTTP, and return objects from your data source as text. To specify the service endpoint, insert the following XML as a child node of the `system.servicemodel` node:

```
<services>
    <service name="DerbyNamesService.DerbyService">
      <endpoint binding="webHttpBinding"
          contract="DerbyNamesService.IDerbyService"/>
    </service>
  </services>
```

To make the service return XML for easy consumption by mobile devices, insert the following XML as a child node of the behaviors node:

```
<endpointBehaviors>
  <behavior>
    <webHttp defaultOutgoingResponseFormat="Xml"/>
  </behavior>
</endpointBehaviors>
```

The final web.config should look like this:

```
<?xml version="1.0"?>
<configuration>
  <system.web>
    <compilation debug="true" targetFramework="4.0" />
  </system.web>
  <system.serviceModel>
    <services>
      <service name="DerbyNamesService.DerbyService">
        <endpoint binding="webHttpBinding"
              contract="DerbyNamesService.IDerbyService"/>
      </service>
    </services>
    <behaviors>
      <endpointBehaviors>
        <behavior>
          <webHttp defaultOutgoingResponseFormat="Xml"/>
        </behavior>
      </endpointBehaviors>
      <serviceBehaviors>
        <behavior>
          <serviceMetadata httpGetEnabled="true"/>
          <serviceDebug includeExceptionDetailInFaults="false"/>
        </behavior>
      </serviceBehaviors>
    </behaviors>
    <serviceHostingEnvironment multipleSiteBindingsEnabled="true" />
  </system.serviceModel>
  <system.webServer>
    <modules runAllManagedModulesForAllRequests="true"/>
  </system.webServer>
</configuration>
```

After all that work, the service is coded and configured. Click the solution and start debugging. Visual Studio will launch the ASP.NET Development Server and launch the system default browser with a URL similar to http://localhost:13610. The number is the port on which the ASP.NET Development Server is delivering requests. Add /DerbyService.svc/PlayerNames to the end of the URL to get the PlayerNames. Figure 3-7 shows the result in Google Chrome.

FIGURE 3-7: Player Names XML result

With the service returning data, you can now have some fun! Using the Chrome Developer Tools will show the service response payload is 3.07KB. You can open the Chrome Developer Tools by using the keystroke Ctrl+Shift+I in Google Chrome. Figure 3-8 shows the Chrome Developer Tools network tab.

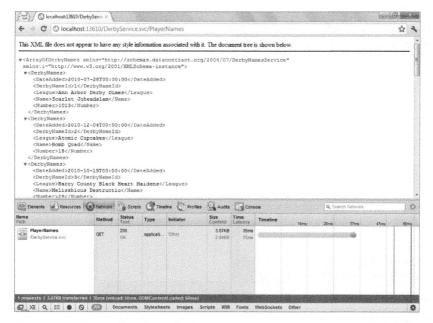

FIGURE 3-8: Chrome Developer Tools network view

An earlier section of this chapter discussed the differences in protocols. Change the protocol to JSON and see what happens. WCF makes this change easy. Open the `web.config` file and find the `webHttp` node under the `behavior` node. Change the `defaultOutgoingResponseFormat` from XML to JSON. The node should look like this:

```
<webHttp defaultOutgoingResponseFormat="Json"/>
```

Then rebuild the project and navigate back to the ASP.NET Development Server URL `/DerbyService.svc/PlayerNames`. On my machine, Chrome developer tools show the response size is now 2.22KB, which is a 28 percent reduction in size from the XML format. This reduction in size will result in faster transfer times, especially for larger data services. I recommended using JSON as the default data format and providing XML only if the requirements demand it.

The next improvement to make is getting URLs that make more sense. The URL `/DerbyService` `.svc/PlayerNames` doesn't look nice. A better URL would be `/RollerDerby/PlayerNames`. ASP.NET routing is the easiest way to get the URL `/RollerDerby/PlayerNames`.

Routing is built into ASP.NET, but to get it to work with the service you need to add one reference. Expand the DerbyNameService project node, right-click References, and select Add Reference to bring up Add Reference dialog box. Select the .NET tab and find `System` `.ServiceModel.Activation`. Click OK to add the `System.ServiceModel.Activation` assembly to the project as shown in Figure 3-9.

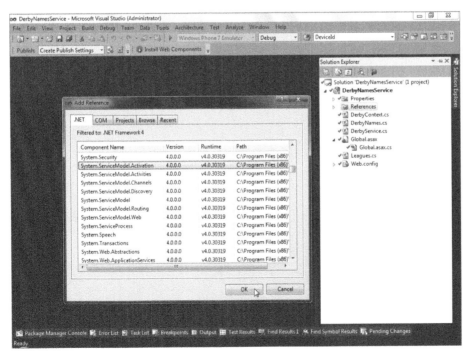

FIGURE 3-9: Add Reference dialog box

Right-click the DerbyNames project and select Add New Item from the menu. From the Add New Item dialog box, select Global Application Class, and click the Add button to add it to the project as shown in Figure 3-10.

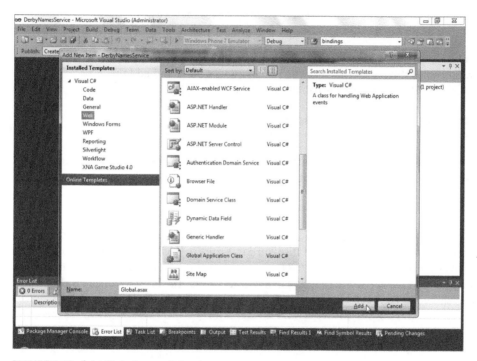

FIGURE 3-10: Add Global.asax dialog box

Find the `Application_Start` method within the `Global.asax` file and add the following line of code within the method:

```
RegisterRoutes(RouteTable.Routes);
```

Below the `Application_Start` method, add the following method:

```
private void RegisterRoutes(RouteCollection routes)
{
    routes.Add(new ServiceRoute("RollerDerby",
        new WebServiceHostFactory(), typeof(DerbyService)));
}
```

The `RouteTable` class is in the `System.Web.Routing` namespace. The `WebServiceHostFactory` and `ServiceRoute` classes are in the `System.ServiceModel.Activation` namespace. Add these using statements at the top of the file to resolve the references:

```
using System.Web.Routing;
using System.ServiceModel.Activation;
```

For ASP.NET routing to work, WCF requests need to flow through ASP.NET. To turn this feature on, open the `web.config` file and find the `serviceHostingEnvironment` element. Add the attribute `aspNetCompatibilityEnabled="true"`. The `serviceHostingEnvironment` element should look like this:

```
<serviceHostingEnvironment multipleSiteBindingsEnabled="true"
    aspNetCompatibilityEnabled="true" />
```

ASP.NET routing also requires the service class be attributed stating it supports ASP.NET compatibility. To enable this, open the `DerbyService.svc.cs` class and add the `AspNetCompatibilityRequirements` attribute like this:

```
[AspNetCompatibilityRequirements(RequirementsMode =
    AspNetCompatibilityRequirementsMode.Required)]
```

The `AspNetCompatibilityRequirements` attribute is in the `System.ServiceModel.Activation` namespace, which requires the following `using` statement:

```
using System.ServiceModel.Activation;
```

After making those changes, compile and run the project. Navigate to the URL `/RollerDerby/PlayerNames` and the same JSON document displayed in Figure 3-7 will display. Since I'm discussing nice-looking URLs (also known as friendly URLS), notice when giving a URL the service doesn't understand such as `/RollerDerby/THIS-PAGE-DOES-NOT-EXIST`, the browser displays the strange looking page as shown in Figure 3-11.

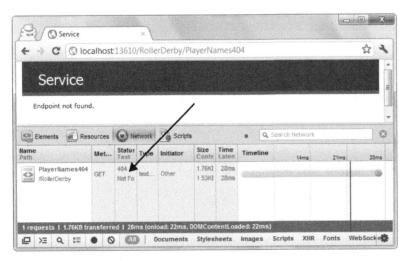

FIGURE 3-11: A typical 404 page

Using Chrome Developer Tools shows the response has the correct 404 code. This is the same result when navigating to the root service: `/RollerDerby`. It would be better if missing pages were controlled by the `DerbyService` class. Fortunately, the `WebGet` attribute applied to the service methods gives control of the URLs.

To deliver a 404 page that doesn't expose the underlying technology as WCF, add the following method to the `DerbyService` class:

```
[WebGet(UriTemplate="*")]
public void ErrorForGet()
{
    throw new WebFaultException(HttpStatusCode.NotFound);
}
```

The method name doesn't matter. The functionality is coming from the `UriTemplate` parameter. The asterisk means if there isn't a better match, run this attributed method for the request. The `HttpStatusCode` class is in the `System.NET` namespace, which requires the following `using` statement:

```
using System.Net;
```

Change the `DerbyService` class so it does not implement the `IDerbyService`. Because it is not using the `IDerbyService`, add the `ServiceContract` attribute to the `DerbyService` class, which requires the following `using` statement:

```
using System.ServiceModel;
```

The final change to remove the response body is a `web.config` change. Find and remove the `Services` node along with its child service node. After rebuilding, running the application, and navigating to `/RollerDerby/THIS-PAGE-DOES-NOT-EXIST`, the page returns a 404 error with an empty body as shown in Figure 3-12:

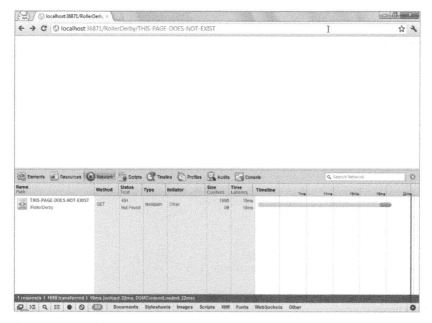

FIGURE 3-12: A 404 page with an empty body

It is important for web services to be discoverable. Users may try to navigate to /RollerDerby. The service is currently configured to give a 404 error at that URL. It would help users to expose the PlayerName and Leagues operations of the service from the /RollerDerby URL so the users can find the supported service operations.

To expose the services, open the DerbyService class and add the following method:

```
[WebGet(UriTemplate="")]
public Stream Root()
{
    WebOperationContext.Current.OutgoingResponse.ContentType = "text/html";
    string html = "<a href=\"PlayerNames\">Player Names</a><br /><a" +
        "href=\"Leagues\">Leagues</a>";
        return new MemoryStream(Encoding.UTF8.GetBytes(html));
}
```

The Stream and MemoryStream classes are in the System.IO namespace, and the Encoding class is in the System.Text namespace. Add these two using statements:

```
using System.IO;
using System.Text;
```

After building the project, running it, and navigating the browser to /RollerDerby, users are able to discover the operations the RollerDerby service provides. In Chrome, the page looks like Figure 3-13.

The final code for the DerbyNamesService should look like this:

```
using System.Collections.Generic;
using System.IO;
using System.Linq;
using System.Net;
using System.ServiceModel;
using System.ServiceModel.Activation;
using System.ServiceModel.Web;
using System.Text;

namespace DerbyNamesService
{
    [AspNetCompatibilityRequirements(RequirementsMode =
        AspNetCompatibilityRequirementsMode.Required)]
    [ServiceContract]
    public class DerbyService
    {
        [WebGet(UriTemplate="/PlayerNames")]
        public IEnumerable<DerbyNames> PlayerNames()
        {
            var names = new DerbyContext().DerbyNames.ToList();
            return names;
        }

        [WebGet(UriTemplate="/Leagues")]
```

FIGURE 3-13: Discoverable service URLs

```
        public IEnumerable<Leagues> Leagues()
        {
            var leagues = new DerbyContext().Leagues.ToList();
            return leagues;
        }

        [WebGet(UriTemplate = "*")]
        public void ErrorForGet()
        {
            throw new WebFaultException(HttpStatusCode.NotFound);
        }

        [WebGet(UriTemplate = "")]
        public Stream Root()
        {
            WebOperationContext.Current.OutgoingResponse.ContentType = "text/html";
            string html = "<a href=\"PlayerNames\">Player Names</a><br />
                <a href=\"Leagues\">Leagues</a>";
            return new MemoryStream(Encoding.UTF8.GetBytes(html));
        }
    }
}
```

The final `web.config` should look like this:

```xml
<?xml version="1.0"?>
<configuration>
  <system.web>
    <compilation debug="true" targetFramework="4.0" />
  </system.web>
  <system.serviceModel>
    <behaviors>
      <endpointBehaviors>
        <behavior>
          <webHttp defaultOutgoingResponseFormat="Json"/>
        </behavior>
      </endpointBehaviors>
      <serviceBehaviors>
        <behavior>
          <serviceMetadata httpGetEnabled="true"/>
          <serviceDebug includeExceptionDetailInFaults="false"/>
        </behavior>
      </serviceBehaviors>
    </behaviors>
    <serviceHostingEnvironment multipleSiteBindingsEnabled="true"
        aspNetCompatibilityEnabled="true" />
  </system.serviceModel>
 <system.webServer>
    <modules runAllManagedModulesForAllRequests="true"/>
  </system.webServer>
</configuration>
```

As shown in this section, WCF is a flexible framework capable of delivering consumable web services to clients. The downside of using WCF for web services is the complexity of the technology stack. With all the flexibility WCF provides, using it to deliver text data over HTTP is using only a small percentage of the framework.

Using Open Data Protocol (OData)

The Open Data Protocol (OData) is a web protocol for querying and updating data in a standard way. OData has many querying capabilities such as getting the count, expanding related entities, paging, and many filter options. Read about the capabilities on http://www.odata.org. Microsoft created the technology and has released it under the Open Specification Promise, which means Microsoft has granted everyone license to use the OData technology. OData is a great choice for web services that create, read, update, and delete data without complex business rules. OData has especially advanced querying capabilities that make it flexible for many projects.

This walkthrough assumes the following software is installed:

➤   Visual Studio 2010

➤   IIS 7.5

➤   Entity Framework 4.0

➤   SQL Server 2008 R2

1.   Open Visual studio and select File ➪ New Project.

2.   From the New Project menu, select ASP.NET Empty Web Application.

3.   Name the service **ODataDerbyService** and click OK, as shown in Figure 3-14.

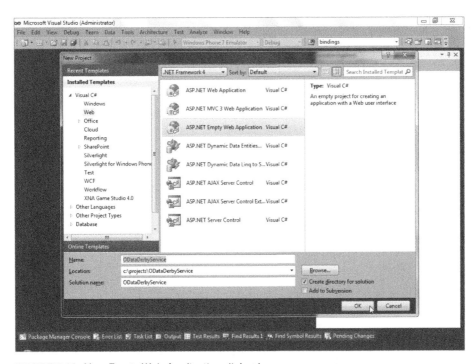

FIGURE 3-14: New Empty Web Application dialog box

To deliver data from the service, this example uses Entity Framework. Entity Framework is an Object Relational Mapper that has been released by Microsoft. What that means is that it will bind your database to C# objects directly without the user needing to do any of the heavy lifting.

Right-click the ODataDerbyService project and select Add New Item.

From the Templates tree, find Data and then select the ADO.NET Entity Data Model template. Enter **DerbyData.edmx** for the name and click the Add button as shown in Figure 3-15.

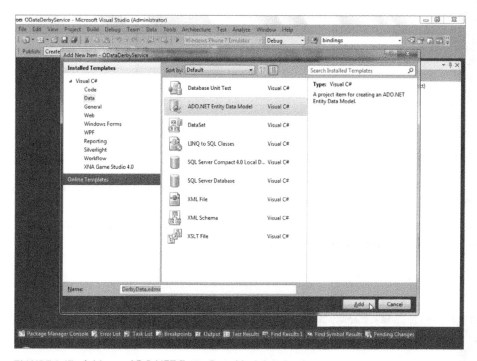

FIGURE 3-15: Add new ADO.NET Entity Data Model dialog box

On the first screen of the Entity Data Model Wizard, select Generate from Database and click Next. On the next screen of the wizard, click the New Connection button. If you are connecting to SQL Server on the same machine as you are developing on it refer to it by the local instance address. For the server name enter a dot (.). For the database name select DerbyNames from the drop-down list. Then click OK as shown in Figure 3-16.

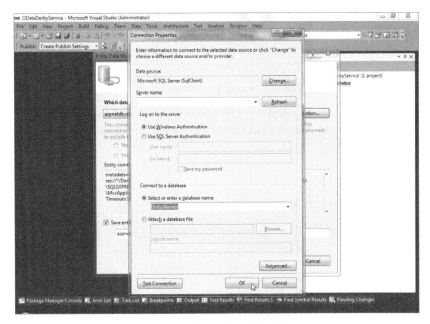

FIGURE 3-16: Database Connection Properties dialog box

After clicking OK on the Connection Properties dialog box, Visual Studio will be back in the Entity Data Model Wizard. Click Next to continue.

On the Choose Your Database Objects step of the wizard, check Tables, leave the rest of the settings at their defaults, and click Finish, as shown in Figure 3-17.

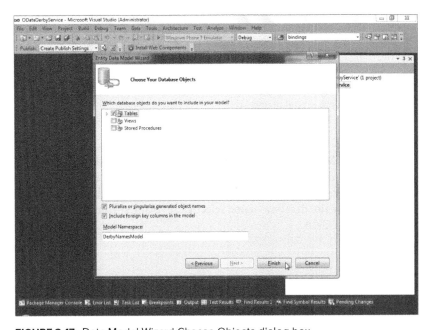

FIGURE 3-17: Data Model Wizard Choose Objects dialog box

With the data model created, the next step is to add the OData service. Right-click the ODataDerbyService project and select Add New Item. From the Add New Item dialog box, in the Installed Templates tree select the Web node and then select WCF Data Service. Name it **DerbyService.svc** and then click the Add button as shown in Figure 3-18.

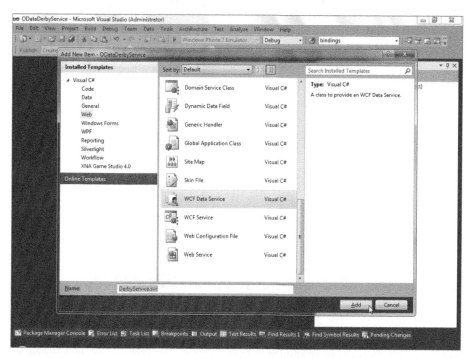

FIGURE 3-18: Add new WCF Data Service

Visual Studio has done almost all of the work to make OData expose the database as a web service. To make the service access the data model created earlier, open the `DerbyService.svc.cs` class and find the comment `/* TODO: put your data source class name here /*`. Replace that comment with `DerbyNamesEntities` like this:

```
public class DerbyService : DataService<DerbyNamesEntities>
```

Now the service is connected to the data. However, by default OData doesn't expose any of the data for security reasons. To expose the two tables from the model, uncomment this line:

```
config.SetEntitySetAccessRule("MyEntityset", EntitySetRights.AllRead);
```

and change the string `"MyEntityset"` to `"*"` like this:

```
config.SetEntitySetAccessRule("*", EntitySetRights.AllRead);
```

The final `DerbyService.svc.cs` file should look like Figure 3-19.

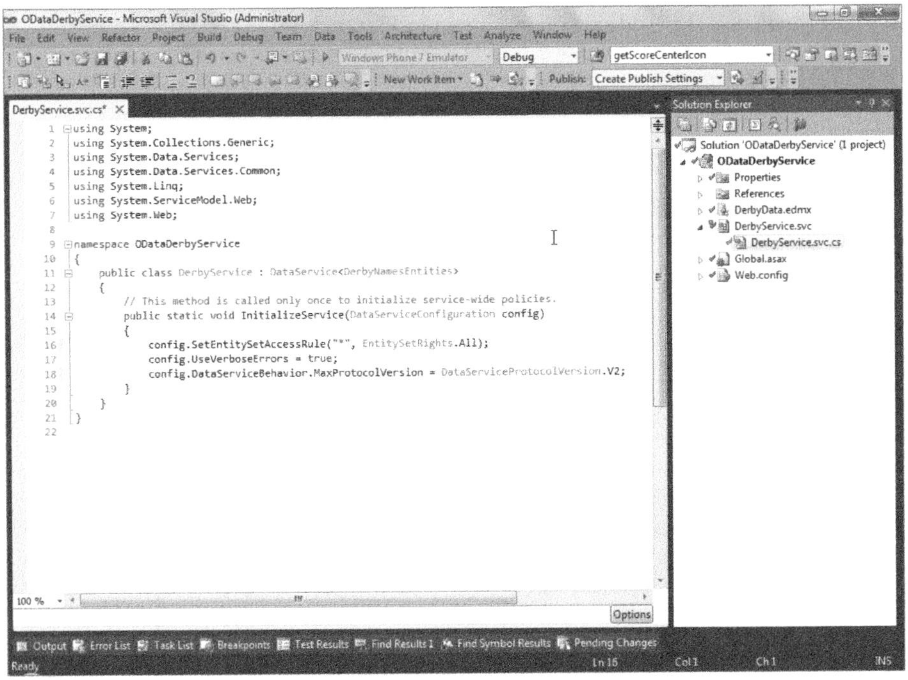

FIGURE 3-19: The final `DerbyService.svc.cs` file

That is all the configuration required to configure an OData service. Build the project, run the project, and if Visual Studio doesn't point the browser to the `DerbyService.svc` URL, navigate to /DerbyService.svc/. Figure 3-20 shows results in Google Chrome.

OData is showing `DerbyNames` and `Leagues` collections are available.

In the browser address bar add /DerbyNames after `DerbyService.svc`. The service responds with an XML document showing the `DerbyNames` from the database. Notice the `DerbyNames` XML document isn't color coded — this is because the content type request header is `application/atom+xml` instead of `application/xml`. OData uses the Atom and AtomPub format to represent collections. Also notice the `DerbyNames` XML

FIGURE 3-20: Chrome displaying service results

document has links like `<id>http://localhost:25457/DerbyService.svc/DerbyNames(1)</id>`. That link is to the URL showing the `DerbyName` with a primary key of 1. This starts to show the power of OData. OData provides many querying capabilities. The document is telling consumers how to query the service for a particular instance of a collection item.

To expand upon the querying capabilities, enter this URL:

```
/DerbyService.svc/DerbyNames?$filter=League%20eq%20'Lansing%20Derby%20Vixens'
```

The query string is telling the OData service to return items from the `DerbyNames` collection where `League` is equal to "Lansing Derby Vixens." OData responds by returning all the players in the system from the Lansing Derby Vixens league as shown in Figure 3-21.

FIGURE 3-21: Chrome displaying query results

OData does have the capability to return JSON. Unfortunately, the WCF Data Services implementation does not implement the `$format` query parameter specified in the OData specification. Instead, the WCF Data Services implementation responds with JSON only when the HTTP accept request header is set to `"application/json"`. Unfortunately, some programming platforms do not support changing request headers. The following procedure shows how to make the service return JSON without modifying the request headers on the client.

First, the service code needs to have access to all incoming requests before the requests are put into the OData pipeline. To get access to the requests, right-click the ODataDerbyService project and select Add New Item. In the Add New Item dialog box Installed Template tree, select Web. From the Templates select Global Application Class. Click the Add button to create the codefile in the project as shown in Figure 3-22.

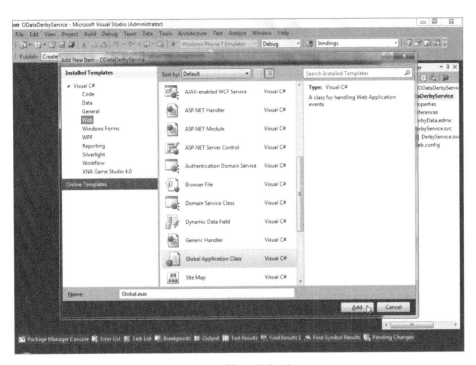

FIGURE 3-22: Add New Global Application Class dialog box

The Global class has a method named Application_BeginRequest, which is called when an HTTP request enters the application. This is a good spot to change the HTTP accept request header before WCF Data Services processes the request. To change the request header, insert the following line in the Application_BeginRequest method:

```
protected void Application_BeginRequest(object sender, EventArgs e)
{
    HttpContext.Current.Request.Headers["accept"] = "application/json";
}
```

Unfortunately, the ASP.NET Development Server does not allow modifying the request headers, but IIS 7.5 does. For this method to work in the debug environment requires using IIS Express instead of the ASP.NET Development Server. To change the environment, right-click the ODataDerbyService project and click Properties. From the properties window navigation tree select the Web tab. In the Web tab find the Servers section and select the radio button for Use Local IIS Web Server. Mark the Use IIS Express checkbox and accept the Project URL, as shown in Figure 3-23.

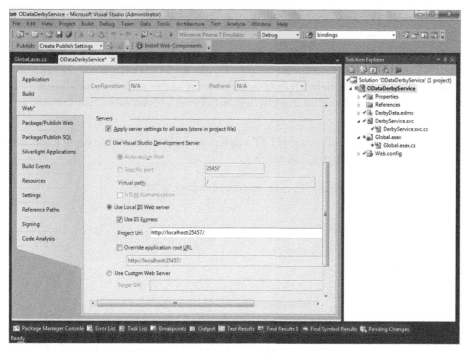

FIGURE 3-23: ODataDerbyService Project Properties dialog box

Close the property window to save the changes. Build the project, run it, and change the browser URL to /DerbyService.svc/DerbyNames?$filter=League%20eq%20'Lansing%20Derby%20 Vixens'.

The document is now returned in JSON instead of XML as shown in Figure 3-24.

```
{
"d" : [
{
"__metadata": {
"uri": "http://localhost:25457/DerbyService.svc/DerbyNames(10)", "type": "DerbyNamesModel.DerbyName"
}, "DerbyNameId": 10, "Name": "C3KO", "Number": "6106", "DateAdded": "\/Date(1272758400000)\/", "League":
"Lansing Derby Vixens"
}, {
"__metadata": {
"uri": "http://localhost:25457/DerbyService.svc/DerbyNames(11)", "type": "DerbyNamesModel.DerbyName"
}, "DerbyNameId": 11, "Name": "Frisky Business", "Number": "Purrfect 10", "DateAdded":
"\/Date(1272758400000)\/", "League": "Lansing Derby Vixens"
}
]
}
```

FIGURE 3-24: Chrome showing JSON result

For this query, changing the format to JSON resulted in a 75 percent reduction in the size of the document.

OData also enables inserting and updating data. Open the `DerbyService.svc.cs` file and change the `config.SetEntitySetAccessRule` second parameter from `EntitySetRights.AllRead` to `EntitySetRights.All`. This will make all data in all tables readable and writable. To set rights on a specific table use a line like this: `config.SetEntitySetAccessRule("tableName", EntitySetRights.All);`

To insert a player name, submit the following HTTP request programmatically or using a tool like Fiddler (discussed in the later "Debugging" section):

```
POST http://localhost:25457/DerbyService.svc/DerbyNames HTTP/1.1
User-Agent: Fiddler
Host: localhost:25457
content-type: application/json
Content-Length: 108

{"Name":"gravityworks",
"Number":"infinity",
"League":"Lansing Derby Vixens",
"DateAdded": "2012/04/30"
}
```

OData is a great choice for applications that are dealing with CRUD operations. Instead of writing boilerplate code to read, update, delete, and insert data, OData gives a robust set of operations with little work.

Using ASP.NET MVC 3

ASP.NET MVC is a web framework released by Microsoft. It follows the model-view-controller pattern. This separation provides benefits such as easy testability and providing different views of the same model. These features make ASP.NET MVC a great choice for creating web services.

This walkthrough assumes the following software is installed:

- ➤ ASP.NET 4.0
- ➤ ASP.NET MVC 3
- ➤ Visual Studio 2010
- ➤ IIS 7.5
- ➤ Microsoft SQL Server 2008 R2

To get started you need a project. Open Visual Studio and select File ➪ New Project. From the New Project dialog box, select the Web node from the Installed Templates tree and then select ASP.NET MVC3 Web Application. Name the project **MVCDerbyService** and click OK to create the project as shown in Figure 3-25.

FIGURE 3-25: Create new ASP.NET MVC 3 Web Application Project dialog box

On the New ASP.NET MVC 3 Project Template dialog box, select Internet Application, set the view engine to Razor, and check the Use HTML5 Semantic Markup checkbox. Then click OK to continue. Figure 3-26 shows the configuration screen with the options for this walkthrough.

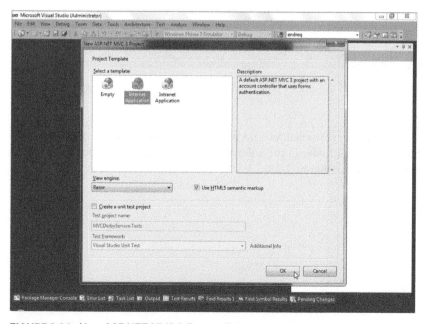

FIGURE 3-26: New ASP.NET MVC 3 Project Template dialog box

For ease of database access this walkthrough uses LINQ to SQL. Using LINQ to SQL requires an additional project reference to System.Data.Linq. To add the reference, right-click the References node of the DerbyNamesService project and select Add Reference. In the Add Reference dialog box click the .NET tab, find System.Data.Linq, and click the Add button as shown in Figure 3-27.

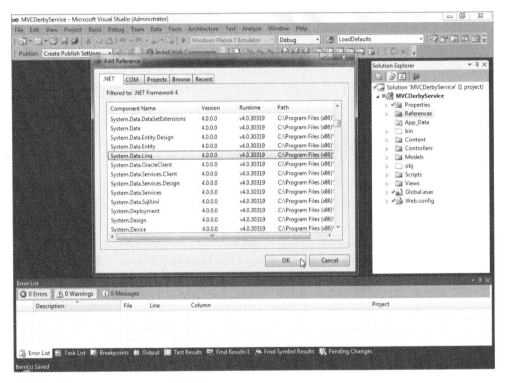

FIGURE 3-27: Add Reference dialog box

After adding the System.Data.Linq reference, you need to create a class to access the data. To add the data access class, find the Models folder in the Solution Explorer. Right-click the Models folder and select Add New Item as shown in Figure 3-28.

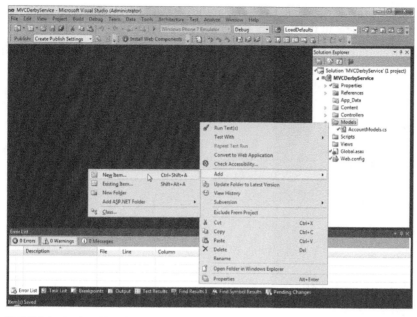

FIGURE 3-28: Add New Item menu

In the Add New Item dialog box, select the Web node from the Installed Templates tree. Then select Class from the Templates, name it **DerbyContext,** and click the Add button as shown in Figure 3-29.

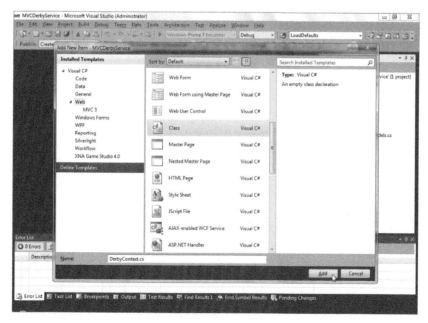

FIGURE 3-29: Add New Class dialog box

The `DerbyContext` class will provide the data. To represent the data as .NET objects, add two more code files, `DerbyNames` and `Leagues`, in the `Models` folder.

The `DerbyNames` class will contain the information on a derby player. Make the `DerbyNames.cs` file contain this code:

```
using System;
using System.Data.Linq.Mapping;
namespace MVCDerbyService.Models
{
    [Table]
    public class DerbyNames
    {
        [Column(IsPrimaryKey = true)]
        public int DerbyNameId;
        [Column]
        public string Name;
        [Column]
        public string Number;
        [Column]
        public DateTime? DateAdded;
        [Column]
        public string League;
    }
}
```

The `Leagues` class will contain information about the derby leagues, such as the league name. Make the `Leagues.cs` file contain this code:

```
using System.Data.Linq.Mapping;

namespace MVCDerbyService.Models
{
    [Table]
    public class Leagues
    {
        [Column(IsPrimaryKey = true)]
        public int LeagueId;
        [Column]
        public string LeagueName;
        [Column]
        public string URL;
        [Column]
        public string StateProvince;
        [Column]
        public string CountryCode;
    }
}
```

The `DerbyContext` will be the class providing access to the database from the `DerbyService` class. Modify the `DerbyContext.cs` code to contain this code:

```
using System.Data.Linq;

namespace MVCDerbyService.Models
{
    public class DerbyContext : DataContext
    {
        public Table<DerbyNames> DerbyNames;
        public Table<Leagues> Leagues;
        public DerbyContext()
            : base("Data Source=.;Initial Catalog=DerbyNames;
              User Id=webUser;Password=webuser;")
        { }
    }
}
```

MVC uses a concept called a controller to route requests. To create a request endpoint, right-click the `Controllers` folder and select Add Controller, as shown in Figure 3-30.

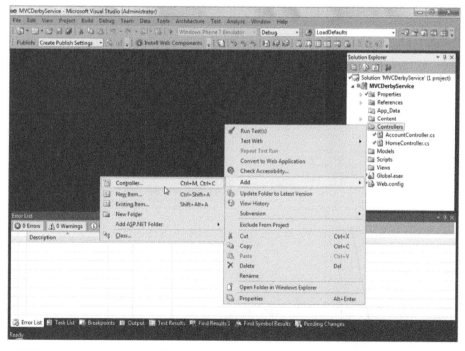

FIGURE 3-30: Add New Controller context menu

In the Add Controller dialog box, name the controller **DerbyServiceController** and select the Empty controller template.

Modify `DerbyServiceController.cs` to contain the following code:

```
using System.Collections.Generic;
using System.Linq;
using System.Web.Mvc;
using MVCDerbyService.Models;

namespace MVCDerbyService.Controllers
{
    public class DerbyServiceController : Controller
    {
        public ActionResult DerbyNames()
        {
            DerbyContext dc = new DerbyContext();
            List<DerbyNames> names = dc.DerbyNames.ToList();
            return Json(names, JsonRequestBehavior.AllowGet);
        }
    }
}
```

One controller class with one method is all MVC requires to create an HTTP endpoint. Build and run the project. Visual Studio will open a web browser with a localhost URL. Add `/DerbyService/DerbyNames` to run the preceding code. The results in Chrome are shown in Figure 3-31.

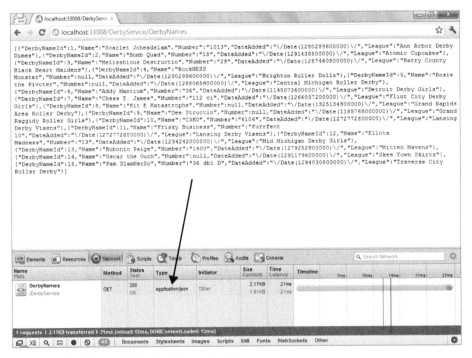

FIGURE 3-31: Chrome displaying the content type

Figure 3-31 shows MVC correctly set the content type to `application/json`.

What if the service needs to return XML? It would be nice to have an `XmlResult` class providing functionality similar to the `JsonResult` class. Unfortunately, MVC does not ship with an `XmlResult` class, but we can easily build one.

The `DerbyNames` method is returning a `JsonResult`, which is a type of `ActionResult`. To create an `XmlResult` class, first add a `Results` folder to the MVCDerbyService project to keep the project well organized.

Right-click the `Results` folder and add a new class named `XmlResult`. The contents of the `XmlResult` class should look like this:

```
using System.Web.Mvc;
using System.Xml.Serialization;

namespace MVCDerbyService.Results
{
    public class XmlResult : ActionResult
    {
        private object payload { get; set; }

        public XmlResult(object data)
        {
            payload = data;
        }

        public override void ExecuteResult(ControllerContext context)
        {
            XmlSerializer serializer = new XmlSerializer(payload.GetType());
            context.HttpContext.Response.ContentType = "text/xml";
            serializer.Serialize(context.HttpContext.Response.Output, payload);
        }
    }
}
```

MVC uses routes to match incoming request URLs to the appropriate controller. To enable returning XML, open the `Global.asax.cs` file in the root of the solution. Find the `RegisterRoutes` method and add `routes.MapRoute("format","{controller}/{action}.{format}");` between the two existing route statements.

```
public static void RegisterRoutes(RouteCollection routes)
{
    routes.IgnoreRoute("{resource}.axd/{*pathInfo}");

    routes.MapRoute( "format", "{controller}/{action}.{format}");

    routes.MapRoute(
        "Default", // Route name
        "{controller}/{action}/{id}", // URL with parameters
        new { controller = "Home", action = "Index",
        id = UrlParameter.Optional } // Parameter defaults
    );
}
```

With the route in place it is time to change the controller to respond to the format information. Open the `DerbyServiceController.cs` file and modify it like this:

```
using System.Collections.Generic;
using System.Linq;
using System.Web.Mvc;
using MVCDerbyService.Models;
using MVCDerbyService.Results;

namespace MVCDerbyService.Controllers
{
    public class DerbyServiceController : Controller
    {
        public ActionResult DerbyNames(string format)
        {
            DerbyContext dc = new DerbyContext();
            List<DerbyNames> names = dc.DerbyNames.ToList();
            if (string.Compare(format, "xml") == 0)
            {
                return new XmlResult(names);
            }
            return Json(names, JsonRequestBehavior.AllowGet);
        }
    }
}
```

After building and running the project, navigating to `/DerbyService/DerbyNames.xml` displays the same document in XML instead of JSON.

This approach of specifying the format in the URL works and provides advantages, for example being able to have anchor links to PDF and comma separated value (CSV) representations, but the HTTP specification has MIME types for content negotiation. Content negotiation enables the client to request the information as well as the format of the information. For example, web browsers request text/html. For correctness and expected behavior the service should return HTML, XML, or JSON depending on what the client requests in the accept header. If the service does not support the requested type, the service should return a 406 error code specifying the valid values for the header, such as HTML, XML, and JSON.

Supporting different request headers will require a new result class. Add an `AcceptHeaderResult` class in the `Results` folder. Open the `AcceptHeaderResult.cs` file and replace the generated file contents with the following code:

```
using System.Web.Mvc;

namespace MVCDerbyService.Results
{
    public class AcceptHeaderResult : ActionResult
    {
        private object payload { get; set; }

        public AcceptHeaderResult(object data)
        {
```

```
            payload = data;
        }

        public override void ExecuteResult(ControllerContext context)
        {
            string accept = context.HttpContext.Request.Headers["accept"].ToLower();

            ActionResult result = null;
            if (accept.Contains("text/html" ))
            {
                context.Controller.ViewData.Model = payload;
                result = new ViewResult() { TempData = context.Controller.TempData,
                    ViewData = context.Controller.ViewData };
            }
            else if (accept.Contains("application/json"))
            {
                result = new JsonResult() { Data = payload, JsonRequestBehavior =
                    JsonRequestBehavior.AllowGet };
            }
            else if (accept.Contains("text/xml"))
            {
                result = new XmlResult(payload);
            }
            else
            {
                result = new HttpStatusCodeResult(406, "Type not supported.");
            }
            result.ExecuteResult(context);
        }
    }
}
```

To use the new `AcceptHeaderResult` class you need to modify the `DerbyService` controller to use it. Modify the `DerbyServiceController.cs` file like this:

```
using System.Collections.Generic;
using System.Linq;
using System.Web.Mvc;
using MVCDerbyService.Models;
using MVCDerbyService.Results;

namespace MVCDerbyService.Controllers
{
    public class DerbyServiceController : Controller
    {
        public ActionResult DerbyNames()
        {
            DerbyContext dc = new DerbyContext();
            List<DerbyNames> names = dc.DerbyNames.ToList();
            return new AcceptHeaderResult(names);
        }
    }
}
```

Using a tool like Fiddler (discussed in the next section) enables you to modify the application headers to test the XML and JSON responses. To get the same JSON response from before, issue the following HTTP request:

```
GET http://localhost:33008/DerbyService/DerbyNames HTTP/1.1
Host: localhost:33008
Accept: application/json
```

To make the system respond with the unsupported error code, issue the following HTTP request:

```
GET http://localhost:33008/DerbyService/DerbyNames HTTP/1.1
Host: localhost:33008
Accept: invalid
```

On the ASP.NET Development Server, the nice message specifying the supported types of text/html, text/xml, and application/json is not displayed. The message text displays on IIS 7.5 and IIS Express.

This gives a nice framework to easily add new endpoints. To add the `Leagues` endpoint, add the following method to the `DerbyServiceController.cs` file:

```
public ActionResult Leagues()
{
    DerbyContext dc = new DerbyContext();
    List<Leagues> names = dc.Leagues.ToList();
    return new AcceptHeaderResult(names);
}
```

Adding that code snippet makes the JSON and XML HTTP requests work correctly. To add the HTML view, find the `DerbyService` folder underneath the `Views` folder. Right-click the `DerbyService` folder and select Add View. Name the view **Leagues**.

Open the `Leagues.cshtml` file and modify it as shown in the following code snippet:

```
<h2>Leagues</h2>

    @foreach (var item in @Model)
    {
        <div>
            <span>@item.StateProvince</span> - <span>@item.LeagueName</span>
        </div>
    }
```

To make this service discoverable, add content at /DerbyService. This requires a change to the `DerbyServiceController` and an additional view. In the `DerbyService` subfolder of the `Views` folder, add a new view named **Index**. Put the following code in the view:

```
@{
    ViewBag.Title = "Index";
}

<h2>Index</h2>
```

```
<div>
    @Html.ActionLink("DerbyNames", "DerbyNames")

</div>
<div>
    @Html.ActionLink("Leagues", "Leagues")
</div>
```

After adding the index file you need to hook it up. To enable the endpoint, open `DerbyServiceController.cs` and add the following method:

```
public ActionResult Index()
{
    return View();
}
```

After making those changes, navigating to `/DerbyService` shows a link for `DerbyNames` and a link for `Leagues`.

This section has shown how easy it is to create a consumable service in ASP.NET MVC. The technology is geared toward making websites, but the extensible and pluggable nature of the technology makes it a great choice for creating consumable services.

Using the Linux Apache MySQL PHP (LAMP) Stack

Web services are cross platform. This section shows how to configure a web server on Linux to retrieve data from a MySQL database and leverage a technology called OData to deliver querying functionality with little work. OData is a web platform that enables create, read, update, and delete operations over HTTP. OData is used to expose information from systems such as relational database, file systems, and traditional websites using existing web technologies such as HTTP, XML, and JSON. Think of it as exposing parts of your database to the World Wide Web.

This walkthrough assumes the following software is installed:

- ➤ Ubuntu 11.10
- ➤ Apache2 with URL rewrite mode
- ➤ PHP-5.4
- ➤ MySQL
- ➤ Symfony 2.0
- ➤ PHP5s XSL extension
- ➤ PHP Extension and Application Repository (PEAR)

To use OData on MySQL, first you need a data source, meaning someplace where the data is contained. Download the file named `MySQL-Create-DerbyNames-Database.sql` from the download section for this book at `http://www.wrox.com`. This document contains a script that will create the DerbyNames database, which consists of a leagues table and a derby names table.

To execute the script from a terminal, run the following command to log into the MySQL admin console:

```
mysql -u root -p
```

Enter the root password when MySQL prompts for a password.

From the MySQL command prompt, execute the script by entering the following command:

```
source DerbyNames.sql
```

After creating the database, the next task is to download the OData Producer Library for PHP. The OData Producer Library is software that will expose the MySQL database as an OData source. Download it from http://odataphpproducer.codeplex.com/.

Unzip the file contents and copy the OData Producer Library files to /var/www/OData and ensure the /var/www/OData directory has an Index.php file.

Next, PHP needs to know where the OData library is located. To configure PHP to look for the OData Producer Library for PHP, create an OData.ini file in /etc/php5/conf.d$. After creating the file, type in the following line of code and save the file:

```
include_path = ":/var/www/Odata:/var/www/OData/library";
```

For the OData library to handle a request, Apache needs to hand the request to OData. By default, on the Microsoft Windows .NET stack OData services end in .svc. To keep that convention on this Apache configuration, modify /var/etc/apache2/httpd.conf by adding these lines:

```
<Directory "/var/www">
    <IfModule mod_rewrite.c>
    RewriteEngine on
    RewriteRule (\.svc.*) OData/Index.php
    </IfModule>
</Directory>
```

The OData Connector for MySQL will examine a MySQL database and produce all the PHP code files necessary for read-only OData operations except one — the OData connector for MySQL does not create the code for IDataServiceStreamProvider. IDataServiceStreamProvider is used to deliver binary data, for example an image or a video, through the OData Producer Library.

The OData Connector for MySQL requires a specific piece of software called Doctrine Object Relational Mapper. This software is an Object Relational Mapper (ORM). For those unfamiliar with it, an ORM represents database tables as programming language objects.

Using the PEAR package manager, the Doctrine Object Relational Mapper can be installed using the following commands:

```
sudo pear channel-discover pear.doctrine-project.org
sudo pear install doctrine/DoctrineORM
```

With the prerequisite ORM installed, it is time to download the OData Connector for the MySQL library. The OData Connector library is built to generate PHP code files to perform OData operations against a MySQL source. You can download the package from http://odatamysqlph-pconnect.codeplex.com. The following steps are for V 1.0.

Navigate to the directory the package downloaded to and unzip it. Open a terminal and navigate to the unzipped package directory.

To generate the code files, execute the following command:

```
php MySQLConnector.php /db=DerbyService /srvc=DerbyService /u=webUser
/pw=webuser /h=localhost
```

Running the MySQLConnector.php script states:

```
EDMX file is successfully generated in the output folder.
Do you want to modify the EDMX file-/home/smithd98/Downloads/MySQLConnectorV1.0
/ODataConnectorForMySQL/OutputFiles/Northwind/NorthwindEDMX.xml(y/n):
```

Press N and the Return key to indicate no.

The terminal will print the following success messages:

```
MetadataProvider class has generated Successfully.
QueryProvider class has generated Successfully.
DataServiceProvider class has generated Successfully.
DSExpressionProvider class has generated Successfully.
Service.config file has generated Successfully.
```

Copy the generated files into the /var/www/OData/services/DerbyNames directory with the following two commands:

```
sudo mkdir /var/www/OData/services/DerbyNames
sudo cp ~/Downloads/MySQLConnectorV1.0/ODataConnectorForMySQL
/OutputFiles/DerbyNames/* /var/www/OData/services/DerbyNames/
```

One of the files generated by the MySQLConnector script is service.config.xml. This file specifies the configuration information to correctly activate the service. Unfortunately, the service.config.xml file generated doesn't work correctly on Linux. To work on Linux it needs to be modified slightly.

The contents of the /var/www/OData/services/DerbyNames/service.config.xml file generated by the library are:

```xml
<?xml version="1.0"?>
<configuration>
 <services>
  <Service Name="DerbyNames.svc">
    <path>Services\DerbyNames\DerbyNamesDataService.php</path>
    <classname>DerbyNamesDataService</classname>
    <baseURL>/DerbyNames.svc</baseURL>
  </Service>
 </services>
</configuration>
```

The contents of the `/var/OData/services/DerbyNames/service.config.xml` Service element need to be copied into the `/var/www/OData/services/service.config.xml` services element as a child element.

After copying it in there, you need to make some slight changes:

1. Change the `Service` node to lowercase.

2. Replace the backslash (\) in the path node with a forward slash (/) so the paths are valid on Linux.

3. Change `Services` to lowercase in the path node.

After making those changes, the file should look like this:

```
<?xml version="1.0"?>
<configuration>
 <services>
  <service Name="DerbyNames.svc">
    <path>services/DerbyNames/DerbyNamesDataService.php</path>
    <classname>DerbyNamesDataService</classname>
    <baseURL>/DerbyNames.svc</baseURL>
  </service>
 </services>
</configuration>
```

Use a web browser to navigate to `http://localhost/DerbyNames.svc/DerbyNames`. Firefox will display an XML document, as shown in Figure 3-32.

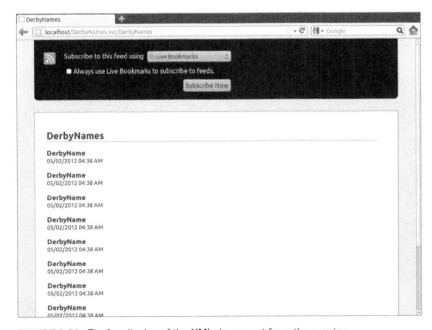

FIGURE 3-32: Firefox display of the XML document from the service

If the browser displays an error like this:

```
Warning: Cannot modify header information - headers already sent by
(output started at /var/www/OData/services/DerbyNames/
DerbyNamesQueryProvider.php:390 in /var/www/OData/Dispatcher.php on
line 205
```

edit the file `/var/www/OData/services/DerbyNames/DerbyNamesQueryProvider.php` by removing line 326. In the version I have there is a bug putting an empty line at the end of the file (after the `?>`).

Save the file and then reload `http://localhost/DerbyNames.svc/DerbyNames` in the browser. The XML document shown in Figure 3-32 should display.

With everything working correctly it is time to take advantage of OData features! First, use JSON instead of XML to reduce the size of the data returned by the OData service calls. To change the format to JSON, use the following URL:

```
http://localhost/DerbyNames.svc/DerbyNames?$format=json
```

This time the browser displays the raw JSON, as shown in Figure 3-33.

FIGURE 3-33: JSON output from service

Another feature of OData is that it enables querying data over HTTP. To query the service for all the players in the Lansing Derby Vixens league, enter the following URL in the Firefox web browser:

```
http://localhost/DerbyNames.svc/DerbyNames?$filter=Leagues eq 'Lansing Derby
Vixens'&$format=json
```

Firefox displays the only two players in the database from the Lansing Derby Vixens League, as shown in Figure 3-34.

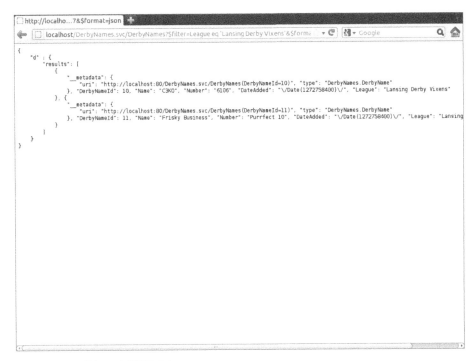

FIGURE 3-34: Filtered JSON data

OData enables developers to quickly expose read, write, update, and delete operations through web services. This chapter touched a bit on OData's querying capabilities. The querying capabilities would take many hours of development time to get the same functionality OData provides. These querying capabilities make the service flexible, which speeds up development because the service doesn't need to be constantly modified to meet new requirements. To learn more about the OData specification and features that were not shown in this chapter, visit `http://odata.org`.

This section walked through creating a sample database, configuring Apache for OData, installing the OData library, and configuring the OData library. OData is a good choice to use for web services that need to provide create, read, update, and delete (CRUD) operations because it provides so much functionality and flexibility for such a small effort.

DEBUGGING WEB SERVICES

Despite your best intentions, all developers are not perfect and the web service you create will not work exactly correct the first time you try to test it. This section discusses methods to figure out what is going wrong.

Tools

Understanding why a web service is not working correctly can be difficult because most of the code running is standard software and not code written by you or your team. Most of the code delivering web services consists of the libraries being leveraged, the platform the code is running on, the web server code running, and the operating system code.

Fiddler

When debugging web services, it is important to have the capability to see the raw requests and responses. Fiddler is a free Windows tool that does just that. Find installation instructions and the download at `http://www.fiddler2.com`.

Fiddler shows the raw HTTP traffic for the Windows system on which it is running. This means the tool will show the raw HTTP service request and HTTP response if the system running Fiddler is the one making the request. Unfortunately, when developing mobile applications, Fiddler will not be able to show the HTTP traffic because it is coming from an external device. Fiddler has another feature called Composer that allows the creation and execution of a raw HTTP request. The Composer feature enables testing and debugging of services. Getting the request and response to behave as expected is often the first place I start when debugging a misbehaving web service. I configure the Fiddler request builder to go against my localhost, which also enables me to set breakpoints in my code. After the request and response are working correctly, I ensure my code is passing data that matches what I've produced in Fiddler.

The two most important features of using Fiddler to debug web services successfully are the filters and Composer. When Fiddler is running it captures all the HTTP traffic on the machine on which it is running. This is typically too much data, which obscures the web calls that are important. Fiddler has the concept of filters, which enable a user to hide HTTP traffic that is not of interest. I usually use the Hosts filter to show only traffic from localhost and `http://www.GravityWorksDesign.com` as shown in Figure 3-35.

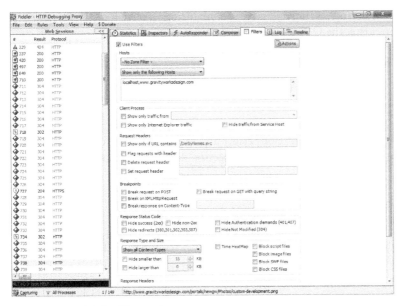

FIGURE 3-35: Fiddler Filters tab

The other feature I use all the time is Composer. Composer enables putting together the exact HTTP request to have executed. This is useful for understanding why a web service call isn't working, especially requests that use HTTP accept headers, because those requests cannot be executed by a default web browser.

Figure 3-36 shows using Fiddler to build an HTTP POST request to add a player to the WCF service created earlier in the chapter.

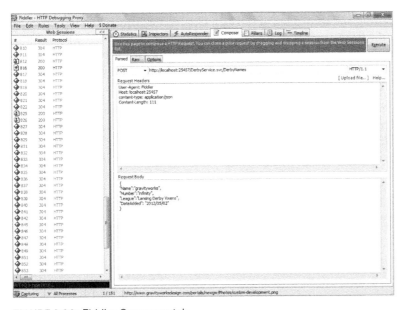

FIGURE 3-36: Fiddler Composer tab

Fiddler is a must-have tool for debugging on the Windows platform.

Wireshark and MAC HTTP Client

When developing services on the Macintosh platform I use the Mac HTTP client to test web service requests. Unfortunately, it does not capture traffic like Fiddler. When I need to capture traffic on Macintosh or Linux platforms I turn to Wireshark (http://www.wireshark.org/download.html), a free, open source debugging tool that is much more advanced than Fiddler or the Mac HTTP client. Wireshark is an advanced packet analysis tool used for HTTP traffic analysis as well as any other network traffic, such as debugging IP phones. For my simple needs of just debugging HTTP web calls, the additional features and complexity of Wireshark make it harder for me to use. For those not developing web services on the Windows platform, Wireshark will be a crucial tool. Figure 3-37 shows Wireshark in action on Linux.

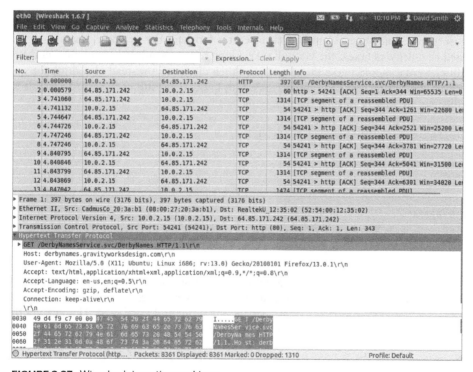

FIGURE 3-37: Wireshark in action on Linux

Advanced Web Service Techniques

This section covers two advanced web service techniques: Web Sockets and Web Service Callbacks. These techniques are not required for consumable web services, but can help services run efficiently.

Web Sockets

The HTTP protocol is designed for servers to respond to client requests. The client asks for a resource and the server delivers that resource. A problem arises if the server wants to deliver a resource to the client. For example, a stock viewing site like `http://www.google.com/finance?q=p` would be more valuable if it were able to update data on the client when the stock data changes. Today the most supported way to do this is by having the client continually ask the server "Do you have any new data for me?" This is wasteful because oftentimes the answer is no. That method is known as polling. Using Web Sockets a web server is able to deliver new data to the client without the client having to ask for the new information.

As of this writing Web Sockets are an emerging technology that not all browsers support. As support becomes more mainstream, web applications for things like e-mail, weather, traffic information, and so on will benefit from the ability for servers to notify clients when there is more current information.

Web Service Callbacks

Sometimes a web service needs to call another one after it is finished. For example, if a web service is exposed that delivers faxes, the fax will take a long time to send. When submitting the fax request, the calling service should make the request and then disconnect instead of waiting for the result. However, the calling service eventually needs to know the result of the fax. To enable this web service, callbacks are used. Consider the following POST request:

```
POST http://faxservice.com/fax/000123456 HTTP/1.1
Host: faxservice.com
content-type: application/json
Content-Length: 107

{
"faxId": "9839384",
"OnComplete": "http://www.gravityworksdesign.com/faxresultreceiver",
"MessageBody":"sending a fax"
}
```

The requester submits that HTTP POST request to inform the fax service to make a fax to `000123456`. After the fax service executes that request and gets a result, it calls the `OnComplete` service at `http://www.EXAMPLE.com/faxresultreceiver` passing the result and the `faxId`. This enables the original requester to match that `faxId` and result with the request it initiated.

SUMMARY

This chapter covered a lot of ground. Initially the chapter discussed overall web service concepts before diving into specific implementations of example services on a variety of technologies. The first walkthrough created an OData web service on the Linux platform. The next set of walkthroughs focused on three Microsoft technologies on the Windows platform: WCF, OData, and ASP.NET MVC.

After understanding the walkthroughs, you learned that OData is a good choice for creating CRUD services without complex business logic very quickly. You have learned WCF provides a lot of functionality and customization, but much of it is not needed for web services. You have learned ASP.NET MVC is a great platform for developing web services with complex business logic, because it provides extreme flexibility without complex features getting in the way.

The chapter wrapped up by discussing techniques for debugging services and some advanced web service techniques. The service implementations are intended to give readers a good starting point for creating consumable web services which will work for mobile applications and other applications.

Now that you know how to design and implement web services, the next chapter discusses mobile user interface design. The chapter focuses on issues like effective use of screen real estate, accessibility, and designing for the different platforms.

Mobile User Interface Design

WHAT'S IN THIS CHAPTER?

➤ Using the screen real estate efficiently

➤ How the user perceives design elements

➤ Social aspect of mobile interfaces

➤ Accessibility

➤ Design patterns

➤ Designing for the platforms

Design falls into the category of craftsmanship: you do something until you are good at it, and then keep doing it until you are better. But many developers are too excited to solve the next functionality puzzle to spend much time with interface questions like appropriate color contrast or font. Don't miss out on amazing design puzzles.

The latest generation of mobile devices are portable enough to carry at all times, connected to voice and data networks, and contextually aware by using sensors and networks to preemptively complete tasks.

Current mobile limitations include bandwidth, times when users cannot access wireless Internet or phone networks, as well as a lack of technical capabilities, such as Flash, on many mainstream mobile devices. These constraints give application creators the opportunity to focus each application on a precise set of features. Mobile application creators can also use exciting new interactions with motion and gestures: zooming, swiping, tapping, turning, and shaking. These capabilities offer the chance to innovate.

Technology is changing and no device has a guaranteed market share in perpetuity, providing the easy excuse that the next device might change everything anyway. But like learning the syntax of one programming language and applying this knowledge to learn the next industry standard, good design transcends next season's toy. Developers who understand the people who will use an application and the information users need will craft better applications no matter where technology goes next.

So, let's talk design.

This chapter will introduce the mobile design context, detailing ways to use screen real estate efficiently. The rest of the discussion is divided among the people, the data, and the device. From Gestalt principles to accessibility on mobile devices, this chapter covers understanding your users. A discussion of design patterns and content structure introduces mobile information design, using illustrations and real-world examples. An overview of platform-specific tips and resources ends the chapter, with "Understanding Mobile Platforms."

EFFECTIVE USE OF SCREEN REAL ESTATE

The first step to use the smaller interfaces of mobile devices effectively is to know the context of use. Who are the users, what do they need and why, and how, when, and where will they access and use information?

Mobile design is difficult, as developers try to elegantly display a telescoped view of almost limitless information. But user experience issues are amplified on mobile interfaces. Cognitive load increases while attention is diverted by the needs to navigate, remember what was seen, and re-find original context. Cognitive load is the mental effort to comprehend and use an application, whatever the inherent task complexity or information structure may be.

Effectively use screen real estate by embracing minimalism, maintaining a clear visual hierarchy, and staying focused.

Embrace Minimalism

Limit the features available on each screen, and use small, targeted design features. Content on the screen can have a secondary use within an application, but the application designer should be able to explain why that feature is taking up screen space. Banners, graphics, and bars should all have a purpose.

Use a Visual Hierarchy

Help users fight cognitive distractions with a clear information hierarchy. Draw attention to the most important content with visual emphasis. Users will be drawn to larger items, more intense colors, or elements that are called out with bullets or arrows; people tend to scan more quickly through lighter color contrast, less-intense shades, smaller items, and text-heavy paragraphs.

A consistent hierarchy means consistent usability; mobile application creators can create a hierarchy with position, form, size, shape, color, and contrast.

Stay Focused

Start with a focused strategy, and keep making decisions to stay focused throughout development. A smaller file size is a good indicator of how fast an application will load, so the benefits of fighting feature creep extend beyond in-application user experience.

Focused content means users won't leave because it takes too long for the overwhelming amount of images per screen to load. And users won't be frustrated with the number of links that must be cycled through to complete a task. Text-heavy pages reduce engagement as eyes glaze over and users switch to another application.

If people have taken the time to install and open an application, there is a need these users hope to meet. Be methodical about cutting back to user necessities. Build just enough for what users need, and knowing what users need comes from understanding users.

UNDERSTANDING MOBILE APPLICATION USERS

While standing in line at the bank or a restaurant, people pull out their mobile devices to check in, entertain, and consume another dose of content. You can borrow metaphors from the real world, like a trash can or recycle bin holding deleted files; favor industry standards and make sure interface metaphors are appropriate to the device.

Don't be afraid to take new risks, but look to past design concepts to frame new ideas.

The Gestalt principles have had a considerable influence on design, describing how the human mind perceives and organizes visual data. The Gestalt principles refer to theories of visual perception developed by German psychologists in the 1920s. According to these principles, every cognitive stimulus is perceived by users in its simplest form. Key principles include proximity, closure, continuity, figure and ground, and similarity.

Proximity

Users tend to group objects together. Elements placed near each other are perceived in groups; as shown in Figure 4-1, people will see one group of three gears, and one group of two gears. Many smaller parts can form a unified whole.

FIGURE 4-1: Proximity

Icons that accomplish similar tasks may be categorically organized with proximity. Place descriptive text next to graphics so that the user can understand the relationship between these graphical and textual objects.

Closure

If enough of a shape is available, the missing pieces are completed by the human mind. In perceiving the unenclosed spaces, users complete a pattern by filling in missing information. Figure 4-2 illustrates the concept of closure: people recognize a triangle even though the figure is not complete.

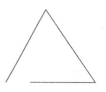

FIGURE 4-2: Closure

Harness the closure concept to create icons with a strong primary silhouette, without overloading users on pixelated and overdone details. In grid patterns with horizontal and vertical visual lines, use closure to precisely show the inside and outside of list items.

Continuity

The user's eye will follow a continuously-perceived object. When continuity occurs, users are compelled to follow one object to another because their focus will travel in the direction they are already looking.

FIGURE 4-3: Continuity

When people see Figure 4-3, they perceive the horizontal stroke as distinct from the curled stroke, even though these separate elements overlap. Smooth visual transitions can lead users through a mobile application, such as a link with an indicator pointing toward the next object and task.

Figure and Ground

A figure, such as a letter on a page, is surrounded by white space, or the ground. In Figure 4-4, the *figure* is the gear icon, and the *ground* is the surrounding space.

FIGURE 4-4: Figure and ground

Complex designs can play with the line between "figure" and "ground," but mobile interfaces speed user frustration with unclear distinctions. Primary controls and main application content should maintain a distinct separation between figure and ground.

Similarity

Similar elements are grouped in a semiautomated manner, according to the strong visual perception of color, form, size, and other attributes (see Figure 4-5). In perceiving similarity, dissimilar objects become emphasized.

FIGURE 4-5: Similarity

Strict visual grids confuse users by linking unrelated items within the viewport. The layout should encourage the proper grouping of objects and ideas.

The Social Aspect of Mobile

We all want to be connected, and to share something with the world. Social networking and social media outlets collect and distribute chunks of content from people across the globe, adding value to the user experience while spreading ideas and building reputations through trusted social networks.

Connect with Existing Outlets

It can certainly help spread the word about an application when users share in-application content with a wider audience. Count on users to share achievements or interests when "tweet results" or "like article" options are available. It might also be beneficial to simplify sharing and retrieving content from current network connections. This requires API integration according to the integrated network.

If socialization is not the primary function of an application, beware of feature creep as well as overwhelming users with cluttered interfaces. A single "share" button can open a pop-up box with sharing options, which saves space and simplifies adding or removing options.

If any person really must build new social outlets without leveraging existing platforms and APIs, I will not discourage you from building the next great thing. But focus the interface on providing something newer or better than what has already been done.

Usability

If a function cannot be discovered, is too small to read, or is not large enough to be selected, an application is not usable. With real-world distractions and limited dexterity, usable applications are the ones users will return to.

In a perfect world, usability considerations would be a regular, ongoing part of the whole process, checking how pixels and fingers interact in the real world (many a button has looked great in the mock-up design, only to be too small for actual people to use). This star life cycle is optimal: with evaluation as the center of the star, and various design and development tasks as branches of that evaluation process, this encourages ongoing iterations as user needs are discovered. Remember that it's better to do too little than nothing at all. If all else fails, hand over an application to a friend and see what happens when they try to use it.

Determining and Reaching the Target Audience

Research and determine the target audience: Who are they, what do they need, and how can they get it? It is important to consider the different hardware and usage patterns, whether holding an iPad with two hands in a meeting or thumbing through menus on the bottom of an Android phone screen.

Mobile applications can connect people with the world around them, providing personalized functionality. Popular applications include social networking; weather or traffic; consumable content such as music or news; productivity, education, and enrichment; and games.

Usable mobile applications help users perform tasks that are appropriate for mobile devices. Mobile tasks can involve quickly finding current information under some deadline (perhaps even an emergency), often requiring privacy and communication with other people. Usability therefore starts during mobile strategy, when stakeholders determine that the target audience will use the application functionality on mobile devices.

Designing for Gestures

If it is difficult to discover gestures to tap, pinch, swipe, and zoom across an application, this means average users will be missing out on those great features developers spent time building.

One simple solution is a pop-up box to announce the first time each gesture-prompted feature becomes available. Avoid swipe ambiguity: user error rates will be higher if the same swipe gesture can prompt multiple actions on the same screen.

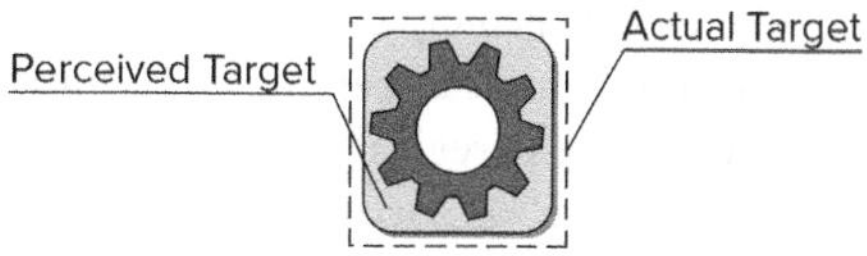

Be sure to consider the perceived versus the actual target area when designing for mobile gestures. The actual target area for touch input may be larger than the perceived target area as seen on the screen as shown in Figure 4-6. When there is no nearby gestural action, accommodate for finger sizes and user error by extending

FIGURE 4-6: Perceived target versus actual target

the actual input area into the white spaces beyond buttons and tabs. As much as possible, design dead space to reduce errors from touching nearby target areas.

Error Protection and Correction

Without a mouse, touch-screen navigation through menus, buttons, links, and scrolling is more prone to user errors. Be sure to include an "undo" or "back" option.

Every process should be designed to protect user input. Develop a log to preserve input history, and design the interface to simplify information retrieval. It can be difficult, and it is usually frustrating, to reproduce time-consuming data lost to accidental destruction, whether data is lost by user error or otherwise.

Implicit data protection avoids information loss, such as a hard stop between taps to slow text deletion. Explicit protections recover data with an undo option, and abandoned forms can be repopulated with recently entered data.

Save data as often, and in as much detail, as possible. Because mobile users become easily distracted or bored, always be prepared to stop application processes.

Accessibility

An application that is easier for people to use with poor or diminished vision, limited dexterity, or a cognitive impairment will be easier for all people to use. Consider accessibility as a way to reach more users, as well as a better way to reach existing users. Find better ways to build features for the entire intended audience.

Similar to the Web Content Accessibility Guidelines (WCAG) 2.0 POUR (perceivable, operational, understandable, and robust) principles, Mobile Web Best Practices (MWBP) is a World Wide Web Consortium standard defining a set of five checkpoints for mobile accessibility:

> **Overall Behavior:** Independent of specific device features, the guidelines for a general mobile experience.

> **Navigation and Links:** The ease of user interaction with hyperlinks on the mobile device interfaces.

> **Page Layout and Content:** How content is designed on each page, and how chunks of content are laid out for accessible consumption.

> **Page Definition:** Defining content areas for mobile device interpretation.

> **User Input:** Considerations of available mobile device input methods.

The POUR principles were created for mobile web interfaces, but apply to all mobile viewports and mobile user experiences. Common barriers to users with disabilities — whether content and features are perceivable, operable, understandable, and robust — are detailed by the W3C at http://www.w3.org/WAI/mobile/experiences.

Human life spans are increasing, and medical science cannot yet overcome our biology. So application creators who do not account for people with accessibility issues are designing themselves out of the future. Leverage the built-in features of various mobile devices, and test applications with assistive technology to validate the effective use of application features.

Hearing

Moderate to profound hearing loss can make it difficult for many people to communicate with a standard telephone, but many mobile devices offer features that make promising progress.

For moderate hearing loss, adjustable volume control offers a simple way to connect with mobile content. However, most solutions are focused on visual alerts: incoming or missed messages in call logs, text messages, on-screen prompts, and hardware-specific features such as blinking alert lights.

Vision

Many users depend on tactile, audio, or other sensory alerts to access resources using mobile devices. People with low vision through complete blindness may benefit from sliding or flipping a phone to answer and end calls (rather than a touch-screen button), and are likely to consider the hardware first. Popular and industry-standard devices without a flip or slide may be modified to meet the needs of low-vision users. Mobile application creators can consider adjustable font sizes, color contrast, and backlit displays.

Tactile markers on keyboards and other hardware-specific buttons can help orient users to available inputs. Where such hardware is not available, haptic feedback — kinesthetic indication, generally by device vibration, that the user has activated a control — provides feedback that a button has been pressed. Audible feedback and notifications can include action confirmation, such as low battery or incoming calls.

A great resource to find more accessibility recommendations for vision and other accessibility topics can be found at http://www.mobileaccessibility.info/.

Speech

Aid users with speech-related accessibility issues with output-related functionality using text features. Text messaging, email, and predictive text are popular solutions.

Consider allowing users to save text inputs to reuse personalized outputs. "I am leaving the office now" could be recycled from a personalized dashboard within a social mobile application.

Dexterity

Many people have difficulty for various reasons with the fine controls on a mobile device.

A hands-free mode can limit how much the phone must be held to properly navigate, which benefits low-dexterity users as well as busy cooks, lost drivers, and distracted parents. Voice recognition is an increasingly common way to manage hands-free controls. Limiting text input has a similar effect: autocompletion is increasingly common, and incredibly valuable.

It is not necessary to avoid twisting and pinching for complex gestural interactions, but designers and developers must be aware that the features and functionality behind such movements will be inaccessible to many. Therefore, consider if what these gestures prompt is integral to the use of an application; if so, multiple ways to access that function may be in order.

Reduce unnecessary error correction from low dexterity by enabling a setting where selecting any button will complete an important and time-sensitive function, such as answering a phone call while using another application.

Cognition

From birth to trauma to age-onset impairments, a large number of mobile devices are used by people with cognitive accessibility issues. Clear navigation and simple instructions are incredibly important, and help all users.

Any feature to reduce the cognitive load — the amount of information users must hold in their memory — is helpful. Associating images or photographs with long lists of information such as contacts can be helpful. Anticipate the information that users are seeking and allow shortcuts and prerecorded commands. Enable user customization to include audio, visual, and tactile alerts, as well as audio, visual, and tactile feedback as users navigate application features.

UNDERSTANDING MOBILE INFORMATION DESIGN

The visual display of information is how people connect with loved ones, colleagues, and friends. It is how we know our gas tank is almost empty or that we can cross the street. Mobile devices offer an exciting space to design information, fitting personalized and real-time data into tightly-constrained screens. But keep audience goals in mind when crafting an application, because mobile devices are not generally used for extensive browsing or complex searches.

This section covers charming, but not overwhelming, your audience with a discussion of key mobile design patterns. Because information design requires information, the structure and use of textual content also appears at the end of this section.

Information Display

A microwave has a simple display. When the timer alerts us the popcorn is done, we can check to see if the bag looks adequately puffed, and then open the microwave door and popcorn bag to start eating. People identify signals, interpret the meaning of these signals, determine the goal according to these interpretations, and then carry out an action until the goal is reached.

Go beyond returning user-requested data, and choose a personality that sets an application apart. The power to charm users can overstep redundant applications in industry-standard markets. Clean silhouettes on application screens that do not crowd designs will display information in the ideal manner. Overly detailed designs do not suit mobile users, who are often microtasking, influenced by urgent and new surroundings, and looking for a quick fix for boredom.

Design Patterns

Hardware and operating systems become irrelevant far quicker than design that reaches users. A design pattern recycles and repurposes components, reusing the best ideas. More than time efficiency, patterns have been refined by use. Look to patterns, and maintain a pattern library that works for you, but look to the user and the purpose of an individual design above any best practices.

Navigation

Good design makes it clear how users can move through and use application features.

Annunciator Panel

An *annunciator panel*, seen at the top of Figure 4-7, gives information on the state of a mobile device. Though each mobile device will provide a slightly different panel, developers can modify or suppress the annunciator panel — which lists the hardware features such as network connection and battery power — within an application. Because the information in this area is only notifications, application users will not usually have any direct interaction with the annunciator panel.

FIGURE 4-7: Annunciator panel

Fixed Menu

A menu that remains fixed to the viewport as users roam content is useful in many situations:

➤ When users need immediate access to frequently selected functionality on multiple screens

➤ When a revealable menu is already used on the same screen

➤ When a lack of controls, conflict with key interactions, or low discovery makes a revealable menu a poor choice

Because fixed menus are always accessible (at the bottom and top of Figure 4-8), users can interact with page content as needed; keep in mind the small screen real estate, and limit any fixed menus to the absolute necessities.

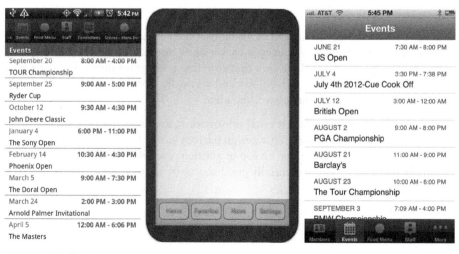

FIGURE 4-8: Fixed menu

Do not stack multiple fixed menus on top of each other, and reconsider the size and scope of an application if you have a fixed menu at both the top and bottom of a screen. The style, such as whether the menu goes across the top or bottom of the viewport, will be largely determined by the mobile device.

Expandable Menu

When all function options for one page cannot fit on the viewport, an expanding menu can provide selectively available options: a full menu similar to the one shown in Figure 4-9 will reveal once prompted. A gesture, like a swipe or double tap, may prompt the reveal as well as selecting an on-screen icon. Soft keys — hardware buttons connected to on-screen labels — may also prompt a menu to reveal. Users often benefit from multiple access options, especially for the harder-to-find gestural prompts.

Users may exit a menu using a back button, a close button that is part of the revealed menu list, or by toggling with the same gesture or soft key that prompted the reveal. Try to keep close functionality on the screen while the menu is revealed.

FIGURE 4-9: Expandable menu

Scroll

As in the case of a revealable menu giving additional functionality, there will often be more content on a screen than can be seen in the device viewport.

It is best to limit scrolling, limiting application screens to the size of the viewport whenever possible. Some types of apps you develop will require scrolling to present data to the user effectively, such as an email client. When scrolling must occur, check that the design communicates the area that can be scrolled, the current context of a user, and the ratio of the current view to the total content available.

Easy navigation keeps people connected, instead of losing users to navigational frustrations. Only in-focus items should be able to scroll. Make an application more immersive, incorporating gestures such as tilting to scroll through content. Make sure that scrolling takes place only on a single axis, if possible. When scrolling must occur both horizontally and vertically, consider providing a thumbnail of the user's place within the entire scrolling area.

The vertical list (Figure 4-10) simply displays textual information, and is the foundation of information display on many mobile devices. This design pattern works the same no matter how many results are returned. By stacking one line on top of another, each item takes up an entire line; this can be horizontally inefficient, but a potentially good source of white space.

FIGURE 4-10: Vertical list

An endless list of information breaks large data sets into manageable, consumable sizes within the viewport. One portion of content fills the screen, and when users either scroll to the end of a list (predictive retrieval) or select a "more" button (explicit retrieval), the application pulls more data from the server to the device (see Figure 4-11).

If there is an error generating information with predictive retrieval, the application will use explicit retrieval, with users selecting a "refresh" button to load more content.

Reduce the user's awareness of loading content by preloading content just beyond the screen when possible. To create great endless lists, monitor performance and data usage during production to find the best balance of prefetched and displayed content.

FIGURE 4-11: Endless list

Graphical data — profile photos, category icons, status indicators — can clarify content lists. Use position as well as size, contrast, and other identifiers to show the visual importance of elements that users utilize to sort information.

Selecting the thumbnail can lead to different functionality than the other content in a list item, but a thumbnail list (Figure 4-12) will have the same interactions as any other vertical list.

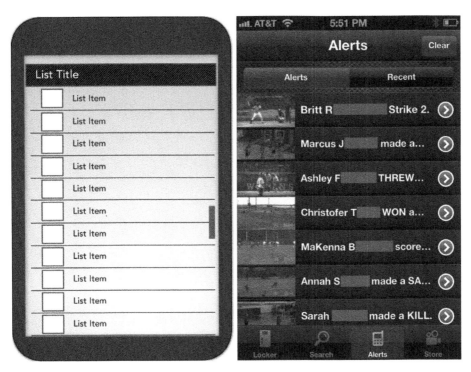

FIGURE 4-12: Thumbnail list

Thumbnails can be replaced by a default icon when a specific image is not available, but the value of the graphical indicator diminishes as more icons are not individually identifiable. Use icons and images to emphasize clarity and categorical distinction — embracing a strong and varied silhouette — over personality or generic graphics.

An expandable list, shown in Figure 4-13, reveals additional, valuable content for selected (touched) list items without leaving the current view.

The content that was visible before the reveal should remain unchanged; the top of the list will remain unchanged and the selected item will expand downward, as in Figure 4-13.

New information can be revealed as an animation whenever possible, aligning users with the structure and context of the expanded content areas. Higher-priority information, whether the revealed content or the list item title, should be set apart with size, color, or contrast.

FIGURE 4-13:
Expandable list

When application information is a group of images that are all or mostly unique, consider using a thumbnail grid (see Figure 4-14). You can use little to no text, and users can either scroll vertically or horizontally through the grid.

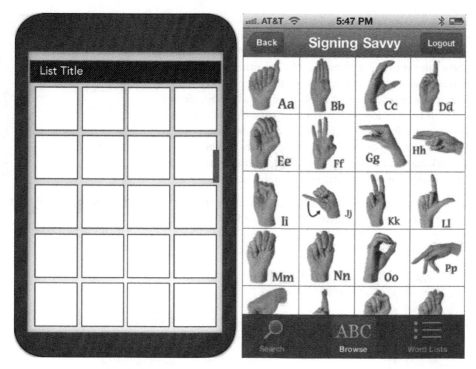

FIGURE 4-14: Thumbnail grid

Clearly identify in-focus or selected items with some type of visual indicator such as color, zoom, text label, or otherwise when the selected item does not immediately bring users to a new screen. Be sure to consider the accessibility of these distinctions, from color contrast to animation.

Users may scroll by gesture, device tilt, or on-screen buttons. Choose a different pattern if live-scrolling — a pixel-by-pixel response to user input — is not possible.

Notifications and Feedback

If the user needs new information, application creators must use notifications. These prompts pause ongoing tasks, and enable users to change processes and behaviors according to the new information or feedback.

Feedback is the user-perceived result of an interaction, providing immediate confirmation like a color change, message, or being led to a new page. Delayed feedback leads to user frustration and redundant, often error-inducing input; confirmation feedback is useful when user data could otherwise be lost, and should be indicated with a distinct change in state from the initial view.

Notification can inform a user (presenting a single button to close the notification), offer the ability to cancel a process or correct an error, or give multiple options from which to select. A user should never be presented with more than three options from any notification.

Users could be notified they must log in to access application features. Security is often overused, but if only authorized individuals should have access to application features — such as a personalized "favorites" collection — users may need to create an account or verify credentials in a login area. Obscuring passwords is not as important in mobile applications. The likelihood of data-entry mistakes outweighs the security concerns of small, easy-to-move screens. User expectations do, however, shape the perceived trustworthiness of an application. One solution is to briefly display each character either for a moment or until the next key is pressed, and then mask characters as dots. In a personal mobile device context, users should need to log in only the first time they access an application, and not on subsequent visits. However, users could be prompted to reenter their password within the application when completing high-risk transactions, such as making a bank withdrawal. Figure 4-15 is an example of a simplistic mobile login screen.

If the user must make a decision, or there is a risk of human error, a confirmation presents users with a choice. As shown in Figure 4-16, clearly and simply present the available options.

FIGURE 4-15: Log in

FIGURE 4-16: Confirmation

Because a notification forces users to read, decide, and act on a prompt to continue their task, users become frustrated with excessive confirmations.

Notifications, like those depicted in Figure 4-17, catch user attention to indicate that further action may be required, or that an action (such as a download or an update) has been completed. Visual design can be complemented with notification tones, a single and repetitive sound that may change frequency over time.

Some application screens should not be obscured or disrupted by notifications, such as mediacentric functionality like music players and video.

Try to group multiple prompts in a single view, so that no prompt obscures another important piece of information. Serialize redundant

FIGURE 4-17: Notification

prompts: if three friends favorite your latest announcement, a single notification prompt should say clearly say "you have three favorites," instead of three separate notifications.

Content and Controls

Input mechanisms, the controls users manipulate to enter or modify data, can be enhanced during the design process by keeping a few key concepts of mobile usability. Use standard controls, which positively shape user perceptions of an application. Consider giving distinct personality with custom graphics or textures on controls, to invite touch interaction with screen depth.

Mobile platforms differ on the minimal size of any touch point; controls to navigate, select, and read content should be large enough for a finger to press without error. If users are most likely to hold a mobile device from the bottom with one hand, then frequently selected points in the interface are more usable when placed toward the bottom of the screen. Put these primary controls in reach of users' thumbs, and create wide-enough controls that left-handed users can use buttons and tabs as easily as right-handed users. Information at the top of the screen will be out of the immediate comfortable reach of the average thumb: display less commonly selected functionality at the top of the screen. Figure 4-18 is an example of an app that contains multiple controls on a single screen; notice how each control can still be accessed within comfortable reach of the average thumb.

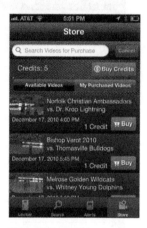

FIGURE 4-18: This application enables a variety of controls across the screen.

Be sure to minimize the need to enter data to access application features, especially text entry, which is often time-consuming and frustrating. Where data entry is actually necessary, consider the cross-platform differences in touch controls, and scale content for the various screen sizes and resolutions.

Reveal Content

You can display content either as a full page or revealed in context. When you use a full-page layout, the user should not need to constantly bounce back and forth between pages: all necessary information to use the features on that page should be displayed on that very page. If content might help users decide how to proceed, a quickly revealed, in-context design (such as a pop-up box) may be the better design choice.

A pop-up box, shown in Figure 4-19, is a modally presented piece of information that overlays the current screen and disrupts an ongoing user task. It is useful for displaying a small amount of information, but should keep an association with the current screen and task.

Users will request information, and this narrowed-down content should be displayed in a concise and useful way.

Display a range of information, from graphics to text, in an array such as an ordered list. Information can be contextually presented as an addition

FIGURE 4-19: Pop-up box

to other information, and be prioritized or sortable as shown in the two examples in Figure 4-20 (for smaller mobile devices) and in Figure 4-21 (for a larger mobile device).

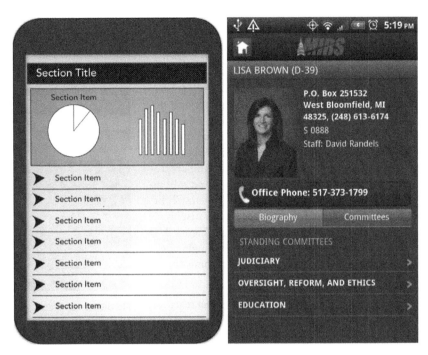

FIGURE 4-20: Returned result detail

FIGURE 4-21: A profile in landscape view on an iPad

A hierarchy of content (see Figure 4-22) shows the parent-child relationship of information within the context of a larger information set. Large amounts of data can be structured in a way that is relevant and readable. Precise labels and distinct structure helps users to explore, opening and closing content to find their way around the presented information.

Expandable panes, shown in Figure 4-23, reveal a small amount of content without leaving the context of the current application screen. Though the expanding functionality will not work on some lower-end or older devices, the additional information or interactive elements can enhance user experience.

However application information is displayed, lengthen the value of the application by replenishing content, adding levels or features, and building a community around the application.

FIGURE 4-22: Hierarchy

Intervening Screens

Between delivering personalized functionality and life-changing brilliance to users, there will be times that content must load, or a device becomes locked while the user looks up from their device. During those times, be sure to include application branding with the title of the application, and do not display information from any previous screen. In this section you learn about designing for intervening screens, beginning with the home and idle screens.

The Home and Splash Screen

The home and splash screens show a default set of available information when the application starts, or after a task has been completed. Make it clear when users are on the homepage with a distinctly different screen.

FIGURE 4-23: Expandable panes

The first screen of an application is a great opportunity for branding, as well as a potential point of frustration for impatient users. Minimize the use of long, over-animated splash screens and slow-to-access main features. One way to reduce wait time and increase user value is to store the last-opened screen, and display that screen the next time the application is opened. A useful design method to disguise slow launch times is to use the splash screen image (see Figure 4-24) as the application background: users will perceive a quicker entry to application features.

Parallax scrolling, where foreground and background content move at different speeds, will make the screen appear to have more depth. This technique helps users understand their current location within an application, and invite more immersive engagement.

Because frequent navigation to the home screen encourages users to jump between pages and between applications, avoid depending on the home screen for the continuous use of primary features. It is also preferable to send users to another actionable screen with some notification of the

FIGURE 4-24: Example splash screen

completed task instead of an idle screen: idle screens often send the message a task is complete, encouraging users to jump to another application.

The home screen is where important, frequently used features are highlighted, sometimes with branding and advertisements. As shown in Figure 4-25, the home screen layout can comfortably include up to three columns; content may include a logo, connect to key features, and link to deeper information.

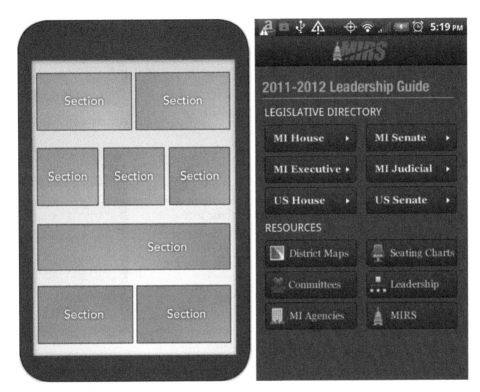

FIGURE 4-25: Home screen

The Loading Screen

An in-progress, "loading" screen signals when new data is loading, whether the user logs in to an account, enters search criteria, or is receiving an automated alert. Develop applications to load as quickly as possible to avoid showing the loading screen, but design to accommodate application limitations.

Include the estimated position in progress (as shown in Figure 4-26), and avoid showing information from the previous screen while newly requested data is loading. To shape user perceptions of load times and give the appearance of quicker data retrieval, place the progress indicator over a screen shot of the last screen. When there is sufficient delay, you can display advertising on the loading screen.

FIGURE 4-26: Loading screen

Advertising

Project stakeholders need to pay the bills, and advertising can certainly help. But application creators must find a balance of attention and integration to avoid two common mistakes: too-obvious advertising, and advertising that is confused for application content.

Set apart advertisements with a strong border, a different color or distinct texture for the background, a full-width box, or — when the advertisement is smaller than the screen width — a different alignment than application content.

Advertising styles and guidelines will vary across platforms, but advertisements must generally:

➤ Be clearly differentiated from application content.

➤ Remain unobtrusive to application features.

➤ Be actionable, and allow user interaction.

➤ Be legible.

➤ Use consistent styles and layout throughout application screens.

Advertisements may scroll within application content, or be locked (as in Figure 4-27) to the viewport. Avoid animated advertisements, which distract from primary tasks and information.

Whether content is paid advertising, curated by application administrators, or a help screen, the best content is useful content.

FIGURE 4-27:
In-application advertisements

Content Structure and Usage

Mobile application users are there to consume, produce, and share content: it does not matter how pretty or useful the application may seem to stakeholders if content is worthless to users.

Users need to quickly locate and effectively use information. Page layouts must therefore reflect the mental models that users understand. Label key elements to make it clear where users are, in context of where they can go, as well as how to complete the current process. These content titles should always be horizontal, and set apart with a different background or surrounding box. Be sure to maintain consistent capitalization, using either sentence or title case throughout all headers. Titles can include icons, but these should be descriptive of the content, and not needlessly redundant or vague.

Structured, templated designs are valuable to great user experience: when people can predict which information will appear on what screen, users can more easily manipulate and navigate through mobile screens.

Information Architecture

Give every application a strong foundation by organizing, labeling, and identifying all content that users will perceive. The most common structure is the parent-child relationship of a hierarchy. A growing segment of interactive content is *faceted*, tagging chunks of content with attributes that can be filtered during regular application use. Application creators and stakeholders generally know their message, and can lead users through content with an optimal hierarchy. But the benefits of personalized and sortable information cannot be ignored. Consider classifying information by name, sequence, a fixed relationship between values, the distance between values, geographic location and proximity, goals, or categorical subject matter.

When categorizing nonfaceted information, limit ambiguity with exclusive categories. It helps to take note of the most important category (a user role such as "student," a common action like "share") and keep all items in that menu the same theme ("student" and "teacher," or "find" and "share"). Be sure to balance the breadth, the user's ability to scan the page according to viewport size, and depth of the architecture. Limit the scope to a depth of two to three levels down.

Wayfinding, or how users will orient themselves in a space and move around it, is generally managed by paths, nodes, edges, landmarks, and districts.

Consistent, simple navigation elements help users find and use the best information an application has to offer. Decide what information is necessary, because too many options can be dangerously frustrating to users. Mobile users consume information and complete simple, linear tasks; jumping between tasks and comparing information are still more common to desktop user experiences. But do not discount the future of mobile, and the possibility of complex information seeking and content production.

Typography

The central focus of every application will often be textual content. The fonts used in any design are far less important than the way traditional typography methods are used throughout a mobile application.

Vector shapes will be rasterized on devices as fonts are converted to comply with device formats. Even newer devices, which now enable more than bitmap fonts, can make angles look pixelated. Technology is improving, but even the most high-end devices still have some degree of pixilation, so be sure to consider this limitation during design.

Size, shape, contrast, color, and position all matter. Type elements, and the relationship between type elements, should be immediately findable, consumable, and usable. Though sans serif fonts are generally considered easier to read on a viewport, serif or slab serif fonts have a proper place, such as bringing emphasis to a header (see Figure 4-28).

FIGURE 4-28: Serif, sans serif, and slab serif fonts

Text layout and alignment should follow certain readability guidelines. In a left-to-right language, left alignment is preferred over justified or center alignment. Because of the thin screen space, bullet lists are easier to scan than tables, and single-column layouts will generally work best.

Mobile interfaces compound the issues of web interfaces, and add new environmental factors and use cases. Interactive and dynamic interfaces enable exciting new design capabilities, such as animated notifications. But just because it's neat doesn't mean it is a good idea. If users only glance down at their screen when an animation is at a low-visibility point, they miss important information.

Plain Language

"Plain language" is the idea that content producers should speak in the language of their users, in a way that is clear and understandable to the audience. Content usability is one of the most important factors for task success, and plain language is usable language. Because of the limited space of a mobile device screen, these tips are especially relevant to mobile application creators:

➤ Omit unnecessary words. Take the first draft and cut it in half, and then see if you can cut it in half again (you probably can).

➤ Use the simplest form of a verb.

➤ Use short, simple words; avoid jargon and abbreviations.

➤ Use pronouns.

For more guidelines and in-depth examples, see `http://www.plainlanguage.gov`.

Mobile devices have tightly restricted widths; when determining readability, font size generally matters more than the number of characters per line. Precision is key to successful mobile content. Mobile plain language best practices also include:

➤ Focus keywords to the beginning or top of any screen.

➤ Use the same voice, preferably active voice, throughout the interface. Try to also use the same tense, when practical.

➤ If a product must be referenced, use a consistent product name.

➤ Correct unnecessarily mean or passive-aggressive error messages and task prompts.

➤ Avoid redundant content.

Plain language, and much of mobile design, is not about "dumbing down" the interface; it's about elegant precision. In the next section, you'll learn about sending a clear message over various industry-standard platforms.

UNDERSTANDING MOBILE PLATFORMS

Developers can take advantage of native functionality across mobile devices. More than a smaller, weblike interface, an Android, BlackBerry, WP7, or iOS device can make phone calls as well as record and transmit contextual information like geolocation.

As bad as it is to work into any particular corner, we all have comfort zones and favorite platforms. Just keep in mind that this fragmentation is bad for marketing, design, and user experience; this same market fragmentation is absolutely terrible for application creators to solve exciting new puzzles. Be aware of comfort zones and safety nets, and get ready to evolve.

Android

Android has a diverse ecosystem, with fewer institutionalized restrictions and a wider variety of mobile devices than other popular systems. The Android user base has grown to be a strong competitor in the mobile market, but the flexibility of Android design can introduce new issues. Development of the Android operating system is led by Google, and backed by a global and growing user base. Google maintains user interface guidelines in an online repository at `http://developer .android.com/guide/practices/ui_guidelines/index.html`.

Interface Tips

Get started on Android application design with these hints:

➤ Android convention is to place view-control tabs across the top, and not the bottom, of the screen.

➤ Use the main application icon for temporal, hierarchical navigation, instead of a "back" button and main icon link to the home screen.

➤ Don't mimic user interface elements or recycle icons from other platforms. For instance, list items should not use carets to indicate deeper content.

➤ Parallax scrolling is common in Android applications.

➤ Android development can extend to home-screen "widget" tools.

Accessibility

Google provides guidelines and recommendations, such as testing with the often-preinstalled and always-free TalkBack. Accessibility design guidelines are listed on the Android Developer website (`http://developer.android.com/guide/topics/ui/accessibility/index.html`), and further discussed by the Google "Eyes Free" project (`http://eyes-free.googlecode.com/svn/trunk/ documentation/android_access/index.html`).

iOS

Apple maintains strict design standards, which are detailed and updated online. iOS interface documentation and general mobile design strategies are available from Apple, including design strategies and case studies, at `http://developer.apple.com/library/ios/#documentation/ UserExperience/Conceptual/MobileHIG/Introduction/Introduction.html`.

The iOS-specific user interface element usage guidelines detail standard elements and behaviors: `http://developer.apple.com/library/ios/#documentation/UserExperience/Conceptual/ MobileHIG/UIElementGuidelines/UIElementGuidelines.html`.

Interface Tips

Apple can reject an application from the official App Store because of design problems. Follow the current guidelines closely, starting with these tips:

➤ iPhone users generally hold from the bottom of the device, so main navigation items should be in reach of user thumbs.

➤ Target areas for controls should be a minimum of 44 x 44 points.

➤ Support standard iOS gestures, such as swiping down from the top to reveal the Notification Center.

➤ Larger iPad screens are great for custom multi-finger gestures, but non-standard gestures should never be the only way to reach and use important features.

Accessibility

See Apple's Accessibility Programming Guide (`http://developer.apple.com/library/ios/#documentation/UserExperience/Conceptual/iPhoneAccessibility/Accessibility_on_iPhone/Accessibility_on_iPhone.html`) for detailed guidelines on VoiceControl, Speech Synthesis, and VoiceOver. Accessible touch and gestural controls are available on the iPad and later-generation iPhones; screen magnification and color contrast adjustments are also available.

BlackBerry OS

BlackBerry OS is often the mobile device of choice in government or corporate environments. BlackBerry includes native support of corporate emails; and runs on many devices with hard keypads, which is favored by users with accessibility issues as well as late adopters to touch-screen interfaces. Search through BlackBerry user interface guidelines according to device type and version, at `http://docs.blackberry.com/en/developers/subcategories/?userType=21&category=BlackBerry+UI+Guidelines`.

Interface Tips

When designing a BlackBerry mobile application, keep these standards in mind:

➤ Use BlackBerry UI components, not the tabs or other components of alternate platforms.

➤ Use standard interaction behaviors for an intuitive experience.

➤ Link common tasks to the BlackBerry track pad according to standard actions:

  ➤ **Press the track pad:** Default option, like revealing the menu

  ➤ **Press and hold track pad:** Activate available pop-up box

  ➤ **Press track pad and select Shift:** Highlight content

  ➤ **Press track pad and select Alt:** Zoom

  ➤ **Move finger along track pad:** Cursor or mouse will move accordingly

Accessibility

BlackBerry mobile devices include text-based push-delivery messages, closed captions on multimedia content, and hearing-aid compatibility for hearing accessibility issues. Low-vision users can use the Clarity theme and other screen adjustments, and benefit from tactile keyboards. Predictive text and AutoText aid users with mobility and cognitive issues.

Best practices and device capabilities are maintained online at `http://docs.blackberry.com/en/developers/deliverables/17965/Accessibility_825872_11.jsp`.

Windows Phone 7

Developed by Microsoft, Windows Phone 7 (WP7) is a currently smaller contender, focused on consumer markets. Using the "Metro" theme, features are divided into "Live Tiles" that link to applications.

Microsoft maintains design-impacting requirements for hardware, including six dedicated hardware buttons (back, start, search, camera, power, and volume), at least 4 GB of Flash memory, and Assisted GPS.

Microsoft also keeps a collection of WP7 design resources. See `http://msdn.microsoft.com/en-us/library/ff637515(v=vs.92).aspx` for more details.

Interface Tips

Windows Phone 7 interfaces are minimalist, using empty space to lend clarity to the application.

➤ WP7 uses movement over gradients for on-screen elements to immerse users in the application experience.

➤ Users will enter a WP7 application from a "tile," which can display dynamic and real-time information. Tile images should be in the PNG format, 173 pixels × 173 pixels at 256 dpi.

➤ Do not use a "back" button to navigate back the page stack. All WP7 devices have a dedicated hardware button that should always be used instead.

➤ Give users a distinctly WP7 experience. Panorama controls slide horizontally through panes, and pivot controls list panes users can visit. Uniform Page Shuffle presents nonhierarchical information users can shuffle through; "leaf-blowing turn" flips content area into focus, scattering and tilting tiles leaving focus.

Accessibility

WP7 devices include many standard accessibility features, such as color and contrast adjustment to themes for low-vision users. Many, but not all, devices are compatible with TTY, TDD, and hearing aids.

Learn more about the basics of WP7 accessibility at `http://www.microsoft.com/windowsphone/en-us/howto/wp7/basics/ease-of-access-on-my-phone.aspx`.

The full Accessibility and Ergonomic Guidelines for Windows Phone 6.5 are a good in-depth start, and are available at `http://msdn.microsoft.com/en-us/library/bb158589.aspx`.

Mobile Web Browsers

If a mobile application sends users to a website, that website should be optimized for mobile browsers. Similarly, mobile web applications should follow key mobile design methods. A great resource for design best practices for mobile web browsers is published by the W3C; see `http://www.w3.org/TR/mobile-bp/`.

Interface Tips

More detail is included in Chapter 5, but here are a few quick tips to get started:

➤ Test for a consistent experience when websites are accessed from a variety of mobile browsers.

➤ Provide minimal navigation at the top of the page, and use consistent navigation mechanisms.

➤ Do not change or refresh the current window, or cause pop-ups, without informing the user and providing the means to stop it.

➤ Limit content to what the user has requested, and what the user's device can display by avoiding large image files.

➤ Specify default input formats; when possible, provide preselected defaults.

Accessibility

The W3C Web Accessibility Initiative provides introductions, solutions, and further resources to create accessible mobile websites and mobile web applications. Learn more at `http://www.w3.org/WAI/mobile/`.

USING THE TOOLS OF MOBILE INTERFACE DESIGN

Design is a craft, and the tools shape how any individual's craft will develop. Some tools are discussed in this section, but be confident enough in yourself to stick to the tools that work for you; also, be confident enough in your craft to try new things. And always be looking for new things to try: your next favorite tool may already be available.

User Acceptance Testing

Understand your users — their behaviors, and their goals — with accurate measurement and thorough analysis. User Acceptance Testing (UAT) is an organization-specific, and a project-specific, process. But the right tools help application designers qualitatively and quantitatively know what users are doing, and what stakeholders are getting wrong.

Information Capture

Document user inputs and reactions the old-fashioned way by taking notes as users complete tasks. Video recording can archive tests for later review, but cameras should not distract user focus.

Larger budgets can get access to eye-tracking and screen-capture software. Established testing environments will be using these emulators on a desktop environment with keyboard and mouse navigation; be aware that interscreen interactions will suffer from the incorrect context. But applications may be run in emulator environments for precise data on where users looked, and when, on a screen-specific basis.

Task Analysis

Standard user acceptance testing procedures apply to the mobile context. Testers will continue to monitor results until time, budget, or questions run out.

Information Design Tools

Creating the mobile application interface requires a range of tools, and only by using a tool can designers learn their best toolset. This section briefly discusses some information design tools.

Sketching and Wireframes

Sometimes we need to go analog, shaping ideas on paper before focusing on the pixels. Storyboard application screens to outline features and flow, focusing on the big picture. Save wasted time developing the wrong thing the right way by involving all key stakeholders in the sketching and wireframing process. Mobile stencils are even on the market to help nondoodlers pencil in ideas before turning to computer screens.

A wireframe is a rough outline of each application's framework. Stay focused on functionality during wireframing; these easy-to-share, easy-to-edit files are just a skeleton of the design. A simple image will do, but tools such as Balsamiq Mockups (http://www.balsamiq.com/) let designers drop boilerplate widgets (including scroll bars, tabs, and image placeholders) into a wireframe editor.

Mock-up Designs

When you are ready to consider colors and fonts, you can build the mock-up design concept in Adobe Creative Suite (preferences vary between PhotoShop, FireWorks, and Illustrator). The final images of buttons and icons will be pulled from the final mock-up design, but details will solidify only after some experimentation.

Look to existing stencils for a streamlined process that does not re-create the wheel. Yahoo (http://developer.yahoo.com/ypatterns/about/stencils/) is one personal favorite; many organizations and designers regularly post new files, such as Windows Phone 7 design templates from Microsoft (http://go.microsoft.com/fwlink/?LinkId=196225).

Prototype

"Perfection is the enemy of good," and designs that start as ugly prototypes quickly progress to elegant, usable applications. The most primitive start is a most important iteration. Platform-specific tools are available, such as the Interface Builder or Xcode for iOS, but HTML and CSS are a standard and simple way to quickly build prototypical interactions.

On-device Testing

One of the most important tools during design will be the physical device. Buy, or borrow, the devices an application will run on.

Simulators and Emulators

Simulators and emulators are important when the hardware is unavailable and the service contracts for devices are prohibitively expensive. A simulator uses a different codebase to act like the intended hardware environment. An emulator uses a virtual machine to simulate the environment using the same codebase as the mobile application.

It can be cost prohibitive to test on many devices, making emulators incredibly useful. Emulators can be run in collaboration with eye-tracking software already available in most testing labs, but an emulator lacks the touch experience of a mobile application. At an absolute minimum, use one of the target devices for user testing at this level.

During design, development, testing, and demonstration, these tools are incredibly valuable. Emulators are discussed in more depth in Chapter 5.

SUMMARY

Focus on the mobile context, understand your users, create information designs according to successful design patterns, and take care to meet platform-specific requirements or constraints.

The most important part of every interaction will be the user, so test with the user. Engage interaction with platform-specific methods such as gradients in iOS and movement for Windows Phone 7. Effectively use limited screen real estate to build consistent, precise screens. Look to industry standards before taking a risk and trying new things. Current design and prototyping tools allow effective iterations and "what if I tried . . ." moments. But most important, have fun.

In Chapter 5, you apply some of the design techniques used for mobile applications while creating mobile websites.

5

Mobile Websites

WHAT'S IN THIS CHAPTER?

➤ How to Choose a Mobile Web Development Option

➤ Creating Adaptive Mobile Websites

➤ Creating Dedicated Mobile Websites

➤ Creating Mobile Web Apps

People are using their mobile phone browsers more and more every day to find information about businesses, make product decisions and purchases, and even determine the quality of a business based on what they can find online. Recently, I needed to call a business to change an appointment. I searched for the company in my mobile Safari browser, only to find the site would not load because it was built entirely in Flash. Annoyed, I opened up my Maps program to find the business location, because the Google map listings always have associated contact information. For some reason, this company did not have its map listings up to date, and no phone number was included with the address. Finally, I was able to track down the phone number on my third attempt using my White Pages app. But this was way too difficult!

With the proliferation of mobile browsers, people need to be able to access your website and, at a minimum, be able to browse it smoothly to find the information they need. Taking it a step further and providing an optimal mobile user interface (UI), or specialized mobile content, can provide a great experience and enhance the reputation of your organization.

You have several different strategies and techniques to choose from for your mobile website, some of which provide quick and easy solutions for getting an optimized mobile presence up and running. Creating a mobile website depends on the functionality of your current website, the platform and development standards with which it was created, and the purpose that users have for visiting the website. This chapter discusses different options for developing your mobile website, and how to get started with each technique.

CHOOSING A MOBILE WEB OPTION

If your organization is itching to be mobile, but doesn't have a focused purpose or resources to develop a mobile app, a mobile website can be a great place to start. You can approach a mobile website project in several ways, which are discussed in depth later on. *Adaptive mobile websites* automatically adjust your current website when viewed on mobile screen sizes, modifying the layout, sizing, and spacing to make it more mobile-friendly. *Dedicated mobile websites* require a completely separate mobile website, and *mobile web apps* employ HTML5 functionality and specific UI elements to create an app-like experience on the web.

You need to analyze some things about your organization and its current website before choosing a mobilization strategy, as discussed in the following sections.

Why Do People Use Your Website on Mobile Devices?

For restaurants and local retail stores, this question can be pretty easy to answer. People are already out and about, and they need to know your location, your phone number, or more information about what they will find at your store. (*What's on the menu? Do you carry the product I'm searching for? How much will it cost if I go there?*) A mobile website that makes it extremely easy to access information is critical in these situations, and can potentially cost sales if people can't find what they are looking for.

Some websites are less likely to be needed by people browsing on their mobile devices, such as a commercial construction company: it's unlikely that a customer will make a decision to work with a construction company based on mobile website experience. But there's no reason that less critical mobile websites should not provide a smooth mobile experience.

What Can Your Current Website Accommodate?

Different mobile website techniques use existing desktop websites more than others. It's important to know how the current website was built and what the platform capabilities are when choosing a mobile development technique. For example, if the desktop website is built entirely in Flash, you will have to develop a separate, dedicated website for mobile devices to accommodate non-Flash mobile browsers, such as iPhones. (Or you might consider revamping the entire website to eliminate Flash, but that's another story.)

Desktop websites built using clean, modern development standards — external style sheets and semantic, div-based HTML — can work well as the base for an adaptive website design, because existing elements are easily manipulated through CSS.

If your website is built on a content management system (CMS), you can check for any mobile options available on the platform. More CMS platforms are focusing on facilitating great mobile sites. As a start, most include some sort of template system for the site designs. Templates make it easier to apply sitewide mobile modifications because changes made to a theme file instantly apply to the entire site, which means less time updating individual pages. Global style sheets create a default place for mobile CSS changes to be added for the entire site.

Most theme-based CMS systems are starting to introduce mobile-friendly themes that you can use and modify to provide your site with both a desktop and mobile optimized experience. Some CMS systems provide other tools to help with things like mobile browser testing, mobile detection and redirection, and mobile menu modifications.

The following sections provide some CMS system mobile functionality examples.

WordPress

Some specific WordPress themes automatically apply a different mobile theme to their blog sites when viewed on mobile devices. Many of the available WordPress themes are considered mobile-ready, and come with mobile versions. The default WordPress theme automatically applies an alternate mobile theme plus a View Full Site link is included to get back to the full desktop website.

Drupal

Drupal has many themes and modules that you can piece together to create a mobile website version. The WURFL (`http://drupal.org/project/wurfl`), Mobile Plugin (`http://drupal.org/project/mobileplugin`), and Mobile Tools (`http://drupal.org/project/mobile_tools`) modules can assist with mobile detection, redirection, theme-switching, and image scaling. Read more about Drupal mobile options here: `http://www.mediacurrent.com/blog/going-mobile-drupal`.

DotNetNuke

The latest DotNetNuke versions include built-in tools for mobile detection, redirection, and a mobile template that provides a few layout changes for phone and tablet browsers. It also has a nice, built-in emulator for mobile browser testing.

Lots of tools are available that are making dynamic mobile sites easier. Basic HTML and CSS websites can also be modified with mobile CSS. If you have an older website, or a lot of custom-developed functions or complicated features, it might be difficult to adapt your current website, and a dedicated site may be the way to go.

How Much Do You Want to Provide for Mobile Users?

If you want mobile users to access basically the same information as they would on a desktop browser, a mobile website is the direction to go. That technique allows you to hide some elements and rearrange the majority of your site for a better mobile UI. Content is identical and updated through the same editing process.

If you know that mobile users won't need to access a large amount of your website content, a dedicated mobile website would be a good solution. Design a mobile-specific website from the ground up, addressing specific organizational requirements and the needs of on-the-go customers. A dedicated mobile website will benefit from a thorough mobile marketing strategy, and can use modified content targeting mobile users in an optimal UI.

A mobile web app would be appropriate with a focused feature for mobile users, provided through a web browser instead of a downloadable app. Offer robust functionality on multiple platforms, and avoid the restrictions of app stores with a mobile web app.

The following table lists the pros and cons of the various mobile web development options.

	ADAPTIVE MOBILE WEBSITE	DEDICATED MOBILE WEBSITE	MOBILE WEB APPLICATION
Pros	• Maintain only one website • Quick and least expensive to implement • Provide improved mobile user interface	• Good website performance • More perfected mobile UI • Fairly inexpensive to implement	• A website that can behave like an app • Less development cost than native app • Works across platforms
Cons	• No use of native device functionality • Not optimal performance • Some layout restrictions	• No use of native device functionality • Maintain two websites	• Not in app stores • Can't use all mobile features

Now that you can choose which development technique to use, lets look closely at how each one works.

ADAPTIVE MOBILE WEBSITES

An adaptive mobile website is a great first project for mobile, and it allows steps to be taken incrementally toward an optimal mobile UI. Adaptive mobile websites use CSS media queries to serve different style sheets based on the size or type of browser or device detected viewing the site (see Figures 5-1 and 5-2). With CSS, content and presentation layers are kept separate; media queries change website layout and appearance without content modification. No browser detection or site redirection is needed; the optimal website layout appears automatically when media query parameters are met. As already mentioned, the key to a smooth, responsive mobile website project is a well-coded existing website to manipulate.

FIGURE 5-1: Adaptive website example, viewed in a full-sized desktop browser

Get Your Queries in Place

Media queries are the core of adaptive mobile websites. This section explains how to choose what media type or feature to target, and then explains different ways to add your media query to your site.

Choose Your Target

To apply a media query to a website, first determine in what situations you will target a browser to apply your mobile changes. One way to target browsers is by media type. Media types have been in the W3C's specifications for many years, and more types continue to be added. The following is a list of all the media types now available. Some you likely recognize, but others are more obscure.

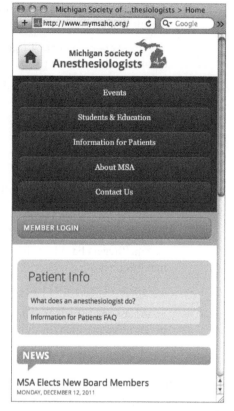

> ➤ all: Covers all device types.

> ➤ braille: Intended for braille tactile feedback devices.

> ➤ embossed: Intended for paged braille printers.

> ➤ handheld: Targets devices that are considered mobile, with smaller screens and limited bandwidth.

> ➤ print: Intended for paged material and documents viewed on-screen in print preview mode, or output to an actual printer.

FIGURE 5-2: Adaptive website example, viewed in a mobile-sized browser

> ➤ projection: Intended for large-scale, projected presentations.

> ➤ screen: Targets common-sized desktop computers with color screens.

> ➤ speech: Intended for speech synthesizers.

> ➤ tty: Intended for media using a fixed-pitch character grid (such as teletypes, terminals, or portable devices with limited display capabilities).

> ➤ tv: Targets television-type devices (low resolution, color, limited-scrollability screens, sound available).

Media types offer numerous uses, but this chapter discusses only all and handheld. The other way to target a browser for mobile styling is by media feature. Available media features are:

> ➤ aspect-ratio: Targets based on the ratio of the value of the width media feature to the value of the height media feature. Accepts min/max prefixes.

> ➤ color: Targets based on the number of bits per color component of the output device. Accepts min/max prefixes.

➤   color-index: Targets based on the number of entries in the color lookup table of the output device. Accepts min/max prefixes.

➤   device-aspect-ratio: Targets based on the ratio of the value of the device-width media feature to the value of the device-height media feature. Accepts min/max prefixes.

➤   device-height: Targets based on the height of the rendering surface of the output device. Accepts min/max prefixes.

➤   device-width: Targets based on the width of the rendering surface of the output device. Accepts min/max prefixes.

➤   grid: Targets with a query for whether the output device is grid or bitmap.

➤   height: Targets based on the height of the display area of the output device. Accepts min/max prefixes.

➤   monochrome: Targets based on the number of bits per pixel in a monochrome frame buffer.

➤   width: Targets based on the width of the display area of the output device. Accepts min/max prefixes.

➤   orientation: Targets by portrait or landscape orientation.

➤   resolution: Targets based on the resolution of the output device, that is, the density of the pixels (dots per inch, or dpi). Accepts min/max prefixes.

➤   scan: Targets the scanning process of "tv" output devices.

Media features more than double the number of ways to target browsers, and give more fine control with the ability to combine targeted features and properties. And, not, and only can be included for combinations of requests.

So how do you decide the best way to target for mobile? I recommend targeting all media types, and using the width media feature to apply your styles once a browser is smaller than a set width. For example:

```
@media all and (max-width: 480px) {… }
```

This means whenever a browser is less than 480 pixels wide, any CSS properties defined inside this media query will then apply.

You can also target small desktop monitors or tablets with a combination of widths:

```
@media all and (min-width:480px) and (max-width: 800px) {… }
```

Or widescreen monitors:

```
@media all and (min-width:1400px) {… }
```

This targeting method gives finer control over when styles will apply, as opposed to the handheld media type, and this technique also makes testing easier by enabling you to test in a desktop browser. Also, some newer mobile devices have excluded themselves from the handheld distinction in order to serve full-feature websites, because modern mobile devices have this capacity.

Link to Your Media Queries

Once you determine how to target your mobile website, you have several ways to add your media query to the site. We recommend including your mobile CSS directly inside your global style sheet:

```
@media handheld {
/* Mobile styles go here*/
}
```

You can also link to a separate mobile style sheet in your HTML file:

```
<link rel="stylesheet" href="mobile.css", type="text/css" media="handheld" />
```

Or, import your mobile CSS from a global CSS file:

```
@import url("mobile.css") handheld;
```

The first option is easiest to start with because the styles will apply instantly if the other styles in that style sheet are working correctly. There's no need to add any files; simply add your mobile styles into an existing CSS file. You will want to put this section at the end of your style sheet, so all normal CSS styles will apply first and mobile styles will then be added. This technique is also best for performance, because only one style sheet will be loaded. Additionally, the `@import` technique isn't well supported in older versions of Internet Explorer, so that's another reason it should be avoided.

Remember the Viewport

Another important detail is needed to ensure mobile browsers render a site correctly. A viewport meta data tag ensures that mobile browsers on different devices zoom properly to the right size of your site. Otherwise, if you have a 300px-wide mobile site, the browser might still render it on a 1000px-wide canvas if a viewport is not defined. To add the viewport, simply add this property to the `<head>` tag of all pages:

```
<meta name="viewport" content="width=device-width, initial-scale=1.0,
maximum-scale=2.0"/>
```

Inside the `content` property, several things are happening, and several options are defined. The `width` property is set to render the site at the width of the device, with the website scaled to its normal size on load. The maximum scale is set so touchscreen mobile users can zoom the site to two times its normal size. This example is my preferred setup, but you can make changes as desired. For instance, setting `maximum-scale` to 1.0 prevents users from zooming in on the site at all.

Figures 5-3 and 5-4 show a mobile web page with and then without the proper viewport setting:

FIGURE 5-3: Mobile web page example with viewport properly set

FIGURE 5-4: Mobile web page example with viewport not set

The Inevitable Internet Explorer Fix

Media queries are part of the CSS3 W3C specification, and are well supported across platforms. At the time of writing, they had support at least three versions back in Firefox (since 3.6), Chrome (since 17), Safari (since 5), Safari iOS (since 3.2), Opera (since 11.6), Opera Mobile (since 10), and the Android browser (since 2.1). Unsurprisingly, the gap is seen in Internet Explorer, which has supported the feature only since Internet Explorer 9. Though global usage of Internet Explorer 8 or below is at least 30 percent (source: http://www.caniuse.com), if you are using media queries only for mobile sites, the main worry is Windows Phone 7, which comes with an Internet Explorer 7 equivalent browser. Version 7.5 comes with Internet Explorer 9, so going forward it's in the clear. With a mobile market share of around 2 percent, Windows Phone is not a drastic concern, but there is a JavaScript workaround to get media queries rendering in older mobile (and desktop) Internet Explorer browsers:

```
<!--[if lt IE 9]> <script src="http://css3-mediaqueries-js.googlecode.com/
svn/trunk/css3-mediaqueries.js"></script> <![endif]-->
```

The script parses your CSS and applies the media query styles, and can be tested in real time on Internet Explorer, including when you resize the window.

Add Mobile Styles

Once the media query is in place, it's time to decide how to change the website for mobile browsers.
It is a good idea to create mock-ups of how you would like your website to look on mobile, but it's
important to know the limitations of this technique, and it may be helpful to test out some changes
in the code first.

Adding Your Changes to @Media

The basic process for changing your website for mobile browsers is to place CSS styles for the
mobile site inside your @media tag. These styles will apply to your site when the defined media type
or feature properties have been met. You can reduce the number of columns, modify the width of
content areas, increase the size of buttons and links, and hide items not needed for mobile.

In the following example, you can see that the regular site header has a width of 960px. But when
the site is viewed on a small, mobile screen, the media query applies a new width of 320px, which
will override the original width. For the logo, an alternate mobile logo image is loaded as a CSS
background image, and the size of the div is also reduced.

Here's an example of some regular website CSS, defining a header that is 960px wide and 105px tall, with
a background image. The site logo is 312px by 102px, and also loaded as a background image in CSS:

```
#header {
float:left;
width:960px;
height:105px;
background:url(images/header-bg.jpg) no-repeat;
}

h1#logo, a#logo {
width:312px;
height:102px;
background:url(images/logo.png) no-repeat;
float:left;
margin:0;
padding:0;
}
```

Here's an example of the mobile website CSS, applied to the same elements when a browser width
is under 480px wide. Now the header is set to 320px wide and 65px tall. The same float and
background properties will still apply on the mobile version, but the height and width set in the
media query section will override the regular CSS (as long as the regular CSS appears first in
the style sheet).

```
@media all and (max-width: 480px) {
#header {
width:320px;
height:65px;
}


h1#logo, a#logo {
width:160px;
height:100px;
background:url(images/mobile-logo.png) no-repeat!important;
margin:8px 0 0;
}
}
```

This is the process followed throughout the adaptive mobile site code: simply change the CSS for each element to fit into the mobile screen size and modify the site styles. You can add @media styles for one set of properties or multiple properties to optimally change the site appearance for several devices:

```
@media all and (max-width: 480px) {
/*phone styles go here*/
}

@media all and (min-width:480px) and (max-width: 800px) {
/* tablet styles go here */
}
```

Change Your Width

The first thing you'll want to do is set a smaller width for the entire website. If you are used to designing fixed-width websites, you can also design mobile fixed-width sites. Set the width of any containing divs on your site to smaller width, such as 320px (that would fit a portrait orientation iPhone screen perfectly). With the right viewport, a mobile site with a fixed width automatically scales to fit wider or narrower screens with everything scaled proportionally. If you turn your phone to landscape mode, everything gets slightly bigger to fit the width.

Alternatively, you can set div widths to 100 percent for the mobile website. This means that instead of the entire site scaling up or down for different screen sizes, the content areas simply become wider or narrower. Font sizes remain the same, and content areas have different lengths based on how much content fits on each line.

Choosing a fixed or fluid mobile website width depends on your preference for user experience on different devices and screen sizes, as well as your preference for development techniques. Fluid mobile layouts are more flexible and provide a better use of space on varying screen sizes, but you have more variables and factors to test through development than with a single, fixed mobile site version.

With either width setting, make sure that all divs are set to widths less than your determined fixed width, or are all set to a percent for fluid widths. Make sure no desktop site div widths, such as 500px or 800px, persist on the mobile website, because they will break outside of the set mobile site width and create horizontal scrolling.

DEALING WITH TABLES

A related element to watch out for is tables. As previously mentioned, if your entire site is built with tables, this technique won't work. Whatever columns are side by side in tables must stay side by side, unlike divs, whose positions can easily be manipulated.

Additionally, even if you have a correctly used table of data on the site, it can cause layout problems.

If a width is not set on the table or its columns, the table will try to shrink to fit inside its containing div. But if the table contains a lot of columns, or long elements of content (such as a URL), it will still break out of the right side of the site and cause horizontal scrolling. This is a situation in which you have to decide the best thing to do for your project. Can the content be easily switched to divs, and do you have the project resources to do this? If yes, this is the best plan of action for your ideal mobile site design.

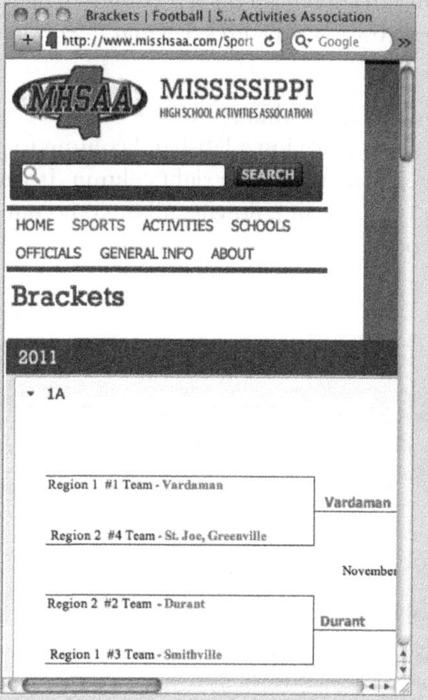

If it would be too time-consuming, or if it would not make sense to move the data out of a table, leaving a few isolated pages with this issue might not be a deal breaker (see Figure 5-5). Mobile users will still be able to access and read the content; a bit of horizontal scrolling will simply be required.

FIGURE 5-5: Mobile web page example with table-based content breaking out of the frame. (Although this example content should not be laid out using tables, in this situation, the project scope did not include modifying this previously developed HTML content.)

Flow Your Columns

Once you have set the width for the entire site, you'll want make sure all of the contained divs flow into one continuous column because the available width is so small on a mobile phone. If your divs are already floated, this part should be easy. If two divs were floated next to each other in the desktop website, the second div will automatically position itself after the first div once the containing div no longer has enough room to fit both side by side. This is why table-based websites don't work well with this technique: all columns will still be positioned next to each other no matter how small the containing div is.

The order of mobile website content is controlled by the HTML content order. This can be seen as one of the limitations of a dynamic mobile website. If a desktop website contains two columns, all content in the left column must appear before any content in the right column on the mobile website (see Figures 5-6 and 5-7). There is no way to switch the order of HTML content using CSS.

Knowing this, one thing to take into consideration is the placement of any side menus. If you have a menu placed in a left-hand column for all inside pages, this menu would appear before any of the page content from the right column. If you are willing to live with this kind of restriction (which I usually am), flowing all of your content into one, usable website column is a pretty easy process.

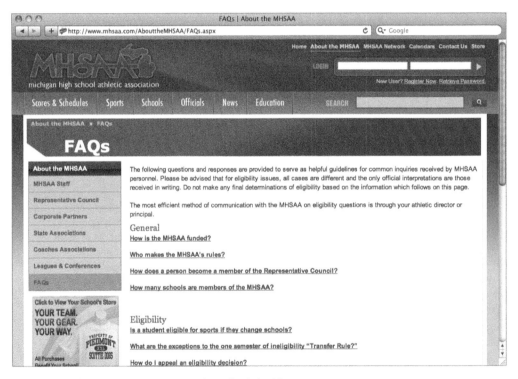

FIGURE 5-6: Desktop web page example with a left-side menu

In Figure 5-7, the left menu appears before the main content. The small advertisement has been hidden below the menu (you'll see how to do this in the next section), otherwise that also would have appeared before the main content.

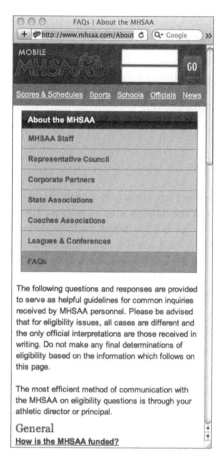

FIGURE 5-7: The same web page example when viewed at a mobile screen size

Hide Content

Another thing to do while planning your mobile website is determining content areas that are not needed on the mobile site. For items that you want to hide for mobile, it's as easy as adding `display:none` to the CSS for a class or ID that surrounds only that content.

> **HIDDEN CONTENT IS STILL *ACTUALLY* THERE**
>
> It's important to note that hiding content with CSS does not remove the content from your website completely. Content with the `display:none` property will still be loaded with the page, but hidden using CSS. This means that using `display:none` will not help improve the speed of your mobile website, but only decrease the content viewed by the users to improve the mobile UI and their ease of browsing.

Some things that are best to hide on mobile include image rotators, any Flash, and any images that are simply supplemental to the design and don't add to the understanding of the page content.

You can also choose to hide entire sections of content that aren't important for mobile website users. For example, you can hide supplemental content in a side column or footer blocks, or hide testimonials, social media links, or a persistent contact form for pages on which users wouldn't need them. Especially if content is repeated on every page, think about whether it's actually important, or just supplemental column filler. You may even decide to hide a side menu if the main navigation is sufficient for getting around the site.

Simplify Your Header

Wise use of website real estate that is "above the fold" is even more important on a mobile website than a desktop version. Mobile browser bars may allow users to see only an area as little as 200px in height before having to scroll. One of the most important things to do is design and simplify your website header to just get the most pertinent information across. Use a smaller logo. Remove contact information unless it's critical for your mobile users (I'm talking to you, restaurants and retail stores). Hide slogans, links that are useful only on a desktop ("Print this page"), and even search bars.

Make sure that the header tells users what site they are on, then make sure they can quickly get to the information they really want. Figures 5-8 and 5-9 show changes in a website header between desktop and mobile site versions. The slogan is removed, the menu is compacted onto two lines, and the large image rotator is hidden on the mobile site.

FIGURE 5-8: Desktop website homepage example with all content visible

Modify Menus

Determining how to position the mobile website's main menu is arguably one of the trickiest and most important elements to address. If a horizontal main menu contains only a handful of items, it may be possible to leave the links listed horizontally in one or two rows, as shown in Figure 5-9. Make sure the links are large enough, with enough spacing, that they can be easily hit on a touchscreen: no more than four or five items in a row, and no more than two rows.

Or a menu created as an unordered list could be restyled so that each item goes on its own line, becoming a vertical menu (Figure 5-4 is one example). This would do the trick:

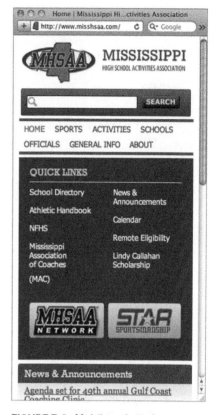

FIGURE 5-9: Mobile website homepage example, with elements like the image rotator and slogan hidden

```
ul li {
    display:block;
    width:100%;
}
```

A third option is to use completely different HTML code for a menu on desktop and mobile. You can change a menu rendered inside an unordered list on desktop to a drop-down list on mobile. A drop-down list needs only a little bit of space, and mobile devices have developed very user-friendly ways of handling them. It's possible to display different menu code on mobile. In your desktop CSS code, set your normal styling for the <ul> elements, and set display:none for your <select> elements. Inside the mobile media query styles, do the opposite: set <ul> to display:none and include any desired styling and display:inline for your <select> element.

```
/* Desktop Menu CSS */
nav select {display: none; }
nav ul li {float: left; list-style: none; }
nav ul a {color: #fff; display: block; }

/* Mobile Menu CSS */
@media all and (max-width: 480px) {
    nav select {display: inline; }
    nav ul {display: none; }
}
```

Of course, adding duplicate code for mobile can increase the size of your site and requires maintaining two menus, so it is not ideal. Using JavaScript, you can automatically convert the type of list displayed between a <ul> and <select> element. The following example uses the jQuery framework, which allows you to select and append HTML elements without a great deal of logic.

Start with the menu code set as an unordered list:

```
<nav>
  <ul>
    <li>Item 1</li>
    <li>Item 2</li>
  </ul>
</nav>
```

Add this JavaScript to the `<head>` of your HTML file to specify the two separate menu types, and when to use them:

```
<script type="text/javascript">
// Create the dropdown base
$("nav a").addClass("mm-add");

$("<select />").appendTo("nav");

// Create default option "Go to..."
$("<option />", {
  "selected": "selected",
  "value"   : "",
  "text"    : "Go to..."
}).appendTo("nav select");

// Populate dropdown with menu items
$("nav a.mm-add").each(function() {
  var el = $(this);
  $("<option />", {
    "value"   : el.attr("href"),
    "text"    : el.text()
  }).appendTo("nav select");
});

// Make sure it all works
$("nav select").change(function() {
  window.location = $(this).find("option:selected").val();
});
</script>
```

This technique is a great option for creating a space-saving mobile menu. Thanks to Chris Coyier of CSS-tricks.com (http://css-tricks.com/convert-menu-to-dropdown) for creating this technique. Figures 5-10, 5-11, and 5-12 show this technique in action, switching menu styles from unordered list to drop-down list, between desktop and mobile.

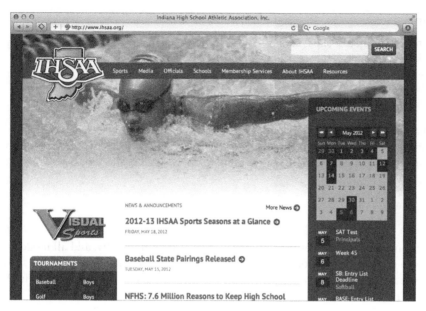

FIGURE 5-10: Website homepage example with a full menu, using an unordered list

FIGURE 5-11: Same website homepage example with a select box replacing the unordered list for the menu, when viewed at a mobile screen size

FIGURE 5-12: On iOS devices, the select box automatically brings up an easy to use spinner as a standard UI element

Review Your Content

Once the basic template of your mobile site is set up — header, footer, site width, and columns — review the content and make sure everything is where it should be. Text-heavy pages should not have many issues. Custom website features, such as an events calendar or a contact form, may need a bit of caressing.

Scale Media

A common element that may break out of mobile site constraints is images. If you have a containing div set to 300px, and an image that is, or has dimensions set to, 400px wide, the image will extend outside of the div to maintain its full size. Luckily, there is a quick fix to apply to all of the images on your site:

```
img {
    max-width: 100%;
}
```

This little bit of CSS ensures that no images break outside of any surrounding div, and all modern browsers will scale down content proportionally that have a max-width set. The `max-width: 100%` CSS property can also be applied to other media such as `video`, `object`, and `embed` to constrain the size at which they are displayed.

Once again, scaling an image using CSS does not change the size of the media that has to be loaded by the browser. A 600x400, 200k image shown at 300x200 on mobile is still a 200k element loading on the website. Some tools have emerged lately that can help improve bandwidth by changing the actual size of media files on mobile devices.

Adaptive Images

Adaptive Images (`http://adaptive-images.com`) from Matt Wilcox is an excellent, drop-in JavaScript and PHP script solution that automatically resizes actual image file sizes to the specific dimensions at which they are viewed. This creates the ideal scenario: lightweight, easy to implement, and does all the work for you on the fly. Combining adaptive images with `max-width: 100%`; should cover all the bases — display *and* load images at the optimal size. Just follow these steps and you're done:

1. Download the latest version of Adaptive Images from `http://adaptive-images.com/download.htm`.

2. Add the included `.htaccess` and `adaptive-images.php` files to the server document-root folder.

3. Add one line of JavaScript into the `<head>` of your site: `<script>document.cookie='resolution='+Math.max(screen.width,screen.height)+'; path=/';</script>`.

4. Add your CSS Media Query values into `$resolutions` in the PHP file.

5. Add images as you normally would, at their desktop website size.

This solution works only on websites using Apache 2 and PHP 5.x, but others have adapted the technique in other languages, including .NET and ColdFusion. View the download page `http://adaptive-images/download.htm`) for an up-to-date listing of Adaptive Images ports and plugins.

This technique was built off an earlier option created by the Filament Group called Responsive Images (`https://github.com/filamentgroup/Responsive-Images`). This technique requires you to create and upload images at multiple sizes to your website, add a query to all images' src elements, and then add JavaScript to test screen width and load the correct image. This technique also requires Apache and PHP. Obviously, creating and uploading duplicate images and changing all image files' URLs is cumbersome and time-consuming. One of the main reasons to use the adaptive mobile website technique is that it is easy to apply to an entire site with just CSS changes. I personally would not want to take the time necessary to apply this technique to an existing website with many images, but it's important to know your options and understand how techniques are progressing.

Testing Made Easy

Testing adaptive mobile websites is extremely easy, especially if you are targeting your media queries for all devices with max-width criteria as discussed earlier:

```
@media all and (max-width: 480px)
```

This means you can simply resize your browser to less than 480px wide, and you'll instantly see your website with the mobile CSS styles applied on your desktop screen. It's convenient to do a majority of testing right on your desktop as you code. Some mobile emulators are available to enhance testing from your desktop. Screenfly (http://quirktools.com/screenfly) uses a proxy server to mimic devices as you view a website. Enter a website address and preview the website on a number of different device screen sizes and resolutions (see Figure 5-13). Screenfly's proxy server mimics the user agent string of a selected device, but does not emulate device behavior such as zoom. There is also a Firefox plug-in called User Agent Switcher (https://addons.mozilla .org/en-US/firefox/addon/user-agent-switcher) that does just what it says: it allows Firefox to emulate the user agents of other browsers, such as iPhone or Internet Explorer.

FIGURE 5-13: Screenfly's emulator with desktop, tablet, mobile, and television view options

Testing on a desktop browser or emulator is convenient, but there is no comparison to native mobile browsers for working out all the kinks and small details. For example, desktop browsers will not accurately portray the left and right margin space that appears in a mobile phone browser. Using a regular desktop browser might always show some space on each side, but when you check on your phone, text might run right up to each edge if specific margins or padding were not added in the CSS. Don't wait until the last minute to test your website on a variety of smartphones. And if you don't have a slew of mobile devices for your own testing purposes, be sure to seek out a few friends who are willing to poke around the website for you.

Break Out of Mobile (or Not?)

Depending on how far you go with your adaptive mobile website, you may or may not choose to include a link back to your "regular" website. If you keep the majority of website content and just modify the display for mobile users, a link to the standard desktop website shouldn't be necessary. Think about all the changes you have made for the mobile website, and make sure there is nothing that someone might seek out and be unable to find on the mobile website. If your mobile website version is well tested, easy to navigate, and still contains most of your desktop website content, people should have no reason to switch back to a desktop version.

If you've chosen to hide a lot of content or entire pages in your adaptive mobile site, linking to the desktop website may be useful. To do this, you need to use a separate style sheet for your mobile device styles, and a bit of Javascript to "break out" of the mobile styles and view the regular webpage. The following example uses a JavaScript file named `breakout.js` that performs this functionality.

```
<script type="text/javascript"
src="http://www.website.com/js/breakout.js"></script>

<span id="FullSite">View Full Website</span>
<span id="MobileSite">View Mobile Website</span>
```

Include spans with `id`s that can be called in the JavaScript, one to view the full website, and one to view the mobile website. Inside your media query CSS, use `display:none` on the `span` `id`s to set them to be visible only when viewing the mobile or full site versions, to link to the opposite.

The following JavaScript code assumes that the jQuery framework has already been loaded. After the HTML page has been loaded, the jQuery document ready function is called, and our logic checks to see if the user has "broken" out of mobile. This is performed in the `shouldWeBreakOutOfMobile` function, which simply checks to see if a certain cookie exists (which is written when user opts to break out of mobile):

```
$(document).ready(function () {
    if (shouldWeBreakOutOfMobile() == true) {
        breakOutOfMobile(document.URL, false);
    }
    else {
        $('head').append('<meta name="viewport" content="width=device-width, initial-
            scale=1.0, maximum-scale=2.0" />');
        applyMobileStyle();
    }
}
```

If the user has broken out of the mobile, the `breakOutOfMobile` function is called, which will remove the mobile CSS file and then refresh the page without the mobile style applied:

```
function breakOutOfMobile(urlToRedirectTo, redirect) {

    $("LINK[href*='" + MOBILE_STYLE_SHEET + "']").remove();

    if (redirect == true) {
        setTimeout(function () { window.location = urlToRedirectTo; }, 1000);
    }
}
```

If the user is not broken out of mobile, you append a meta tag for the viewport, and then apply the mobile CSS File:

```
$('head').append('<meta name="viewport" content="width=device-width, initial-
    scale=1.0, maximum-scale=2.0" />');

applyMobileStyle();
```

There are also two `click` functions that are important to note as well. When the `FullSite` span tag is clicked using this method, the following logic is called:

```
$("#FullSite").click(function (e) {
    breakOutOfMobileFromLink();
    saveBreakOutOfMobileCookie();
});
```

This `click` event will break the user out of the mobile version using the technique described previously, as well as write a cookie to the users browser indicating they have broken out of the mobile. So if they try to view another page, it will not be rendered as a mobile page again. The following method saves the cookie to accomplish this.

```
function saveBreakOutOfMobileCookie() {
    document.cookie = COOKIE_NAME + "=" + "Break Out Of Mobile; path=/; expires=Monday,
    04-Apr-2020 05:00:00 GMT";
}
```

The second important `click` function is the `MobileSite` span. This logic will apply the mobile CSS file, and then delete the cookie that indicates the site is rendering the desktop version.

```
$("#MobileSite").click(function (e) {
    applyMobileStyle();
    deleteBreakOutOfMobileCookie();
});
```

Here is the entire JavaScript defining the break out of mobile method, using cookies to ensure users stay in their current mode once they click a link:

```
var MOBILE_STYLE_SHEET = "mobile.css";
var COOKIE_NAME = "BreakOutOfMobile";

$(document).ready(function () {
    if (shouldWeBreakOutOfMobile() == true) {
        breakOutOfMobile(document.URL, false);
    }
```

```
        else {
            $('head').append('<meta name="viewport" content="width=device-width, initial-
                scale=1.0, maximum-scale=2.0" />');
                applyMobileStyle();
        }

        $("#FullSite").click(function (e) {
            breakOutOfMobileFromLink();
            saveBreakOutOfMobileCookie();
        });

        $("#MobileSite").click(function (e) {
            applyMobileStyle();
            deleteBreakOutOfMobileCookie();
        });
});

function applyMobileStyle() {
    $('head').append("<link rel='stylesheet' href=" +
    MOBILE_STYLE_SHEET + " type='text/css' />");
}

function breakOutOfMobileFromLink() {
    breakOutOfMobile(document.URL, true);
}

function breakOutOfMobile(urlToRedirectTo, redirect) {
    $("LINK[href*='" + MOBILE_STYLE_SHEET + "']").remove();

    if (redirect == true) {
        setTimeout(function () { window.location = urlToRedirectTo; }, 1000);
    }
}

function deleteBreakOutOfMobileCookie() {
    document.cookie = COOKIE_NAME + '=; path=/; expires=Thu, 01-Jan-70 00:00:01 GMT;';
}

function saveBreakOutOfMobileCookie() {
        document.cookie = COOKIE_NAME + "=" + "Break Out Of Mobile; path=/
        ;   expires=Monday, 04-Apr-2020 05:00:00 GMT";
        }

function shouldWeBreakOutOfMobile() {
    var tmpRtn = false;
    var breakOutCookie = document.cookie.indexOf(COOKIE_NAME);

        if (breakOutCookie != -1) {
            tmpRtn = true;
        }

    return tmpRtn;
}
```

Taking It Further: Complete Responsive Websites

Now that you've seen how to use media queries to develop an *adaptive* mobile-specific website, you can expand upon some of these techniques to create a fully *responsive* website. Instead of modifying the fixed-width desktop website to create a fixed-width mobile website, a fully responsive website utilizes percentage-based widths and margins for a flexible grid layout.

This is very similar to the "liquid layouts" from years past, long despised by designers for their unpredictable appearances and lack of layout control. But combined with media queries and other new discoveries, designers are embracing responsive websites as the future of web design — meeting the needs of all different screen and device types while giving designers the fine control over details they want.

Some web designers have even started advocating designing for mobile first. Start with the small screen, strip your site down to the essentials, and build from there. This idea might sound a bit scary, but judging by the proliferation of smartphones and tablets, it's really not very extreme.

Because creating a fully responsive website would generally require a full site redevelopment, and introduces a lot of detailed coding techniques, it is out of the scope of this book to explain the entire process. Ethan Marcotte's *Responsive Web Design*, part of the A Book Apart series, details the techniques if you are interested in learning more. Also check out Media Queries (`http://mediaqueri.es`) for inspiration. They provide a wonderful gallery of responsive website designs, displaying screenshots of each website as they appear at different screen or browser widths (see Figure 5-14).

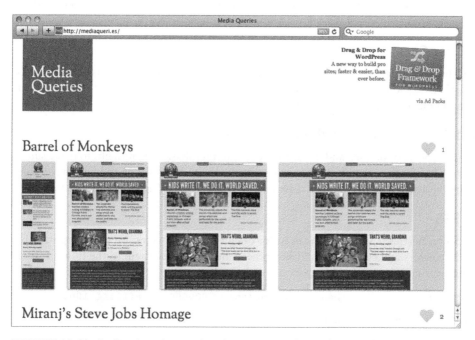

FIGURE 5-14: Media Queries, showcasing sites optimized for desktop, tablet, and mobile devices using responsive web design

Now that we know how to create an adaptive mobile website, the next mobile site alternative we will discuss is a dedicated mobile website.

DEDICATED MOBILE WEBSITES

With a dedicated mobile website, most of the concepts discussed for a dynamic mobile site still hold true. You need to decide how you want to change, rearrange, or remove content from your website for the mobile version. The difference is that you will be building the dedicated mobile website from the ground up, so you have very few restrictions and it is easier to pay attention to the details that create the optimal mobile browsing experience. This is also a good opportunity to undertake a fully responsive site design, to cover the range of phone and tablet device differences.

When planning a brand new mobile website, designing ahead is a must. A designer does not need to think about restrictions like the flow of columns: there is much more freedom to design a mobile site as perfectly as possible. Start with a modifying your sitemap to include only the pages that people will need when browsing your mobile site. You may choose to have only a small number of key pages on the mobile site. This might allow the menu to fit horizontally across the mobile site, when the desktop version may have had too many links to do so.

Because a dedicated website will not mirror desktop content, it is also a good idea to cater site content to mobile users. Rewrite mobile content to be shorter, and appeal to any mobile-specific user needs.

Some guidelines to follow when planning and building your dedicated mobile website are outlined in the following sections.

Keep Files Sizes Small

Avoid using 32-bit PNG images, as these have the largest file size of image types used on the web. Use JPG and GIF files, and if you need transparency use 8-bit PNG files. 8-bit files support alpha transparency and render fine in modern mobile browsers.

Increase the Size of Elements in the User Interface

Optimize size and spacing of buttons and links; a good rule of thumb is, quite fittingly, to make sure users can hit buttons easily with their thumbs when testing the site. Make sure buttons and links have large hotspots that are the actual link area, and increase font sizes and line spacing for the mobile version.

Leverage CSS3

Many new CSS3 properties that reduce the need for design element images are well-supported by modern mobile browsers and can speed up development. Be sure to use them to the fullest extent when designing your mobile website. Here are a few examples:

➤ **Gradients:** `background: linear-gradient(top, #000000 0%,#ffffff 100%);`

➤ **Border Radius (rounded corners):** `border-radius: 15px;`

➤ **Box Shadow:** `box-shadow: 10px 10px 5px #888;`

➤ **Text Shadow:** `text-shadow: 2px 2px 2px #000;`

Retina Images

With iPhone 4's retina display added to the mix, the best way to create images for mobile websites has now changed. Gone are the days of the 72dpi standard web image. Because the retina display doubles the potential resolution users can see, simply double the size of your `<img>` source files to serve retina resolution images. To display an icon at 32x32 pixels, create the file at 64x64 pixels, and set the image size properties to 32x32:

```
<img src="/my-icon.png" width="32px" height="32px" />
```

It is important to note that this will serve double the amount of data than what can be used on non-retina displays. You can also use media queries to target iPhone 4's retina display and serve only the double resolution images to applicable devices:

```
<link rel="stylesheet" type="text/css" href="/retina.css" media="all and
(-webkit-min-device-pixel-ratio: 2)" />
```

Then, in the retina-specific CSS, you can load a background image that is 64x64 pixels, and specify its dimensions as 32x32 using the `background-size` CSS property.

Detection and Redirection

To redirect users to the mobile website, you can use a basic JavaScript option based on screen size, similar to using media queries:

```
<script type="text/javascript">
    <!--
            if (screen.width <= 500) {
                document.location = "mobile.html";
            )
    //-->
</script>
```

This redirects users to your mobile website homepage when their screen widths are below the set dimensions. In this example, `mobile.html` is the mobile homepage file, which will be displayed when the website is viewed from any screen less than 500px wide — whether tablet or phone.

Users can also be redirected through JavaScript that detects the user agent. Several scripts are available to use, depending on the language with which your website is built. `http://detectmobilebrowsers.com` has a collection of downloadable scripts for fifteen different languages.

Link Back to the Desktop Site

Generally, content is greatly reduced on a dedicated mobile website compared to the desktop website, so it is important to provide a link back to the regular website version. Because a dedicated mobile website has a unique URL, it's easy to add links between the two versions. Use a media query and `display:none` to ensure the link to the desktop version appears only when someone is viewing the site from a mobile device.

Testing

Most of the same testing methods apply for a dedicated mobile website as they do for a responsive one. You can review the initial work on a scaled-down desktop browser, and use emulators like Screenfly. Native mobile devices should definitely be used for testing the website interface and usability. It is also important to test the detection and redirection to the mobile website using several major mobile device platforms.

Adobe Shadow (`http://adobe.com/shadow`) is a great tool to assist with on-device website testing. With it you can pair native iOS and Android devices with your computer wirelessly. Then when you refresh your site on your desktop while using the Shadow extension for Google Chrome, the native mobile browsers will automatically sync and refresh as well. You can also remotely inspect your site as rendered on the mobile browsers through your desktop browser.

W3C MOBILEOK CHECKER

Another tool that can check if your website is mobile-friendly is the W3C mobileOK Checker (`http://validator.w3.org/mobile`). The Checker gives a site a percentage score (out of 100) based on a number of web standards and mobile best practices. It also explains any errors or areas in need of improvement. I would caution not to stress too much if your site performs poorly with the Checker, though. I had a hard time finding any websites, including the dedicated mobile websites of prominent businesses, that scored over 50 percent. As an example, Huffington Post (`www.huffingtonpost.com`) appears and functions quite nicely in mobile browsers, but scores just 25 percent in the Checker.

Some factors that trigger critical or severe errors in the Checker are not that serious, in my opinion. Any iFrames on your website cause a critical error in the Checker, although most modern smartphones will render iFrames just fine. In fact, using the recommended embed code from YouTube requires an iFrame, instead of embedding a Flash `<object>`. This was designed in large part so that YouTube could detect browser video support and serve HTML5 videos to mobile browsers that don't support Flash.

Responsive mobile websites will have a harder time scoring well with the Checker because they still have to deal with all of the existing content and code of the desktop website. A dedicated mobile website development project can pay closer attention to fulfilling the W3C mobile recommendations. The mobileOK Checker is still a useful tool, and it is important to be aware of what mobile best practices the W3C recommends. Review the Detailed Report from the Checker and think carefully about how beneficial addressing each error will be for the website.

The next mobile website option this chapter discusses is a mobile web app, which is meant to function closer to a native mobile app than a normal website.

MOBILE WEB APPS WITH HTML5

Mobile web apps can provide useful alternatives to native mobile apps. With a plethora of new tools harnessing the HTML5 and JavaScript capabilities of modern mobile browsers, dynamic web applications can stand up to any native app. It can take much less time for an experienced web developer to create a mobile web app that works across platforms than to develop the same app natively for the same variety of device platforms.

What Exactly Is HTML5?

HTML5 is really just HTML, and the evolving of the language for easier creation of web applications. Although some features and specifications are new, it is not meant to create a global shift to a "new" language. The goal of HTML5 is to create standards that are compatible across browsers and provide ways to develop web features using open source methods that previously required proprietary technologies. It aims to maintain backward compatibility, and not break current HTML web pages.

Whereas previous iterations of HTML and XHTML kept adding more strict syntax and less room for error, HTML5 scales back requirements, creating a more open environment for creating web pages. Starting with the `doctype`, HTML5 is overtly simple:

```
<!doctype html>
```

That's it. All you have to do to technically be using HTML5 is use this `doctype`, and it isn't likely to change anytime soon. Though HTML5 sounds like a version number, the compatibility factors guiding HTML5 mean that things like the `doctype` should become standard, and one less thing web developers have to worry about when making sure their websites and applications work for everyone.

HTML5 introduces many features that you can utilize in your mobile web apps to create a more native mobile web experience. At its core, HTML5 introduces new structural elements with more semantic meaning than `<div>`s:

➤ `<header>`: For a group of introductory aides. This is defined by content, not position, so you can have a `<header>` for your entire site and also a header within a blog post.

➤ `<nav>`: For major site navigation (not just groups of links). Again, could be used multiple times on a page.

➤ `<hgroup>`: To aid with document outlining, can be used to wrap multiple, subsequent headers (for example, an `H1` title and `H2` subtitle).

➤ `<section>`: Used to group semantically related content.

➤ `<article>`: For self-contained related content. (A rule of thumb: Think "Could this be an RSS item?")

➤ `<footer>`: Information about the `footer`'s containing element (copyright, author). Like `<header>`, `<footer>` can be used for an entire site, or multiple elements within it.

➤ `<aside>`: A sidebar related to adjacent content (not just an unrelated side column).

These new structural elements create the base of any modern, semantically rich website or web application. To compete with a native app, you can use more advanced HTML5 features in a mobile web app, which are discussed in a little bit.

And What Exactly Is a Mobile Web App?

Whereas a mobile website exists to improve the mobile functionality of an existing website, a mobile web app exists to perform a specific mobile function. A mobile web app should be more comparable to a native app than to a website. A web app cannot handle some functions, or might not have the capability to access the device to perform them. Some of the situations that would require a native application development include:

➤ Resource and graphic-intensive games

➤ Accessing the device camera, microphone, address book, or media library

➤ Apps to be sold through app markets for payment

➤ Sending push notifications

➤ Running as a background service

If the app doesn't need to do any of these things, creating the app on the web is a great option. When you decide to create a mobile web app, at its core you'll still be developing a mobile website. You can use many of the already-discussed techniques like adaptive images and media queries. Like a dedicated mobile website, a mobile web app will most likely be designed only for mobile phones and possibly tablets. You'll still be creating all of your HTML pages and can use media queries to target different orientations and screen sizes. Then, using HTML5 and JavaScript, you can add advanced functionality that more closely relates to a native app.

How Do You Use HTML5 in a Mobile Web App?

If you're not looking for any of the aforementioned capabilities in your mobile app, then HTML, CSS, and JavaScript might very well provide all the necessary tools to create a well-designed, full-fledged mobile web app. This section looks at some of the HTML5 features you *can* use to help you create native-like, mobile web apps.

New Form Input Types

These HTML5 specifications are easy to understand, quick to implement, and a no-brainer to use right away. Instead of the basic `<input type="text">`, new input types can provide a streamlined experience in modern mobile browsers, and can also aid in form validation:

➤ `<input type="email">`: This markup tells browsers that they should accept the field entry only if a valid e-mail address format is followed. On iPhone, the device keyboard that is brought up for this field includes the at (@) and dot (.) symbols on the main screen, making it easier to quickly enter the correct information (see Figure 5-15). The keyboard on Android will not be modified, though.

➤ `<input type="url">`: This tells browsers to check for a valid web address format. A special keyboard with a ".com" button appears on iPhone; Android's keyboard remains the same.

➤ `<input type="tel">`: Although varying telephone number formats mean there's no validation added, this brings up a number keyboard screen on some mobile devices, including iPhone and Android (see Figure 5-16 for iPhone example).

➤ `<input type="number">`: Allows only numbers to be input, and shows numeric keyboards and number spinner controls on some devices and browsers.

➤ `<input type="date">`: The goal here is for browsers to provide native date pickers to replace JavaScript widgets, and standardize valid input formats.

➤ `<input type="time">`: Validates a 24-hour time input format.

➤ `<input type="datetime">`: Validates a precise date and time.

➤ `<input type="range">`: Renders a slider in some browsers.

➤ `<input type="search">`: Expects a search to be performed, and renders with a specific style in some browsers, like Safari.

➤ `<input type="color">`: Can provide a native browser color picker, although not well-supported by browsers yet.

FIGURE 5-15: The specialized keyboard that is brought up on iPhones for <input type="email">

FIGURE 5-16: The number pad keyboard that is brought up on iPhones for <input type="tel">

Backward compatibility is in full effect with these elements, so you don't have to worry about forms breaking in older browsers. If a browser doesn't recognize an input type, it just falls back to a regular text input field. There's no reason not to use these input types in a mobile web app to provide a better user experience.

New form attributes have also been introduced to help replace common JavaScript widgets:

- ➤ `required`: Can be placed on `<textarea>` and most input fields; browsers won't allow the form to be submitted if the field is empty.

- ➤ `placeholder`: Puts default text in the input box that automatically clears once the user's focus is on that field.

- ➤ `min` and `max`: Constrains the range of values that can be entered in a field, such as a number or date range.

- ➤ `multiple`: When used on an input type such as e-mail, allows multiple addresses to be added in a comma-separated format.

- ➤ `step`: When used on a spinner, can control the increment of options that are shown.

Offline Storage

HTML5 offline storage provides a way to save data on the client side even when there is no Internet connection. Once data has been downloaded to the device, a manifest file can be used to cache files locally, such as options and actions the user made. When the Internet connection is restored the data can synchronize back to the server. Data cannot be downloaded from the server if the Internet connection is lost, but many aspects of a mobile web app experience can continue unchanged with offline storage. This is an important element for behaving more like a native mobile app, because many apps don't require an Internet connection to fully function.

The Cache Manifest

A manifest tells the browser what it needs to store on its local cache. Once the browser has stored the files in its cache, the web app can continue to use the files when the user is offline. The manifest can also specify files that should *not* be cached, and provide fallbacks when assets are missing.

To get started, simply add the manifest attribute to the `<html>` element, and point it to the file containing your application manifest:

```
<html lang="en"  manifest="/webapp.manifest">
```

Your manifest file must begin with a declaration of CACHE MANIFEST, which tells your browser that what follows is the source to a manifest file. Next, the files are listed within categories, also known as namespaces.

```
CACHE MANIFEST

CACHE:
index.html
myscripts.js
```

```
mystyles.css

FALLBACK:
/ offline.html

NETWORK:
liveinfo.html

# version 1
```

CACHE, quite obviously, tells the browser all of the files that should be cached.

FALLBACK tells the browser how to handle files that are not cached. If anything matches the URL on the left, and is not in the manifest, and can't be accessed due to lack of connection, it will be replaced with the file on the right. In this case, if any URL is specified besides index.html, then show offline.html. This can be used to prevent users from accessing specific parts of the mobile web app that do require an Internet connection, serving users a special page instead.

NETWORK explicitly tells the browser any files that must have an Internet connection to be accessed. By default, anything not listed in the CACHE will fall in this category, and it can be specifically stated using a wildcard asterisk (*).

Last, a comment is included that tells the browser to reload the contents of the manifest. To do this, something needs to change in the contents of the file to force a reload.

To serve the manifest correctly, the file must have the extension .manifest, and it must have the right MIME type. You'll need to change HTTP headers and include something like this in your mime.types file (when using an Apache server):

```
Text/cache-manifest manifest
```

Once the manifest file is in place, when a browser accesses the site it parses the HTML file, processes the manifest file, requests the assets in the manifest file (regardless of whether it received these along with the initial HTML file), and caches the specified files. Then, if the browser reloads when the Internet connection is lost, and nothing in the manifest file has changed, the browser will detect that it has local cache and serve the page from the files saved locally.

Geolocation

Plenty of mobile web user scenarios can benefit from geolocation. For example, many online retail store locators now have a "use my current location" option. This will conveniently bring up the closest stores to a user's current location in one click, instead of having to enter a city or ZIP code.

The JavaScript Geolocation API uses GPS or network IP information to find the physical location of users. It exists inside the navigator object, is simple to work with, and allows you to enhance a mobile web app in very native ways. To start, you can quickly find the current location of your user with the getCurrentPosition JavaScript method. Or, watchPosition checks at regular intervals to see if the user's position has changed.

It's important to note when using geolocation in a web app that browsers prompt users to make sure they accept the app's use of their position information. If users refuse, an error handler is returned, so make sure that your app addresses that scenario appropriately.

The success handler that is returned if the user accepts the app's use of getCurrentPosition or watchPosition includes a Position object containing two properties: timestamp and coords. Using the coordinate data, you can easily map user position on a graphical interface, like Google Maps. The following JavaScript added to your HTML file will get the coordinates for the user's current location for displaying on a map:

```
<script>
function getLocation() {
  if (navigator.geolocation) {
    navigator.geolocation.getCurrentPosition(functon(position) {
      var coords = position.coords;
      showMap(coords.latitude, coords.longitude, coords.accuracy);
    });
  }
}
</script>
```

Canvas

The Canvas API provides 2-D drawing capabilities for a wide range of mobile web applications: drawing tools, games, emulators, and more. It uses HTML and JavaScript to bring dynamic, native drawing and animation, without any need for Flash. The depth of Canvas development capabilities can fill a large book, and already has. The *HTML5 Canvas Cookbook* by Eric Rowell is an excellent resource, from getting started with paths and drawings to advanced animation and game development.

Make Your Mobile Web App Even More Native

Because your mobile web app is still running in a browser, you'll have things like the browser navigation bar taking up screen real estate, and forcing certain options to be available to users, where a native app might have a specialized navigation bar instead. The subsequent sections discuss additional techniques that can make a mobile web app function more like a "native" mobile app.

Add to Home Screen

On iPhone and iPad, the mobile WebKit browser includes an easy way to bookmark a website, adding it as an icon on the device home screen. This is another detail that can make a mobile web app seem more like a native app, with a one-touch access icon, just like any other app on the home screen. Any website can be added to the iOS device home screen; the problem is that the majority of users don't know how to add these shortcuts to their devices.

Matteo Spinelli created a JavaScript project that prompts users to add a site to their home screen (see Figure 5-17), with a bubble intuitively positioned next to the native browser button where users must perform this function (http://cubiq.org/add-to-home-screen). It mimics YouTube's initial use of such a feature, with options including the message text to display, bubble appearance frequency, and bubble animation effects. It also includes a style sheet so designers can easily customize button appearance.

The following two lines simply need to be added to the <head> of the mobile web app's HTML. The script checks the user's device, operating system and version, and displays the bubble only in appropriate configurations:

```
<link rel="stylesheet" href="path/to/add2home.css">
<script type="application/javascript" src="path/to/add2home.js"></script>
```

FIGURE 5-17: The Add to Home pop-up on a mobile web app

More iOS Tips and Tricks

iPhone and iPad have provided several other proprietary properties their browsers will recognize that help create a more native mobile web app experience:

```
<meta name="apple-mobile-web-app-capable" content="yes" />
<meta name="apple-mobile-web-app-status-bar-style" content="black" />
<link rel="apple-touch-icon" href="iphon_tetris_icon.png"/>
<link rel="apple-touch-startup-image" href="startup.png" />
```

To explain each of these:

➤ `apple-mobile-web-app-capable`: A cue to the webkit browser that this web page is behaving as a mobile, potentially offline, web app.

➤ `apple-mobile-web-app-status-bar-style`: Hides the browser status bar by scrolling the screen down to the start of the web page on page load. The status bar will still appear when a user scrolls all the way up. This also hides the navigation bar when the app is offline.

➤ `apple-touch-icon`: Points to the mobile web app icon image to appear on the device home screen.

➤ `apple-touch-startup-image`: Points to the mobile web app startup image.

jQuery Mobile

jQuery Mobile (`http://jquerymobile.com`) is another wonderful tool that helps make great mobile web UIs. jQuery Mobile provides an HTML5-based, touchscreen-optimized user interface framework for cross-platform mobile devices. Based on the established jQuery and jQuery UI foundations, it's lightweight and easily themeable.

To get started, simply link to the jQuery and jQuery mobile scripts and the default style sheet:

```
<link rel="stylesheet"
href="http://code.jquery.com/mobile/1.0/jquery.mobile-1.0.min.css" />

<script type="text/javascript" src="http://code.jquery.com/jquery-1.6.4.min.js">
</script>

<script type="text/javascript"
src="http://code.jquery.com/mobile/1.0/jquery.mobile-1.0.min.js"></script>
```

Instead of making the jQuery Mobile interface look like the iPhone or Android interfaces, jQuery Mobile has an independent UI style that looks good and functions nicely on all mobile browsers. jQuery also provides a *Themeroller* tool, where designers select desired colors and styles and a style sheet is generated automatically (`http://jquerymobile.com/themeroller`).

Besides slick mobile styling, jQuery Mobile provides rich form controls, layouts for lists and overlays, and UI widgets such as toggles, sliders, and tabs. Check out the Quick Start Guide for step-by-step instructions (`http://jquerymobile.com/demos/1.0/docs/about/getting-started.html`).

SUMMARY

It is important for organizations to spend time when creating a mobile strategy to find out exactly which model fits best for their business domain. Starting down the wrong path can be costly as well as ruin a company's reputation. This chapter has stressed the importance of a mobile web presence, whether it's improving a current website on mobile using media queries, or developing a new, full-fledged mobile web app. The provided introduction to each technique should give your organization the tools it needs to successfully get started on the mobile web.

Now that you understand various ways to create a mobile website, the following chapters will explain how to develop various mobile applications, starting with Android.

Getting Started with Android

WHAT'S IN THIS CHAPTER?

➤ Deciding to target Android as your mobile platform

➤ Getting the tools you need to develop Android

➤ Creating a new project

➤ Creating the Derby project in Android

Android Inc. was initially started in 2003, out of a frustration with the smartphone market as it existed at the time. It was acquired by Google in 2005.

The hardware side of Android is supported by the Open Handset Alliance (OHA), which is a conglomeration of many handset manufacturers, and the software is maintained by the Android Open Source Project, which is led by Google.

Android had its first major release in late 2008; the first major phone company to support it was T-Mobile, and the original handset was the HTC Dream (G1).

The Android OS was built on a modified Linux kernel and applications are written in Java. By using Java as the development framework for the applications, Android enables you to develop your application on all major platforms.

By leveraging the Eclipse IDE, Android affords the user almost the exact same user experience for development on all major OS platforms.

Additionally, when researching Android you may come across the name Dalvik. It is the virtual machine that runs on the Android device, and your applications run within it. What does this mean to developers? Because your applications run inside this virtual space, it provides a level of security to the base OS. Also, Dalvik has been designed with performance in mind. As of Android 2.2 it also provides just-in-time compilation to your apps (because Dalvik requires specially compiled .dex files and not just the standard .class files generated in a normal Java compilation).

WHY TARGET ANDROID?

Among the many reasons to target the Android platform, first and foremost is cost. On average you can get an Android smartphone for a fraction of the cost of an iPhone. They may not have commensurate features, but thrift is a major component for new smartphone buyers.

Next is flexibility. More types of Android devices are available, so if your application fits a specific niche market, there is probably a device that would support your needs already in production. At the time of writing, there are effectively two iOS devices (iPhone/iPod touch and iPad); four if you include the retina display versions, versus roughly 15 form factors to develop for.

If you are already a Java developer, adding Android to your repertoire is a snap. What Java is to Android, Cocoa is to CocoaTouch and C# is to Silverlight. All of the frameworks that mobile developers use are a combination of subsets and supersets of the functionality of a given technology.

Identifying an application that exists on another platform but does not yet exist on Android is another perfectly good reason to target Android. That being said, you should do some research, because if a developer has targeted iOS or BlackBerry as the primary platform, you have to assume that Android is potentially on the horizon.

WHO SUPPORTS ANDROID?

HTC, LG, Motorola, and Samsung are the major players in the Android smartphone market. Archos, Dell, Samsung, and Toshiba hold the largest pieces of the Android tablet market. You should note that Amazon's Kindle Fire and Nook Color are up-and-comers and use a customized version of the Android tablet (Version 3) OS on their devices.

ANDROID AS COMPETITION TO ITSELF

Because Android was designed to be run on many different types of devices, created by many different manufacturers (as opposed to the closed system that Apple has maintained), it has left itself open to the will of said manufacturers. Because of the open nature of the Android OS, it is commonplace for manufacturers to create vendor-specific builds of Android, and when this happens you are beholden to them for OS updates. Additionally in these custom builds, vendor-specific limitations have arisen such as the vendor-specific market. You then have another hurdle to cross when releasing your application for sale to the public because some devices may not be able to purchase it because of these limitations.

Another issue that has cropped up is the lack of over-the-air (OTA) distribution of OS updates by cellular carriers. Often your device is perfectly capable of running a later version of the Android software, but carriers are often slow to distribute that to their customers.

Multiple Markets and Market Locks

Depending on your version of Android, and depending on the manufacturer of a given device, you may find yourself locked into using a vendor-specific Android marketplace. Additionally, application vendors can list their application not only on Google Play or vendor-specific marketplaces, but also on the Amazon App Store. You often find on cheap and imported Android devices a version of Google Play that is maintained by the manufacturer. They pick and choose what applications are available from the whole set in the marketplace. You should develop as you expect to be available to all Android devices; just note when purchasing large quantities for an enterprise deployment that you will have to watch out for these inconsistencies.

The version of the Android SDK that you need to support depends on what devices you want to support. If you want to target most phones available right now, you should support Android 2.2 or 2.3. "Gingerbread" (2.3) is the last widely available version for those devices. The Android 3.x versions are for tablets, such as the Samsung Galaxy Tab. The Android 4.x versions are the newest, and are a combination of the Android 2.x and Android 3.x functionality meant to pull back on the version splintering seen in devices, but not many devices currently in release support it.

Once you have decided on a version to deploy your application against, you need to set up your development environment. In the next section you will learn all about configuring your IDE, Java and Android SDKs, and building emulators.

GETTING THE TOOLS YOU NEED

This section paraphrases the installation instructions from the Android Developer section, and we added some personal notes from our experiences.

Downloading and Installing JDK

The first thing that you need to do to develop Android applications is to visit `http://www.oracle .com/technetwork/java/javase/downloads/index.html` and ensure that you have the Java JDK installed. Because so many different acronyms and versions appear on the Java download website, Figure 6-1 points you in the direction you need to get past all of the potential distractions on that site.

The JDK is the Java Development Kit. You need this package to do any Java development on your machine, Android or otherwise. Be sure to look for the Java Platform, Standard Edition JDK.

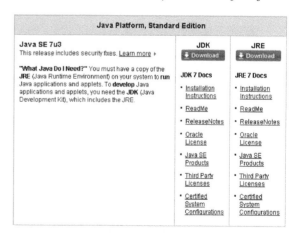

Downloading and Installing Eclipse

After you have successfully installed the JDK, you will need a development environment.

FIGURE 6-1: JDK download page

The open source IDE Eclipse is recommended by Android directly in its documentation. You are not limited only to Eclipse, but the tooling has been honed over time to be the easiest solution to get up and running. Figure 6-2 shows the Eclipse download page (`www.eclipse.org/downloads`). Download the version of Eclipse Classic that is appropriate for your operating system.

FIGURE 6-2: Eclipse download site

Downloading and Installing the Android SDK

After you have installed the Eclipse IDE, you need to install the Android Software Developer Kit (`http://developer.android.com/sdk/index.html`). This includes all the tools necessary to build Android apps, because the SDK is not built directly into Eclipse. Figure 6-3 shows the Android SDK download page; make sure to get the right version for your OS.

FIGURE 6-3: Android SDK download page

Don't use the installer for 64-bit Windows. Just get the zip file and unzip it to `c:\Android`. *At the time of writing the installer package has difficulty finding the Java SDK installed on the machine.*

For Mac deploy it to `/android` *in your root volume.*

Downloading and Configuring the Eclipse ADT Plug-in

After you have installed the Android SDK you need the ADT plug-in. What this does is add the features necessary to create Android Projects (and Android Test Projects), because they are not bundled with the base Eclipse install. Additionally, the plug-in adds debugging tools to Eclipse to help during the Android development process. Figure 6-4 shows the interface for installing the ADT plug-in. You will also use this interface when upgrading ADT. The tooling generally gets a revision when a new version of the Android OS is released.

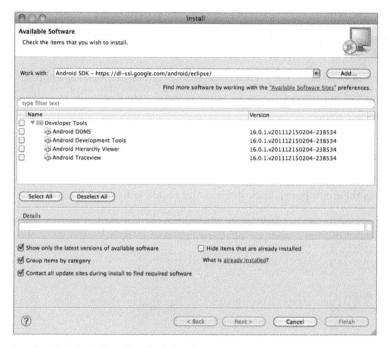

FIGURE 6-4: Installing the ADT plug-in

Use the Update Manager feature of your Eclipse installation to install the latest revision of ADT on your development computer. Follow these steps:

1. Start Eclipse and select Help ⇨ Install New Software.

2. Click Add in the top-right corner.

3. In the Add Repository dialog box that appears, enter **ADT plug-in** for the name and the following URL for the location: `https://dl-ssl.google.com/android/eclipse/`.

4. Click OK. If you have trouble acquiring the plug-in, try using "http" in the Location URL instead of "https" ("https" is preferred for security reasons).

5. In the Available Software dialog box, select the checkbox next to Developer Tools and click Next.

6. The next window shows a list of the tools to be downloaded. Click Next.

7. Read and accept the license agreements and then click Finish. If you get a security warning saying that the authenticity or validity of the software can't be established, click OK.

8. When the installation completes, restart Eclipse.

Once you have downloaded the ADT plug-in you need to set it up to talk to the Android SDK that you downloaded earlier. This allows Eclipse to build, run, and debug Android applications without needing to open a terminal or command shell. Figure 6-5 shows where you need to add the link to the Android SDK in the Eclipse preferences.

After you've successfully downloaded the ADT, the next step is to modify your ADT preferences in Eclipse to point to the Android SDK directory (see Figure 6-5):

1. Select Window ➪ Preferences to open the Preferences panel. In Mac OS X, click Eclipse ➪ Preferences.

2. Select Android from the left panel.

3. You may see a dialog box asking whether you want to send usage statistics to Google. If so, make your choice and click Proceed. You cannot continue with this procedure until you click Proceed.

4. For the SDK Location in the main panel, click Browse and locate your downloaded SDK directory.

5. Click Apply and then click OK.

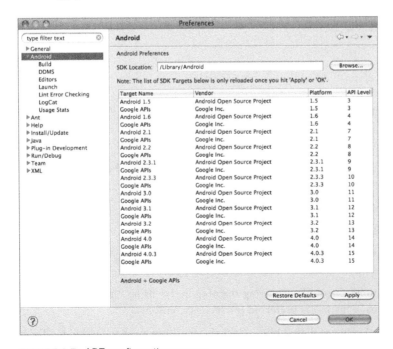

FIGURE 6-5: ADT configuration screen

Installing Additional SDK Components

The last step in preparing your development environment for Android is to download additional Android OS packages. This enables you to build applications that target that OS, and also gives you the tools you need to emulate a device running that OS on which to test all of your applications, whether or not they have been targeted to that OS version. Figure 6-6 shows just how many options you have when looking to target Android OS versions.

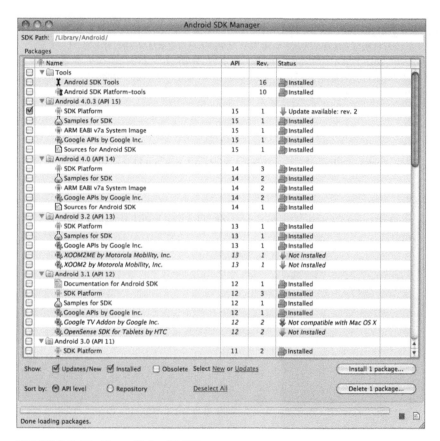

FIGURE 6-6: Working with the SDK Manager

Correctly configuring and using this tool will ensure that you have all the latest SDKs and utilities afforded to you. Note that you will not necessarily need all of the versions of the SDKs listed in Figure 6-6; this was merely to illustrate the full breadth of your options.

Loading the Android SDK Manager in Eclipse takes only a few steps:

1. Open Eclipse.

2. Select Window ⇨ Android SDK and AVD Manager.

3. Select Available Packages in the left panel. This reveals all of the components that are currently available for download from the SDK repository.

4. Select the component(s) you'd like to install and click Install Selected.

5. Verify and accept the components you want (ensure each one is selected with a green checkmark) and click Install. The components will now be installed into your existing Android SDK directories.

 I recommend that you download and install an Android 2.2.x, Android 2.3.x, and Android 3.x version. This will give you the latest two handset-specific versions of Android, and the current tablet version of Android. As Android 4.0 is so new, you may choose to get it, but understand that you may need to purchase a newer device to test apps targeted to that version.

Development

The following sections discuss the application layout and Android app development.

Creating a New Project

First things first — you need to create a new Android project. The line highlighted in Figure 6-7 is the type of project you want.

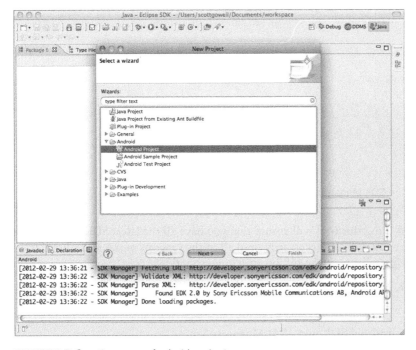

FIGURE 6-7 Creating a new Android project

First you need to name your application and add it to a workspace. Think of a workspace as the folder in which your application resides. Figure 6-8 illustrates what the New Android Project screen looks like.

After you have named your application you will need to give it a package name, set the minimum SDK required to run your application, and name the initial Activity that will run when your application runs. If you want to add a test project to your workspace, you can do so at this time. Figure 6-9 shows a completed Application Info step in the new project wizard.

An important note at this point: Make sure that your package name is unique. The standard format for package names is `com.companyName.applicationName`. This must be unique because that is how it is known on the Android device and in the Android Market. When you make updates you can make them only within your package name. If you change your package name there will be no upgrade path between versions.

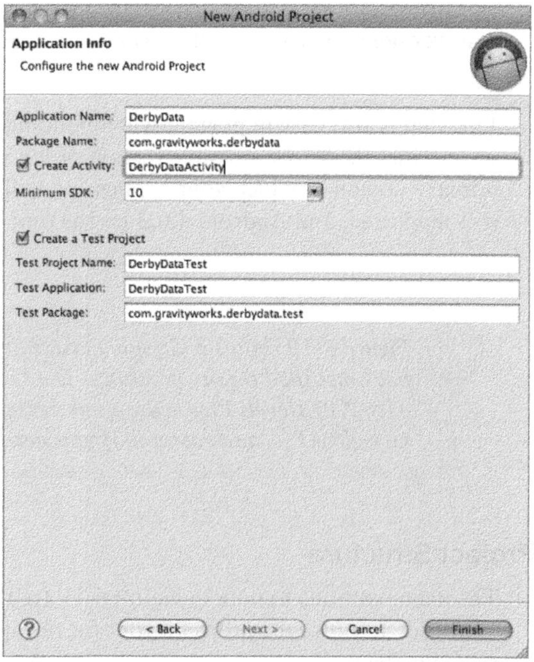

The minimum SDK required is generally set when you are leveraging a permission or piece of functionality that did not exist when the core Android version was released, or if you want to target a specific type of device (tablet versus handset). The major jumps are between 1.6 and 2.1, 2.3 and 3.x, and 3.x and 4.x. Figure 6-10 shows you all of the SDKs that you have installed that you can target when creating your application. Please note that the reason this screen is full of SDKs is because I took the time to download them all for demonstration purposes.

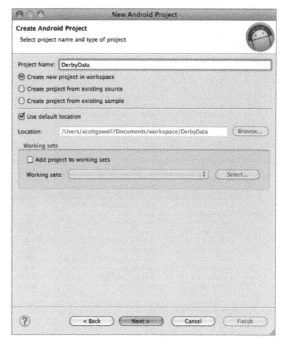

FIGURE 6-8: Naming your project

FIGURE 6-9: Configuring application information

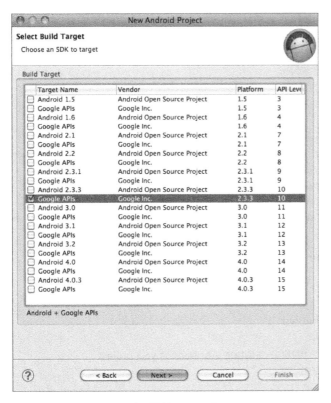

FIGURE 6-10: Choosing the SDK version for your app

This step is also very important when building your application. The minimum SDK version you set specifies the lowest possible version of the SDK in which your application will run, and it is the primary version in which your application will run. Android 1.5 is the lowest version of the SDK still supported, and Android 4.0.3 (at the time of this writing) is the highest.

 Figure 6-10 shows a Google version of the SDK alongside all of the versions I have installed on my machine. The Google APIs add additional functionality to each API Level. Please use your best judgment when deciding whether to use the Google APIs, and research if you need the functionality they provide.

Project Structure

The major sections to note in Figure 6-11 are the `src` and `res` folders and the `AndroidManifest .xml` file. It shows the project layout for the application that I have been building in the previous steps.

All of your code lives within your src folder, under your Package Namespace. The res folder holds layouts and resources for different hardware specs. HDPI, LDPI, and MDPI are the resolutions for which you can create images. The layout subfolder holds all of your XML layouts. These are how your application gets rendered. The code will be how to populate these layouts. All of your XML layouts are stored in the layout subfolder of res, and your code will be linked under the namespace in your src folder of the project view.

The Android Manifest is the heart of your application. It holds the entire configuration of your app (Figure 6-12) — the permissions you request (Figure 6-14), the application attributes (Figure 6-13), and links to instrumentation to be attached to your app. You can edit this in Eclipse's Manifest Editor or in XML (Figure 6-15) because that is how it is saved.

FIGURE 6-11: Basic project structure

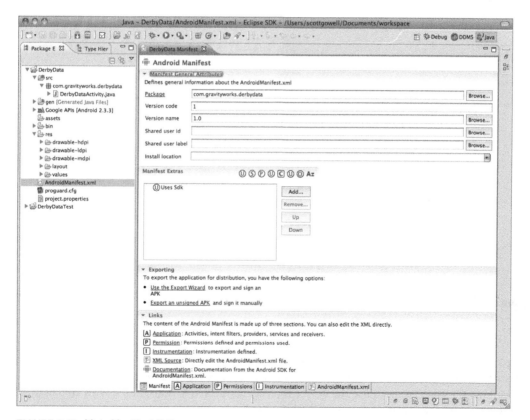

FIGURE 6-12: Main Manifest Editor

The Manifest Editor is where the initial information of your application is stored when you create it. This interface also has links to export your application. Exporting is necessary when submitting your app to Google Play. In Eclipse there is a specific menu option and wizard that expedites the submission process.

Figure 6-13 shows all of the base properties that can be set for a given application in the app's `AndroidManifest.xml` file. The most common properties to edit are the Label (the text shown under the icon, often referenced in a resource file) and Icon (the icon shown in the launcher UI of your device, the icon your users will click on to launch the app).

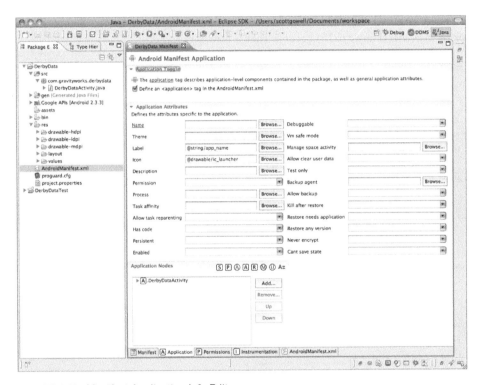

FIGURE 6-13: Manifest Application Info Editor

The spartan view shown in Figure 6-14 is the Permissions Editor. Here you can add permission requests to your application. The most common one is `android.permission.INTERNET`, which allows the application to use the device Internet connectivity. This, along with GPS and accelerometer, are the permissions you will add to the Derby Names application.

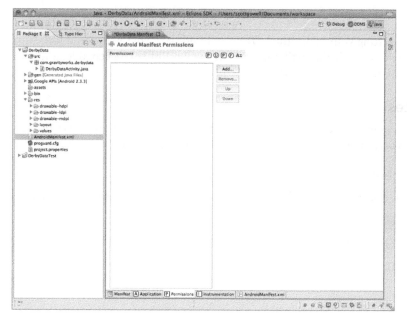

FIGURE 6-14: Android Manifest Permissions Editor

Last is the XML Editor shown in Figure 6-15. As you make changes in the other tabs they are reflected here. If you feel more comfortable editing the XML by hand you can use this interface to add, update, and remove properties as you see fit.

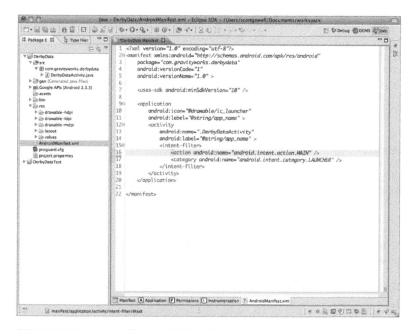

FIGURE 6-15: Android Manifest XML Editor

Android Basics

You have two options for starting your application. You can build the layout you would like to populate, or you can build the code that will populate the layout. Either is acceptable; it just depends on what you feel most comfortable with.

Creating User Interfaces

This section describes the common widgets that come with Android, and shows examples of the different layout elements you can use to coordinate the flow of your application's activities.

Basic Android UI Elements

All of the basic elements in Android are stored in the `android.widgets` namespace in the SDK.

The most commonly used elements include:

➤   **Button:** This is a standard button element.

The following XML specifies the layout of the Button widget:

```
<Button
    android:layout_height="wrap_content"
    android:layout_width="wrap_content"
    android:id="@+id/button"
    android:text="Click Me"
    android:onClick="btnClick" />
```

Code: This code is necessary to handle the `click` event noted in the XML layout.

```
public void btnClick (View view) {
    //Do Something.
}
```

➤   **TextView:** When I see this I want to think *text box*, but it isn't a text box. `TextView` is effectively the same as a label in other languages. It is just a place to display text.

Layout:

```
<TextView
    android:id="@+id/textview"
    android:layout_width="fill_parent"
    android:layout_height="fill_parent"
    android:text="Hello World"/>
```

Code:

```
TextView tvToShow = (TextView)this.findViewById(R.id.textview);
tvToShow.setText("Ta-Dah!");
```

➤   **EditText:** This is the text box widget. You can edit the contents of the text box and save those values in code.

Layout:

```
<EditText
    android:id="@+id/txtUsername"
    android:hint="Username"
    android:layout_width="fill_parent"
    android:layout_height="wrap_content" />
```

Code:

```
EditText txtUserName = (EditText) findViewById(R.id.txtUsername);
String username = txtUserName.getText().ToString();
```

➤ **CheckBox:** This is a standard checkbox element.

Layout:

```
<CheckBox android:id="@+id/checkbox"
    android:layout_width="wrap_content"
    android:layout_height="wrap_content"
    android:text="Checkbox Text" />
```

Code:

```
final CheckBox checkbox = (CheckBox) findViewById(R.id.checkbox);
checkbox.setOnClickListener(new OnClickListener() {
    public void onClick(View v) {
        if (((CheckBox) v).isChecked()) {
            //It's Checked
        }
else {
            //Not Checked
        }
    }
});
```

➤ **RadioButton:** This is a standard radio button element. To really get the most bang for your buck, though, you need a RadioGroup.

Layout:

```
<RadioGroup
    android:layout_width="fill_parent"
    android:layout_height="wrap_content"
    android:orientation="vertical">
    <RadioButton android:id="@+id/radio_uno"
        android:layout_width="wrap_content"
        android:layout_height="wrap_content"
        android:text="1 - Uno" />
    <RadioButton android:id="@+id/radio_dos"
        android:layout_width="wrap_content"
        android:layout_height="wrap_content"
        android:text="2 - Dos" />
</RadioGroup>
```

Code:

```
private OnClickListener radioButtonOnClick = new OnClickListener() {
    public void onClick(View v) {
        RadioButton rb = (RadioButton) v;
// Do with it what you will
        //rb.getText();
    }
};

//This assigns this event to the radio buttons.
    RadioButton radio_uno = (RadioButton) findViewById(R.id.radio_uno);
    RadioButton radio_dos = (RadioButton) findViewById(R.id.radio_dos);
    radio_uno.setOnClickListener(radio_listener);
    radio_dos.setOnClickListener(radio_listener);
```

Figure 6-16 shows all of the major UI widgets.

➤   **ListView:** This is the element you use if you want to
    show lists of data. You can overload its display and
    put lots of elements in each row, or you can just bind
    a text item and a value to each. The trick is using an
    `ArrayAdapter<T>` where T is the type of object that you
    want bound. Additionally, creating a layout XML for
    how you want each item displayed is a good strategy.

    Layout:

```
<ListView
    android:id="@+id/lstWords"
    android:layout_width="fill_parent"
    android:divider="#ddd"
    android:dividerHeight="1px"
    android:paddingBottom="67dp"
    android:layout_height="fill_parent" />
```

FIGURE 6-16: Major UI elements all together

Code:

```
static final String[] words = new String[]{ "Hello", "World" };
lstWords = (ListView)findViewById(R.id.lstWords);
lstWords.setAdapter
new ArrayAdapter<String>(this.getApplicationContext(),R.id.list_content,words));
```

Basic Android Layouts and Views

➤   **FrameLayout:** This is very simplistic and can really contain only a single UI element. You
    can, in fact, have multiple elements but they overlap each other by default.

    The example code shown here is rendered in Figure 6-17:

```
<?xml version="1.0" encoding="utf-8"?>
<FrameLayout
    android:id="@+id/frameLayout"
    android:layout_width="fill_parent"
    android:layout_height="fill_parent"
    xmlns:android="http://schemas.android.com/apk/res/android">
<EditText
    android:id="@+id/widget46"
    android:layout_width="wrap_content"
    android:layout_height="wrap_content"
    android:text="EditText"
    android:textSize="18sp" />
</FrameLayout>
```

This is a simple `FrameLayout` that contains a single `EditText` widget with the text "EditText."

LinearLayout: This lays out your UI elements along a given direction: horizontal or vertical. Figure 6-18 is a linear layout, which contains four consecutive TextView widgets along the vertical.

FIGURE 6-17: FrameLayout rendered

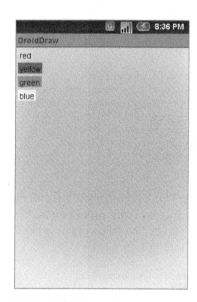

FIGURE 6-18: LinearLayout rendered

Example:

```
<?xml version="1.0" encoding="utf-8"?>
<LinearLayout
    android:id="@+id/widget59"
    android:layout_width="fill_parent"
    android:layout_height="fill_parent"
    android:orientation="vertical"
    xmlns:android="http://schemas.android.com/apk/res/android">
```

```
<TextView
    android:id="@+id/widget60"
    android:layout_width="wrap_content"
    android:layout_height="wrap_content"
    android:background="#ffaa0000"
    android:layout_marginTop="5dp"
    android:layout_marginLeft="5dp"
    android:text="red" />
<TextView
    android:id="@+id/widget63"
    android:layout_width="wrap_content"
    android:layout_height="wrap_content"
    android:background="#ffaaaa00"
    android:layout_marginTop="5dp"
    android:layout_marginLeft="5dp"
    android:text="yellow" />
<TextView
    android:id="@+id/widget64"
    android:layout_width="wrap_content"
    android:layout_height="wrap_content"
    android:background="#ff00aa00"
    android:layout_marginTop="5dp"
    android:layout_marginLeft="5dp"
    android:text="green" />
<TextView
    android:id="@+id/widget65"
    android:layout_width="wrap_content"
    android:layout_height="wrap_content"
    android:background="#ff0000aa"
    android:layout_marginTop="5dp"
    android:layout_marginLeft="5dp"
    android:text="blue" />
</LinearLayout>
```

➤ **TableLayout:** Think tables in HTML and this is the type of organization you get with this layout. `TableLayouts` contain rows and columns, representing a grid, and you can put other UI elements into it. The following code results in a table with two rows, each with two cells, and is visualized in Figure 6-19:

```
<?xml version="1.0" encoding="utf-8"?>
<TableLayout xmlns:android="http://schemas.android.com/apk/res/android"
    android:layout_width="fill_parent"
    android:layout_height="fill_parent"
    android:stretchColumns="1">
    <TableRow>
        <TextView
            android:text="Hello"
            android:padding="3dip" />
        <TextView
            android:text="World"
            android:gravity="right"
            android:padding="3dip" />
    </TableRow>
```

```
        <TableRow>
            <TextView
                android:text="Goodbye"
                android:padding="3dip" />
            <TextView
                android:text="User"
                android:gravity="right"
                android:padding="3dip" />
        </TableRow>
    </TableLayout>
</TableLayout>
```

➤ **RelativeLayout:** This is the most complex layout of the four mentioned in this section. You specify relationships between UI elements to lay out your interface.

The following code represents a simple form with a TextView acting as a label for a blank EditText widget, with Cancel and OK widgets docked beneath EditText relative to the right screen boundary:

FIGURE 6-19: TableLayout rendered

```
<?xml version="1.0" encoding="utf-8"?>
<RelativeLayout
    android:id="@+id/widget37"
    android:layout_width="fill_parent"
    android:layout_height="fill_parent"
    xmlns:android="http://schemas.android.com/apk/res/android">

    <TextView android:id="@+id/label"
            android:layout_width="fill_parent"
            android:layout_height="wrap_content"
            android:text="Type here:" />

    <EditText android:id="@+id/entry"
            android:layout_width="fill_parent"
            android:layout_height="wrap_content"
            android:background="@android:drawable/editbox_background"
            android:layout_below="@id/label" />

    <Button android:id="@+id/ok"
            android:layout_width="wrap_content"
            android:layout_height="wrap_content"
            android:layout_below="@id/entry"
            android:layout_alignParentRight="true"
            android:layout_marginLeft="10px"
            android:text="OK" />

    <Button android:layout_width="wrap_content"
            android:layout_height="wrap_content"
            android:layout_toLeftOf="@id/ok"
            android:layout_alignTop="@id/ok"
            android:text="Cancel" />
</RelativeLayout>
```

Figure 6-20 shows how this code renders on an Android device.

Having seen the various UI elements, now is the time to get the rest of your development environment configured to be able to debug your app.

Creating an Android Virtual Device

You need to create an Android Virtual Device (AVD) in order to debug your application in the emulator, because this "device" is what the emulator runs. Creating an AVD is quite easy. Eclipse includes a tool called AVD Manager (click Window Manager ➪ AVD Manager). You need to name your AVD instance, choose its OS version (Target), pick a skin (with which you can customize the look and feel of the emulator) and resolution, and specify the hardware details for the device (amount of RAM, size of SD card, and sensors like Accelerometer and GPS). Once you have configured it to your specifications, click Create AVD and you are all set.

FIGURE 6-20: RelativeLayout rendered

For most purposes, the stock AVD skins are fine for debugging, but if you would like to emulate a specific device (tablet or handset) either for demonstration purposes or because you want it to feel like the device you are developing for, you can use a custom skin. Although you can always set the hardware properties to mirror those of the device you are using, there is an online community (www.xda-developers.com) dedicated to making custom skins for use with the AVD. Using your favorite search engine, type the model and make of the Android device you want to emulate, and most likely you will find a custom skin out there for it. Creating a new AVD with the appropriate specs and then selecting this skin gives you an emulator that looks just like the device you are testing for.

Debugging

Debugging in Eclipse is easy. Instead of running your application, you click Debug As and you are off and running. Set breakpoints in your code by selecting them by the gutter next to the line numbers, and as your code progresses it will break at all your steps.

In addition to breakpoint-based debugging, you also have access to the Dalvik Debug Monitor Server (DDMS) perspective in Eclipse (see Figure 6-21). You can use DDMS to view the heap usage for a given process (your running app or anything running inside the virtual machine), track memory allocation of objects inside an app, interact with the filesystem of the device running the app (emulator or actual), view running threads for an application, profile methods using tracing, read log messages using LogCat, and emulate phone and sensor data (SMS, phone calls, location [GPS]), as shown in Figure 6-22.

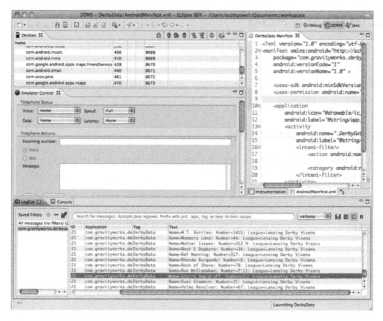

FIGURE 6-21: DDMS perspective

In Figure 6-22 you see the Emulator Control pane. In this pane you can spoof an incoming number to your emulator, to test how your application deals with that. You can also simulate text messages. The bottom pane in that page has a way to configure your GPS manually. This allows you to test location-based code without having to move your device.

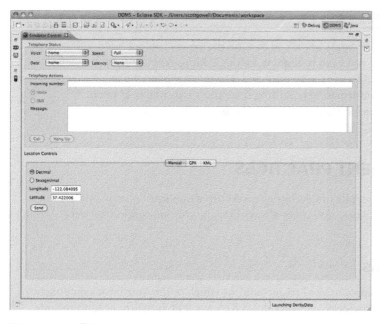

FIGURE 6-22: Faking out your emulator

CONNECTING TO THE GOOGLE PLAY

This section explains what is necessary to publish your application to the Google Play. There is also the Amazon Android Marketplace, which has other requirements. But because it may be more of a marketing choice than a development choice, we decided to go with the explanation of the basic Google Play distribution process.

Getting an Android Developer Account

Signup is a snap for a dev account. Just make sure you have a Google account (Gmail, or Google Apps), $25 (one-time registration fee), head to `https://play.google.com/apps/publish/signup`, and you are all set.

Signing Your Application

Signing your application with Eclipse is a relatively simple process:

1. Right-click your project in the Package Explorer and select File ⇨ Export.

2. Select Export Android Application.

3. Complete the steps of the wizard and you will have a keystore, and a signed release build of your app ready for the market.

When you have created your keystore, make sure to guard it safely. It is the file you will use to sign your application every time you update, and if you lose it you cannot upgrade your application in Google Play.

SIGNS OF THE TIMES

When you are signing your application you can use the export tooling built into Eclipse. However, if you need to request a Google Maps API key for your application, you will need to use the keytool and jarsigner applications to get the hash of your signature. Information regarding these tools is available at `http://developer.android.com/guide/publishing/app-signing.html`.

ANDROID DEVELOPMENT PRACTICES

This section covers the fundamentals of developing an Android application, explaining the permissions in the Manifest and how you must always manage your navigation between Activities using the back stack.

Android Fundamentals

When developing an Android app you need to account for which of the four basic components (Activities, Services, Content Providers, and Broadcast Receivers) of apps you need to include.

Activities

Activities are the individual screens in your application. All of the functionality that is exposed in the UI for that screen lives in the scope of that Activity.

Services

Services are components that run in a background thread. Common usages for services are to hold long-running processes, or for functions that can happen in parallel with the application (playing music from your library, or updating a web service). Be aware that when you have an application running in the background it can take processing power from the device, though contrary to popular thought it does not affect your battery life.

Content Providers

Content providers are interfaces to the offline storage that you have within your app. If you create a suite of applications you may want to have a single point for holding all of your data. You can also leverage the Content Providers built into the Android OS. The standard set of providers in the OS allows you to get content from the Calendar, Contacts, Media Store, Messaging, and Voice Mail applications.

Broadcast Receivers

Broadcast receivers are components that respond to system messages. You would use a Broadcast Receiver to catch events like the screen turning off, or the battery reaching a critical level. A common use for a Broadcast Receiver is for querying the status of the network (Wi-Fi or cellular) so that you can display the appropriate messaging to the user.

Fragments as UI Elements

Starting in Android 3.x, there has been a shift in design elements to account for the significant differences between the screen sizes of tablets versus handsets.Whereas normally UI design for mobile devices is very rigid, Fragments add a level of flexibility. Fragments themselves live as a subactivity that you can reference in multiple places in your application. Fragments live within the scope of their parent activity, but can be used in multiple activities.

Ask for Permission

The users of your application must approve of what functionality you want to leverage on their device. To prompt the user for what you need, and so that your device will behave as designed, you need to add permission requests in your application's manifest. Visit `http://developer.android .com/reference/android/Manifest.permission.html` for a list the various permissions you can request when developing.

Depending on what version of the OS you are targeting you are afforded additional permissions. One of the newest permissions available is `READ_SOCIAL_STREAM`, which enables you to access the user's social stream. One of the oldest permissions is your ability to set the given time zone, using, you guessed, it `SET_TIME_ZONE`.

If you try to run a piece of code in the emulator and it should be responding to firing events or listening to hardware, and it isn't, make sure you have requested permission in your app. Additionally, do not request every possible permission. Applications that do this are often considered malware or at least not trustworthy by the layperson.

Mind the Back Stack

Unlike iOS-based devices, all Android devices have a hardware back button. What this means is that there is something physical on the device that interrupts the UI and takes the user to the previous action. This is known in the *back stack*. It can be likened to a browser history or a copy/paste clipboard. How this differs from those, though, is that it must be stateful (to provide the least jarring UI to your users). You must understand that you need to persist the state of the View when returning to it from the back stack. Additionally, if the current view affects the state of the previous view, you must update it accordingly without requiring the user to click a UI element; it needs to be able to be updated when the user backs up the stack.

Now that this chapter has covered all the major sections of development in Android, the next section will show how to build the demo Derby app in Android.

BUILDING THE DERBY APP IN ANDROID

The idea of the Derby app is to build the same app over all of the mobile platforms covered in this book. The Android version is very similar to the other versions you have built thus far or will build in future chapters.

The requirements are to list the roster from the Lansing Derby Vixens roller derby team as the primary function, and then list all the roller derby teams in the world with the ability to see their team rosters.

Common Interactions

The main ways to get your users around your app, and to let them know when events happen or issues arise is by using well-managed UI navigation (and the back stack), and timely use of notifications.

UI Navigation and Using Back Stack

Because Android devices are equipped with a dedicated hardware back button, you need to make certain considerations as you pass from activity to activity within your application. The states of activities are stored in a back stack that persists and allows users to walk back through the navigation one button click at a time. Extras are stateful objects held within Intents that are the primary way that you communicate between activities. Considered "the glue between activities" (http://developer.android.com/reference/android/content/Intent.html) Intents provide a simple storage mechanism that can be retrieved and set, and are passed between two activities.

Use the GetExtra command to retrieve simple and complex objects from one activity to another using an Intent.

You can select the extras you want to refer to individually from the Intent. For example:

```
String id = getIntent().getStringExtra("id");
String name = getIntent().getStringExtra("name");
```

Or you can get all of the objects you passed along as a `Bundle`:

```
Bundle extras = getIntent().getExtras();
String userName;
String id;

if (extras != null) {
    userName = extras.getString("name");
    id = extras.getString("id");
}
```

Use the `PutExtra` command to put the object you want to pass between activities. You can pass simple or complex objects. You need to use Extras only when you want to pass data between activities. It is not necessary to set a complex state transfer process if you don't need that data.

```
String username = "DerbyUser";
String id = "derbyuser42";
Intent newIdea = new Intent(this, newIdea.class);
newIdea.putExtra("username", username);
newIdea.putExtra("id", id);
startActivity(newIdea);
```

Notifications

You have lots of ways to display content to your users: either in your Base UI or through different types of notifications. What follows is an explanation of toasts and alerts.

Toasts

A toast is a quick notification that displays (by default) in a gray translucent box over your UI.

```
Context context = getApplicationContext(); //Find the application you are currently
running
CharSequence text = "Greetings from the App!"; //This is the message you want to share.
int duration = Toast.LENGTH_SHORT; //This is a constant in the SDK for a quick
notification
Toast toast = Toast.makeText(context, text, duration); //Create the toast object
toast.show(); //Display it for the duration now.
```

Alerts

Simpler even than toasts, alerts are very similar to JavaScript alerts in that they pop a modal form with which you have very little ability to interact. You can set a button to represent affirmation, declination, and cancellation alerts. The following snippet of code shows how to do that:

```
//Create a new AlertDialog using its builder respective to the current context.
new AlertDialog.Builder(this)
```

```
.setTitle("Alert Title") //Set Title for the Alert
.setMessage("Is this the message you expected?") //Set Message for the alert
.setNegativeButton("No", null) //Set the Declination Button (Optional)
.setPositiveButton("Yes", null) //Set the Affirmation Button (Optional)
.setNeutralButton("Who Cares", null) //Set the Cancellation Button (Optional)
.show(); //Display the alert now.
```

Like all things in Android, you can customize notifications. You can find more information on customizing them at http://developer.android.com/guide/topics/ui/notifiers/index.html.

Offline Storage

Even though the bulk of Android devices are smartphones — which afford users an always-on, always-connected experience — many reasons exist to store data on the device versus querying the a service remotely. For simple or small pieces of data you can use Shared Preferences; for larger data sets that may include complex objects, you can use SQLite.

SQLite

SQLite is a flat-file database that runs inside the Android framework. You can use it to store large object graphs or significant amounts of data so that you aren't constantly connecting to a remote source.

This is the base class for instantiating your SQLite instance in your Android app:

```
public class PersistingData extends Activity{
    private static final String DATABASE_NAME = "DerbyData";
    private SQLiteDatabase db;
    private DatabaseOpenHelper dbhelper;

    /** Called when the activity is first created. */
    @Override
    public void onCreate(Bundle savedInstanceState) {
        super.onCreate(savedInstanceState);
        ConnectToDatabase(this.getApplicationContext());
    }

    public void ConnectToDatabase(Context context){
        dbhelper = new DatabaseOpenHelper(context, DATABASE_NAME, null, 1);
    }

    public void DB_Open() throws SQLException{
        db = dbhelper.getWritableDatabase();
    }

    public void DB_Close(){
        if (db != null){
            db.close();
        }
    }
}
```

This is a helper class to handle creating the database for you based on a predefined schema:

```
public class DatabaseOpenHelper extends SQLiteOpenHelper{

    public DatabaseOpenHelper(Context context, String name,
            CursorFactory factory, int version) {
        super(context, name, factory, version);
    }

    @Override
    public void onCreate(SQLiteDatabase db) {
        String loadSchema =
            "CREATE TABLE DerbyNames" +
            "( DerbyNameId integer primary key autoincrement," +
            "name TEXT, Number TEXT, League TEXT, DateAdded DateTime);";
        db.execSQL(loadSchema);
    }

    @Override
    public void onUpgrade(SQLiteDatabase db, int oldVersion, int newVersion) {

    }
}
```

SharedPreferences

`SharedPreferences` is a set of key-value pairs saved on your device that is helpful for storing instance-specific data as it pertains to the app. The main concern is the level of privacy that you impose upon it. If you make it world-readable its value can be accessed by any application should another application query against your key. This function is an example of leveraging `SharedPreferences` to store application preference for the user:

```
SharedPreferences sharedPreferences = getPreferences(MODE_PRIVATE);
SharedPreferences.Editor editor = sharedPreferences.edit();

public void savePreferenceToSharedPreferences(String key, String value){
    editor.putString(key, value);
    editor.commit();
}

public String loadPreferenceFromSharedPreferences(String key)
{
    String tmpRtn = sharedPreferences.getString(key, "");
    return tmpRtn;
}
```

Web Service

In Chapter 3 you developed a web service for the Derby application to call. This section goes over what you need to do to consume this information. In this example you write out the data to the log:

```
public class DerbyDataActivity extends Activity {
    /** Called when the activity is first created. */
    @Override
```

```
    public void onCreate(Bundle savedInstanceState) {
        super.onCreate(savedInstanceState);
        setContentView(R.layout.main);

        getLansingDerbyVixens();
    }
```

In the following part you are loading up the activity, and telling it to run your
getLansingDerbyVixens function.

```
public  void getLansingDerbyVixens() {
    String requestURL = "http://derbynames.gravityworksdesign.com/DerbyNamesService.svc/
DerbyNames?$filter=League%20eq%20'Lansing%20Derby%20Vixens'";

Log.i("DerbyData", "getSurvey-Starting");
    try {
        URL webRequest = new URL(requestURL);
        URLConnection tc = webRequest.openConnection();
        BufferedReader in = new BufferedReader(new InputStreamReader(tc.
getInputStream()));

        Log.i("DerbyData", "- before loading JSON");
        StringBuilder surveyJSON = new StringBuilder();
        String currentLine = "";
        while ((currentLine = in.readLine()) != null) {
            surveyJSON.append(currentLine);
        }
```

This continuing function makes a webRequest to your service, takes the content of the response,
and reads it in as a string. Because your service returns JSON you can deserialize each item in your
JSON string to a DerbyName object using your getDerbyDataFromJSON function.

```
if (surveyJSON != null) {
    Log.i("DerbyData", "getSurvey-Have Data");
    ArrayList<DerbyName> derbyNames = getDerbyDataFromJSON(surveyJSON.toString());
```

Next you iterate through the returned ArrayList<DerbyName> object and print each item's
properties in the log.

```
for(DerbyName item : derbyNames ){
                Log.i("DerbyData", String.format("Name=%s: Number=%s: League=%s",
   item.getName(), item.getNumber(), item.getLeague()));
    }
        }
    }
    catch(Exception e) {
        Log.e("DerbyData", "Error getting data" + e.getMessage());
    }

Log.i("DerbyData", "finished");
}
```

This function takes the JSON string and deserializes it into an `ArrayList` of `DerbyName` objects. You iterate through the contents of the returned objects and assign them to properties inside an instance of a `DerbyName` object, then add it to the `ArrayList` to be returned to your main function.

```java
public static ArrayList<DerbyName> getDerbyDataFromJSON(String surveyDerby) {
    ArrayList<DerbyName> tmpRtn = new ArrayList<DerbyName>();

    Log.i("DerbyData", "getDerbyDataFromJSON-Starting");

    try {
        JSONObject fullJsonObject = new JSONObject(surveyDerby);
        JSONArray jsonNames = fullJsonObject.getJSONArray("d");

        // loop through each json derby name
        for (int i = 0; i < jsonNames.length(); i++) {
            DerbyName derbyName = new DerbyName();

            JSONObject result = jsonNames.getJSONObject(i);

            derbyName.setDerbyNameId(result.getInt("DerbyNameId"));
            derbyName.setName(result.getString("Name"));
            derbyName.setNumber(result.getString("Number"));
            derbyName.setLeague(result.getString("League"));

            tmpRtn.add(derbyName);
        }

    } catch (JSONException e) {
        Log.e("DerbyData",
"getDerbyDataFromJSON-Error converting JSON to Derby Name" + e.getMessage());
    }

    Log.i("DerbyData", "getDerbyDataFromJSON-Finished");

    // return
    return tmpRtn;
}

}
```

The following class is the `DerbyName` object you have created to hold the data you get from the web service. You have effectively created an entity to equate to a single item from the service.

```java
public class DerbyName {
    private int DerbyNameId;
    private String Name;
    private String Number;
    private String League;

    public int getDerbyNameId() {
        return DerbyNameId;
    }
    public void setDerbyNameId(int derbyNameId) {
```

```
            DerbyNameId = derbyNameId;
    }
    public String getName() {
        return Name;
    }
    public void setName(String name) {
        Name = name;
    }
    public String getNumber() {
        return Number;
    }
    public void setNumber(String number) {
        Number = number;
    }
    public String getLeague() {
        return League;
    }
    public void setLeague(String league) {
        League = league;
    }
}
```

Long-Running Tasks over the Web

Please be aware that if you are going to be downloading a lot of data over any web request, or if you are in a high-latency situation, you might want to look into using the AsyncTask (http://developer.android.com/reference/android/os/AsyncTask.html) for handling long-running tasks on a background thread. If your main thread hangs for roughly five seconds, you can receive a message like the one shown Figure 6-23.

GPS

The following function connects to your device's GPS (if available) and displays a toast of your latitude and longitude when you go past its set threshold:

FIGURE 6-23: Common error when your Service times out

```
public class SensorsGPS extends Activity {
    /** Called when the activity is first created. */
    @Override
    public void onCreate(Bundle savedInstanceState) {
        super.onCreate(savedInstanceState);
        setContentView(R.layout.main);

        /* Use the LocationManager class to obtain GPS locations */
        LocationManager locManager = (LocationManager) getSystemService(Context.
LOCATION_SERVICE);
        LocationListener locListener = new MyLocationListener();
```

```
            locManager.requestLocationUpdates(LocationManager.GPS_PROVIDER, 0, 0,
    locListener);
    }

    /* Class My Location Listener */

    public class MyLocationListener implements LocationListener
    {
        @Override
        public void onLocationChanged(Location loc) {
            loc.getLatitude();
            loc.getLongitude();

            String Text = "My current location is: " + "\nLatitude = " + loc.getLatitude()
    + "\nLongitude = " + loc.getLongitude();
            Toast.makeText(getApplicationContext(), Text, Toast.LENGTH_SHORT).show();
        }

        @Override
        public void onProviderDisabled(String provider)
        {
            Toast.makeText(getApplicationContext(), "GPS Disabled", Toast.LENGTH_SHORT).
    show();
        }

        @Override
        public void onProviderEnabled(String provider) {
            Toast.makeText(getApplicationContext(), "GPS Enabled", Toast.LENGTH_SHORT).
    show();
        }

        @Override
        public void onStatusChanged(String provider, int status, Bundle extras) {}
    }
```

Accelerometer

In order to track motion and position of the Android device you will leverage the device's built-in accelerometer as it monitors the x, y, and z axes of the device.

Following is a basic Activity that monitors the Accelerometer in your device:

```
    public class SensorsAccel extends Activity {
        /** Called when the activity is first created. */
        @Override
        public void onCreate(Bundle savedInstanceState) {
            super.onCreate(savedInstanceState);

            /* do this in onCreate */
            mSensorManager = (SensorManager) getSystemService(Context.SENSOR_SERVICE);
            mSensorManager.registerListener(mSensorListener, mSensorManager.
    getDefaultSensor(Sensor.TYPE_ACCELEROMETER), SensorManager.SENSOR_DELAY_NORMAL);
```

```java
            mAccel = 0.00f;
            mAccelCurrent = SensorManager.GRAVITY_EARTH;
            mAccelLast = SensorManager.GRAVITY_EARTH;
    }

    private SensorManager mSensorManager;
    private float mAccel; // acceleration apart from gravity
    private float mAccelCurrent; // current acceleration including gravity
    private float mAccelLast; // last acceleration including gravity

    private final SensorEventListener mSensorListener = new SensorEventListener() {
        public void onAccuracyChanged(Sensor sensor, int accuracy) {}

        @Override
        public void onSensorChanged(SensorEvent se) {
            float x = se.values[0];
            float y = se.values[1];
            float z = se.values[2];

            mAccelLast = mAccelCurrent;
            mAccelCurrent = (float) Math.sqrt((double) (x*x + y*y + z*z));

            float delta = mAccelCurrent - mAccelLast;
            mAccel = mAccel * 0.9f + delta; // perform low-cut filter
        }
    };

    @Override
    protected void onResume() {
        super.onResume();
        mSensorManager.registerListener(mSensorListener, mSensorManager.
getDefaultSensor(Sensor.TYPE_ACCELEROMETER), SensorManager.SENSOR_DELAY_NORMAL);
    }

    @Override
    protected void onStop() {
        mSensorManager.unregisterListener(mSensorListener);
        super.onStop();
    }
}
```

SUMMARY

This chapter outlined the best reasons to target Android as your framework. It covered how to get your development environment configured, gave you solid examples of best practices while developing your application and connecting with the Google Play, and finally how to implement the Derby application with all its respective functionality within Android.

Chapter 7 will cover these same topics using the iOS stack, for targeting iPhone, iPod touch, and iPad devices. Please note that development will require a computer running OSX.

7

Getting Started with iOS

WHAT'S IN THIS CHAPTER?

- ➤ History of iOS
- ➤ Getting an iOS development setup
- ➤ Objective-C Basics
- ➤ iOS Project Basics
- ➤ Implementing the Derby App

This chapter is not intended to make you an expert iOS/Objective-C/Cocoa Touch developer; it's intended to give you an idea of what it takes to create a mobile application on the iOS platform. In our everyday interaction with developers, we have found that many developers dread learning Objective-C, the native language used to create iOS applications. At technical conferences, we have often sat in on beginning-level sessions on how to develop iOS applications, where the presenter has said, "This is very difficult, you don't want to do it." We have no idea why some of the developer community thinks this way. Code is code (unless you are working with a functional language, but that's a topic for a different day). Learning a new programming language/framework takes time and a bit of passion — if you are reading this book, we have no doubt in our mind that you can obtain some more Objective-C resources and have what you need to become an Objective-C developer.

THE IPHONE CRAZE

The first iPhone was revealed at the Mac World conference in early January 2007, and later released in June of that year. Initially, third-party native applications were not allowed. Apple executives argued that developers could build web (HTML/CSS) applications that would behave like native iPhone apps. Developers pushed back, and in October 2007 Apple announced an SDK that allowed developers to create native iPhone applications. Many argue that Apple's decision to allow developers to create native applications was based on the fact that the Android platform was going to be hitting the market soon, and was an extremely open and flexible platform in which developers could do things that they could not within iOS. The decision to allow native apps within iOS created a new business model for developers, where small projects after work hours have turned into full-fledged companies. As of February 2012, the Apple App Store contained more than 725,700 applications, which have collectively been downloaded more than 25 billion times.

Since June 2007, iPhones have helped drive the mobile boom. Apple converted a generation of iPod users to iPhone users with simple and effective user interface practices, and made its product "cool." In May 2010, 59 percent of all mobile web data consumption in the U.S. came from iPhones. The iPhone was a game changer: a personal organizer, gaming platform, web browser, and a phone all in one small package.

Apple in Its Beauty

When Steve Jobs introduced the world to the iPhone he proclaimed it as a revolutionary product that would change everything, with a brand-new "multi-touch" interface as breakthrough and as breathtaking as the mouse interface that was introduced in the 1960s. We agree with this statement, and feel that it was the iPhone that kick-started the mobile boom. The iPhone was marketed to consumers, and its ease of use made just about everybody want one.

At the time of its release, the core uniqueness of the iPhone went far beyond its web browser and tightly integrated web functionality. It was six core ideas (outlined in the following list) that changed software applications and websites. Although there were "smartphones" on the market at the time of release of the iPhone, it was not until after the iPhone was released that smartphone manufacturers realized the importance of all of these features being combined to provide a great mobile development platform.

> **Always on the Internet:** A platform that had Internet access wherever cell phone coverage was available opened the door for a new type of application to be developed. Without this functionality, applications such as foursquare (an app that allows you to "check in" to locations) would not exist. This core concept is easy for developers to develop for; the most difficult part is coming up with an application idea.
>
> **Location-aware:** The iPhone also introduced a platform that could detect where you were based on your location. Apart from privacy concerns, this feature has been well received in the developer and user community. Whether it's a mapping application or an application that lets you tag photos with your location, this feature opened tremendous opportunity for developers to develop location-based apps that did not have to run on a standalone GPS.
>
> **Orientation-aware:** In addition to location awareness, the iPhone offered a platform that could now detect where in space the device existed. The app that made this feature popular is Urbanspoon. Urbanspoon displays a random restaurant in your area based on criteria

that you set. If you do not like the restaurant that it picks, you can "shake" the phone and it will choose another one. This is a new type of UI feature that makes interfaces easier to use.

The mobile gaming industry has also taken full advantage of the iPhone's orientation awareness, releasing many games that allow you use the device as the control stick; for example, moving the iPhone left and right in a race car game makes the car turn left and right, making it feel as though you are actually using a steering wheel.

Innovative input: The iPhone also represented a platform that could detect multiple fingers as input, as well as a wide range of gestures such as swipe up, swipe down, tap, double tap, and so on. With new input types, new UI patterns emerged helping make the small screen of the mobile device easier to deal with.

High-quality, scalable screen: A huge selling point for the iPhone is its high-resolution screen on which movies and photos can be viewed with stunning picture quality.

Power consciousness: Because the iPhone runs on battery, you as a developer need to watch the power consumption of your application. Loops within your code can cause the CPU to work hard, and when the CPU works hard it takes more power, causing your application to drain the device's battery, which could result in negative comments from users. Years ago, developers worked to keep the size of applications small; for mobile development, you should pay close attention to how an application is coded, and ensure it doesn't use too much power.

Apple Devices

Throughout the years, Apple has produced many different types of mobile devices. From the iPod classic to the iPhone, Apple has created great products, but has not always opened these products up for developers to create apps for or modify them. For the purpose of this chapter, we are going to discuss iPhone, iPod touch, and the iPad. Although each of these devices runs a version of iOS, it's important to note that older devices may not be able to run the latest version of iOS. For example, if your company tasked you with creating an app for your sales department and the entire sales team had iPhone 3Gs, you could not take advantage of the great features in iOS 5.0, because these devices run only in iOS 4.2.1 and below.

iPhone

The iPhone may well be the reason why you are reading this book. Since its introduction in 2007, the iPhone has helped fuel the mobile boom that is currently underway. It has been the thorn in the side of many IT departments, from networking issues (employees bringing their own devices to work, which raises security concerns) to development issues (making your applications run on iOS). From 2007 to December 2011 five devices have been released. It's important to understand the close relationship between the iOS hardware and software. Meaning, not all versions of iOS will run on all iOS hardware. As device hardware becomes dated, Apple stops releasing iOS updates. Table 7-1 shows iOS hardware with the version of iOS that shipped with the device and the maximum version that can be installed on the device.

TABLE 7-1 iPhone Hardware and iOS Versions

DEVICE	SHIPPED IOS VERSION	MAX IOS VERSION
iPhone	iOS 1.0	iOS 3.1.3
iPhone 3G	iOS 2.0	iOS 4.2.1
iPhone 3GS	iOS 3.0	
iPhone 4	iOS 4.0	
iPhone 4S	iOS 5	

iPod Touch

After the release the original iPhone, Apple added a new product to the iPod product line: the iPod touch. This device was built on iPhone technology, looked identical to the iPhone, and used the same 480×320 multitouch screen, but it was not a phone. This was a great option for consumers who wanted the iPhone experience, but did not want to pay the fees for a cell phone contract. Because of its lack of cellular connectivity, this device could access the Internet only through a wireless Internet connection. Table 7-2 shows iOS hardware with the version of iOS that shipped with the device and the maximum version that can be installed on the device.

TABLE 7-2 iPod touch Hardware and iOS Versions

DEVICE	SHIPPED IOS VERSION	MAX IOS VERSION
1st generation	iOS 1.1	iOS 3.1.3
2nd generation	iOS 2.1.1	iOS 4.2.1
3rd generation	iOS 3.1.1	
4th generation	iOS 4.1	

iPad

Introduced in January of 2010, the iPad was another revolutionary product from Apple. When the iPad was first released, many argued it was just a big iPod touch, which was partially true. You could purchase a cellular data plan so that the device could access data but not phone service. The same great UI that made the iPhone and iPod Touch famous was now available with a 1024×768 screen size.

The iPad pushed the mobile boom even more, with many industries seeing the benefit that a tablet computer could provide. With two models containing different data storage sizes and access to cellular data, the iPad is leading the way in tablet computing. Table 7-3 shows iOS hardware with the version of iOS that shipped with the device and the maximum version that can be installed on the device.

TABLE 7-3 iPad Hardware and iOS Versions

DEVICE	SHIPPED IOS VERSION	MAX IOS VERSION
iPad	iOS 3.2	
iPad 2	iOS 4.3	
iPad 3	iOS 5.1	

GETTING THE TOOLS YOU NEED

Developing for iOS is not a matter of opening up your favorite text editor and going to town. You may need to do a bit of planning, with the first (and most expensive) being hardware. Depending on your development intentions you may need to pay Apple for the honor of being an iOS developer as well.

Hardware

Oftentimes we are asked, "Do I really need to have a Mac?" The answer is yes. To develop iPhone, iPod, and iPad applications you must have a Mac. The iPhone SDK runs only on Mac OS X. The only sanctioned hardware for iPhone, iPod, and iPad development is an Intel-based Macintosh.

If you are having a hard time justifying the cost of the hardware, we have had great luck with getting refurbished machines direct from Apple at the following URL:

```
http://store.apple.com/us/browse/home/specialdeals/mac
```

Because we work in many different languages and platforms each day, all of the developers we work with have Mac computers. The developers we work with mainly in .NET like to say the Macs are the best Windows machines they have ever had.

Program Levels

If you do not have an Apple Developer account, you can create a free account at `https://developer.apple.com/`. Having the Apple Developer account allows you to create iOS applications and run them locally on your machine using the iOS Simulator. To deploy applications you have created to a physical device (iPhone, iPad, iPod Touch) you must belong to the iOS Developer program. This is where the money comes in. These programs and prices change from time to time, so please use the following only as a guide, and check `https://developer.apple.com/programs/start/ios/` before making any mission-critical decisions.

iOS Developer Program

This program level allows developers to distribute apps in the App Store as an individual, a sole proprietor, a company, an organization, a government entity, or an educational institution. The cost for this program is $99 a year, and you are allowed to name 100 devices within your iOS Developer account (which is covered in the device section of this chapter).

iOS Developer Enterprise Program

This program level allows developers to develop proprietary apps for internal distribution within your company, organization, government entity, or educational institution. The cost for this program is $299 a year. This level of the program will not allow you to distribute apps through the App store, but allows ad hoc distributions (distribute directly to a device without using the App Store) to devices in your organization. A valid Dun & Bradstreet (DUNS) number is required, and this program level will take a little bit longer to get enrolled in. We have seen this process take well over a month before acceptance into the program.

iOS Developer University Program

This program level allows higher-education institutions to create teams of up to 200 developers that can develop iOS applications. This program level is free, and allows for programs to be tested on physical devices, but does not allow for ad hoc or App Store deployment.

The iOS Provisioning Portal

No matter which level of Apple Developer program you registered for, you will have access to the iOS Provisioning Portal. This is the section of the iOS Developer Center that allows you to create the files necessary to deploy development and distribution (production) builds onto physical devices.

Certificates

During the development process of your iOS app, you will more than likely create both a development and a distribution certificate. These certificates are used to digitally sign the app, and verify you are who you say you are. Figure 7-1 shows the iOS Provisioning Portal Certificate section, found within the iOS developer account web interface; here both development and distribution certificates are created.

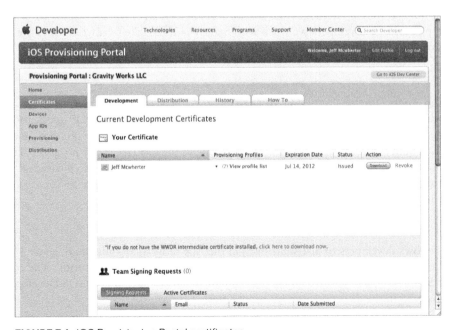

FIGURE 7-1: iOS Provisioning Portal certificates

App IDs

Each iOS application that you create (that you intend to deploy to a device) needs to be identified on the App IDs section of the iOS Provisioning Portal. The app ID that is created is a unique ID that contains a number from Apple and then a bundle identifier that you specify. The bundle identifier is usually in the format com.companyname.appname. As you start to develop more applications, they tend to become messy in this interface, as shown in Figure 7-2.

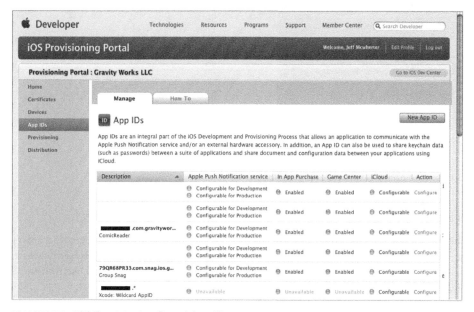

FIGURE 7-2: iOS Provisioning Portal App IDs

Devices

The Devices section in the iOS Provisioning Portal section allows developers to maintain a list of devices in which their iOS applications will be developed. These are the devices that are either used for testing your app or for ad-hoc deployments. The number of devices that you can register on this screen relates to the type of Apple Developer account level you selected. For example, if you registered at the iOS Developer level, you will be able to add 100 devices. This number is 100 per year, meaning if you add 100 devices and then delete 10, you are still out of spaces for accounts until you re-enroll in the program the following year, which will still only have a maximum of 100 devices.

This can become problematic if you are developing iOS applications for multiple customers who have not set up accounts for themselves. It's important to manage and plan ahead for the amount of devices you will need. Figure 7-3 shows that there is room for only 16 more devices in this account.

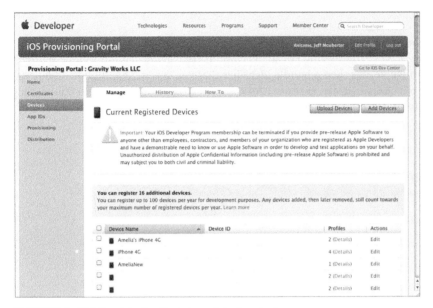

FIGURE 7-3: iOS Provisioning Portal provisioning devices

Provisioning Files

After the certificate, the app ID, and devices have been created/added, you can then create a provisioning profile. The provisioning profile combines the information about which apps/certificates can be installed on which devices. As with certificates there will be a Development and Distribution version. Figure 7-4 shows the Provisioning section within the iOS Provisioning Portal.

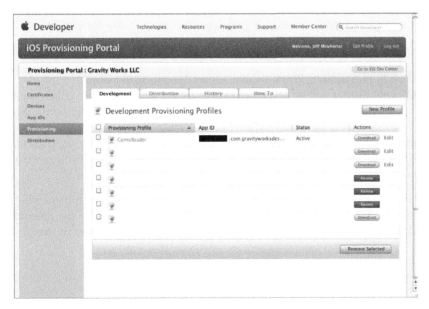

FIGURE 7-4: iOS Provisioning Portal Provisioning Profile

With all of the Apple administrative tasks complete with regard to setting up an account and obtaining provisioning profiles and certificates, you can move on to installing the xCode IDE and starting to work with the iOS SDK.

xCode and the iOS SDK

To create native iOS applications, you will need to install both the xCode IDE as well as the iOS SDK. Although you can obtain xCode by using the App Store within Mac OS X, we recommend downloading xCode and the SDK from the downloads section in the iOS Dev Center as shown in Figure 7-5.

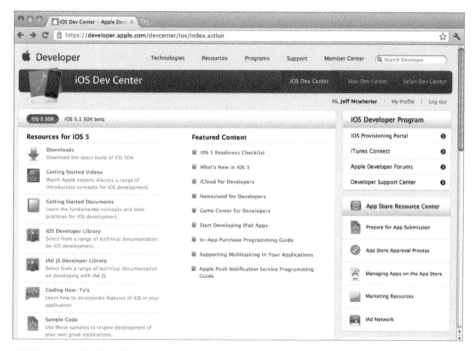

FIGURE 7-5: iOS Dev Center

Installation

After you follow the steps to install xCode, you should have the xCode IDE as well as a great deal of other useful development tools installed to /Developer/Applications, as shown in Figure 7-6.

FIGURE 7-6: Development tools

You can start xCode from this directory or by using spotlight. After you start xCode, you should see a screen similar to the one shown in Figure 7-7.

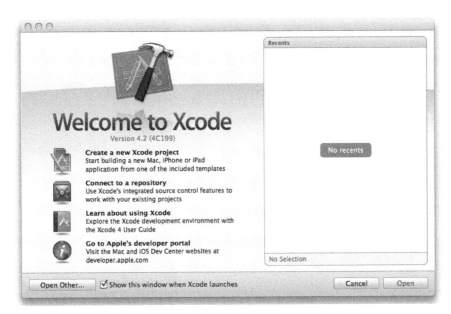

FIGURE 7-7: xCode startup screen

Components of the iPhone SDK

The iPhone SDK includes a great number of tools that help create iOS for apps. These tools range from debugging and profiling to developing. This section lists the most common tools that we use that are included in the iOS SDK.

xCode

xCode is Apple's Integrated Development Environment (IDE) for creating Objective-C applications. xCode enables you to manage, author, and debug your Objective-C projects.

Dashcode

Dashcode is an IDE that enables you to develop web-based iPhone/iPad applications and Dashboard widgets. This product is not in the scope of this book as it is considered an advanced topic.

iPhone Simulator

This tool provides a method to simulate an iPhone or iPad device on your Mac, for use with testing your iOS applications.

Interface Builder

The Interface Builder, or IB, is a visual editor that is used for designing the user interface for your iOS application.

Instruments

Instruments is a suite of tools that helps you analyze your iOS application and monitor for performance bottlenecks as well as memory leaks in real time while attached to an iOS device or iOS Simulator.

The iOS Human Interface Guideline

The iOS Human Interface Guideline (HIG) document is one of the most valuable tools to the iOS developer. The iOS HIG describes guidelines and principles that help the iOS developer design a superlative user interface and user experience. It is very important for new iOS developers to read through this document; if you do not develop using the UI principles found in the HIG, your application could be rejected when submitted to the Apple App Store.

The UI standards that Apple puts in place for developers can cause heated conversation. One side of the argument is that developers are locked into obeying a set of rules that cost time and money to learn and implement. The other side of the argument is that Apple has provided a standard UI for applications that have been created for the platform, thus giving the user a great experience no matter who creates the app.

You can find the iOS HIG at `http://developer.apple.com/library/ios/#documentation/ UserExperience/Conceptual/MobileHIG/Introduction/Introduction.html#/apple_ref/ doc/uid/TP40006556`.

With the xCode IDE and iOS SDK installed, you can now examine what exactly makes up an iOS project with respect to files and code.

IOS PROJECT

By now you may be thinking that you need to follow a lot of steps before you start creating an iOS application. This may be the reason many seasoned iOS developers try to steer new developers from the platform. Although it takes a lot of steps to get going, they are not complicated or difficult; it's just a matter of learning them and why they exist, which is covered in the remainder of this chapter.

With all of the "setup" out of the way, we can focus on getting into the IDE and looking at code.

Anatomy of an iOS App

iOS .app files, the files that are actually deployed to the iOS device, are just a set of directories. Although there is an actual binary for the iOS application, you can open the .app file and find the images, meta data, and any other resources that are included.

Views

iPhone apps are made up of one or more views. Views usually have GUI elements such as text fields, labels, buttons, and so on. You can build a view built using the Interface Builder tool, which enables you to drag and drop controls on the view, or you can create a view entirely with code.

Code That Makes the Views Work

Because iOS applications follow the MVC design pattern, there is a clean break between the UI and code that provides the application code.

Resources

Every iOS application contains an icon file, an info.plist file that holds information about the application itself and the binary executable. Other resources such as images, sounds, and video are also classified as resources.

Project Structure in Depth

When an iOS project is created within xCode, the IDE creates a set of files that are ready to run. These files provide the basics of what is needed to get going with a new project. Figure 7-8 shows the files that are created for a new project named DeleteMe.

Main.m

As with any C program, the execution of Objective-C applications start from the main() function, which is the main.m file.

AppDelegate.m

FIGURE 7-8: Anatomy of an iOS app

The AppDelegate receives messages from the application object during the lifetime of your application. The AppDelegate is called from the operating system, and contains events such as the didFinishLaunchingWithOptions, which is an event that iOS would be interested in knowing about.

MainStoryBoard.storyboard

This is where the user interface is created. In past versions of xCode/iOS the user interface was stored within .xib (pronounced NIB) files. Although this method is still supported, Storyboards are a great improvement over .xib files for applications with complex navigation and many views.

Supporting Files

The supporting files directory contains files such as the `plist` setting files (which contain customizable application settings), as well as string resource files that are used within your app.

Getting to Know the xCode IDE

It's important to use the correct tool for the job, regardless of whether you are constructing a house or constructing an application. If you are new to xCode, there will be a bit of a learning curve to becoming proficient with the IDE, but xCode is a top-notch IDE with many features for you to discover.

Navigators

The left side of the xCode window is known as the navigator area. A variety of navigators enable you to list the contents of your project, find errors, search for code, and more. The remainder of this section introduces the Project Navigator, the Search Navigator, and the Issue Navigator.

Going from left to right, the project navigator is the first of the xCode navigators; the icon looks like a file folder. The Project Navigator simply shows the contents of your project or workspace, as shown in Figure 7-9. Double-clicking a file in the Project Navigator opens the file in a new window, and single-clicking opens the file within the xCode workspace.

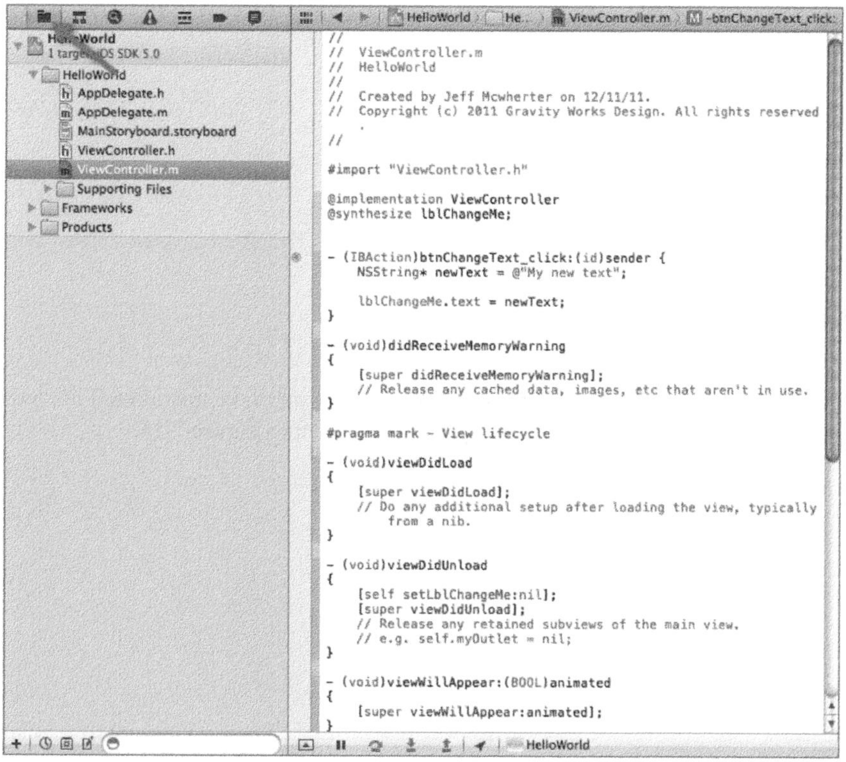

FIGURE 7-9: Project Navigator

The Search Navigator helps you locate text within your project or workspace as shown in Figure 7-10.

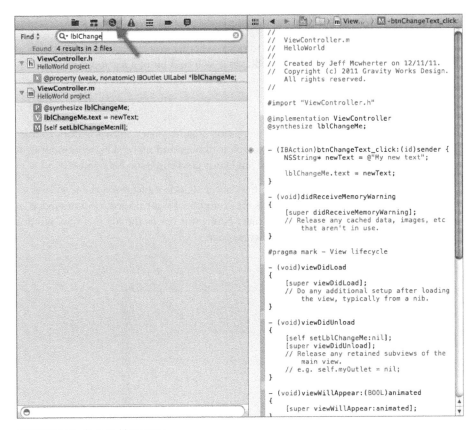

FIGURE 7-10: Search Navigator

The Issue Navigator lists project warnings and errors in real time as you make mistakes. This navigator shows any issues preventing your code from compiling, as shown in Figure 7-11.

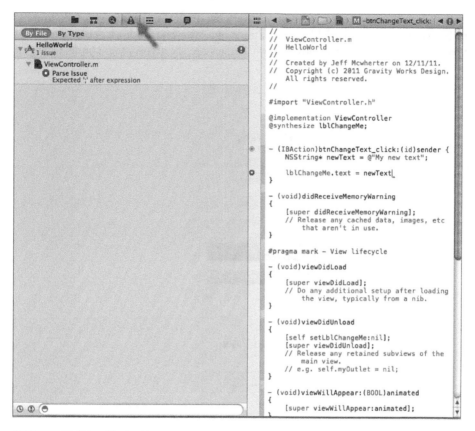

FIGURE 7-11: Issue Navigator

Storyboards

In iOS versions prior to iOS 5, developers needed to create a separate XIB file for each view of their application. A XIB file is an XML representation of your controls and instance variables that get compiled into the application. Managing an application that contains more than a few views could get cumbersome.

iOS 5 contained a new feature called storyboards that enables developers to lay out their workflow using design tools built within xCode. Apps that use navigation and tab bars to transition between views are now much easier to manage, with a visual representation of how the app will flow. Transitions and segues are used to switch between views, without ever having to code them by hand.

With Storyboards, you will have a better conceptual overview of all the views in your app and the connections between them. Figure 7-12 is an example of a Storyboard for an application that contains a tab bar for navigation to three other views. Segues are the arrows that connect the views.

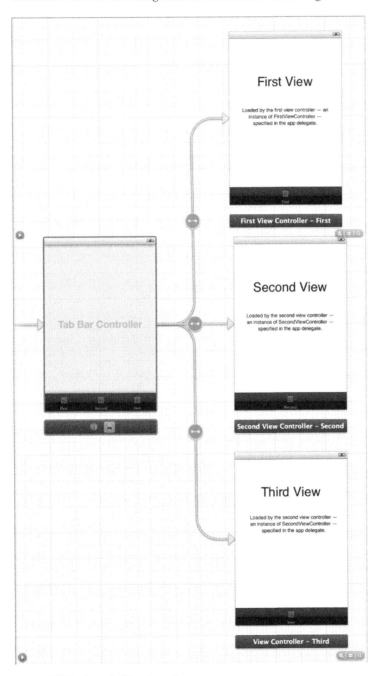

FIGURE 7-12: Sample Storyboard

DEBUGGING IOS APPS

A bug discovered in the field is much more expensive to fix than bugs that are found on a developer's machine or during the quality assurance process. Modern-day IDEs provide a great deal of tooling that helps developers find issues in their code before it reaches production.

The term "debugging" was made popular by Admiral Grace Murray Hopper, who was working on a Mark II computer at Harvard University in August 1945, when colleagues discovered a moth stuck in a relay that was causing issues with the system. She made the comment they were "debugging the system."

The iOS Simulator

Developers use the iOS Simulator as their first way of finding issues with the code they just created. The iOS Simulator enables developers to run their iOS applications on their Macs without having to have a physical iOS device. The Simulator is a great tool for testing your apps quickly. The iOS Simulator is very quick to load, compared to other simulation tools for other mobile platforms. The iOS Simulator is also a great tool for HTML/CSS experts to have installed as well to test mobile webpages rendered within the mobile Safari web browser. Figures 7-13 and 7-14 show the Simulator simulating an iPhone and iPad, respectively.

FIGURE 7-13: iOS Simulator simulating an iPhone

FIGURE 7-14: iOS Simulator simulating an iPad

By no means is the Simulator the only tool you should use for testing your app. Although the Simulator is great for testing some things, it lacks in other areas. Not all applications that are available on a physical iOS device are available within the Simulator. Besides that, memory, performance, accelerometer, and camera functionality cannot be tested reliably in the Simulator.

One nice feature of the iOS Simulator is the ability to test various iOS versions, as shown in Figure 7-15.

FIGURE 7-15: iOS Simulator version options

 The iOS Simulator is not an emulator. An emulator tries to mimic the behavior of a real device. The iOS Simulator simulates real behavior of the iOS device, but relies on various libraries that are installed on the Mac, such as QuickTime, to perform renderings so that it looks like an actual iPhone. Applications that are deployed to the iOS Simulator are compiled to x86 code, whereas on a real iOS device the code would be compiled to ARM-based code.

Debugging Code

As with many modern-day IDEs, Apple and the xCode team have put a great deal of time and effort into creating a set of tools to aid developers in their quest for hunting bugs.

When it boils down to it, developers want tools that make their life easier — tools to step through the code, view log messages, as well as see the state of their variables. xCode provides tools for these features, and much more.

The debugging tools within xCode are located at the bottom of the workspace window. If you do not see the debugging tools, you can click View ➪ Debug Area ➪ Show Debug Area from the xCode menu (see Figure 7-16) to make the debugging tools visible.

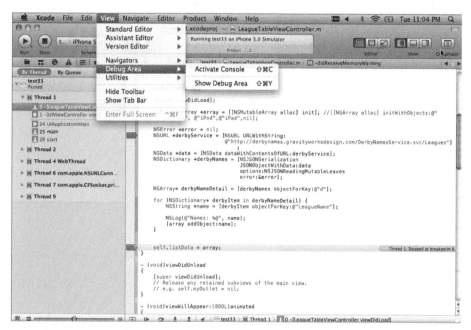

FIGURE 7-16: The Debug area

Local Window

When the debug area is enabled, the local window shows you a list of all of the variables that are currently within scope of your current breakpoint, and enables you to view details about each variable. Figure 7-17 shows the local window, and you can see that an object named `derbyNameDetail` that is of type `NSCFArray` contains 908 elements within the array.

FIGURE 7-17: The local window

Breakpoints

You can set breakpoints by clicking on the "gutter" next to the line of code where you would like the application to break. Breakpoints can be enabled and disabled; disabled breakpoints have an opaque blue color, whereas active breakpoints are a solid blue, as shown in Figure 7-18.

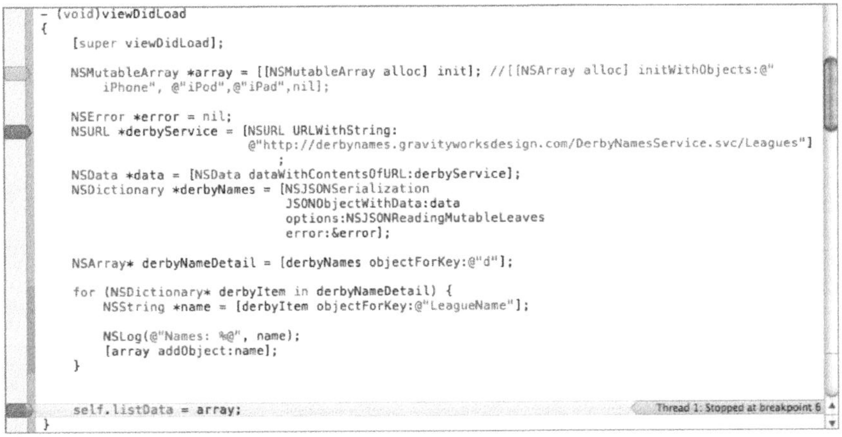

```
- (void)viewDidLoad
{
    [super viewDidLoad];

    NSMutableArray *array = [[NSMutableArray alloc] init]; //[[NSArray alloc] initWithObjects:@"
        iPhone", @"iPod",@"iPad",nil];

    NSError *error = nil;
    NSURL *derbyService = [NSURL URLWithString:
                          @"http://derbynames.gravityworksdesign.com/DerbyNamesService.svc/Leagues"]
                          ;
    NSData *data = [NSData dataWithContentsOfURL:derbyService];
    NSDictionary *derbyNames = [NSJSONSerialization
                               JSONObjectWithData:data
                               options:NSJSONReadingMutableLeaves
                               error:&error];

    NSArray* derbyNameDetail = [derbyNames objectForKey:@"d"];

    for (NSDictionary* derbyItem in derbyNameDetail) {
        NSString *name = [derbyItem objectForKey:@"LeagueName"];

        NSLog(@"Names: %@", name);
        [array addObject:name];
    }

    self.listData = array;                          Thread 1: Stopped at breakpoint 5
}
```

FIGURE 7-18: Breakpoints added to the gutter

The top of the debug area contains the Breakpoint toolbar, with tools that enable you to Step Over, Step Into, Step Out, and continue execution of your code. These tools are located in the Debug Area's toolbar, as shown in Figure 7-19.

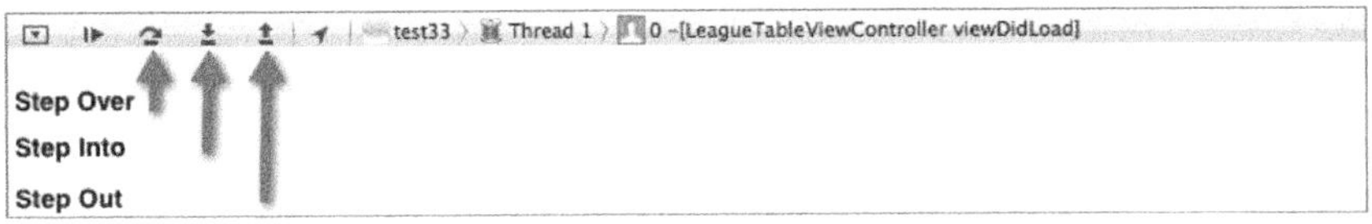

```
                    test33 > Thread 1 > 0 -[LeagueTableViewController viewDidLoad]
Step Over
Step Into
Step Out
```

FIGURE 7-19: Breakpoint toolbar

Output

The output section of the Debug Area gives important information about the execution of the app, as well as displays any log messages you may add in your code. Figure 7-20 shows the application output of an application that logged information received from a web service.

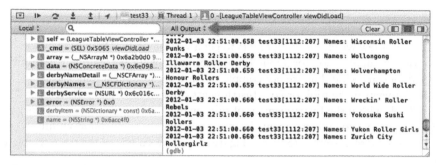

FIGURE 7-20: Output window

Call Stack

When hunting for bugs, it's useful to follow the execution path of a particular feature, in hopes of finding the issue. Figure 7-21 shows the stack trace window within xCode.

```
0 -[LeagueTableViewController viewDidLoad]
1 -[UIViewController view]
2 -[UIViewController contentScrollView]
3 -[UINavigationController _computeAndApplyScrollContentInsetDeltaForViewController:]
4 -[UINavigationController _layoutViewController:]
5 -[UINavigationController _startTransition:fromViewController:toViewController:]
6 -[UINavigationController _startDeferredTransitionIfNeeded]
7 -[UINavigationController _viewWillLayoutSubviews]
8 -[UILayoutContainerView layoutSubviews]
9 -[UIView(CALayerDelegate) layoutSublayersOfLayer:]
10 -[NSObject performSelector:withObject:]
11 -[CALayer layoutSublayers]
12 CA::Layer::layout_if_needed(CA::Transaction*)
13 CA::Context::commit_transaction(CA::Transaction*)
14 CA::Transaction::commit()
15 +[CATransaction flush]
16 _afterCACommitHandler
17 __CFRUNLOOP_IS_CALLING_OUT_TO_AN_OBSERVER_CALLBACK_FUNCTION__
18 __CFRunLoopDoObservers
19 __CFRunLoopRun
20 CFRunLoopRunSpecific
21 CFRunLoopRunInMode
22 GSEventRunModal
23 GSEventRun
24 UIApplicationMain
25 main
26 start
```

FIGURE 7-21: The call stack window

Instruments

Suppose you've spent the last few weeks working nights to get a version of an iOS app ready for release, but after you use your application for about 15 minutes, it stops for no reason. You think it may be a memory leak of some kind, but are not completely sure because the log messages were pretty cryptic. Instruments is the tool for you. Instruments can be found in the Developer ⇨ Application directory. Tools within the Instruments tool suite enable you to track down memory issues and help find slow-running code. Instruments is one of our favorite tools found within xCode, because it helps us find those hard-to-replicate issues. Figure 7-22 shows a few of the trace templates that are available for iOS.

FIGURE 7-22: Instruments analysis tools

OBJECTIVE-C BASICS

Objective-C is an object-oriented language based on the C programming language. Objective-C adds Smalltalk-style messaging, which throws even the seasoned polyglot programmer for a loop when starting with this language. Objective-C was created in the early 1980s by Brad Cox and Tom Love, and gained popularity when Steve Jobs and NeXT licensed the language from them, and made Objective-C the main language on NeXT's NextSTEP operating system.

Objective-C requires developers to declare a class in an interface and then define the implementation, something that non-C developers find off-putting about the language. If you are comfortable developing in C languages, Table 7-4 will help you find your bearings when getting started with Objective-C.

TABLE 7-4: Equivalencies between C languages and Objective-C

C/C++	OBJECTIVE-C
#include "library.h"	#import "library.h"
this	self
private:	@private
protected:	@protected
public:	@public
Y = new MyClass();	Y = [[MyClass alloc] init];
try, throw, catch, finally	@try, @throw, @catch, @finally

Classes

The interface of Objective-C classes is defined in a header file for each interface. Usually the filenames of the header match the class name. For example, you can create a header file named dog.h:

```
@interface Dog : Animal {
    // instance variables
}

// Method declarations

@end
```

You are telling the compiler that a new class named Dog, which is a subclass of animal, is being declared. Any instance variables are declared between the curly brackets, and methods are declared between the end of the curly bracket and the @end keyword.

The actual implementation of the Dog class would look like this:

```
#import "dog.h"
@implementation Dog
// method definitions
@end
```

Instance Variables

The attributes that are declared between the curly brackets are instance variables. Instance variables are declared like local or global variables, but have a different scope. Instance variables by default are visible in all instance methods of a class and its subclasses.

Methods

Methods can be declared as either instance methods or class methods. Instance methods are called by sending a message directly to the instance of the class, which means you need to have your own instance of the class before you can call these methods. Instance methods are prefixed with a minus sign (-). The following is an example of the declaration for an instance method that returns the name of the animal, and takes no parameters:

```
-(NSString) getNameOfAnimal;
```

A class method does not require an instance of a class. You call a class method by sending a message to the unique class object. C# or Java developers may recognize class methods as static methods. The following method returns an array containing a list of all nonextinct animals:

```
+(NSArray) getNonExtinct();
```

Calling Methods

You may have noticed that Objective-C is heavy on the use the brackets. In Objective-C, methods are not *called* in the traditional sense; their objects are *sent* messages. The syntax for sending messages is to enclose the name of the object and the message with square brackets:

```
[object method];
[object methodWithInput:input];
```

Methods can return values:

```
output = [object methodWithOutput];
output = [object methodWithInputAndOutput:input];
```

Objective-C 2.0 provides a dot-notation that can be used to invoke methods. Many new Objective-C developers like this syntax because it looks like other languages in which they are more proficient.

Implementation in Non-Dot Notation:

```
int lastLocation = [myAnimal getLastLocation];
```

Implementation in Dot Notation:

```
int lastLocation = myAnimal.getLastLocation;
```

Control Structures

Oftentimes when learning a new language, we like to look at the control structures to get an idea of how to implement these types of structures.

If Statements

If statements are pretty straightforward in Objective-C. The following example checks to see if an array of animal names contains a name "luna":

```
NSArray *animalNames = ...
NSString* nameOne = @"luna";

if ( [animalNames containsObject: nameOne] )
{
    ...
}
else
{
    // do something else
}
```

For Loops

The standard C for loop can be used to iterate over an enumerable object such as an array in Objective-C. The following example loops over an array of animal objects and prints their location to the console screen:

```
NSArray *animals = ...
NSUInteger animalCount = [animals count];

for (j=0; j < animalCount; j++ )
{
    NSLog([[animals objectAtIndex: j] getLastLocation]);
}
```

Fast Enumeration

Objective-C 2.0 also gives us new syntax for a control structure called Fast Enumeration. Fast Enumeration is easier for developers to code, and runs faster than other traditional loops such as for and while loops.

```
NSMutableArray *animals = ...

for (Animal *singleAnimalObject in animals )
{
    NSLog([singleAnimalObject getLastLocation]);
}
```

Try Catch

Error handling is one of those developer religious debates that we are not going to get into in this chapter. We will tell you that exception handling in Objective-C is expensive, and was designed for catching programmer errors or other nonrecoverable problems. If you can test for an error condition in advance, you should do so rather than catching exceptions. Your code will run must faster.

The following example illustrates the structure of exception handling in Objective-C:

```
@try {
    // code that may cause the exception
}
@catch (NSException *e) {
    //exception is caught and logic should be added to handle the exception
}
@finally {
    // code that should be executed no matter if an exception has occurred or not.
}
```

Now that the Objective-C basics are covered, you can dive in and create your first native iOS app with Objective-C and the iOS SDK.

HELLO WORLD APP

Before you can run, you need to walk. We are not huge fans of creating Hello World–type apps, but with the iOS SDK and Objective-C so different from many other application frameworks, we felt it made sense.

This section illustrates the steps needed to create a simple iOS application that contains a label and a button. When the button is touched, the text in the label changes. This allows us to explain xCode and the various tools contained within xCode that are required when making an iOS application.

Creating the Project

After opening xCode, create a Single View Application project type found under the iOS project types, as shown in Figure 7-23. When you select a Single View Application, xCode generates the files you need to start creating an iOS app that has only one view.

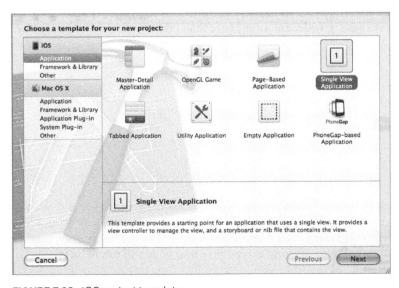

FIGURE 7-23: iOS project template

After you select a project template, you are prompted to enter the project level options as shown in Figure 7-24.

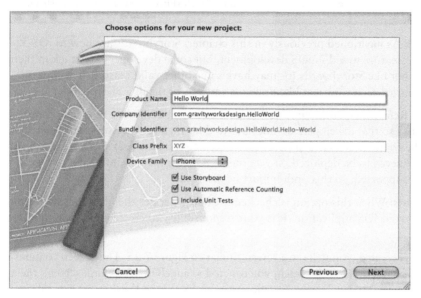

FIGURE 7-24: iOS project options

For this example, enter a product name of **Hello World,** target the iPhone, set the company identifier to whatever you choose, and leave the default settings for the rest.

Product Name

xCode uses the product name you enter to name your project and the application. If you want your application name to show up differently in iOS, there is an option in the `.plist` file to set the display name of the app.

Company Identifier

This identifier is used to generate the bundle identifier for the iOS app. The company identifier is usually something like `com.gravityworksdesign`.

Bundle Identifier

The bundle identifier is automatically generated for you and is a combination of the product name and company identifier. This identifier is used when provisioning your app to be installed on devices. The bundle identifier is unique to an app, and the Apple developer tools will not allow you to provision an app when an existing app is using the same bundle identifier.

Class Prefix

The text you enter into the Class Prefix field is prefixed to the filenames and class names of all header and implementation files.

Device Family

This option enables you to target which type of device your application will run on: iPhone, iPad, or Universal. Universal allows your application to be run on both iPhone and iPad. Beneath Device Family are three checkboxes:

➤ **Use Storyboard:** As mentioned previously in this chapter, Storyboards are new to iOS 5. They are a great feature to aid in iOS development, but some developers are stuck in their ways, and may not like Storyboards (or may have some other valid reason). This option creates .xib files for each view just like previous versions of the iOS SDK/xCode.

➤ **Use Automatic Reference Counting:** A new feature to iOS 5, automatic reference counting manages memory so that developers do not have to do it themselves. Automatic reference counting can be considered a type of garbage collection mechanism. If you are creating an application that needs to be deployed on versions of iOS less than 5, automatic reference counting is not supported, so this option must be disabled.

➤ **Include Unit Tests:** When this option is checked, xCode generates the file structure for a set of unit tests for your iOS application. It is your responsibility to create and maintain these unit tests.

After the project has been created, you will see a screen similar to Figure 7-25. This screen contains the project level options for your app. On this screen, you can add a launch image (splash screen), the app icon, target-specific device orientations, target-specific versions of iOS, and the list goes on and on.

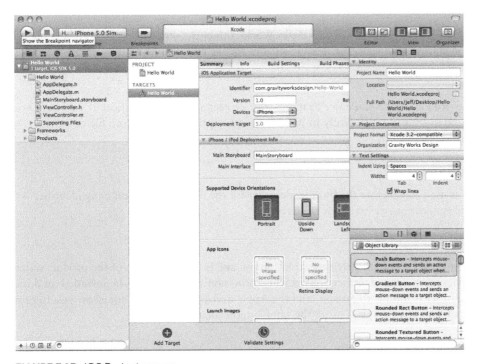

FIGURE 7-25: iOS Project screen

You do not have to do anything on this screen for the Hello World app.

Creating the User Interface

The user interface is fairly simple for this app. It has a label and a button. We are not going to get fancy with any UI elements, but feel free to explore and extend the application to get a feel of your first iOS app.

Controls in the View

From the Project Navigator, select the MainStoryboad.storyboard file. You then need to put a label control on the view. You can find the controls that you have access to on the bottom right of the IDE in the Object Library. Find the label control, and drag the control to the storyboard. Your app should look similar to Figure 7-26 now.

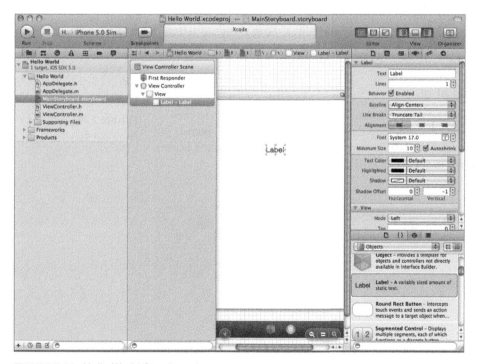

FIGURE 7-26: Hello World Storyboard

When you click the label in the storyboard, you should see settings that are specific to that control in the upper-right side of xCode in the Identity Inspector. The Identity Inspector is a settings tool, which enables you to control font color, size, and other options specific to the control you are working with. Figure 7-27 shows the Identity Inspector interface when editing the settings for a button.

The next step is to add a button to the view. Buttons are added like the label control, by dragging the control onto the view. In this example set the button text to say Change Label.

Wiring Up the Controls

By this point you should have a view that contains two controls: a label and a button. If you run your application, you should see the interface you developed in the iOS Simulator, but you have not told the application to do anything yet. Wiring up the controls to events can be tricky for new developers on this platform.

The first thing you want to do is to show the Assistant Editor. You can toggle this editor on and off by selecting the "Tuxedo" button near the upper-right side of the IDE, as shown in Figure 7-28.

Depending on where you have the Assistant Editor set to show, yours may be placed differently than the following screenshots. To change where exactly on the screen the Assistant Editor shows, you can select View ⇨ Assistant Editor from the xCode menu and then select where you would like the editor to show.

Defining the Label

The next step is a bit tricky. You need to define your controls in the header file. To do this, hold down the Control key on the keyboard, and click and drag your label control from the storyboard to the header file that is shown in the Assistant Editor (see Figure 7-29).

FIGURE 7-27: xCode control-specific settings

FIGURE 7-28: Toggling the Assistant Editor

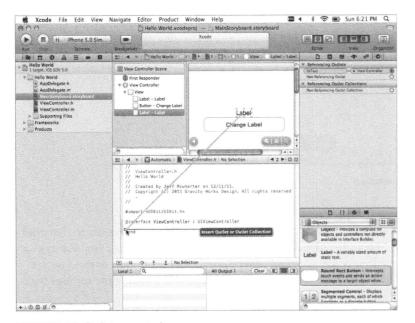

FIGURE 7-29: Defining controls

Once you release the mouse, a dialog box appears asking you to name the object. We like to follow Hungarian notation for control names, so name the label **lblChangeMe** as shown in Figure 7-30.

FIGURE 7-30: Naming the control

Wiring the Button

Wiring the event for the button is similar to defining the event. If you right-click the button you see a dialog box similar to the one shown in Figure 7-31.

You are most interested in the Touch Up Inside event, which is the event that occurs when a finger is raised off the control. This is where you want to add logic . To do this, simply click the circle next to the Touch Up Inside event, and drag it to the Assistant Editor as shown in Figure 7-32. As with the label, you are prompted for a name; name this one **btnChangeText_click**.

FIGURE 7-31: Right-clicking a control

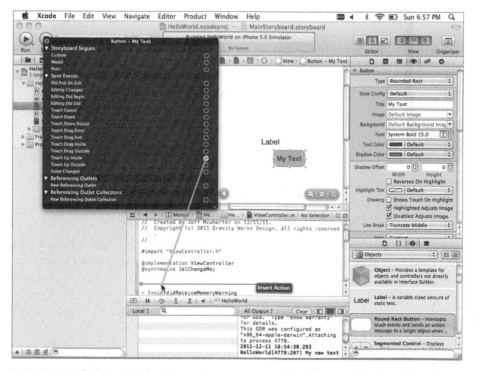

FIGURE 7-32: Defining the Touch event

Writing the Code

With the UI completed and wired up, you can now tell your app what you want the Touch event to do when touched. To do this, open the ViewController.m file, and add the following method:

```
- (IBAction)btnChangeText_click:(id)sender {
    NSString* newText = @"My new text";

    lblChangeMe.text = newText;
    NSLog(newText);
}
```

This code defines a new string, sets the label text to the new string, and then logs the new string to the event viewer. If you followed the steps correctly, your app should look similar to Figure 7-33 in your iOS Simulator, and you should see a log file similar to Figure 7-34 in the output window of xCode.

FIGURE 7-33: Completed
Hello World iOS app

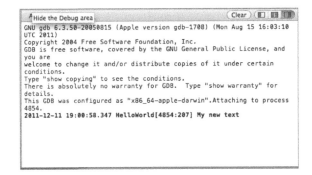

FIGURE 7-34: Output of the Hello World app

Like all Hello World–type apps, the intention was to give you an idea of the project structure and basic interaction between the UI and code. To build upon this, the next section tackles a more complex native iOS app.

BUILDING THE DERBY APP IN IOS

The idea of the Derby App is to build the same app over all of the mobile platforms covered in this book. The iOS version is very similar to the other versions that you have built thus far or will build in future chapters.

The requirements are to list the roster from the Lansing Derby Vixens roller derby team as the primary function, and then list all the roller derby teams in the world with the ability to see their team rosters.

User Interface

The derby app contains a list of data, so you use table views throughout the application to show the information to the user. Start by creating a new tabbed application within xCode as shown in Figure 7-35.

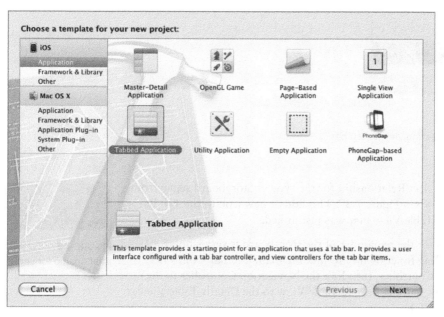

FIGURE 7-35: Creating a tabbed app

By default xCode creates a new iOS application that contains a Storyboard with tabbed navigation. Your project needs to contain three table views and one Navigation controller. The table views are used to the list the data about the derby teams and rosters, and the navigation controller enables you to create a "back stack" that will allow users to navigate back to the team names table view, when finished viewing the team's roster data. Start by dragging three Table View Controllers from the Object Library onto the storyboard, and then remove the views that were added by default.

Once the previous views are removed and the table views are added, you need to connect them to the navigation controller. To do this, Control-click the Tab Bar Controller icon on the Tab Bar View, within the Storyboard, and drag it to the new view as shown in Figure 7-36.

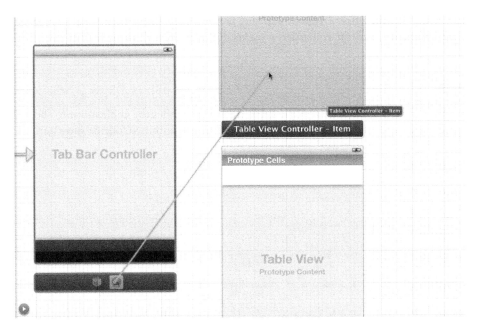

FIGURE 7-36: Connecting view to tab bar

When prompted, select Relationship for the type of Storyboard segue from the dialog box shown in Figure 7-37. This adds a new icon to the Tab Bar Controller for the Table View that was just linked.

Setting the segues for the remainder of the storyboard is very similar. Use the Control-drag functionality to link the main Tab Bar Controller to the Navigation Controller, then link the Navigation Controller to the League Table View, and the League Table View to the Details Table View as shown in Figure 7-38.

FIGURE 7-37: Selecting relationship for segue

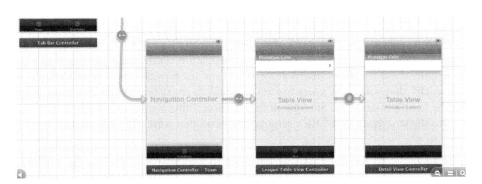

FIGURE 7-38: Linking the Navigation Controller for the leagues

The segue that is created from the Leagues view needs to have an identifier of "Details." This enables you to trigger this particular segue from within code. To do this, click the segue (the arrow between the Leagues Table View and the Details Table View), and open the Identity Inspector. In the Identifier box enter **Details** as shown in Figure 7-39.

When you have completed this task, you should have a storyboard that looks similar to Figure 7-40. For complete code samples, visit this book's page on http://www.wrox.com and click the Download Code tab.

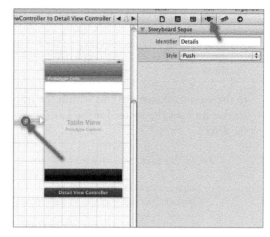

FIGURE 7-39: Adding an identifier to a segue

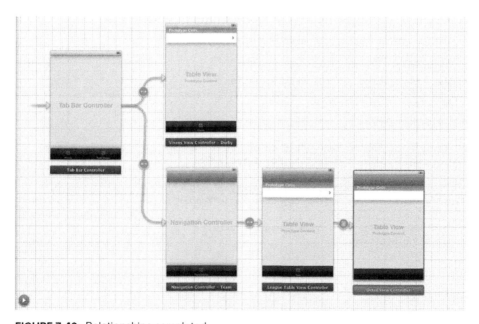

FIGURE 7-40: Relationships completed

Team Roster

With the storyboard in place, you can now write the code to populate the table views. Start with the Team Roster tab, which will go out to a web service, and obtain a list of all the Lansing Derby Vixens.

First create a new class named `VixensViewController`:

```
@interface VixensViewController : UITableViewController
@property(nonatomic, retain) NSArray *listData;
@end
```

In the `viewDidLoad` method within the implementation file, add your logic to go out the web service and get the roster for the Lansing Derby Vixens. Notice the filter criteria contained within the URL.

```
- (void)viewDidLoad
{
    [super viewDidLoad];
    NSMutableArray *array = [[NSMutableArray alloc] init];

    // go out to the service and get the data
    NSError *error = nil;
    NSURL *derbyService = [NSURL URLWithString:
        @"http://derbynames.gravityworksdesign.com/DerbyNamesService.svc/
        DerbyNames?$filter=League%20eq%20'Lansing%20Derby%20Vixens'"];

    NSData *data = [NSData dataWithContentsOfURL:derbyService];

    // Use native functions to parse the JSON
    NSDictionary *derbyNames = [NSJSONSerialization
    JSONObjectWithData:data options:NSJSONReadingMutableLeaves error:&error];

    NSArray* derbyNameDetail = [derbyNames objectForKey:@"d"];

    // loop through all of the derby objects only add the name object to the array
    for (NSDictionary* derbyItem in derbyNameDetail) {
        NSString *name = [derbyItem objectForKey:@"Name"];
        NSString *league = [derbyItem objectForKey:@"League"];
        NSString *number = [derbyItem objectForKey:@"Number"];

        NSLog(@"Names: %@-%@-%@", name, league, number);
        [array addObject:name];
    }


    self.listData = array;
}
```

iOS 5 is the first version of the iOS SDK that contains built-in support for parsing JSON strings. This is great because you do not have to depend on a third-party tool. The last line in the method `self.listData = array;` sets the data that you will use to bind the data to the table view.

For the table view to know how many rows it needs to select, you must implement the `numberOfRowsInSection` method. In this case, just return the count of the number of items in the `listData` array, which is the array that you populated when the view loaded.

```
- (NSInteger)tableView:(UITableView *)tableView numberOfRowsInSection:(NSInteger)section
{
    return [self.listData count];
}
```

The magic really happens in the `cellForRowAtIndexPath` method. This method is called for the number of times that was returned in the `numberOfRowsInSection`. In the code, you create a new cell, get the data for the correct position in the `listData` array, and then return the cell you created, which will be added to the table:

```
- (UITableViewCell *)tableView:(UITableView *)tableView
cellForRowAtIndexPath:(NSIndexPath *)indexPath
{
    static NSString *CellIdentifier = @"Cell";

    UITableViewCell *cell = [tableView dequeueReusableCellWithIdentifier:CellIdentifier];
    if (cell == nil) {
        cell = [[UITableViewCell alloc] initWithStyle:UITableViewCellStyleDefault
            reuseIdentifier:CellIdentifier];
    }

    // Configure the cell...
    NSUInteger row = [indexPath row];
    cell.textLabel.text = [listData objectAtIndex:row];

    return cell;
}
```

Details

The next class you need to create is `DetailViewController`. This is the code that drives the details that are displayed when a team name is selected.

```
#import <UIKit/UIKit.h>

@interface DetailViewController : UITableViewController

@property (nonatomic, retain) NSString *data;
@property (nonatomic, retain) NSArray *listData;

@end
```

The logic for this is very similar to what you just implemented for the roster view, but you are adding a new string named `data`, which holds the string value of the team for which you want to receive the roster. This string is passed into this view, allowing you to filter which roster is shown. You need to implement both the `numberOfRowsInSection` and `cellForRowAtIndexPath` methods exactly as you did with the roster view.

You can see that the `viewDidLoad` code is very similar, but you take the data string, encode it for URL use, and then append it to your URL that filters which team to get the roster for:

```
- (void)viewDidLoad
{
    [super viewDidLoad];

    // build our URL to get the data from
    NSString* url = @"http://derbynames.gravityworksdesign.com/DerbyNamesService.svc/
        DerbyNames?$filter=League%20eq%20'";
    NSString* escapedUrlString = [data stringByAddingPercentEscapesUsingEncoding:
        NSASCIIStringEncoding];
    NSString *urlToGetData = [NSString stringWithFormat:@"%@%@'",
        url,escapedUrlString];

    // get the data
    NSMutableArray *array = [[NSMutableArray alloc] init];
    NSError *error = nil;
    NSURL *derbyService = [NSURL URLWithString: urlToGetData];
    NSData *rosterData = [NSData dataWithContentsOfURL:derbyService];
    NSDictionary *derbyNames = [NSJSONSerialization JSONObjectWithData:rosterData
        options:NSJSONReadingMutableLeaves error:&error];


    // process the data
    NSArray* derbyNameDetail = [derbyNames objectForKey:@"d"];

    for (NSDictionary* derbyItem in derbyNameDetail) {
        NSString *name = [derbyItem objectForKey:@"Name"];
        NSString *league = [derbyItem objectForKey:@"League"];
        NSString *number = [derbyItem objectForKey:@"Number"];

        NSLog(@"Names: %@-%@-%@", name, league, number);
        [array addObject:name];
    }

    // return the data
    self.listData = array;
}
```

Leagues and Team Names

Listing all of the team names is very similar to the code you just created for displaying the roster and
the details. Start by creating a new class named `LeagueTableViewController`:

```
#import <UIKit/UIKit.h>

@interface LeagueTableViewController : UITableViewController
@property(nonatomic, retain) NSArray *listData;
@end
```

The `viewDidLoad` method will look very similar, but notice the URL you are using this time, which
is different from the previous URL. This URL returns a JSON string containing the team names.

```
- (void)viewDidLoad
{
    [super viewDidLoad];

    NSMutableArray *array = [[NSMutableArray alloc] init];

    // go out to the service and get the data
    NSError *error = nil;
    NSURL *derbyService = [NSURL URLWithString:
        @"http://derbynames.gravityworksdesign.com/
        DerbyNamesService.svc/Leagues"];
    NSData *data = [NSData dataWithContentsOfURL:derbyService];

    // Use native functions to parse the JSON
    NSDictionary *derbyNames = [NSJSONSerialization
        JSONObjectWithData:data options:NSJSONReadingMutableLeaves
        error:&error];

    // loop through the derby objects returned only add the name object to the array
    NSArray* derbyNameDetail = [derbyNames objectForKey:@"d"];

    for (NSDictionary* derbyItem in derbyNameDetail) {
        NSString *name = [derbyItem objectForKey:@"LeagueName"];

        NSLog(@"Names: %@", name);
        [array addObject:name];
    }

    self.listData = array;
}
```

What's new in this view is the functionality to select a row. When the row is selected, a new view that contains the list of team members for that derby team is opened. To accomplish this you first need to implement the `didSelectRowAtIndexPath` method. In your method you get the cell and then call the `performSegueWithIdentifier` method.

```
- (void)tableView:(UITableView *)tableView didSelectRowAtIndexPath:(NSIndexPath
    *)indexPath
{
    UITableViewCell *cell = [self tableView:tableView cellForRowAtIndexPath:indexPath];

    [self performSegueWithIdentifier:@"Details" sender:cell];
}
```

After the user selects the table row, you need to pass the data in the cell that the user touched to the details view, which will show the roster for that particular team. The `performSegueWithIdentifier` method is the code that actually switches the views for you. In this case, you are following a segue with the name of `Details`. Before the transfer is performed, you set the destination controller of the segue to a new `DetailViewController` and set the data property on the detail view to the contents of the cell, in this case the name of the derby team for which you want to see the roster.

```objectivec
- (void)prepareForSegue:(UIStoryboardSegue *)segue sender:(id)sender
{
    if ([segue.identifier isEqualToString:@"Details"])
    {
        DetailViewController *detailView = segue.destinationViewController;
        UITableViewCell *dataCell = (UITableViewCell *)sender;
        [detailView setData:dataCell.textLabel.text];
    }
}
```

After all of the code has been added to the new View Controllers you created, you need to go back to the Storyboard and attach them as shown in Figure 7-41. You do this using the Identity Inspector found near the upper right of the screen when you are viewing the storyboard. Map each view to the correct class that was created.

With this logic in place, you should now have a working Derby App created natively with iOS. Your app should look similar to Figure 7-42.

FIGURE 7-41: Attaching a class to a View

FIGURE 7-42: Completed Derby application

This section of the iOS chapter covered creating a native iOS mobile app using xCode and Objective-C. The Derby app example covers the major functionality that a mobile developer would encounter when creating an app, such as creating UI and communicating with an external data service. By no means does this section give complete coverage as to what it takes to be an iOS developer, but it should lead you in the right direction.

OTHER USEFUL IOS THINGS

The two example projects up to this point have provided the basics for creating iOS applications that will go out to a web service and render the collected data on the screen. By no means do we feel that we have covered every possible situation you may need to develop a solution for, so we wanted to finish this chapter by providing a few more short examples that will help you out when discovering how the iOS framework works.

Offline Storage

Even if your application is using a web service for retrieving information, at some point you may need to save information on the device. Depending on the size and type of data, you have a few different options.

Plist

Property lists are the simplest way to store information on the device. In the Mac world, many applications use the plist format to store application settings, information about the application, and even serialized objects. It's best to keep the data contained in these files simple and small, though.

The following example finds the path to a plist stored in the supporting files directory, with a name of example. It then loads the plist into a dictionary object, and loops through each time writing the contents of each item in the plist to the debug console.

```
- (void)getValuesFromPlist
{
    // build the path to your plist
    NSString *path = [[NSBundle mainBundle] pathForResource:
        @"example" ofType:@"plist"];

    // load the plist into a dictionary
    NSDictionary *pListData = [[NSDictionary alloc] initWithContentsOfFile:path];

    // loop through each of the Items in the property list and log
    for (NSString *item in pListData)
        NSLog(@"Value=%@", item);

}
```

If you want to get a single item out of the plist the code is very similar. The following example creates a function named outputSinglePlistValue that takes in the name of the item you want to output, itemName. You then just use the objectForKey method to get the value of a specific key in the dictionary that was returned.

```
- (void)outputSinglePlistValue: (NSString*) itemName
{
    // build the path to your plist
    NSString *path = [[NSBundle mainBundle] pathForResource:
```

```
        @"example" ofType:@"plist"];

    // load the plist into a dictionary
    NSDictionary *pListData = [[NSDictionary alloc] initWithContentsOfFile:path];

    NSString *value = [pListData objectForKey:itemName];

    NSLog(@"Name=%@-Value=%@", itemName,value);
}
```

To write to the `plist` file, again you need to load the plist into a dictionary, this time a mutable dictionary that will allow you to make changes. You can use the `setValue` method to change the value of a key, and then write the `plist` database to a file named `example`.

```
- (void)writeToPlist
{
    NSString *path = [[NSBundle mainBundle] pathForResource:
        @"example" ofType:@"plist"];

    NSMutableDictionary* pListData = [[NSMutableDictionary alloc]
        initWithContentsOfFile:path];

[pListData setValue:@"Modified Value" forKey:@"Test1"];
    [pListData writeToFile:path atomically: YES];
}
```

Core Data

If the data that you need to persist on the device is nontrivial, meaning there is a great deal of it or its complex, Core Data is the way to go. Core Data is described by Apple as a "schema-driven object graph management and persistence framework." Core Data is not an ORM (Object Relational Mapper). Core Data is an API that abstracts the actual data store of the objects. Core Data can be configured to store these objects as a SQLite database, a plist, custom data, or a binary file. Core Data has a steep learning curve, but is well worth learning more about if your app will have a great deal of data held within.

GPS

One of the great benefits to mobile devices is the GPS functionality. Once you are able to get over the hurdles of learning the basic functions within the iOS platform, starting to work with the GPS functions can be a great deal of fun.

The GPS functions are located in the CoreLocation framework, which is not added to a new project by default. To do this, you will need to click the Build Phases tab on the project settings page as shown in Figure 7-43.

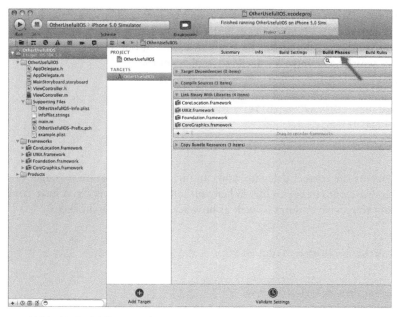

FIGURE 7-43 Build Phases tab

Once on the Build Phases tab, expand the Link Binary With Libraries section, and click the + button. You are then prompted with a list of frameworks to add. Select the CoreLocation.framework as shown in Figure 7-44.

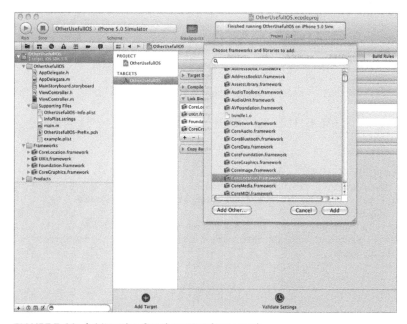

FIGURE 7-44: Adding the CoreLocation framework

With the reference to the CoreLocation framework in place, you are now ready to start working with the GPS functionality. Start with the `ViewController.h` file. The `CLLocationManager` class will send out updates anytime the location is changed. These updates are sent out using the delegate pattern, which simply means your view controller needs to implement the `CLLocationManagerDelegate` protocol.

```
@interface ViewController : UIViewController
<CLLocationManagerDelegate>{
    CLLocationManager *locationManager;
}
```

Once your header file implements the correct delegate, you can initialize the location manager in the `ViewDidLoad` method of the `ViewController.h` file. When you initialize this class, you have control over how frequently you want to receive updates as well as how accurately you want them.

```
// GPS Example
locationManager = [[CLLocationManager alloc] init];
locationManager.delegate = self;
locationManager.distanceFilter = kCLDistanceFilterNone;
// get GPS DatalocationManager.desiredAccuracy =
    kCLLocationAccuracyHundredMeters;
[locationManager startUpdatingLocation];
```

The last step you need to perform is to implement the method that is called whenever the location has changed. In this method you convert the raw GPS data that is sent from iOS to the common format of Degrees, Minutes, and Seconds, and then log the latitude and longitude:

```
- (void)locationManager:(CLLocationManager *)manager
    didUpdateToLocation:(CLLocation *)newLocation
    fromLocation:(CLLocation *)oldLocation
{
    // turn the raw lat info into degrees, minutes, seconds
    int latDegrees = newLocation.coordinate.latitude;
    double latDecimal = fabs(newLocation.coordinate.latitude - latDegrees);
    int latMinutes = latDecimal * 60;
    double latSeconds = latDecimal * 3600 - latMinutes * 60;

    NSString *latitude = [NSString stringWithFormat:@"%d° %d' %1.4f\"", latDegrees,
        latMinutes, latSeconds];
    NSLog(latitude);

    // turn the raw long into degrees, minutes, seconds
    int longDegrees = newLocation.coordinate.longitude;
    double longdecimal = fabs(newLocation.coordinate.longitude - longDegrees);
    int longMinutes = longdecimal * 60;
    double longSeconds = longdecimal * 3600 - longMinutes * 60;
    NSString *longitude = [NSString stringWithFormat:@"%d° %d' %1.4f\"", longDegrees,
        longMinutes, longSeconds];

    NSLog(longitude);
}
```

When you run this example project you are prompted from iOS whether you want to allow this application to use your current location, as shown in Figure 7-45. The Simulator will return the GPS location for Cupertino, California. So if you are looking for more accurate data, you will need to deploy the app to a physical iOS device.

SUMMARY

This chapter spent a great deal of time describing the iOS platform. After reading this chapter, you should be comfortable installing xCode and getting started developing and debugging your first iOS app. Developing for iOS should not be rushed into. Even though corporate executives are pushing development teams to create applications for the iOS platform, you should take a step back and make sure it really makes sense.

Apple has helped push the world into the mobile boom that we are in now, and it is constantly innovating and pushing the mobile industry. Choosing one platform helps developers focus their skills, but locks them into that platform. Apple is known for not being kind to developers, by providing tools that are not the easiest to work with. However iOS fits into your strategy, be aware that Apple has a large market share, and will be around for a long time.

FIGURE 7-45: iOS prompts for use of current location

The following chapter will take a dive into what it takes to develop the same type of mobile app on the Windows Phone 7 platform.

Getting Started with Windows Phone 7

This chapter covers the basics of developing for Windows Phone 7 — how to acquire the tooling and basic design patterns, and preparing to distribute your application to the marketplace. During this chapter you are expected to configure your development machine to run Windows, install Visual Studio and the Windows Phone 7 SDK, and go over the examples from the Derby App. This chapter also covers the specific situations in which Windows Phone 7 breaks away from other smartphone platforms.

NEW KID ON THE BLOCK

Although the Windows Mobile 6.5 design was significantly different from the last major version (6.1), it had been lambasted by critics as change for change's sake. It used design elements from the Zune UI at that time. It was never part of Microsoft's mobile platform blueprints, and was released as a stopgap until the release of Windows Phone 7. It has now been superseded by Windows Embedded Handheld 6.5 for Enterprise Handheld Devices.

Windows Phone 7 is not the next iteration of the Windows Mobile platform, but is its successor. It has been built specifically for the Qualcomm Snapdragon processor family. Since being launched in November 2010 it has had two major revisions. The first, NoDo, primarily added copy-and-paste functionality. The second, Mango, added an update to the included mobile browser and multitasking for third-party developed apps. Whereas iOS and Android have a passive or reactive dashboard for their applications, Windows Phone 7 embraces a proactive approach with constantly updating tiles for application- and context-specific information.

Because Windows Phone 7 was launched three and a half years after the iPhone, it has benefitted from the lessons learned by older revisions of iOS. Windows Phone 7 is still a young platform but it is opening a new channel for .NET developers to provide applications, and its success or failure is a long way off.

Metro

Metro is a design language that Microsoft developed around the Segoe font family to be applied to its entire software stack.

It is patterned on International Typographic Style, with content organized into logical groups. Menus are replaced with panes of content, which are grouped into hubs.

The current versions of the Xbox 360 Dashboard Interface and website, the next version of the Windows operating system, and the next version of Visual Studio all implement the Metro style.

With Metro, Microsoft took a drastically different approach to mobile interfaces than it had done in the past. It is obvious Microsoft took an approach to be innovative, by not following in the UI footsteps that Apple and Android had recently set. The interface puts a strong emphasis on typography, something that had not stood out in past Microsoft software, and it uses its signature Metro font for much of the interface and navigational elements. It uses more text and images for navigating the interface, as opposed to iconography. It uses a freer-flowing, horizontal scrolling layout for most of its apps, as opposed to set screens where you navigate from one to another.

The strong design and interface standpoint that Microsoft took is commendable, and attention to typography in particular is much appreciated by designers. But judging from its market share, the risk has not paid off — at least not yet. The drastically different interface of Metro can be a deterrent when looking to transfer an existing iPhone or Android app to Windows Phone 7.

Though themes and accent color customizations are not specific to Metro, I think now is the time to discuss it. Users can choose either a light or dark theme for their device, and can choose from 10 different accent colors. When editing UI elements and setting their default colors, note that in certain circumstances text may be difficult to read or effectively invisible. When using the Light theme, text defaults to a dark color, and when using the Dark theme, text defaults to a light color. You also can leverage built-in system resources to bind specific accents and default color values to your UI elements.

The benefit of this is shown in Figure 8-1. By using a default style in the Derby App (shown later), when you update the theme on your device, the application automatically updates the styles respective to that theme. The left half of the image is from running the application with the Dark theme, and the right is running the application with the Light theme. I did not have to change a line of code. You can find more information on working with these resources on the MSDN library at `http://msdn` `.microsoft.com/en-us/library/ff769552(v=vs.92).aspx`.

FIGURE 8-1: Two themes with no extra code

Application Bar

The Application Bar is Windows Phone 7's answer to iOS's `UITabBar` and Android's `TabHost`. It can contain icon items (maximum four) and/or menu items.

Some common uses for items in the Application Bar are to pin the current view to the main tile bar (loads your app in a preset state), or to add functionality to the application that cannot be handled with the standard set of touch events.

You can create a global App Bar in XAML (stored in your application's App.xaml file), or in code in your application page, which will show on all pages. Figure 8-2 shows the default view of an Application Bar.

In the XAML for any page you want the global created bar you must add a reference to it as a resource in the PhoneApplicationPage element.

FIGURE 8-2: Global Application Bar

MAINAPP.XAML PAGE ELEMENT

```xml
<phone:PhoneApplicationPage
    x:Class="GravityWorks.DerbyApp.WP7.MainPage"
    xmlns="http://schemas.microsoft.com/winfx/2006/xaml/presentation"
    xmlns:x="http://schemas.microsoft.com/winfx/2006/xaml"
    xmlns:phone="clr-namespace:Microsoft.Phone.Controls;assembly=Microsoft.Phone"
    xmlns:shell="clr-namespace:Microsoft.Phone.Shell;assembly=Microsoft.Phone"
    xmlns:controls="clr-namespace:Microsoft.Phone.Controls;
assembly=Microsoft.Phone.Controls"
    xmlns:d="http://schemas.microsoft.com/expression/blend/2008"
    xmlns:mc="http://schemas.openxmlformats.org/markup-compatibility/2006"
    mc:Ignorable="d" d:DesignWidth="480" d:DesignHeight="800"
    FontFamily="{StaticResource PhoneFontFamilyNormal}"
    FontSize="{StaticResource PhoneFontSizeNormal}"
    Foreground="{StaticResource PhoneForegroundBrush}"
    SupportedOrientations="Portrait" Orientation="Portrait"
    shell:SystemTray.IsVisible="False"
    ApplicationBar="{StaticResource MyGlobalAppBar}">
```

APP.XAML RESOURCES

```xml
<!--Application Resources-->
<Application.Resources>
    <shell:ApplicationBar x:Key="MyGlobalAppBar" IsVisible="True"
IsMenuEnabled="True">
<shell:ApplicationBarIconButton IconUri="/appbar.map.direction.rest.png"
Text="Vixens" Click="ApplicationBarIconButton_Click" />
        <shell:ApplicationBar.MenuItems>
            <shell:ApplicationBarMenuItem Text="Menu Item" />
        </shell:ApplicationBar.MenuItems>
    </shell:ApplicationBar>
</Application.Resources>
```

If you want to have a page-specific Application Bar you can create one in your page's constructor. Figure 8-3 shows the icon and menu item. The Application Bar starts minimized and expands when you click the ellipsis. The click event for both items in the figure pop up a message box with the text "Alert." Page-specific Application Bars are good for context-sensitive functions such as non-discoverable UI functions (double-click events) or events that have no direct touch event associated with them. The following code shows how to render the Application Bar shown in Figure 8-3.

FIGURE 8-3: Page-specific Application Bar

```
public MainPage()
{
    InitializeComponent();
    LoadApplicationBar();
    this.Loaded += new RoutedEventHandler(MainPage_Loaded);
}

private void LoadApplicationBar()
{
    ApplicationBar = new ApplicationBar();

    ApplicationBar.Mode = ApplicationBarMode.Minimized;
    ApplicationBar.Opacity = 1.0;
    ApplicationBar.IsVisible = true;
    ApplicationBar.IsMenuEnabled = true;

    ApplicationBarIconButton button1 = new ApplicationBarIconButton();
    button1.IconUri = new Uri("/images/blankicon.png", UriKind.Relative);
    button1.Text = "button 1";
    ApplicationBar.Buttons.Add(button1);
    button1.Click += event_Click;

    ApplicationBarMenuItem menuItem1 = new ApplicationBarMenuItem();
    menuItem1.Text = "menu item 1";
    ApplicationBar.MenuItems.Add(menuItem1);
    menuItem1.Click += event_Click;
}

private void event_Click(object sender, EventArgs e)
{
    MessageBox.Show("Alert");
}
```

Tiles

Tiles are the UI elements in Windows Phone 7 that render in the main menu when pinned. Think of pinning as adding a shortcut to your phone's menu to an application. If you don't configure any secondary app tiles programmatically, when the application is pinned it will show the App Icon and the Tile Title from the Project Properties as shown in Figure 8-4. This is known as the Application Tile.

```
private static void LoadTileInfo()
{
    StandardTileData data = new StandardTileData
    {
        Title = "Derby Names Tile",
        Count = 42,

        BackTitle = "Gravity Works",
        BackContent = "Derby Names App"
    };

    ShellTile.ActiveTiles.First().Update(data);
}
```

FIGURE 8-4: Default tile

When you create a tile for your application you can update it programmatically. These Active Tiles add additional interactivity to your app while it is *tombstoned*, or between application loads (tombstoning is explained in more detail in the next section). You can configure the title for the front and back sides (as of Windows Phone 7.1; before that it was only one-sided), a badge count on the front (Figure 8-5), and text content on the back (Figure 8-6). You can also configure backgrounds for both faces. Resolution of these tiles is 173 × 173 pixels and images will be stretched to that size. You can use `.png` or `.jpg`, but only `.png` will allow transparency.

FIGURE 8-5: App Tile front

You can use the ShellTile APIs (`http://msdn.microsoft .com/en-us/library/hh202948(v=vs.92).aspx`) to update the application tile, or create, update, or delete active tiles from user interaction. Push Notifications with the correct XML format will update the tile. You can also schedule a set of updates to your tiles

FIGURE 8-6: App Tile back

using ShellTileSchedule APIs. Inside your schedule you can set interval, links to remote content for your update, start time, and recurrence limits.

Your application can also have secondary tiles. These tiles link to specific functionality or views in your app. They are added using the same APIs, but are created as the result of user interaction versus the application tile that will always be there when the app is pinned.

Tombstoning

Tombstoning is Windows Phone 7's answer to multitasking. iOS (as of version 4.x) and Android handle multitasking by putting applications in the background but not freeing up the memory used by the application. When events fire that would put the app in the background (in a multitasking OS), Windows Phone 7 dumps the application out of memory, and the developer can catch the event and save the state of the application. Then when an event is fired to bring the application into the foreground it effectively relaunches the app, this time firing an activated event instead of a launched event. This enables the developer to pass back in the state and get the user right back to where he was. This allows the application to be "multitasked" without persisting the application in memory.

What does this mean for you as a developer?

To save your application and last running page's state dictionary when being tombstoned, all data in these dictionaries must be serializable.

You have two primary ways of storing this data on the device:

➤   The `System.IO.IsolatedStorage` namespace contains the `IsolatedStorageSettings` class, which contains an ApplicationSettings dictionary of key-value pairs. This can persist whether the app was tombstoned or closed.

➤   The `Microsoft.Phone.Shell` namespace contains the PhoneApplicationService.State dictionary. It works between activation and deactivations, but is removed from memory when the application closes.

Now that you understand the idiosyncrasies of Windows Phone 7, you can learn how to get the tools for development.

GETTING THE TOOLS YOU NEED

To develop software for Windows Phone 7 you need a machine running Windows (Vista or Windows 7), Visual Studio 2010, and the Phone SDK, as well as a Windows Phone 7 device to test with.

Hardware

HTC, Nokia, and Samsung are currently manufacturing Windows Phone 7 devices. Device resolutions are 800 × 480 pixels, and most are outfitted with both front- and rear-facing cameras, and screens from 4.3 to 4.7 inches. They are primarily found on GSM carriers.

Visual Studio and Windows Phone SDK

Code for the Windows Phone is written in the .NET Framework, either with XNA (Microsoft's run time for game development), or a custom version of Silverlight (Microsoft's Rich Internet Application framework). User interfaces are created with XAML (eXtensible Application Markup Language).

The Windows Phone SDK works with Visual Studio Express, and will install it if you don't already have it installed. If you have another version of Visual Studio 2010 on your machine it will add the functionality to that install. The SDK also installs a specialized version of Expression Blend set up to work specifically for Windows Phone 7 development. Expression Blend is a tool developed by Microsoft for working with XAML. It provides similar functionality to Visual Studio, though its layout is designed to be more user friendly to designers.

Installation

Microsoft's App Hub (`http://create.msdn.com/`) is the download site for the Windows Phone SDK.

The Windows Phone SDK installer includes:

➤ Visual Studio 2010 Express for Windows Phone (if you do not have another version of Visual Studio 2010 installed)

➤ Windows Phone Emulator

➤ Windows Phone SDK Assemblies

➤ Silverlight 4 SDK

➤ Phone SDK 7.1 Extensions for XNA Game Studio

➤ Expression Blend for Windows Phone 7

➤ WCF Data Services Client for Windows Phone

➤ Microsoft Advertising SDK

To install the Windows Phone SDK you need:

➤ Vista (x86 or x64) or Windows 7 (x86 or x64)

➤ 4 GB of free disk space

➤ 3 GB of RAM

➤ DirectX 10 or above capable graphics card with a WDDM 1.1 driver

Getting to Know Visual Studio

Visual Studio is the integrated development environment from Microsoft for the .NET Framework. Visual Studio Express for Windows phones is a trimmed-down version of Microsoft's full retail products. It provides developers with everything they need to develop Windows Phone 7 apps. Though the interface may seem daunting to the uninitiated, it has a relatively simple learning curve. You are afforded both a WYSIWYG and text-based editor, as shown in Figure 8-7.

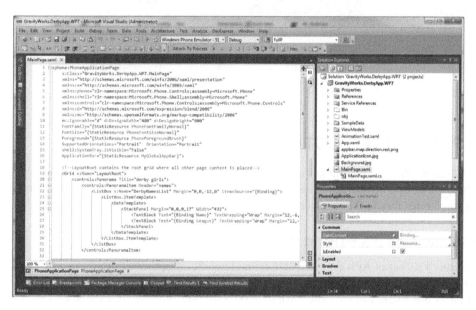

FIGURE 8-7: Visual Studio 2010

Getting to Know Expression Blend

Expression Blend is a user interface design tool developed by Microsoft, with emphasis on a WYSIWYG design for XAML-based projects (Silverlight and WPF). Figure 8-8 shows the Blend UI with the standard tools displayed in a Windows Phone 7 Pivot application.

FIGURE 8-8: Expression Blend for Visual Studio

WINDOWS PHONE 7 PROJECT

Ultimately, a Windows Phone 7 project is similar to a Silverlight project, which is technically a subset of WPF. This section goes over the ins and outs of the Windows Phone 7 project structure, and gives you some resources for adding to the stock controls in the SDK.

Silverlight vs. Windows Phone 7

Silverlight contains a subset of APIs from the .NET Framework, all optimized to run in a browser host so that it can be run cross-platform. The Windows Phone 7 SDK is a subset of that. When porting third-party Silverlight libraries you have to make sure they build against the WP7 version of Silverlight because some of the APIs don't transfer.

Windows Phone 7 contains a fair amount of controls for your application, but they are not all-inclusive. Multiple control toolkits have been released on CodePlex; see `http://silverlight .codeplex.com/` (Microsoft) and `http://coding4fun.codeplex.com/` (independent developer).

Most of the companies that produce control packages for WPF and Silverlight have created Windows Phone 7 control packages as well. Telerik (`http://www.telerik.com/products/windows-phone .aspx`), ComponentOne (`http://www.componentone.com/SuperProducts/StudioWindowsPhone/`), and Infragistics (`http://www.infragistics.com/dotnet/netadvantage/windows-phone .aspx#Overview`) all have prebuilt and skinnable control packs for Windows Phone 7 ranging in price from roughly $100 to $1,500.

Anatomy of a Windows Phone 7 App

This section covers the basic design elements used in Windows Phone 7 application development, and how you can leverage the tools you have at hand to implement them.

Storyboards

Storyboards are Silverlight's control type for managing animations in code. They are defined in a given page's XAML and leveraged using code behind. Uses for these animations are limited only by the transform operations you are allowed to perform on objects. Anytime you want to provide the user with a custom transition between your pages or element updates, you should consider creating an animation to smooth the user experience.

Because storyboards are held in XAML you can either edit them manually or use Expression Blend's WYSIWYG editor.

In Blend, in the Objects and Timelines Pane at the left, click the (+) icon to create a storyboard (see Figure 8-9).

FIGURE 8-9: Storyboards in Blend

Once you have a storyboard, you can add key frames on your time line for each individual element you would like to perform a transformation on. This can include moving objects and changing properties (like color or opacity). After setting up your time line, you can start the storyboard in code.

The name you created for your storyboard will be accessible in code behind.

Pivot vs. Panorama

Both the Pivot and Panorama controls are used to delineate categories and subsets of data. With the Pivot control you get strict isolation of these groupings (see Figure 8-10), with the menu providing discoverable UI to show the other categories. With the Panorama control (Figure 8-11) you get transitions between the groupings with discoverable content on the window boundaries.

FIGURE 8-10: Pivot control

FIGURE 8-11: Panorama control

The Windows Phone 7 Emulator

The Windows Phone 7 emulator (see Figure 8-12) is a very powerful tool. Not just a simulator, the emulator runs a completely sandboxed virtual machine in order to better mimic the actual device. It also comes with some customization and runtime tools to manipulate sensors that are being emulated on the device, including GPS and accelerometer, as well as provide a way to capture screenshots while testing and developing applications.

Debugging Code

I find the debugging experience inside of Visual Studio to be supremely superior to the ones in Eclipse and the third-party frameworks. The load time of the Emulator is quite fast. It acts responsively, and the step-through just works.

FIGURE 8-12: The Windows Phone emulator

BUILDING THE DERBY APP IN WINDOWS PHONE 7

In this section you implement the features of the Derby Names project using Microsoft Visual Studio, while also taking time to learn Windows Phone 7–specific technologies.

Creating the Project

Open Visual Studio and create a new Windows Phone project. For this application, choose Panorama because it offers a UI in which you can share your data. Figure 8-13 shows the New Project window.

FIGURE 8-13: Creating a Panorama project

Once you have created the application, we will step through the Solution (Figure 8-14). In a Panorama application the application is created with the default Panorama background. Visual Studio will create `SampleData` and `ViewModels` for your application. Ultimately, you will be able to remove these from your application when you implement your service communications.

`App.xaml` is the entry point for your application and
`MainPage.xaml` is the page that loads by default.
`ApplicationIcon.png` is the default icon that is shown
when pinned, and it is shown attached to toast notifications.
`SplashScreenImage.jpg` is the default image that shows
when your app is loading, and `PanoramaBackground.jpg` is
a default background created for Panorama apps.

FIGURE 8-14: Solution Explorer

User Interface

The default Panorama application defines its `DataContext`
in XAML. The `DataContext` has first item's binding
associated by default as shown in Figure 8-15. The Panorama
control can be likened to any collection-based UI element
(`UITableView` in iOS or the `ListView` in Android), and the
`PanoramaItems` are the respective rows in that collection
element.

When you feel familiar enough to start working with the
data you will need to create a service reference to the OData
feed. For testing purposes I created a local instance of the
service on my machine, but this will work on remote services
as well, as long as they support public consumption (see
Chapter 3).

```
 1  <phone:PhoneApplicationPage
 2      x:Class="GravityWorks.DerbyApp.WP7.MainPage"
 3      xmlns="http://schemas.microsoft.com/winfx/2006/xaml/presentation"
 4      xmlns:x="http://schemas.microsoft.com/winfx/2006/xaml"
 5      xmlns:phone="clr-namespace:Microsoft.Phone.Controls;assembly=Microsoft.Phone"
 6      xmlns:shell="clr-namespace:Microsoft.Phone.Shell;assembly=Microsoft.Phone"
 7      xmlns:controls="clr-namespace:Microsoft.Phone.Controls;assembly=Microsoft.Phone.Controls"
 8      xmlns:d="http://schemas.microsoft.com/expression/blend/2008"
 9      xmlns:mc="http://schemas.openxmlformats.org/markup-compatibility/2006"
10      mc:Ignorable="d" d:DesignWidth="480" d:DesignHeight="800"
11      d:DataContext="{d:DesignData SampleData/MainViewModelSampleData.xaml}"
12      FontFamily="{StaticResource PhoneFontFamilyNormal}"
13      FontSize="{StaticResource PhoneFontSizeNormal}"
14      Foreground="{StaticResource PhoneForegroundBrush}"
15      SupportedOrientations="Portrait"  Orientation="Portrait"
16      shell:SystemTray.IsVisible="False">
17
18      <!--LayoutRoot is the root grid where all page content is placed-->
19      <Grid x:Name="LayoutRoot" Background="Transparent">
20
21          <!--Panorama control-->
22          <controls:Panorama Title="my application">
23              <controls:Panorama.Background>
24                  <ImageBrush ImageSource="PanoramaBackground.jpg"/>
25              </controls:Panorama.Background>
26
27              <!--Panorama item one-->
28              <controls:PanoramaItem Header="first item">
29                  <!--Double line list with text wrapping-->
30                  <ListBox Margin="0,0,-12,0" ItemsSource="{Binding Items}">
31                      <ListBox.ItemTemplate>
32                          <DataTemplate>
33                              <StackPanel Margin="0,0,0,17" Width="432" Height="78">
34                                  <TextBlock Text="{Binding LineOne}" TextWrapping="Wrap" Style="{StaticResource PhoneTextExtraLa
35                                  <TextBlock Text="{Binding LineTwo}" TextWrapping="Wrap" Margin="12,-6,12,0" Style="{StaticResour
36                              </StackPanel>
37                          </DataTemplate>
38                      </ListBox.ItemTemplate>
39                  </ListBox>
40              </controls:PanoramaItem>
```

FIGURE 8-15: Basic Panorama

Prior to Windows Phone SDK version 7.1, a manual process using the svcutil command-line tool was required to create the service entities. As of 7.1, to reference an OData feed you need only to right-click your project, choose Add Service Reference, enter in the URL of your service (as shown in Figure 8-16), and click Go. After it has found the service it should enumerate the models. You are then allowed to update the namespace and create this reference.

Once you create the service you can start working with the Panorama control to bind the data available from these entities.

After you have made this service, be sure to reference this entity context when your page needs to make calls to the service:

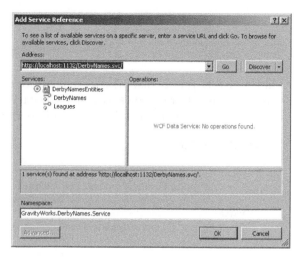

FIGURE 8-16: Service reference for OData

```
readonly DerbyNamesEntities context =
new DerbyNamesEntities(new Uri("http://localhost:1132/DerbyNames.svc/"));
```

Derby Names

To bind data to your Panorama item you need to set the ItemsSource and TextBlock bindings.

Each individual entry in the DerbyNames entity in OData (Figure 8-16) contains properties for Name and League, which you will bind to the TextBlocks in your Panorama item.

ODATA

```
<entry>
    <id>http://localhost:1132/DerbyNames.svc/DerbyNames(29530)</id>
    <title type="text"></title>
    <updated>2012-04-17T01:11:56Z</updated>
    <author>
      <name />
    </author>
    <link rel="edit" title="DerbyName" href="DerbyNames(29530)" />
    <category
term="DerbyNamesModel.DerbyName" scheme=
"http://schemas.microsoft.com/ado/2007/08/dataservices/scheme"
 />
    <content type="application/xml">
      <m:properties>
        <d:DerbyNameId m:type="Edm.Int32">29530</d:DerbyNameId>
        <d:Name>$Yd Vicious$</d:Name>
        <d:Number>5150</d:Number>
        <d:DateAdded m:type="Edm.DateTime">2010-01-15T00:00:00</d:DateAdded>
```

```
            <d:League>TBD (delete 5/10/11)</d:League>
          </m:properties>
        </content>
      </entry>
```

In Figure 8-17 you see that the `ItemsSource` for the `ListBox` has been marked as the binding container, and the two `TextBlocks` in the Data Template have the bindings to the League and Name properties. Please remember that casing is important.

PANORAMA ITEM

```
<controls:Panorama Title="derby girls">
          <controls:PanoramaItem Header="names">
              <ListBox x:Name="DerbyNamesList"
Margin="0,0,-12,0" ItemsSource="{Binding}">
                  <ListBox.ItemTemplate>
                      <DataTemplate>
                          <StackPanel Margin="0,0,0,17" Width="432">
                              <TextBlock Text="{Binding Name}"
TextWrapping="Wrap" Margin="12,-6,12,0"
Style="{StaticResource PhoneTextExtraLargeStyle}" />
                              <TextBlock Text="{Binding League}"
TextWrapping="Wrap" Margin="12,-6,12,0"
Style="{StaticResource PhoneTextSmallStyle}" />
                          </StackPanel>
                      </DataTemplate>
                  </ListBox.ItemTemplate>
              </ListBox>
          </controls:PanoramaItem>
```

WHEN WILL THEN BE NOW?

The Panorama Item has the reference to the `StaticResource` of `PhoneText` `ExtraLargeStyle`. This is what I was mentioning earlier in the "Metro" section. This is a system property that I am leveraging to get the instant UI update when the system theme is changed.

Now that you have the `ListBox` ready to be bound to you can load content from the service.

In the WCF Data Services namespaces you receive access to specialized collections for working from remote data. The `DataServiceCollection<T>` object holds the dynamic entities bound from the web service.

Because you are only querying the base set of data and not passing any parameters to the query, the data binding method is very simple. You first create a collection of type `DerbyName` to hold the data. Bind that collection to the `ItemsSource` property of the list you want the data bound to. Assign a callback to the `LoadCompleted` event on the collection (this is a great place for exception handling), and set your query (in this case `/DerbyNames` because you want all the names on the system). Then you bind the collection asynchronously with the web service by running your query.

DATABINDING FUNCTION

```
private void LoadDerbyNames()
    {
        var derbyNamesCollection = new DataServiceCollection<DerbyName>(context);
        DerbyNamesList.ItemsSource = derbyNamesCollection;
        derbyNamesCollection.LoadCompleted += coll_LoadCompleted;
        var DerbyNamesQuery = "/DerbyNames";
        derbyNamesCollection.LoadAsync(new Uri(DerbyNamesQuery, UriKind.Relative));
    }
```

Calling the `LoadDerbyNames` function from your page's `Load` function results in the UI depicted in Figure 8-17.

Leagues

Each derby team belongs to a league. The entity for `League` is similar to the `DerbyNames` entity, and will make it easy to bind from. The following code block shows an example of a single entity of the `Leagues` type.

FIGURE 8-17: Panorama Item

```
<entry>
    <id>http://localhost:1132/DerbyNames.svc/Leagues(1)</id>
    <title type="text"></title>
    <updated>2012-04-17T20:00:29Z</updated>
    <author>
      <name />
    </author>
    <link rel="edit" title="League" href="Leagues(1)" />
    <category
term="DerbyNamesModel.League" scheme=
"http://schemas.microsoft.com/ado/2007/08/dataservices/scheme"
 />
    <content type="application/xml">
      <m:properties>
        <d:LeagueId m:type="Edm.Int32">1</d:LeagueId>
        <d:LeagueName>5 Cities Roller Kitties</d:LeagueName>
        <d:URL m:null="true" />
        <d:StateProvince m:null="true" />
        <d:CountryCode m:null="true" />
      </m:properties>
    </content>
  </entry>
```

This time you will be using the `LeagueName` property only.

```
<controls:PanoramaItem Header="leagues">
    <ListBox x:Name="DerbyLeaguesList" Margin="0,0,-12,0" ItemsSource="{Binding}">
        <ListBox.ItemTemplate>
            <DataTemplate>
                <StackPanel Margin="0,0,0,17" Width="432">
                    <TextBlock Text="{Binding LeagueName}"
TextWrapping="Wrap" Margin="12,-6,12,0"
Style="{StaticResource PhoneTextExtraLargeStyle}" />
```

```
                </StackPanel>
              </DataTemplate>
          </ListBox.ItemTemplate>
        </ListBox>
    </controls:PanoramaItem>
```

Using effectively the same function for pulling leagues instead of derby names, you bind to the `DerbyLeaguesList` ListBox.

```
        private void LoadLeagues()
        {
          var derbyLeagueCollection = new DataServiceCollection<League>(context);
          DerbyLeaguesList.ItemsSource = derbyLeagueCollection;
          derbyLeagueCollection.LoadCompleted += coll_LoadCompleted;
          var DerbyLeaguesQuery = "/Leagues";
          derbyLeagueCollection.LoadAsync(new
Uri(DerbyLeaguesQuery, UriKind.Relative));
        }
```

Calling the `LoadLeagues` function from your page's `Load` function results in the following UI being displayed in the second panorama item (Figure 8-18).

DISTRIBUTION

To distribute applications in the App Hub you must create a developer account at `https://users.create.msdn.com/Register`. Registration costs $99 per year and allows you to:

➤   Make free, paid, or ad-funded apps and games.

➤   Submit unlimited paid apps to Windows Phone Marketplace.

➤   Submit up to 100 free apps to Windows Phone Marketplace; additional submissions are $19.99 USD per submission.

FIGURE 8-18: Binding to leagues

➤   Expand your reach with worldwide distribution and trial options.

Additionally, all apps are content and code-certified.

Figure 8-19 shows the site for creating a Microsoft Developer account. Note that the Student account type has specific requirements.

Microsoft DreamSpark (`http://www.dreamspark.com/Product/Product.aspx?productid=26`) is a program for students, and gives them a free App Hub account.

Submitting your application to the App Hub is a five-step process. First, you upload your compiled application XAP file. The XAP file is the binary for your application that will be pushed to the phone. To do this you must have a unique name for your application, you must select whether this application is being released to the public or simply being distributed to the App Hub for a private beta test, and you need to specify a version for your app. Next, you must provide an application description (this includes category of app, keywords, detailed description, languages supported, and art assets). Third, you set up your price and select what markets you want to distribute your application in. Next, you provide test information so that the developer in charge of approving your app understands the use cases.

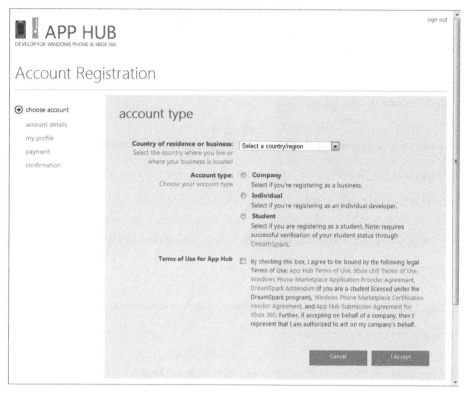

FIGURE 8-19: App Hub registration

Finally, you choose your publishing options (as soon as approved, as soon as approved but hidden, manual publish). You then submit your application for certification.

OTHER USEFUL WINDOWS PHONE THINGS

This section covers persisting data locally, the different types of notifications you can use to interact with your users, the usage of the sensors of the device, and using external resources to improve the quality of your application.

Offline Storage

Windows Phone 7 has the `System.IO.IsolatedStorage` namespace to handle persisting data between application runs. Isolated storage is application-specific storage on the device filesystem.

The simplest means of implementing an isolated storage solution in Windows Phone is to leverage your `PhoneApplicationService`'s state-based events. `Launching` and `Activated` handle application load and resume from tombstone, respectively; `Closing` and `Deactivated` handle application exit and tombstoning, respectively. Making sure that your application loads your isolated storage instance on `Launch` and `Activate`, and saves on `Close` and `Deactivate`, gives you tremendous capability with little effort.

The following code persists a unique identifier to be passed to a web service as part of an authentication token. You first need to declare the property for the unique identifier in your App.xaml.cs (your application's code behind file):

```
public partial class App : Application
{
    public Guid UserAuthToken { set; get; }
}
```

Then you need to add calls in your events to the respective Load and Save functions:

```
private void Application_Launching(object sender, LaunchingEventArgs e)
{
    BindPersistantDataFromIsolatedStorage();
}

private void Application_Activated(object sender, ActivatedEventArgs e)
{
    BindPersistantDataFromIsolatedStorage();
}

private void Application_Deactivated(object sender, DeactivatedEventArgs e)
{
    SavePersistantDataToIsolatedStorage();
}

private void Application_Closing(object sender, ClosingEventArgs e)
{
    SavePersistantDataToIsolatedStorage();
}
```

You then need to use isolated storage in the respective Load and Save functions:

```
private void BindPersistantDataFromIsolatedStorage()
{
    IsolatedStorageSettings appSettings = IsolatedStorageSettings.ApplicationSettings;
    Guid authToken;

    if (settings.TryGetValue<Guid>("authtoken", out authToken))
    {
        UserAuthToken = new Guid(authToken);
    }
}

private void SavePersistantDataToIsolatedStorage()
{
    IsolatedStorageSettings appSettings = IsolatedStorageSettings.ApplicationSettings;

    if (UserAuthToken is Guid)
    {
        appSettings["authtoken"] = (UserAuthToken as Guid).ToString();
        appSettings.Save();
    }
}
```

Windows Phone 7 Isolated Storage Explorer

Available on CodePlex, the Isolated Storage Explorer includes a WPF desktop application and a Visual Studio plug-in to allow developers to manage data held in isolated storage on the device. By adding a reference to the Isolated Storage Explorer Assembly and adding a command in your application launching event you get a per-app instance treating your isolated storage like a folder in Windows.

Notifications

Setting up notifications for Windows Phone 7 is a multistage process. First you must build up a push channel to receive communications within your app. Creating that push channel provides you with a Service URI to post data to. Posting data in specific formats determines what type of message will be displayed to the client app.

```
private void EnablePushNotifications()
    {
        HttpNotificationChannel pushChannel =
HttpNotificationChannel.Find(channelName);

        if (pushChannel == null)
        {
            pushChannel = new HttpNotificationChannel(channelName);

            pushChannel.ChannelUriUpdated += PushChannel_ChannelUriUpdated;
            pushChannel.ErrorOccurred += PushChannel_ErrorOccurred;
            pushChannel.ShellToastNotificationReceived +=
PushChannel_ShellToastNotificationReceived;
            pushChannel.HttpNotificationReceived +=
PushChannel_HttpNotificationReceived;
            pushChannel.Open();

            pushChannel.BindToShellToast();
            pushChannel.BindToShellTile();
        }
        else
        {
            pushChannel.ChannelUriUpdated += PushChannel_ChannelUriUpdated;
            pushChannel.ErrorOccurred += PushChannel_ErrorOccurred;
            pushChannel.ShellToastNotificationReceived +=
PushChannel_ShellToastNotificationReceived;
            pushChannel.HttpNotificationReceived +=
PushChannel_HttpNotificationReceived;
        }

        System.Diagnostics.Debug.WriteLine(pushChannel.ChannelUri.ToString());
    }
```

You can use three types of notifications. The first and simplest is the toast notification. With a toast notification you can pass a title, a string of content, and a parameter. The title will be boldfaced when displayed, the content will follow nonboldfaced, and the parameter will not be shown, but it is what is sent to your application when the user taps on the toast message. This can contain parameters to load on the default page, or a relative link to the page you want loaded when the app loads as a result of the tap.

```
void PushChannel_ShellToastNotificationReceived(object sender, NotificationEventArgs e)
{
        StringBuilder message = new StringBuilder();
        string relativeUri = string.Empty;

        message.AppendFormat("Received Toast {0}:\n", DateTime.Now.ToShortTimeString());

        // Parse out the information that was part of the message.
        foreach (string key in e.Collection.Keys)
        {
            message.AppendFormat("{0}: {1}\n", key, e.Collection[key]);

            if (string.Compare(
                    key,
                    "wp:Param",
                    System.Globalization.CultureInfo.InvariantCulture,
                    System.Globalization.CompareOptions.IgnoreCase) == 0){
                    relativeUri = e.Collection[key];
            }
        }

        Dispatcher.BeginInvoke(() => MessageBox.Show(message.ToString()));
}
```

The second and more complex notification is the tile notification. With the tile notification you can update the application tile content. The XML data that you post contains fields for the title on the front of the tile, front of the tile background image, the count for the badge, the title for the back of the tile, the back of the tile background image, and string of content for the back of the tile.

 The images for the background of the tiles must be local resource URIs. The count for the badge cannot exceed 99.

The third and most developer-centric notification type is raw. With the raw notification type you can pass data directly to the app. It will not be delivered if the application is not running.

```
void PushChannel_HttpNotificationReceived(object sender, HttpNotificationEventArgs e)
        {
            string message;

            using (System.IO.StreamReader reader =
new System.IO.StreamReader(e.Notification.Body))
            {
                message = reader.ReadToEnd();
            }

            Dispatcher.BeginInvoke(() =>
```

```
MessageBox.Show(String.Format("Received Notification {0}:\n{1}",
    DateTime.Now.ToShortTimeString(), message))
    );
}
```

GPS

Windows Phone 7 has built-in functionality for leveraging the geolocation sensors in your device. Using the `System.Device.Location` namespace and tracking the `PositionChanged` event of a `GeocoordinateWatcher` adds a button to your application bar that will tell you the device's distance from our local derby team, the Lansing Derby Vixens.

The Windows Phone emulator has a great interface for mocking GPS location changes while developing and debugging your app, as shown in Figure 8-20.

```
GeoCoordinate DerbyVixensLocation = new GeoCoordinate(42.7337, -84.5469);
    GeoCoordinateWatcher _GeoCoordinateWatcher;

    private void DistanceToVixens()
    {

        try
        {
            _GeoCoordinateWatcher =
new GeoCoordinateWatcher(GeoPositionAccuracy.High)
            {
                MovementThreshold = 10 /* 10 meters. */
            };
            _GeoCoordinateWatcher.PositionChanged +=
GeoCoordinateWatcherPositionChanged;
            _GeoCoordinateWatcher.Start();
        }

        catch
        {
        }
    }

    private void GeoCoordinateWatcherPositionChanged(object sender,
GeoPositionChangedEventArgs<GeoCoordinate> e)
    {
    _GeoCoordinateWatcher.PositionChanged -=
GeoCoordinateWatcherPositionChanged;

    GeoCoordinate current =
new GeoCoordinate(e.Position.Location.Latitude, e.Position.Location.Longitude);
        var metersFromVixens = current.GetDistanceTo(DerbyVixensLocation);
        MessageBox.Show(string.Format("{0:0.00} meters from the Lansing Derby Vixens",
 metersFromVixens));
        _GeoCoordinateWatcher.Stop();
        _GeoCoordinateWatcher.Dispose();
        _GeoCoordinateWatcher = null;
    }
```

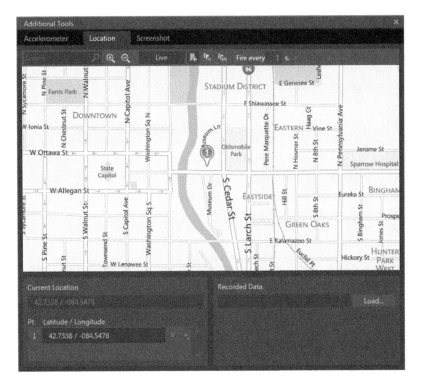

FIGURE 8-20: Location pane

Accelerometer

In addition to GPS, Windows Phone 7 devices are outfitted with an accelerometer. The emulator provides a 3-D interface for simulating accelerometer change events, as shown in Figure 8-21.

You can track the movement of the device by capturing the `ReadingChanged` event on the accelerometer. However, you need to have a delegate to call back to the UI thread if you want to display anything special based on the event. If the application can access the UI thread, the `ReadingChanged` event handler will call the delegate function; otherwise, it will dispatch the event on the UI thread. You must also make sure that when you are done capturing this data, you stop the accelerometer to preserve battery life.

```
private void LoadAccelerometer()
    {
        acc = new Accelerometer();
        acc.ReadingChanged += OnAccelerometerReadingChanged;
        acc.Start();
    }

    delegate void AccelerometerUITextUpdateDelegate(TextBlock accText, string text);
    void AccelerometerUITextUpdate (TextBlock accText, string text)
    {
```

```
            accText.Text = text;
        }

        void OnAccelerometerReadingChanged(object sender,
AccelerometerReadingEventArgs e)
        {
            string accelOutput = String.Format("X:{0} \n Y:{1} \n Z:{2}",
e.X, args.Y, args.Z);
            if (accText.CheckAccess())
            {
                AccelerometerUITextUpdate (accText, accelOutput);
            }

            else
            {
                accText.Dispatcher.BeginInvoke(
new AccelerometerUITextUpdateDelegate (AccelerometerUITextUpdate),
 accText, accelOutput);
            }
        }

    private void AccelerometerDataComplete(){
        acc.Stop();
}
```

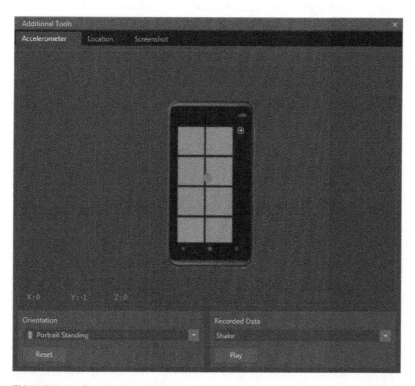

FIGURE 8-21: Accelerometer panes

Web Services

The Derby application is an example of leveraging data over the web to add value to your application. If you don't want to be the central repository for all data exposed to your users, you can leverage web services that exist from other vendors.

As of spring 2011, the Windows Azure Marketplace has more than 16 categories of free and premium data sets that you can consume with content ranging from real estate and mortgage information, to demographics from the UN, to indicators from the World Bank. The data market is available at `https://datamarket.azure.com/`.

SUMMARY

Although the newcomer to the space, the Windows Phone 7 platform has been working hard to implement all of the features expected by a smartphone user, without giving up the Metro design philosophy. Hopefully, you now feel comfortable in the Windows Phone 7 tooling, and can see the parallels between iOS, Android, and Windows Phone 7 when doing UI and back-end development. This chapter covered using sensors, implementing Metro-specific design patterns (such as tiles), calling out to web services, and getting your application submitted for approval to the Marketplace.

This chapter also covered getting the tools you need to develop applications for Windows Phone 7. It covered the UI design patterns found in these applications and discussed how to build your demo application using the .NET Framework and your existing web service. You learned how to leverage the sensors on the device, as well as the framework-specific implementations of offline storage. Finally, you learned the process for getting a developer account and how to prepare to distribute your application.

Getting Started with BlackBerry

WHAT'S IN THIS CHAPTER?

➤ History of BlackBerry

➤ Getting a BlackBerry development setup

➤ Creating mobile apps with BlackBerry for Java

➤ Creating mobile apps with Web Works

➤ Implementing the Derby App

As with the other chapters in the this book, we do not intend to make you an expert BlackBerry developer after reading this one chapter; we simply want to give you the knowledge of the tools you need to develop a BlackBerry application. Of the other platforms discussed in this book, BlackBerry is the oldest but not necessarily the most mature. Over the past few years BlackBerry has been struggling to keep its dominance in the mobile device world, and in doing so has changed the hardware and development platforms in which applications can be created. This has created fragmentation of the BlackBerry platform, and has caused new mobile developers a great deal of grief when researching what languages and tools to use when creating a native BlackBerry application.

Because of this fragmentation of the platform (along with a few other issues you will discover as you read through this chapter), we find BlackBerry to be the most difficult platform for which to develop mobile apps. The goal of this chapter, then, is to help you understand what exactly you are getting yourself into if you have to create a BlackBerry app. This chapter explores the two recommended development paths from Research In Motion (Java and WebWorks) used to create BlackBerry applications.

THE BLACKBERRY CRAZE

The year was 1999. It was the height of the dot-com boom, and companies realized the importance of the Internet and e-mail and were adopting these technologies at a fast rate. Cell phones still had not made it to the general population, and many consumers were still using AOL as their Internet service provider. A company called Research In Motion (RIM) released a small pager-like device that contained functionality for paging, personal organization, and e-mail. Running off of two AA batteries, the BlackBerry 850 was capable of displaying up to eight lines of text at a time. It was the first time for many employees that work was now tied to the side of their belt no matter where they went. Figure 9-1 shows the BlackBerry 850; it was very simple in design, but functional.

FIGURE 9-1: BlackBerry 850, the first BlackBerry model

After the BlackBerry 850, RIM ditched the pager look, and moved toward a bigger PDA-type device. It wasn't until 2003 that the BlackBerry smartphones were released and the BlackBerry really started to gain momentum. BlackBerry devices gained popularity with governments and large corporations because of a software package RIM released called the BlackBerry Enterprise Server. This allowed network administrators to remotely manage users' phones. Connection to the organization's e-mail, remote installation of custom applications, as well as remote deletion of data attracted large organizations to the platform.

As the Internet started making its way into the majority of households in the United States, BlackBerry devices did as well. Having a calendar and e-mail at their fingertips at all times was something many people found appealing. Initially only "tech savvy" people found the thought of this constant line to the Internet appealing, but others started to join in as well, pushing BlackBerry to maintain the top market share in smartphone devices for many years until Google and Apple started to take over in 2011.

BlackBerry Devices

When talking about BlackBerry devices, it important to discuss the BlackBerry operating system (OS) as well. The BlackBerry OS is tied very closely to both the device and the wireless carrier, meaning that the latest version of the BlackBerry OS will not run on every single BlackBerry device under each wireless carrier. To take that a step further, if the device is running in the enterprise, under a BlackBerry server, the enterprise can control the BlackBerry OS version as well.

From a consumer's vantage point, a new BlackBerry is the gift that keeps giving, at least for a while. RIM releases updates to the OS that fix bugs, add new features, and oftentimes improve performance, but which updates actually get installed can be dependent on the device and wireless carrier. This makes keeping track of which OS is on which device a nightmare for developers.

BlackBerry Desktop Software

When it comes to installing a new BlackBerry OS version, and pushing files to the device, the best way to do this is through the BlackBerry Desktop Software program. You can get the BlackBerry Desktop Software from the BlackBerry website at `http://us.blackberry.com/apps-software/desktop/`.

Figure 9-2 shows the summary of a BlackBerry Storm 9530 that has been connected through the software. Notice that the version is 5.0, and even though this device is only two years old, it is no longer able to run the most recent version of the BlackBerry OS because it is now two full versions behind. The BlackBerry Desktop software lists only the updates that are available for a particular device. As with other mobile platforms, it's important that you stay educated as to the latest OS version and features included in the OS that may make your development process easier.

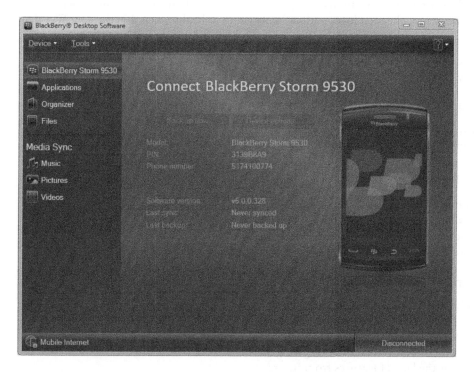

FIGURE 9-2: BlackBerry desktop software

Which BlackBerry OS Version to Develop For

BlackBerry devices as we know them today have been around for almost seven years, and the platform has more devices and OS versions than any other mobile platform. Given that the OS version is tied closely to hardware, and the end user may not even have the ability to upgrade the OS, what is a

BlackBerry developer to do? As a new BlackBerry developer you may have a single device, so you turn to that device when you have questions about how a particular feature works. It's important not to make assumptions, though; if one version of the BlackBerry OS works one way, that does not mean it will work the same in other versions. This paradigm only gets more complex as you are developing your app and testing on other devices. Varying screen sizes, different keyboards, specific carrier settings, and unavailable APIs are issues that make developing for the BlackBerry difficult.

Who Is Using the Application?

The first question to ask is, who is the target market of the application? If you are creating a line of business applications for a larger corporation that has used BlackBerry for years, and has a standard model, then of course you are going to want to develop for that version. This is rarely the case, and we have never been lucky enough to see it. Our clients usually are developing an Android and iOS version, and they want to cover all of the platforms. In this case, the magic OS version you want to develop for is BlackBerry OS 5. More than 85 percent of BlackBerry devices run BlackBerry OS 5 or above. In this case, the application is more than likely going to be distributed in the App World, and it may be a consumer app that users will either pay for or download for free.

This may not be exactly what you wanted to hear, because BlackBerry OS 5 is lacking in many features (mainly revolving around the JavaScript engine) and makes developing in BlackBerry WebWorks, the framework developed by RIM that allows BlackBerry development in JavaScript and HTML, difficult.

In November 2011, the BlackBerry App World reported that 47 percent of users were still using OS version 5, and only 34 percent were using version 6 and higher, as shown in Figure 9-3.

Even though it may be easier for you to develop a BlackBerry version 6 app, you may be doing your client a disservice by allowing only a small percentage of users to access the app.

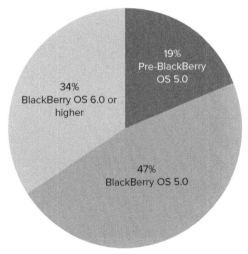

Lowest Common Denominator

By targeting a lower OS version such as 5, your app will be able to run on newer versions such as 6 and 7, allowing more of the users in the market to use your app. One of the largest disadvantages of targeting a lower OS version is the lack of features from future versions. Future OS versions may add new UI widgets that are standard and make your app look like it was developed for the very first BlackBerry.

FIGURE 9-3: BlackBerry App World user OS versions

With the mobile world changing so rapidly, you should be prepared to update interfaces to match OS standards as they advance.

Multiple Builds

Another solution is creating a build for each version you plan to support. If you are creating a BlackBerry application, there's a very good chance that you already have an Android and iOS version, so adding a third BlackBerry version requires a great deal of thought about maintenance costs. The advantage of this approach is that it enables you to match UI and feature sets of new versions as they come out, and not have to worry about backward compatibility.

Change

Sometimes your application will not run on specific versions of the BlackBerry OS or specific devices. Oftentimes targeting a lower BlackBerry OS version creates an inferior product. The BlackBerry App World has settings that allow the developer to target a specific BlackBerry OS and the devices to which the app can be deployed.

With devices and versions changing frequently, BlackBerry provides information to help BlackBerry developers choose a target OS. You can find this information at `http://us.blackberry.com/developers/choosingtargetos.jsp#`.

Screen Resolutions

When it comes to devices, one of the most frustrating issues is the different screen resolutions. For iOS you need to deal with only two sizes, but with BlackBerry you need to account for several screen sizes. Table 9-1 lists the BlackBerry models with their screen resolutions.

TABLE 9-1: Device Screen Resolutions

DEVICE	HORIZONTAL PIXELS	VERTICAL PIXELS
71xx/81xx	240	260
82xx	240	320
83xx/87xx/88xx	320	240
89xx/96xx/97xx	480	360
90xx	480	320
93xx	320	240
91xx	360	400
95xx	360	480
98xx	360	480

BlackBerry Devices and OS Versions

Being a new BlackBerry developer, your BlackBerry device is more than likely not your primary phone. Your device may have been a "hand-me-down" phone given to you, so it's important to find out which version of BlackBerry OS your device can support. Table 9-2 lists BlackBerry devices as well as their input types and max OS versions.

TABLE 9-2: Device OS Versions

OS	MODEL	NAME	INPUT
5	9700	Bold	Track pad 6
5	9650	Bold	Track pad 6
5	9000	Bold	Trackball
5	9630	Tour	Trackball
5	9550	Storm 2	Touch screen
5	9520	Storm 2	Touch screen
5	9530	Storm	Touch screen
5	9500	Storm	Touch screen
5	8900	Curve	Trackball
5	8530	Curve	Track pad
5	8520	Curve	Trackball
5	8350i	Curve	Trackball
5	8330	Curve	Trackball
5	9300	Curve	Track pad
5	9330	Curve	Track pad
6	9800	Torch	Track pad/Touch screen
6	9670	Style	Track pad
6	9780	Bold	Track pad
7	9900	Bold	Track pad/Touch screen
7	9930	Bold	Track pad/Touch screen
7	9350	Curve	Track pad
7	9360	Curve	Track pad
7	9370	Curve	Track pad
7	9810	Torch	Track pad/Touch screen
7	9850	Torch	Track pad/Touch screen
7	9860	Torch	Track pad/Touch screen

BlackBerry Playbook

In April 2011, RIM released the BlackBerry Playbook for sale in Canada and the United States. The Playbook is a tablet-based device sporting a 7-inch display. A year prior, RIM purchased QNX Software Systems, which developed its own operating system for embedded devices. Playbooks use the QNX OS, and contain a different set of APIs than BlackBerry OS. The development story for the BlackBerry Playbook is similar to BlackBerry OS — you have many options, which often makes it confusing to get started. You can even find tools to convert applications created for Android to run on the BlackBerry Playbook. It is out of the scope of this book to discuss developing for the BlackBerry Playbook, but it's important to note that the following platforms can be used to develop applications for it:

➤ Native C\C++

➤ HTML 5 WebWorks

➤ Adobe AIR

➤ Android Runtime

You can find more information about selecting which platform to use for BlackBerry Playbook development in the Platforms section of the BlackBerry Developer Zone at `https://bdsc.webapps .blackberry.com/devzone/platforms`.

GETTING THE TOOLS YOU NEED

If you have ever researched what environment is needed to develop BlackBerry applications, you may have noticed that you can use multiple environments. BlackBerry is an evolving platform, offering developers multiple languages and environments with which to create applications. RIM has not always done a great job of informing developers as to the recommended environment or even strengths of each environment. With the complexity of devices and BlackBerry OS versions, figuring out exactly what environment to develop in often just frustrates new BlackBerry developers. Although RIM has added a great deal of documentation to the BlackBerry Developer Zone, as to the different environments that BlackBerry applications can be developed with, it appears that the future will be much of the same.

RIM is currently planning to base the new BlackBerry OS on QNX, just like the Playbooks. As of June 2012, the name of the OS is BlackBerry OS 10 or just BB10. With not many details being released about BB10, it has been said that BB10 will support the WebWorks environment, which is covered later in this chapter.

BlackBerry Developer Program

One of the most important tools when it comes to BlackBerry development is the BlackBerry Developer website, which is free to join, at `http://developer.blackberry.com`. The BlackBerry Developer website contains a centralized place to download SDKs, participate in forums, and monitor issues pertaining to the development environments as well as the BlackBerry OS. Be aware that this interface changes frequently and is often the first cause of frustration when searching for documentation, because it's not where it used to be.

BlackBerry Partner

RIM/BlackBerry also offers a number of other higher-level paid member types that provide a great deal of other benefits. Programs such the Independent Software Vendor (ISV), Professional Service Providers, and System Integrators member types offer specific tools for each level that may be of benefit to your organization. You can find more information about the various partner levels at `http://partners.blackberry.com`. If you are developing for the enterprise, an ISV account will provide a Service Level Agreement (SLA), in which your BlackBerry ISV representative may be able to assist you with questions that may come up during application development.

Code Signing Keys

It's a good assumption that at some point the BlackBerry application you are creating will be deployed to the BlackBerry App World. In order to do this, your application must be signed with a key from RIM. Also, certain APIs such as persistent store and cryptography require that the app be signed before it can be installed on a device.

It's free to get the signing keys, but it can take a little bit of time, so don't expect to be able to download them right away. Give yourself a few days before you actually need them.

When applying for your BlackBerry code signing keys, it's important to remember the PIN that you used to create them. This PIN is required each time you sign your application. Figure 9-4 shows the signing key order form on the BlackBerry website at `https://www.blackberry.com/SignedKeys/nfc-form.html`.

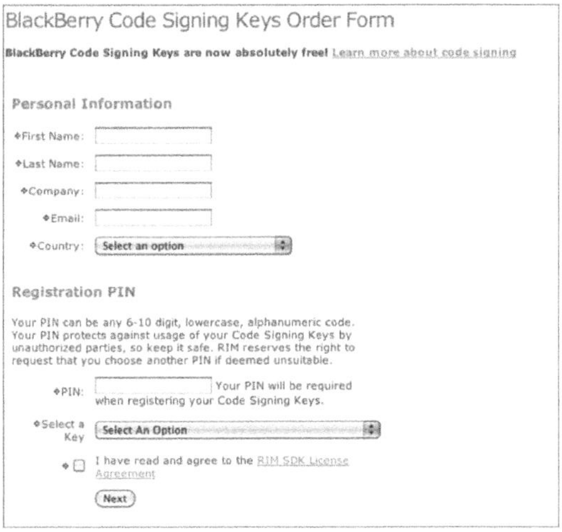

Installing the Signing Keys

Once your application's code signing keys have been approved by RIM, you will receive three e-mails with each one containing a separate signing key. Each key gives access to part of the BlackBerry API, and you should install each one on the same computer. Installing the signing keys is different depending on which environment you choose to work with. The following sections address that under each specific environment.

FIGURE 9-4: BlackBerry Signing Key application

BlackBerry Java Development Environment

If you have been to the BlackBerry Developer Zone, you may have noticed the numerous recommended approaches to creating applications for BlackBerry devices. It can be confusing as to which environment to choose. Currently the Java Development Environment is the most powerful approach. This may not always be the case, but as of today it's important to know how to create BlackBerry applications in this environment. Please note that the BlackBerry simulators will run only on Windows machines.

BlackBerry Java Plug-in for Eclipse

RIM has packaged everything you need for BlackBerry Java development into an Eclipse plug-in. If you already have Eclipse installed, you can find the BlackBerry Plug-in for Eclipse install package on the BlackBerry Developer site at `https://bdsc.webapps.blackberry.com/java/download/eclipse`.

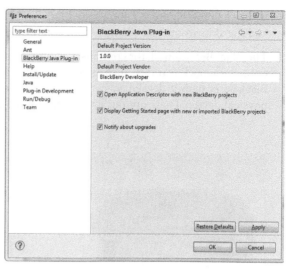

The plug-in includes all of the BlackBerry tools for packaging and signing, as well as the BlackBerry SDKs and the simulators. If you do not have Eclipse installed, RIM offers a download of Eclipse with the plug-in precon-figured as well. When the plug-in is installed correctly, you should see a new set of options entitled BlackBerry Java Plug-in under the preferences, as shown in Figure 9-5.

FIGURE 9-5: BlackBerry Java Eclipse Plug-in

Anatomy of a Java BlackBerry App

If you have developed a Java application before, you already have a good idea of the directory structure and where things will be stored. Figure 9-6 shows a newly created BlackBerry app.

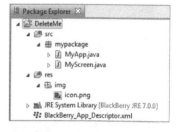

BlackBerry Java apps are structured in a similar manner to other types of Java apps with source code contained within an `src` directory and resources contained with the `res` directory. Within each of these directories contains the files used to make up a BlackBerry Java app.

FIGURE 9-6: Anatomy of a Java BlackBerry app

➤ **MyApp.Java:** This is the entry point of the BlackBerry application. The call to load your first screen will be placed in this file, as well as any other "service" type calls that the application will use. An alternative entry point can be set within the BlackBerry properties within the Alternative Entry Point tab.

➤ **MyScreen.Java:** This is a screen that will be rendered to the user. User interfaces are generated via code, and it's very common to see business logic as well as UI generation logic in the same file, which we highly discourage.

➤ **BlackBerry_App_Descriptor.xml:** This file contains settings specific to the application such as Title, Version, and Description.

The BlackBerry Simulator

RIM puts a great deal of effort into maintaining the different BlackBerry simulators. Because the BlackBerry OS is tightly tied to the hardware, RIM publishes a simulator for each device. Specific device testing is a task that has always plagued mobile developers, but having a simulator for each device type will help you track down device-specific issues more efficiently. Although simulators are never a substitute for a physical device, having a variety of simulators to choose from is very helpful. Figure 9-7 shows the BlackBerry 9930 simulator. Notice the keyboard, screen size, and the skin around the phone — this software is simulating the BlackBerry 9930 Bold.

The BlackBerry Simulator contains a number of tools to help you test your applications. With options to mock features, such as the device being placed in a holster and setting the Camera source, BlackBerry mobile developers can use several options to help test their apps before testing on a physical device. These options are located on the Simulate menu option, as shown in Figure 9-8.

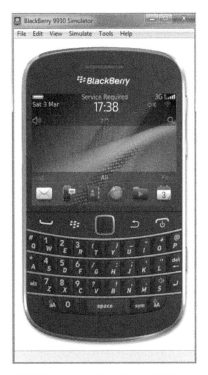

FIGURE 9-7: The BlackBerry 9930 Simulator

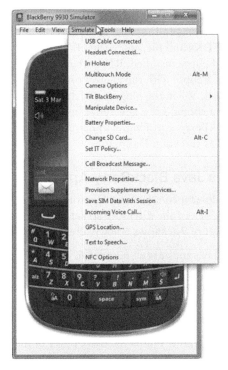

FIGURE 9-8: The BlackBerry 9930 Simulator options

Hello World App

With the plug-in installed, it's time to get to know the BlackBerry tools. In this section, you create a simple Hello World BlackBerry application that contains a label and a button, and you learn the basics of creating an app with the BlackBerry Java Eclipse Plug-in. When the button is touched, the text in the label changes. This will allow you to learn the basics of creating an app with the BlackBerry Java Eclipse Plug-in.

Creating the Project

Within Eclipse, select File ➪ New ➪ Project. When the BlackBerry Java Eclipse Plug-in is installed, you will have an option to create a BlackBerry project. Select BlackBerry Project as shown in Figure 9-9.

After you select the BlackBerry project type, you are prompted for the name of the project and which version of the Java Runtime Environment (JRE) you would like to use, as shown in Figure 9-10.

FIGURE 9-9: Creating a New BlackBerry project

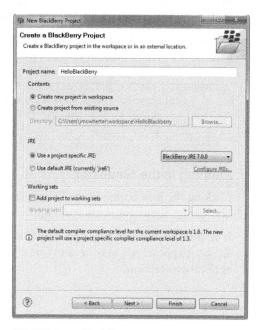

FIGURE 9-10: BlackBerry project settings

Creating the User Interface

Creating the UI for BlackBerry Java apps can get complicated very quickly. Because the UI is built entirely via code, designers don't have full control, and often the UI is left to a developer to implement fully. Developers often "clump" UI and business logic together, which makes understanding the app difficult.

As with most Hello World–type apps, this one is simple, so your business logic is contained within your UI logic. The following logic creates a simple UI that produces a screen with a title of Hello BlackBerry, a blank label, and a button:

```
public MyScreen() {
    // Set the displayed title of the screen
    setTitle("Hello BlackBerry");

    final LabelField lblHello = new LabelField("");
    ButtonField btnHello = new ButtonField("Click Me");


    add(lblHello);
    add(btnHello);
}
```

Notice that the controls are added to the screen with add function, and appear in the order that they were added.

Wiring Up the Controls

BlackBerry fields implement an observer pattern to handle events, meaning all fields can have a listener attached. That listener is notified when a change to the field happens. In this example, the listener is notified when the button is touched or clicked.

The listener is simply going to change the label already placed on the screen to "My New Text." Because it's a small amount of code, you can create and wire your listener all in the same spot:

```
btnHello.setChangeListener(new FieldChangeListener() {
    public void fieldChanged(Field field, int context) {
        lblHello.setText("My New Text");
    }
});
```

Running in the Simulator

Clicking the Run button in the Eclipse menu bar displays the prompt shown in Figure 9-11. Select BlackBerry Simulator to run your app.

If all goes as planned, your app should look similar to the app shown in Figure 9-12. If your app does not appear, you may need to find it on the simulated BlackBerry device under the All applications section.

FIGURE 9-11: Running the project

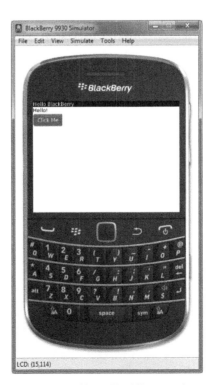

FIGURE 9-12: Hello BlackBerry in the simulator

Basic UI

It is out of the scope of this book to discuss developing a BlackBerry UI with Java in depth, but it's important to note the basics. The UI for a BlackBerry app is created entirely through code. The BlackBerry UI API follows a field/layout manager/screen model:

➤ **Screens:** Only one screen is active per application. Layout Managers are added to screens. Delegate functionality such as menu options are also handled at the screen level.

➤ **Layout Managers:** Layout Managers are a logical grouping of fields that can be used to arrange fields on the screen. Vertical Field Managers, Horizontal Field Managers, Flow Field Managers, and Dialog Field Managers are Layout Managers that you can use. It's also important to note that Layout Managers can be contained within another Layout Manager.

➤ **Fields:** Fields are the building blocks of the UI. Fields are controls such as Buttons and Labels. Every field that you add to your app must belong to a Layout Manager.

Java Micro Edition

BlackBerry applications run within the Java Micro Edition (Java ME, formerly called J2ME). Java ME is a subset of the Java Standard Edition (Java SE) and is very similar to the Java SE, except you may find yourself hunting for objects that do not exist. The Java ME is a trimmed-down version, and is missing some utilities that you may use often in the Java SE. We have found functions revolving around strings and dates to be stripped to the bare bones, and missing a great deal of useful functionality, so be aware of this when you dive into creating a BlackBerry app with Java.

Implementing the Derby App with BlackBerry for Java

The idea of the Derby App is to build the same app over all of the mobile platforms covered in this book. The BlackBerry Java version is very similar to the other versions that you have built thus far or will build in future chapters.

The requirements are to list the roster from the Lansing Derby Vixens roller derby team as the primary function, and then list the other roller derby teams in the world with the ability to see their team rosters.

User Interface

Keeping the user interface abstracted from the business logic is easier said than done when developing BlackBerry aps. Because the UI is generated with code, you will need to think about how you want to abstract your UI as your application grows. For the Derby App, we decided to keep things simple and create one screen that would render both the rosters as well as the leagues and teams, as shown in Figure 9-13.

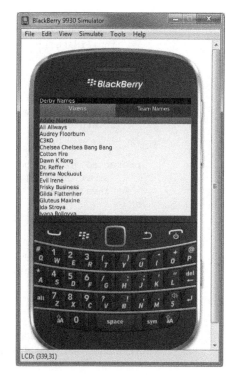

FIGURE 9-13: BlackBerry Java Derby Vixens app

The UI is simple, consisting of a toolbar on the top of the screen used for navigation and a SimpleList control used to list the teams and roster.

Building the Toolbar

We have abstracted the logic required to render the toolbar on the screen into its own function. This function contains a Toolbar Manager control and two Toolbar buttons.

The Toolbar Buttons are added to the Toolbar Manager, and then the Toolbar Manager is added to the screen in the following code. Notice the events for onFocus on each button, which calls the event that should happen when the toolbar button is pressed.

```
public  void buildToolBar() {
    ToolbarManager topToolBar = new ToolbarManager();

    ToolbarButtonField btnLeagues = new ToolbarButtonField(){
        public boolean isFocusable() {
            return true;
        }

        protected void onFocus(int direction) {
            super.onFocus(direction);
            invalidate();

            bindLeagueDataOnScreen();
        }

        protected void onUnfocus() {
            super.onUnfocus();
            invalidate();
        }
    };

    ToolbarButtonField btnVixens = new ToolbarButtonField(){
        public boolean isFocusable() {
            return true;
        }

        protected void onFocus(int direction) {
            super.onFocus(direction);
            invalidate();

            bindTeamDataOnScreen("Lansing Derby Vixens");
        }

        protected void onUnfocus() {
            super.onUnfocus();
            invalidate();
        }
    };

    btnLeagues.setText(new StringProvider("Team Names"));
    btnVixens.setText(new StringProvider("Vixens"));
```

```
        topToolBar.add(btnVixens);
        topToolBar.add(btnLeagues);

        add(topToolBar);
    }
```

Getting the Vixens Roster

When the app is first loaded, call is made out to the Derby web service to obtain the roster for the Lansing Derby Vixens and then binds the data to the SimpleList UI control. The service returns the data in JSON format, exactly the same as the previous examples on other platforms.

Getting the Roster

The following code goes out to the web service, obtains the raw data in JSON format, and then converts into an array of DerbyName objects:

```
private DerbyName[] getDerbyNames(String teamName){
    DerbyName[] tmpRtn = null;
    teamName = replaceAll(teamName, " ", "%20");

    String requestURL = "http://derbynames.gravityworksdesign.com/
        DerbyNamesService.svc/DerbyNames?$filter=League%20eq%20'" +
        teamName + "'";

    String response = NetworkHelper.getDataFromStream(requestURL);
    try {
        JSONObject json = new JSONObject(response);
        JSONArray jsonArray = json.getJSONArray("d");

        int total = jsonArray.length();
        tmpRtn = new DerbyName[total];

        for (int i=0;i<total;i++) {
            String derbyGirlJSON = jsonArray.getString(i);

            tmpRtn[i] = new DerbyName();
            tmpRtn[i].fromJSON(derbyGirlJSON);
        }
    } catch (JSONException e) {
        //TODO: handle error
    }

    // return
    return tmpRtn;
}
```

Recent versions of the BlackBerry SDK include libraries that assist in the parsing of JSON, which makes this task quite simple. In your code you load the raw JSON text into a new JSONObject and then loop through items in the created array, calling a function created on your DerbyName class that will map the raw JSON to the DerbyName object:

```
JSONObject json = new JSONObject(response);
JSONArray jsonArray = json.getJSONArray("d");

int total = jsonArray.length();
tmpRtn = new DerbyName[total];

for (int i=0;i<total;i++) {
    String derbyGirlJSON = jsonArray.getString(i);

    tmpRtn[i] = new DerbyName();
    tmpRtn[i].fromJSON(derbyGirlJSON);
}
```

`fromJSON` is a custom created method found in the `DerbyName` class. This function contains the logic that takes the raw JSON item and maps it to your `DerbyName` object:

```
public void fromJSON(String jsonString) {
    try {
        JSONObject json = new JSONObject(jsonString);

        // build the derby name object from JSON
        setDerbyNameId(json.getInt("DerbyNameId"));
        setName(json.getString("Name"));
        setNumber(json.getString("Number"));
        setLeague(json.getString("League"));
    } catch (JSONException ex) {
        ex.printStackTrace();
    }
}
```

Once the data from the web service has been converted from JSON into an array of `DerbyName` objects, you loop each object and add it to the simple list, which is named `lstDerbyData`:

```
private void bindTeamDataOnScreen(String teamName) {
    clearListItems();
    DerbyName[] derbyData = getDerbyNames(teamName);

    for (int i=0;i< derbyData.length;i++) {
        lstDerbyData.add(derbyData[i].getName());
    }
}
```

Team Names

Team names are loaded in the simple list when the TeamNames button has focus in the toolbar. The team names are loaded very similarly as the Vixens were loaded, but you make a call to a different web service to obtain the team names:

```
private String[] getDerbyLeagues() {
    String[] tmpRtn = null;
    String requestURL = "http://derbynames.gravityworksdesign.com/
        DerbyNamesService.svc/Leagues";
```

```
String response = NetworkHelper.getDataFromStream(requestURL);

try {
    JSONObject json = new JSONObject(response);
    JSONArray jsonArray = json.getJSONArray("d");

    int total = jsonArray.length();
    tmpRtn = new String[total];

    for (int i=0;i<total;i++) {
        JSONObject league = jsonArray.getJSONObject(i);

        tmpRtn[i] = league.getString("LeagueName");
    }
} catch (JSONException e) {
    //TODO: handle error
}

// return
return tmpRtn;
}
```

When the team names are loaded in the simple list, you also set a command that will be fired when the item in the simple list is touched. This adds the functionality that enables you to see the roster for the team when it is selected.

```
private void bindLeagueDataOnScreen() {
    clearListItems();
    String[] leagueData = getDerbyLeagues();

    for (int i=0;i< leagueData.length;i++) {
        lstDerbyData.add(leagueData[i]);
    }

    lstDerbyData.setCommand(new CommandHandler() {
        public void execute(ReadOnlyCommandMetadata metadata, Object context){
            if(context instanceof SimpleList){
                String teamName =((SimpleList)context)
                    .get(lstDerbyData.getFocusRow()).toString();

                    bindTeamDataOnScreen(teamName);
            }
        }
    }, new ReadOnlyCommandMetadata(new CommandMetadata(
        CommandMetadata.COMMAND_ID)), lstDerbyData);
}
```

BlackBerry Eclipse Specifics

If you are used to the Eclipse environment, you will be right at home using this method of creating BlackBerry apps. Debugging and writing code is the same as the other platforms that use Eclipse.

Installing Signing Keys

You can install the BlackBerry signing keys in the Eclipse BlackBerry JDE plug-in by accessing the Signature Tool under the BlackBerry Java Plug-in preferences as shown in Figure 9-14.

Selecting install starts the wizard where you will select each .csi file that you were e-mailed from RIM. After you have installed each of the .csi files, you will be ready to sign your applications as they are built.

It's also important to note that in order to sign your application, the signing tool needs to communicate with RIM over the Internet, and RIM is not shy about sending e-mails when this process happens.

FIGURE 9-14: BlackBerry JDE plug-in Signature tool

BlackBerry Development with WebWorks

WebWorks is another BlackBerry app development approach that enables developers to create BlackBerry apps using standard web technologies, such as CSS, HTML, and JavaScript. You can use whatever IDE that supports HTML/CSS that you are comfortable working with. These WebWorks apps are standalone BlackBerry apps, which means they are not the mobile websites that we talked about in Chapter 5. WebWorks apps are installed locally to the BlackBerry device and do not need to run the HTML on a web server. These apps are packaged into a container that can be viewed by a "headless" browser engine on the BlackBerry device that renders the HTML/CSS for the app.

Depending on the type of app you are creating, this may be a great solution to rapidly develop a BlackBerry app using technologies you are already familiar with. Because WebWorks apps are HTML, existing libraries such as jQuery, Sencha, or other popular JavaScript tools can be imported into your app. WebWorks apps can also take advantage of BlackBerry-specific features and provide the native experience BlackBerry users are accustomed to.

WebWorks SDK

The BlackBerry WebWorks SDK is a set of command-line tools that are used to compile, sign, and package WebWorks projects. The Java SE SDK is a prerequisite, so make sure it is installed before you try to install the WebWorks SDK. You can find the WebWorks SDK at https://bdsc.webapps .blackberry.com/html5/download/sdk.

Anatomy of a BlackBerry WebWorks Project

Because WebWorks projects are created with HTML, you can use your favorite IDE to create and maintain them. For the examples, you will be using Visual Studio. Figure 9-15 shows a newly created WebWorks project.

FIGURE 9-15: BlackBerry WebWorks app

BlackBerry WebWorks apps have a very simple project structure consisting of a few files. This allows you to follow whatever HTML/CSS conventions you may have in place for images and asset files.

➤ **config.xml:** The WebWorks configuration XML file is where settings specific to the app are stored. Settings such as the name, application permissions, and start page are defined in this file.

```xml
<?xml version="1.0" encoding="UTF-8"?>
<widget xmlns="http://www.w3.org/ns/widgets"
    xmlns:rim="http://www.blackberry.com/ns/widgets"
    version="1.0.0.0" rim:header="WebWorks Sample">

    <name>Hello World</name>
    <description>This is a sample application.</description>
    <content src="index.html"/>
</widget>
```

➤ **index.html:** This is the first screen of your app when it loads.

```html
<!DOCTYPE html>
<html>
<head>
    <meta http-equiv="Content-Type" content="text/html; charset=UTF-8">
    <meta name="viewport" content="width=device-width,height=device-
        height,user-scalable=no,initial-scale=1.0">
    <title> Hello BlackBerry </title>
</head>
<body>
    <p>Hello BlackBerry</p>
</body>
</html>
```

The anatomy of a WebWorks project is simple, and we suggest that you follow a common web directory structure strategy when developing your WebWorks app. This structure may look similar to the structure shown in Figure 9-16.

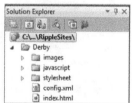

Ripple

FIGURE 9-16: Common web directory structure

Ripple is a mobile environment emulator in a web browser. Ripple enables you to test your BlackBerry WebWorks apps without all the hassle that comes with the BlackBerry simulators. Although Ripple was recently purchased by RIM, Ripple is not just for use with BlackBerry WebWorks projects; it works great for testing PhoneGap (see Chapter 11) projects as well.

Since RIM purchased the Ripple emulator, it has been promoting its use with WebWorks development. Ripple's tools include:

➤ Platform switching

➤ Capability to simulate accelerometer actions

➤ Capability to modify location information

➤ Capability to trigger phone calls

➤ Web Inspector tools

Ripple provides an environment that developers as well as designers will be comfortable with. The app is shown in the middle of the screen, within a mobile phone skin, and the emulator settings are listed along the right and left sides of the phone as shown in Figure 9-17.

The address bar on top of the Ripple emulator enables developers/designers to navigate to the exact screen they wish to work with.

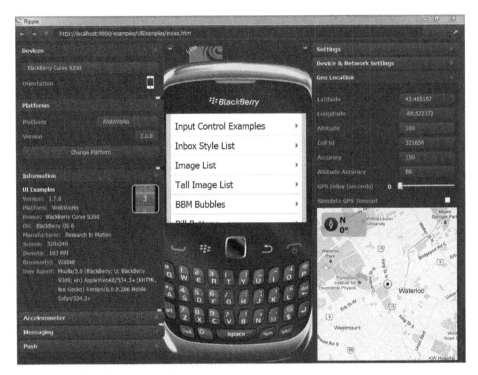

FIGURE 9-17: Ripple testing environment

Because Ripple is a web browser, the first option is to host the HTML files on a server someplace and access them. In most situations that would be cumbersome, and it makes more sense to keep your files local.

To access your mobile app in Ripple from the local filesystem, copy the contents into the RippleSites directory:

➤ Windows XP: `C:\Documents and Settings\<Username>\RippleSites`

➤ Windows 7: `C:\Users\<Username>\RippleSites`

➤ Mac OS: `/Users/<Username>/RippleSites`

After the project has been copied to the RippleSites directory, you can enter http://localhost:9900/<SiteName>. For example, http://localhost/9900/Derby/index.html.

Implementing the Derby App with WebWorks

The requirements with the WebWorks version is to list the roster from the Lansing Derby Vixens roller derby team as the primary function, then list all of the roller derby teams in the world with the ability to see their team rosters.

User Interface

The user interface is created with HTML, making it very easy to change as the app is being created. The Derby app has a toolbar on the top of the screen, and then a list of data as shown in Figure 9-18.

The toolbar in this implementation is simply two HTML anchor tabs within a div. The only thing to note is a CSS class applied to the lnkRoster anchor. This enables you to apply styling that indicates in the toolbar which roster you are working with.

For the list of data, just create an unordered list that will eventually get populated with the information you want to display:

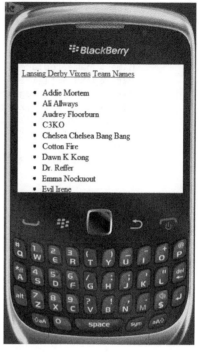

FIGURE 9-18: WebWorks Derby app

```
<body id="mainbody">
    <div id="header">
        <a id="lnkRoster" class="selected" href="roster.html">Roster</a>
        <a id="lnkLeagues" href="index.html">Team Names</a>
    </div>

    <div id="RosterList">
        <ul />
    </div>
</body>
```

Getting the Roster

The first screen that appears when the app starts up is a list of the Lansing Derby Vixens. You use the Roster.html file to list not only the Derby Vixens, but players from other teams as well. It's important to note that all of the logic that is being added is JavaScript and is not WebWorks-specific.

The first thing you do is see if the league name was passed as a query string value. Using the following code, the LeagueName would be 'Test League' if the roster HTML was accessed the following way /roster.html?LeagueName='Test League':

```
var leagueName = getParameterByName("LeagueName");
```

The `getParameterByName` function uses some regular expression magic to filter out and return the requested parameter:

```
function getParameterByName(name) {
    name = name.replace(/[\[]/, "\\\[").replace(/[\]]/, "\\\]");
    var regexS = "[\\?&]" + name + "=([^&#]*)";
    var regex = new RegExp(regexS);
    var results = regex.exec(window.location.href);
    if (results == null)
        return "";
    else
        return decodeURIComponent(results[1].replace(/\+/g, " "));
}
```

If a parameter was not passed in, you default to requesting the Lansing Derby Vixen data and bind it to your unordered list:

```
<script type="text/javascript">


    var leagueName = getParameterByName("LeagueName");

    if (leagueName == "") {
        leagueName = "Lansing Derby Vixens";
        jQuery("#lnkRoster").text(leagueName);
    }

    appendRosterDataOnScreen(getDerbyNames(leagueName),
        "RosterList", true);
</script>
```

In the example, two functions are required to get the roster information from the web service. The `getDerbyNames` function takes in the name of the team for which you want to receive the roster, and builds the URL to the web service:

```
function getDerbyNames(teamName) {
    teamName = teamName.replace(/\ /g, '%20');
    var requestURL = "http://derbynames.gravityworksdesign.com/
        DerbyNamesService.svc/DerbyNames?$filter=
        League%20eq%20'" + teamName + "'";

    return getData(requestURL);
}
```

The `getData` function is a generic HTTP request for data from the web service:

```
function getData(url) {
    var httpReq = new XMLHttpRequest();

    try {
        httpReq.open("GET", url, false);
        httpReq.setRequestHeader("Content-Type", "text/xml; charset=utf-8");
        httpReq.setRequestHeader("Pragma", "cache");
```

```
            httpReq.setRequestHeader("Cache-Control", "no-transform");
            httpReq.send(null);

            if (httpReq.readyState == 4 && httpReq.status == 200) {
                var responseText = httpReq.responseText;

                return responseText;
            } else {
                return null;
            }
        } catch (ex) {
            alert(ex.get_Description);
            return null;
        }
    }
```

Appending the Roster Data to the Unordered List

The data is passed into `appendRosterDataOnScreen` as raw JSON text. Using the JavaScript `eval` function, the JSON is converted into objects containing the roster information. Once the data is in objects, you can loop over them and build the HTML list items that will be injected into the unordered list.

```
function appendRosterDataOnScreen(data, listName, skipHeader) {
    var dataItems = eval("(" + data + ")").d;
    var singleItem = "";
    var list = jQuery("#" + listName).find('ul');

    for (var i = 0; i < dataItems.length; i++) {

        if (skipHeader == null) {
            var headerValue = dataItems[i].Name.substring(0, 1);

            if (m_headerList.indexOf(headerValue) >= 0) {
                headerValue = '';
            }
            else {
                m_headerList.push(headerValue);
                list.append("<li class='letterheader'>" +
                headerValue + "</li>");
            }
        }

        singleItem = "<li title=" + dataItems[i].Name + " >" +
            dataItems[i].Name + "</li>";
        list.append(singleItem);
    }
}
```

Team Names

The methods used to create the Team Names page are very similar, with the only major difference being in the function that builds the list items that are injected into the unordered list.

For the team names, you want to have the ability for the user to select the team, and have the roster for the team load. To accomplish that you create an anchor tag around the list item, linking to the roster page with a query parameter of the team name for which you want to load the roster.

```
function appendLeagueDataOnScreen(data, listName, skipHeader){
    var dataItems = eval("("+ data +")").d;
    var singleItem = "";
    var list = jQuery("#" + listName).find('ul');

    for (var i = 0; i < dataItems.length; i++) {

        if (skipHeader == null){
            var headerValue = dataItems[i].LeagueName.substring(0, 1);

            if (m_headerList.indexOf(headerValue) >= 0 ){
                headerValue = '';
            }
            else {
                m_headerList.push(headerValue);
                list.append("<li class='letterheader''>" +
                    headerValue + "</li>");
            }
        }


        var leagueName = dataItems[i].LeagueName.replace(/\ /g, '%20');
        singleItem = "<a href='roster.html?LeagueName=" + leagueName + "'>
            <li title=" + dataItems[i].LeagueName + " >" +
                dataItems[i].LeagueName + "</li></a>";
        list.append(singleItem);
        }
    }
}
```

Installing Signing Keys from the Command Line

If the Eclipse BlackBerry JDE plug-in is not installed, then signing keys can be installed from the command line using the Signature Tool, which is installed with the BlackBerry WebWorks Packager. This Signature Tool is the same tool that is invoked from the Signature Tool settings in the Eclipse plug-in. You will need to know the full path of the .csi file.

From the command prompt, enter the following command and follow the steps presented:

```
Java -java SignatureTool.ja <.csi file path>
```

OTHER USEFUL BLACKBERRY THINGS

The example projects up to this point have provided the basics for developing a BlackBerry app using both Java and WebWorks. These apps cover getting data from a web service and displaying it on the screen, which is a large part of mobile app development. By no means do we feel we have covered everything that could come up when developing a BlackBerry app, so we wanted to finish this chapter by providing a few examples of common tasks that will help you out when discovering how the BlackBerry development frameworks work.

Offline Storage

There will be times that you will need to store data on the device. This could be because the business rules for your app require offline usage, or just a matter of saving a few settings such as username and password. The BlackBerry development environments support different methods, but for this example we are going to talk about the simplest way to store simple settings.

BlackBerry WebWorks

Within BlackBerry WebWorks, you do not need to use any specific BlackBerry API calls. HTML5 contains local storage functionality that will accomplish your needs.

To store a setting:

```
localStorage.mysetting="My Setting";
```

To retrieve a setting:

```
document.getElementById("Local Storage").innerHTML="My Setting: "
+ localStorage.mysetting;
```

BlackBerry Java

Persistent store objects are used within the BlackBerry Java. The following example commits the value of a string to the persistent store object:

```
public void savePersistentObject(long key) {
    PersistentObject persistentObject =
        PersistentStore.getPersistentObject(key);

    String objectToSave = "My Setting Value";
    persistentObject.setContents(objectToSave);
    persistentObject.commit();
}
```

To retrieve the value you need to cast the object to the correct type, and then you will have use of it:

```
public void getPersistentObject(long key) {
    PersistentObject persistentObject =
        PersistentStore.getPersistentObject(key);

    String myValue = (String)persistentObject.getContents();
}
```

It's important to note that the getPersistentObject methods take a key value, which is a long. Instead of creating your own value to pass it, if you create a string and then right-click in Eclipse, you can convert the string value to a long as shown in Figure 9-19. This will help with keeping your keys consistent.

If you are working with complex or hierarchical data, you may want to look into the objects for SQL Lite, which is supported in both the BlackBerry Java and WebWorks development environments.

Location Services

FIGURE 9-19: Converting a string to long

Location services are one of the great features that mobile developers have to work with. Many apps as we know them would not be used if not for the location services they have integrated. Both the BlackBerry Java and WebWorks have robust functionality for location services.

BlackBerry WebWorks

You do not need to use any BlackBerry API calls within WebWorks; you can simply use HTML5 and JavaScript. You can find the location services under `navigator.geolocation`.

In this example, you get the current location and then show the latitude and longitude in a dialog box:

```javascript
<script type="text/javascript">
    // geolocation is supported
    if (navigator.geolocation !== null) {
        var options;
        navigator.geolocation.getCurrentPosition(success, error, options);
    }
    else {
        alert("Geolocation not supported.");
    }

    function success(position) {
        var time = position.timestamp;
        var coordinates = position.coords;

        var lat = coordinates.latitude;
        var lon = coordinates.longitude;
        var speed = coordinates.speed;
        var alt = coordinates.altitude;
        var acc = coordinates.accuracy;
        var altAcc = coordinates.altitudeAccuracy;
        var head = coordinates.heading;

        alert("You are located at " + lat + ", " + lon);
    }

    function error(error) {
        alert("Error getting location info: " + error.message);
    }
</script>
```

BlackBerry Java

Location services within BlackBerry Java are very robust, offering different methods for retrieving the GPS information, which are defined when creating the Location Criteria object:

➤ **Cell Site:** When the Cell Site method is used, the location is determined only on the location of the cell tower. The accuracy is not as good as other methods.

```
Criteria cellSiteCriteria = new Criteria();
cellSiteCriteria.setHorizontalAccuracy(Criteria.NO_REQUIREMENT);
cellSiteCriteria.setVerticalAccuracy(Criteria.NO_REQUIREMENT);
cellSiteCriteria.setCostAllowed(true);
cellSiteCriteria.setPreferredPowerConsumption(Criteria.POWER_USAGE_LOW);
```

➤ **Assisted GPS:** GPS hardware on the device is used with assistance from the wireless network to help keep power consumption low. This method provides a high accuracy but is slower than the Cell Site method.

```
Criteria cellSiteCriteria = new Criteria();
cellSiteCriteria.setHorizontalAccuracy(Criteria.NO_REQUIREMENT);
cellSiteCriteria.setVerticalAccuracy(Criteria.NO_REQUIREMENT);
cellSiteCriteria.setCostAllowed(true);
cellSiteCriteria.setPreferredPowerConsumption(Criteria.POWER_USAGE_MEDIUM);
```

➤ **Unassisted GPS:** GPS hardware is solely used with this method. Power consumption is higher, but will work when no wireless networks are available.

```
Criteria cellSiteCriteria = new Criteria();
cellSiteCriteria.setHorizontalAccuracy(Criteria.NO_REQUIREMENT);
cellSiteCriteria.setVerticalAccuracy(Criteria.NO_REQUIREMENT);
cellSiteCriteria.setCostAllowed(false);
cellSiteCriteria.setPreferredPowerConsumption(Criteria.POWER_USAGE_HIGH);
```

In the following example you create an unassisted location provider and return the latitude and longitude:

```
public void getLocation() {
    int TIME_OUT = 60;

    // use the device GPS
    Criteria criteria = new Criteria();
    criteria.setVerticalAccuracy(50);
    criteria.setHorizontalAccuracy(50);
    criteria.setCostAllowed(false);
    criteria.setPreferredPowerConsumption(criteria.POWER_USAGE_HIGH);

    try {
        LocationProvider provider = LocationProvider
            .getInstance(criteria);
        Location currentLocation = provider.getLocation(TIME_OUT);

        if (currentLocation != null) {
```

```
            double longitude = currentLocation
                .getQualifiedCoordinates().getLongitude();

            double latitude = currentLocation
                .getQualifiedCoordinates().getLatitude();
        }
    }
    catch (final Exception e) {
        // handle error
    }
}
```

BLACKBERRY DISTRIBUTION

Distribution is one of the biggest issues that new mobile developers face. Most of the issues that revolve around distribution are when a client asks for an app to be created that only their employees can access. Network administrators at medium to large companies control exactly what software is installed on every employee's computer, and it's only natural that they want to control what apps are installed on their phones as well. BlackBerry has always been very friendly to the enterprise, and most of the distribution methods, listed here, have the enterprise in mind:

➤ **Over-the-Air:** A BlackBerry app can be placed on a website where users are directed to download it. This is great for apps created for the enterprise where the users' phones are not controlled by a BlackBerry Enterprise server.

➤ **Desktop:** BlackBerry apps can be installed from the BlackBerry Desktop Manager when the device is connected to the computer via a USB cable. This method is good to get the app on a few phones, perhaps for testing purposes.

➤ **BlackBerry App World:** In 2009 BlackBerry released the App World to the public. This is a central location for BlackBerry users to discover your app. The App World takes a lot of the headache out of deployment issues with BlackBerry and is the recommended solution when your app will be available to the public.

➤ **BlackBerry Enterprise Server:** Many companies that have fully embraced the BlackBerry technologies have a BlackBerry Enterprise Server (BES), which allows IT staff to manage multiple phones in one server environment. BES allows apps to be installed/removed remotely.

SUMMARY

This chapter walked through two of the development methods that you can use for creating BlackBerry applications. BlackBerry Java and WebWorks both offer unique and compelling reasons for using them, with both having upsides and downsides. Deciding which method to use can be a frustrating process, but ultimately depends on the needs of your app.

RIM is innovating and changing how development is performed, which again is extremely frustrating to developers. It's understandable that BlackBerry is trying to define where it stands in the mobile world today. With BlackBerry losing market share at an alarming rate, it's important that you do not dive right into creating a BlackBerry app without ensuring that it is the best business decision. An app aimed at state government or education may be a great fit for BlackBerry. As with all platforms, don't just develop for the platform because everyone else is doing it.

The next chapter discusses developing cross-platform mobile apps using the Appcelerator Titanium platform, and is the first nonnative platform that will be discussed.

10

Getting Started with Appcelerator Titanium

Previous chapters discussed the ins and outs of native mobile application development with the tools that respective companies have available. This chapter covers third-party frameworks for developing mobile applications.

Appcelerator Titanium was released in December 2008, and has been steadily growing in functionality since its release. Starting with its Titanium Developer product, Appcelerator provided a single-point interface to run applications. It tied directly into your emulators (with some configuration) and let users publish to the respective stores, signing your build and creating a distributable package. As features were added to the Native iOS SDK, Titanium released a new, major revision, and each minor version included bug fixes and code to bring parity between Android and iOS.

Appcelerator has been bundling the Titanium Studio product as its main development environment as of version 1.7. You no longer need an external text editor to create your apps. Titanium Studio (a wrapper for the Aptana product that Appcelerator acquired) is a full-featured IDE providing a single place to handle all steps of the development environment and adding what previous versions were missing: a rich debugging solution.

Four versions are available for Titanium. The Community version is free, provides access to the basic API, and offers access to the support community and basic training videos. The Indie version has a cost, for access to the Premium APIs (plug-ins and third-party services). The Professional version has a monthly fee for everything from the past two versions, plus Premium support. Finally, the Enterprise version is for teams with more than three developers, and affords access to classroom training plus all of the features from the other versions. Enterprise pricing requires you to contact Appcelerator directly, and is based on the size of your development staff. Pricing can be found at http://www.appcelerator.com/plans-pricing.

WHY USE TITANIUM?

The primary development languages for Titanium are HTML, CSS, and JavaScript. The compile process generates iOS and Android source code, as well as a distributable binary, respective to each platform. This single API is quite thorough. By leveraging the Titanium framework you get a single way to create all of your UI, transparent to the native codebase. Creating a `Ti.UI.Button` generates a `UIButton` in iOS and an `android.widget.Button` for Android when compiled. Not all UI elements are created equal; Appcelerator has tried to create simple namespace additions to account for native, framework-specific elements not implemented in both platforms.

All base functionality afforded in the framework for both iOS and Android is available in Appcelerator's Kitchen Sink GitHub project: `https://github.com/appcelerator`.

As far as extra functionality, both free and purchasable options are available. Appcelerator offers the Open Mobile Marketplace (`https://marketplace.appcelerator.com/`) for a collection of add-ins you can drop directly into your application.

Appcelerator also has (+Plus) modules for access to APIs for Commerce (PayPal, StoreKit [iOS], In-App Billing [Android]), Communications [Bump, SMS, Urban Airship], Advertising [AdMob, DoubleClick], Media [Brightcove], and Analytics.

Urban Airship, AdMob, DoubleClick, and Brightcove are third-party services, and these premium plug-ins require service agreements with their respective sites to leverage them in Titanium.

An added benefit of this framework is that it also mirrors the Appcelerator Titanium Desktop product to create applications for desktop machines (Mac, Windows, and Linux) with a very similar API.

> ### DOES TITANIUM SUPPORT BLACKBERRY?
>
> One of the most compelling reasons to use Titanium is the number of platforms it can support. We have previously stated that "write once, deploy to multiple platforms" is not a reality. Appcelerator has been saying for more than two years that support for BlackBerry is coming; it launched a closed beta in July 2010 for developing BlackBerry apps using the Appcelerator framework, but it has not been merged into its release distribution yet.
>
> Don't hold your breath for this release. The differences between the BlackBerry OS's are substantial, and creating interfaces that work the same between them would be a very large undertaking.

WHO IS USING TITANIUM?

Appcelerator keeps track of its user base through the login contained within the IDE. When creating projects in Titanium Studio, your login name is registered with your project's App Id, so Appcelerator understands how many apps you are developing. From our knowledge, it doesn't profile your code. Appcelerator does contact members of its developer network conferences, training seminars, and other events. Appcelerator makes sure to let all the developers know when new features and versions are being released.

Every quarter, Appcelerator, along with IDC (an IT market analysis and research firm), release their mobile developer analytics report from information gathered from developer surveys. Figure 10-1 is an example of the type of data included in these reports.

Appcelerator/IDC's most recent survey focused on cloud technologies and their effect on mobile development. Roughly 2,000 developers participate in Appcelerator's Developer Network, and many are part of its Titans program. Titans are developers who use Titanium and have expressed interest in helping grow the brand. Sign-up for the program is free, but you are asked to be active in the community to maintain membership.

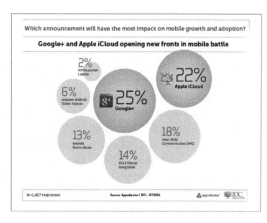

FIGURE 10-1: Appcelerator metrics

Appcelerator also provides a showcase of applications developed with Titanium and organizations using its products. Companies that have been put in the spotlight are covered in the following sections.

NBC

NBC Universal currently uses Titanium for its NBC iPad application: users can view show schedules based on current location, view clips of upcoming and past episodes, can watch full episodes of a few shows in current release. The videos are not downloaded, but streamed to the iPad. The interface has a unique look and feel, while maintaining parity with the branding of the NBC site. Figure 10-2 shows the NBC app in the iTunes App Store. With more than 9,000 ratings, the user base is not small.

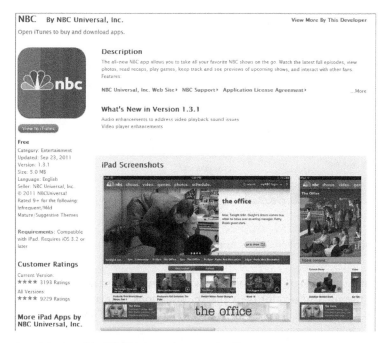

FIGURE 10-2: The NBC Universal app in the iTunes store

GetGlue

Combining social networking with media, GetGlue is a recommendation engine built around a crowd-sourced check-in game. Users pick from preset categories, search for topics, and check in to that topic to rate it based on their tastes; users can also browse what other people said about that topic. Once a few likes and dislikes have been entered, the system provides recommendations based on correlations to other user data. By giving check-in bonuses to people following an event, a media release, or a trending topic, GetGlue incentivizes information gathering to provide these recommendations. GetGlue provides platform-specific interfaces for iPhone, iPad, Android, BlackBerry, and Mobile Web. GetGlue has recently hit the milestone of one million users with a significant portion of traffic coming through its mobile applications. Figure 10-3 shows the GetGlue iPhone version in the iTunes App Store.

FIGURE 10-3: The GetGlue app (iPhone version) in the iTunes App Store.

These two applications show that two different-sized companies with different markets can leverage the tools in Titanium to develop the applications for their specific situations. The next section discusses what you need to do to get the tools necessary to start developing with Titanium.

GETTING THE TOOLS YOU NEED

Getting the tools to develop Titanium is a pretty simple process. The sign-up process is relatively painless, and after completing the free registration you have immediate access to all the support forums and plug-in marketplace. Everything is handled at the Appcelerator site, and the install is a single package.

Installing Titanium Studio

Titanium Studio can be installed on Mac or PC. Chapter 7 discussed installing the tools for iOS development. If you have not already installed this development environment, and the Android Development Environment as discussed in Chapter 6, please review those chapters for getting everything necessary to develop for those platforms. They are a prerequisite for developing those platforms using Titanium. Please note that because the iOS SDK is available only on Mac OSX, you can create iOS apps in Titanium with Titanium Studio only on a Mac.

Go to `http://www.appcelerator.com` and click the Download Titanium button. You are prompted to sign up for an account. Although the Titanium Mobile Framework is free to use, it requires an active developer account. This also allows you access to the forums, support center, and marketplace.

Once Titanium is installed, you need to do minimal configuration the first time you run it.

The first step in configuring Titanium is picking a workspace. Workspace is just a fancy word for a folder to house a project. By default, Titanium puts this folder in your Users Documents folder (see Figure 10-4), but feel free to move it to wherever you want.

You will see this workspace launcher when you open a project for the first time. Once you select a place for the workspace, mark it to use as the default.

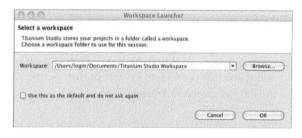

FIGURE 10-4: Choosing your workspace

Adding the Titanium Studio package has made the development process much easier for the amateur or hobbyist programmer and the professional programmer alike, because it is easy to see parallels to modern IDEs.

When the Titanium project was first launched, developers had to use their own text editor with the Titanium Developer application. It acted as a wrapper for some Python scripts that did the builds and launched the emulators. Titanium Studio is a wholly new animal.

People familiar with the look and feel of Eclipse should be right at home in Titanium Studio, because Aptana is a wrapper over Eclipse. That being said, Eclipse must be installed to do Titanium development and native Android development.

Out of the box, you need to add a link to the Android SDK to build your project for Android. Go to Preferences ➪ Titanium Studio ➪ Titanium, as shown in Figure 10-5.

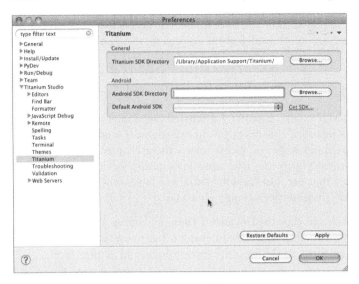

FIGURE 10-5: Configuring the Android SDK

Titanium handles the configuration of the link to the iOS SDK (in Mac OS X) based on queries it can make against the OS. Once you have selected the Android SDK you want to build for, you are ready to create your first project. Creating a project is relatively simple. First choose a workspace and then click the Create Project button on the App Explorer window — by default it is docked to the left, as shown in Figure 10-6.

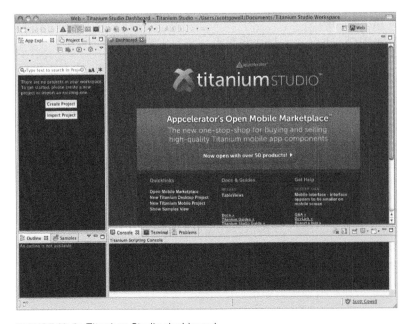

FIGURE 10-6: Titanium Studio dashboard

Fill out the new project form shown in Figure 10-7.

Make sure to fill in the project information as it pertains to your application. Be sure to use the App Id format scheme com.*companyname* .*project.applicationname.*

When picking your App Id, please note the name will be known in perpetuity. It is possible to change this App Id, but you don't want to change the name of your app after you have signed your build or published to the App Markets. The App Id is the unique identifier that Titanium, Google Play, and the iTunes App Store use to determine if you have versioned your product, and if you change the App Id subsequent to release, you can prevent people who have downloaded your app from getting updates.

If you have the iOS SDK installed, and you have added your link to the Android SDK to Titanium

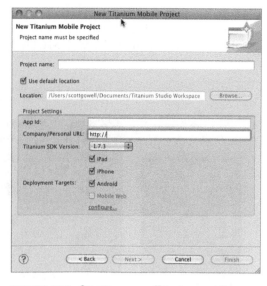

FIGURE 10-7: Creating a new Titanium mobile project

Studio, then the iPad, iPhone, and Android are all available as selectable options at this point.

Once you have completed the new project form, the wizard builds your workspace and drops developers into the TiApp Editor; this enables you to fully customize the Application Configuration file in either a nice graphical interface (see Figure 10-8) or in the XML editor (see Figure 10-9).

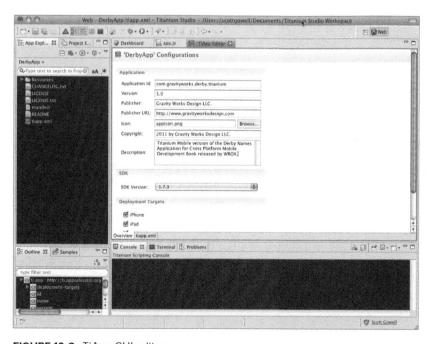

FIGURE 10-8: TiApp GUI editor

Figure 10-8 shows the GUI version of the TiApp Editor. This is an easy point-and-click way to set the values in the TiApp XML file. It exposes the basic options of the configuration file, but for the full feature set you must edit the XML file by hand, as shown in Figure 10-9.

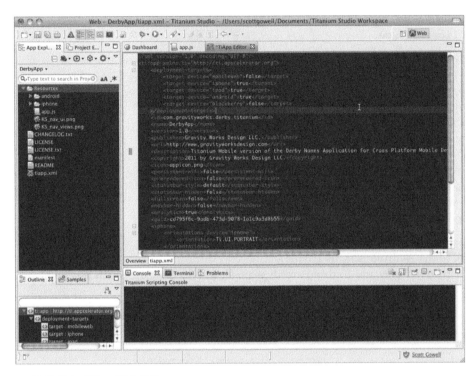

FIGURE 10-9: TiApp XML Editor

At this point you have a "Hello World!" application that can be deployed to any of the target's respective emulators.

Downloading the Kitchen Sink

You can use the Samples tab to import the Kitchen Sink project to get code samples for different UI elements. It takes a second to fetch the latest version of the Kitchen Sink from the Git repository.

Otherwise, you can get it yourself from the Appcelerator GitHub repository (`https://github.com/appcelerator/KitchenSink`).

In the Kitchen Sink application you get an example of all of the UI elements afforded in Titanium with an application you can run in the emulator to test how it will render. This is invaluable when starting, because it can quickly demonstrate the basic navigation as it is handled in the different platforms, and provide the code to account for it.

Development

From this point on the chapter discusses the application layout and gives an explanation of Titanium as a whole.

Project Structure

The layout of the project is displayed in the Application Explorer tab as shown in Figure 10-9. The options are:

➤ **Resources:** All project elements go in this folder. Each separate app pane can be held in a single JavaScript file, to include later. I recommend creating a separate folder for images, styles, and database scripts under this folder.

➤ **android:** This is the folder to use when building specifically for Android. It holds your Android-specific UI elements.

➤ **iPhone:** This is the folder to use specifically when building for iPhone. It holds all of your iPhone-specific UI elements.

➤ **app.js:** This runs when the application is started. It contains all your references to other classes, views, UI elements, and databases, and is where all of your global variables are declared. This is where you include your windows from the resources folder.

Covered next are the basics of Titanium and how you will use it to develop your mobile applications.

Titanium Basics

When you mention JavaScript to most web developers, they cringe. Most times, in fact, it's not JavaScript they hate, it's the document object model (DOM) of most web browsers that causes cross-browser inconsistencies. When it comes down to it, JavaScript is a beautiful language with many advanced programming concepts, taking many concepts from the functional world but staying true to its roots as an OO language. JavaScript was initially created to add interactivity to web pages. Titanium handles UI events and builds the UI as well. JavaScript is a loosely typed language, so all variables and function references are declared with the var keyword.

Variables, classes, and functions are global unless properly namespaced: be sure to remember this when you are naming elements in your application.

Namespaces are how you prevent naming collisions due to the global nature of JavaScript. A namespace is a wrapper that persists your scope.

The following code shows two examples of creating a namespace around a variable and creating a function. The first is the simplest form, directly and specifically creating each part of the object. The second is a more elegant form, initializing the namespace with the intended field and function.

```
var testNS = {};
testNS.name = "Namespace Test";
testNS.hello = new function(){
  return 'Hello from ' + testNS.name;
};
```

or

```
var testNS = {
name: "Namespace Test";
hello: function(){
  return 'Hello from ' + testNS.name;
  }
};
```

Getting into Titanium specifically with JavaScript, you can create a button element to the window with "Click Me" as the title of the button. The next step is to add an event listener to catch the click event. Finally, add the button to the main window and show that window. This is standard practice in Titanium. I recommend that you create a separate file for each window you want to have in your application, and a file that is included to hold all of your UI element declarations. By doing that you can leave the window class itself to event handler functions and other per-page processing functions.

```
Titanium.UI.setBackgroundColor('#000');
var mainWindow = Ti.UI.createWindow({
    title:'Roster',
    backgroundColor:'#fff'
});

var btnHello = Titanium.UI.createButton({
    title: 'Click Me'
})

btnHello.addEventListener('click',function(e)
{
    Titanium.API.info("Button was clicked");
    alert('Hello World!');
});

mainWindow.add(btnHello);
mainWindow.show();
```

Creating User interfaces

`Titanium.include()` is the main way to include views in your application. Effectively no different than a `script` tag in an HTML page, `Titanium.include()` allows for separation of concerns with the resource allocation to happen in one place. Examples of this are shown later in the chapter.

Basic UI Elements in Titanium

All of the elements mentioned in this section are the specifically called out in the Titanium API documentation. I have gone over each individually so that you can feel comfortable with them before starting development.

➤ `ActivityIndicator`: This element is the platform-specific activity throbber represented in the status bar of your device.

➤ `Button`: This is the standard button element.

➤ DashboardItem: This is a very specific element that is rendered in the UI view type DashboardView. It is effectively an image that can be moved around the UI when in a DashboardView, and can have a badge overlay (like the mail icon in iOS).

➤ ImageView: This is the standard image element.

➤ Label: This is the standard UI element for labels. (Noneditable text displayed in your view.)

➤ ProgressBar: Everyone's favorite element to hate, this is a highly customizable UI element to show relative completion metrics.

➤ SearchBar: This is the OS-specific search bar exposed in Titanium. It melds the search button and text field together in a single UI element. It has all of the main event handlers for managing click, change, and blur events.

➤ Slider: This provides granular selection for the user when working with things like volume, opacity, or anything that requires a fine level of control.

➤ Switch: Represented by the on/off slider, and a checkbox on/off on iOS and Android respectively, this is the UI element to represent boolean states.

➤ TextArea, TextField: These are the standard editable text objects. Use TextArea for multi-line and TextField for single line.

Basic UI View Elements in Titanium

The following elements are types of views and containers to be used inside your Titanium app.

➤ AlertDialog: This is the modal window that is created by an alert('message') call. You can also reference it by using the createAlertDialog function.

➤ ScollView: A ScrollView is a section within a window that you want to be able to scroll. It is limited in that it can scroll on only one axis at a time.

➤ ScrollableView: A ScrollableView is a container that holds one or more views that can be scrolled horizontally. This is a control you would use to represent page flips. It also has a built-in paging control that you can use to show the active page index.

➤ View: This is a basic container. It renders on a window, and holds all of your UI objects.

➤ WebView: This is a View that renders valid web content. It allows you to open local or remote content. It is not limited to just HTML; it can open PDF and SVG as well.

➤ Window: This is the highest level container. This is what is used to represent each individual pane of your application.

➤ CoverFlowView: This view creates a slideshow-style view for the images associated with it. It provides a horizontal scroll action by default that lets you cycle through your images.

➤ DashboardView: This view renders DashboardItem objects in a grid like the iOS main screen.

➤ OptionDialog: This view renders a modal to the user with a set of possible selections.

➤ EmailDialog: This view renders a modal containing the OS-specific send email layout.

Basic UI Data/Layout Elements in Titanium

This section covers layout elements that are specifically for data sets and to organize views within your application.

➤ `ButtonBar`, `TabbedBar`, `Toolbar`: These elements are used to represent options that could be used on multiple panes. The `ButtonBar` element renders similarly to most bottom option bars on iOS applications. The difference between the `ButtonBar` and the `TabbedBar` is that the `TabbedBar` persists its state visually.

➤ `Picker`, `PickerColumn`, `PickerRow`: This element and its children are used to create the option picker UI element. By default it renders only a single piece of data per row, but by specifying picker columns in each picker row you can provide many different selectors. `PickerColumns` are items within the `PickerRows` that are children of the picker element.

➤ `Tab`, `TabGroup`: `TabGroups` are containers for tabs, and tabs contain windows. When using a `TabGroup` (while it is active), it is the main container for your UI.

➤ `TableView`, `TableViewRow`, `TableViewSection`: A `TableView` is the standard UI element for holding tabular data. The `TableViewRows` are its children, and the `TableViewSection` allows you to create headers for groups of rows.

➤ `2DMatrix`, `3DMatrix`: These objects hold values for affine transformation matrices. These are used to rotate, scale, and translate (and in 3-D, skew) the objects in a two-dimensional and three-dimensional space, respectively.

Debugging

The `Titanium.API` module provides lots of options for logging of events:

➤ `Ti.API.debug()`: Pass messages to the console that you want to treat as debug notes.

➤ `Ti.API.error()`: Pass messages to the console for error states.

➤ `Ti.API.info()`: Pass messages to the console for success or nondebug.

➤ `Ti.API.log()`: Pass messages to the console for custom severity issues.

➤ `Ti.API.warn()`: Pass messages to the console for when nonerror issues arise.

Titanium Studio is bundled by default from Titanium Mobile SDK 1.7 onward. It is an IDE that contains the build tools from Titanium's original developer package and also has a very powerful debugger. Set a breakpoint and click the green bug to debug in the emulator of your choosing. Also, when running in debug mode, Titanium will break on uncaught exceptions or parse errors. The error messages are generally enough to get you in the right direction, but it can sometimes take a couple of passes to see what they are getting at.

CONNECTING TITANIUM TO THE MARKETS

You will need to have a Developer account for Apple and Android before deploying to the respective app markets. Signing up for an Apple Developer account is explained in Chapter 7, and signing up for Google Play Developer account is covered in Chapter 6.

In the Project Explorer window, depicted in Figure 10-10, right-click the project you want to deploy and select the appropriate deploy action.

To distribute a build to the iTunes App Store you will need to cut a release build. Just like building for development, an option is afforded you in the Titanium Studio interface (see Figure 10-11).

The first four options of this form are outlined in Chapter 7. Next, you must select the SDK version in which you want your final build to be compiled. After that it asks for your Distribution Certificate; this is stored in your keychain. The last option asks where you would like your compiled file to be stored after building.

Figure 10-11 shows the Distribute — App Store option.

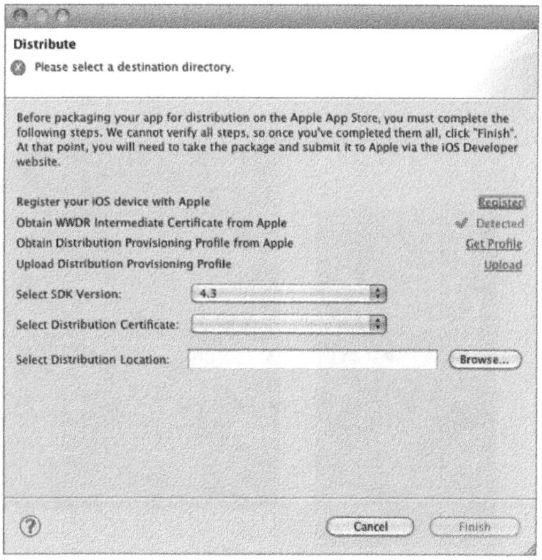

To distribute a build to Google Play, you will need to cut a release build. Just like building for development, you are given an option in the Titanium Studio interface (see Figure 10-12). Your distribution location is the folder where you want your build to be saved. The keystore location is the place on your filesystem where the keystore file is saved. The keystore password is the password that you set up when creating your keystore.

This differs from the iOS flow in that you must also sign your application. A certificate will be generated based on your passphrase, and it will be tied to the App Id set up for the application. Changing the App Id of this application after market release will prevent application updates or maintenance.

Obtaining a key for your application requires the Java KeyTool program, distributed with the Android SDK; instructions for use are available at http://developer.android.com/guide/publishing/app-signing.html#cert.

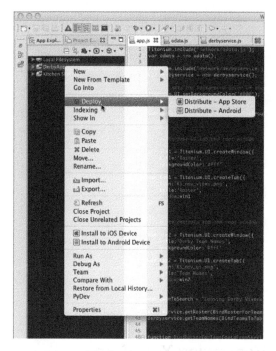

FIGURE 10-10: The Deploy menu

FIGURE 10-11: Setting up iTunes deploy

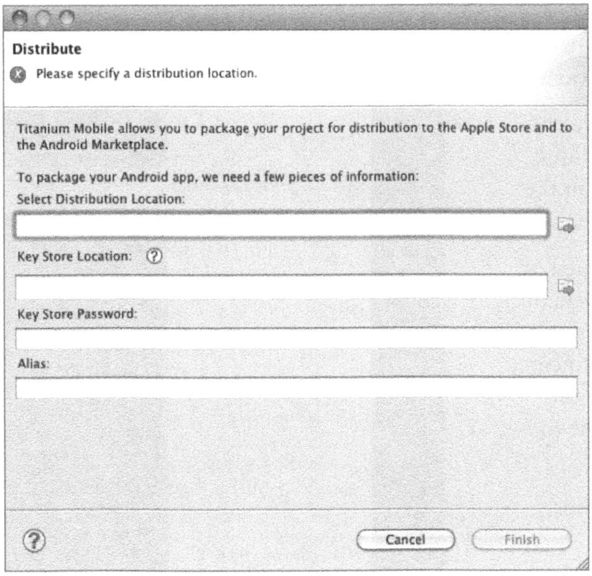

Distribute
Please specify a distribution location.
Titanium Mobile allows you to package your project for distribution to the Apple Store and to the Android Marketplace.
To package your Android app, we need a few pieces of information:
Select Distribution Location:
Key Store Location:
Key Store Password:
Alias:
Cancel
Finish

FIGURE 10-12: Setting up Android deploy

Versioning Your App

Versioning your app is quite simple. Open your `TiApp.xml` file and update the `version` parameter (pointed out in Figure 10-13). This is not exposed in the graphical editor, so you will need to do this by hand. This number will also be used to update your app in the stores.

Dashboard
app.js
Overview
tiapp.xml
Console
Terminal
Problems
Titanium Scripting Console
Outline
Samples

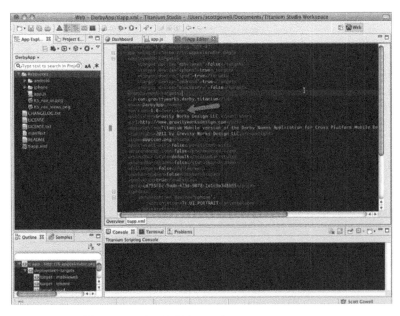

FIGURE 10-13: Version number in TiApp.xml

Once this is set you are ready to begin building your application.

BUILDING THE DERBY APP IN TITANIUM

The same patterns explained in the native application chapters are used to develop the Derby Names application, only this time in Titanium. You create the UI, using some of the device features (GPS, Accelerometer), and communicating with the web service you created in Chapter 3.

Common UI Patterns

This section discusses the basic patterns in mobile applications: standard ways to represent data, make selections, navigation patterns, and display quick alerts to the user.

Tables

The Table UI element is the standard way to display data.

You can bind JSON objects directly to tables (as long as they have a `title` element):

```
var data = [{title:"Row 1"},{title:"Row 2"}];
var table = Titanium.UI.createTableView({data:data});
win.add(table);
```

Or you can bind arrays of `TableViewRow` objects. When you create a `TableViewRow` object you can assign other UI elements to the row as well:

```
function BindTeamsToTable(dataFromService)
{
var dataToBind = [];
Ti.API.info(JSON.stringify(dataFromService));
for (var i=0; i<dataFromService.length; i++)
{
  var leagueName = dataFromService[i].LeagueName;
  var rowToAdd = Ti.UI.createTableViewRow(
  {
     title: leagueName, //main field to be bound and rendered
     hasChild: true //Show child arrow
  }
);
rowToAdd.addEventListener('click', function(){
  teamToSearch = this.title;
  derbyservice.getRoster(BindRosterForTeam, teamToSearch);
  tabGroup.setActiveTab(0);
  });
dataToBind.push(rowToAdd);
}
var table = Ti.UI.createTableView({height: 368, top: 0, data: dataToBind});
win2.add(table);
}
```

If you have large sets of data to bind, this `table` element will be your go-to UI to display the data to your users.

 The Table UI element is significantly different from the HTML table element, so please don't confuse one with the other. Whereas modern web development frowns upon the use of tables for layout, using tables to display data in mobile applications is commonplace.

Pickers

The `picker` UI object illustrates some of the differences between how Titanium generates UI elements for iOS versus Android.

By default, the iOS element represented by this `picker` is a spinner (a date picker in iOS), whereas in Android the element represented by this `picker` is, by default, a drop-down. Titanium handles this by adding the `usespinner` property to the create method for this picker, but here you run the risk of maintaining parity between look and feel inside your app versus look and feel consistent with the OS on which your app is running. Additionally, although you can add custom views to your rows of the `picker` in Titanium, they will not be rendered on the Android version.

```
var picker = Titanium.UI.createPicker();
var dataToBind = [];
dataToBind[0]=Titanium.UI.createPickerRow({title:'Nose'});
dataToBind[1]=Titanium.UI.createPickerRow({title:'Friends'});
//dataToBind[2]=Titanium.UI.createPickerRow({title:'Friend\'s Nose'});
//You can't pick this.
picker.add(dataToBind);
```

 You can find more examples in the Kitchen Sink; try running both the iOS version and the Android version simultaneously to see these differences.

Using a `picker` provides users a uniform way to enter data quickly.

Navigation (Back Stack) and Tab Groups

In iOS you need to have a back button on a child view. It is not only standard in the OS, it is expected. As stated in the Apple Human Interface Guidelines (`http://developer` `.apple.com/library/ios/#DOCUMENTATION/UserExperience/Conceptual/MobileHIG/` `UIElementGuidelines/UIElementGuidelines.html`):

You can use a navigation bar to enable navigation among different views, or provide controls that manage the items in a view.

Use the title of the current view as the title of the navigation bar. When the user navigates to a new level, two things should happen:

➤ *The bar title should change to the new level's title.*

➤ *A back button should appear to the left of the title, and it should be labeled with the previous level's title.*

If users can navigate down a path, developers need to provide a simple way of going back up the stack. Additionally, navigation back up the stack may involve persisting state as well, so be sure to account for whether a given view's state needs to be persisted when retracing a user's steps through the navigation stack. In Android, the hardware back button and the OS persist state and the "back stack" for you. That being said, if you have a back button in your UI, make sure that it is not displayed when on an Android device, because it will be considered unnecessary and sloppy.

When using tab groups the standard UI layout differs between iOS and Android. iOS displays tabs inside apps on the bottom. There is generally a black background with some see-through icons, and the tab highlights blue when selected (either the background of the tab or the icon on top). In Android, the tab navigation is almost always rendered on the top, with black and gray being the colors used to represent active and inactive. This only goes to further demonstrate the need for the Android and iPhone project subdirectories, to distinguish device-based and OS-specific layouts.

```
var win1 = Titanium.UI.createWindow({
    title:'Roster',
    backgroundColor:'#fff'
});
var tab1 = Titanium.UI.createTab({
    icon:'KS_nav_views.png',
    title:'Roster',
    window:win1
});

var win2 = Titanium.UI.createWindow({
    title:'Derby Team Names',
    backgroundColor:'#fff'
});
var tab2 = Titanium.UI.createTab({
    icon:'KS_nav_ui.png',
    title:'Team Names',
    window:win2
});

tabGroup.addTab(tab1);
tabGroup.addTab(tab2);

tabGroup.open();
```

First you create your two basic windows, and bind them to tab elements. Once bound, you add those tabs to the group of tabs. This builds your clickable UI for you.

Modal Forms

Modal forms are most commonly used to break away from your UI while communicating with a third-party source. This could be authenticating with OAuth or OpenID, publishing content to a social network, or anytime you want to lock the UI for the user.

```
var modal = Titanium.UI.createWindow();
modal.open({
modal: true, //Set it as modal
navBarHidden: true, //Hide the UI Chrome
fullscreen: false //Make sure that it isn't rendered full screen.
})
```

The preceding code creates a new modal window. It will show up over top of the current window, and not display any of the standard UI for a window element.

Alerts

There is a lot to be said for the value of a simple alert modal. Calling one is simple. A straight `Javascript:alert('message');` renders out as an OS native message. That being said, it is best not to have this as the only way to communicate data to app users, because alerts block the UI and prevent things from happening behind the scenes. And queuing multiple, successive alerts can potentially put your UI in a very unmanageable state. Tread with caution.

```
var message = "Greetings Program!";
alert(message);
```

You are also afforded the `OptionDialog` view for displaying alerts that require a response. The following code snippet shows how to create an alert that requires a response. Setting the `cancel` property to `-1` denotes that there is no cancel action in the list of potential options:

```
var dialog = Titanium.UI.createOptionDialog({
    title: 'Trick Question - Did you walk to school, or buy your lunch?',
    options: ['Walked to School','Bought my Lunch'],
    cancel:-1
});
dialog.show();
dialog.addEventListener('click', new function(e){
//e.index = index of option selected.
});
```

Once you have built your user interface, you will need to bind data to it. The following options show the ways you can get data onto the device.

Offline Storage

Offline storage refers to any data that you will persist on the device. It can be as simple as a property bag, storing key-value pairs, or updating resource files, or it can be as complex as a full SQLite database.

SQLite

Titanium provides the developer with an interface to store data. This is exposed through the `Titanium.Database` namespace. You can create a database programmatically, but I would recommend installing one from a SQLite script in your resources folder:

```
var db = Ti.Database.install('../derbygirls.sqlite','derbyGirls');
```

Once the database is on the device, make standard CRUD calls using the SQLite syntax:

```
var teamName = 'Lansing Derby Vixens';

var rows = db.execute('SELECT * FROM DerbyNames WHERE TeamName="' + teamName + '"');
var data = [
{title:'' + rows.fieldByName('Name') + ' - ' + rows.fieldByName('JerseyNumber') + ''}];

var derbyNameTable = Ti.UI.createTableView({
    data:data
});

var currentWindow = Ti.UI.currentWindow;
currentWindow.add(derbyNameTable);
```

If you do not need to store relational data sets, but still want to store large pieces of information or content, the option afforded to you is Isolated Storage.

Isolated Storage

In most mobile SDKs you are allowed a sandboxed area of the filesystem most commonly known as isolated storage. Titanium exposes this functionality through its `Titanium.Filesystem` namespace.

Reasons to use isolated storage would be to store resources downloaded remotely or saving large data sets outside of a database environment. The following code looks on the filesystem and if it finds it adds it to the specified window.

```
for (var i = 0; i < derbyTeams.Length; i++)
{
  var teamLogo = Titanium.Filesystem.getFile(derbyTeams[i].TeamId + '.jpg');
  if (!teamLogo.exists())
  {
    Ti.API.error("We have not loaded a logo for this team yet.");
    return;
```

```
    }
    else{
      var logoItem = Ti.UI.createImageView(
        {
        image: teamLogo,
        height: auto,
        width: auto
        });

      win1.add(logoItem);
    }
}
```

Preferences and Settings

Using the Property Bag (Preferences and Settings) is the simplest form of offline storage available. It is mostly used for storing authentication tokens and default display parameters. With the `Titanium.App.Properties` namespace, you can persist these properties between application runs. The following code shows how to save and retrieve properties from the property bag.

```
//Setting the UserName
Ti.App.Properties.setString("username","derbyfan419");
//Getting the Hashed Password from Property Bag
var hashedPassword = Ti.App.Properties.getString("password");
```

Storing lots of information on your device can be time-consuming and difficult to maintain, so often applications query data from a remote location. Web services provide an easy way to retrieve these sets of data.

Web Service

This section shows examples to query from the web service created in Chapter 3, discusses formatting the data to be read by Titanium, and describes some of the "gotchas" that occur in platform-specific calls to a web service.

JSON Is Your Friend

Chapter 3 discussed the technology used to create the web service, but — platforms aside — what you really need to wrap your head around is JavaScript Object Notation (JSON). JSON is a simplified way to store your data in a serializable way over the wire, while still following the structure of the initial object. The service you use outputs JSON to parse in the app. A great resource to see how a JSON object is outlined is the Json Parser Online (`http://json.parser.online.fr/`), as shown in Figure 10-14.

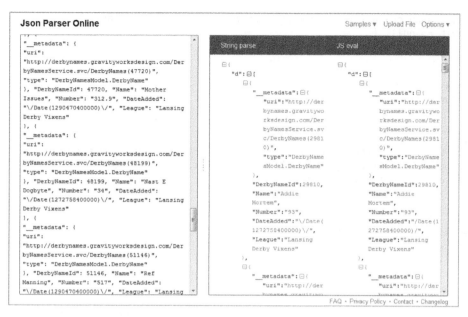

FIGURE 10-14: Json Parser Online

The JSON parser gives you a nice visualization of the object, and shows any parsing errors. Effectively an array of dictionaries (key-value pairs), a JSON object can provide you with an entire object graph with little overhead.

Something to note at this point: when building up URLs to send in an XHR request in Titanium for Android (at least as of Titanium version 1.7), you have to do some postprocessing to it before passing it to be sent. If you are building for iPhone, you don't have to worry. The following code shows the call necessary to format these request strings for Android.

```
if (Titanium.Platform.name == 'android') {
  requestString = requestString.replace(/\s/g, '%20');
}
```

What follows is the `odata` object that holds the `getData` function. When retrieving data from the service, pass the parameters to it, parse the response as JSON, and then pass it to the `successFunction` callback to bind the data to the window:

```
function odata(){
this.getData = function (requestString, successFunction){
    if (Titanium.Platform.name == 'android') {
        requestString = requestString.replace(/\s/g, '%20');
    }
var xhr = Titanium.Network.createHTTPClient();
xhr.onload = function () {
  var response = JSON.parse(this.responseText);
  var result = response.d.results;
```

```
//for some reason oData will return it both ways, in .d and .d.results
  if (result == null) {
    result = response.d;
  }

var gotData = new Date();
  successFunction(result);
};

xhr.onerror = function (e) {
  Titanium.UI.createAlertDialog({ title: 'Error retrieving data', message:
'An error occurred retrieving data. Please try later.' }).show();
  Titanium.API.error(requestString);
};

  xhr.open('GET', requestString);
  xhr.setRequestHeader('Accept', 'application/json');
  var send = new Date();
  xhr.send();

}
```

This class is included in `app.js` so that all other windows can call into it statically if necessary:

```
Titanium.include('network/odata.js');
var odata = new odata();
```

Next is the `derbyservice` class, which is also included in `app.js`:

```
Titanium.include('network/derbyservice.js');
var derbyservice = new derbyservice();
```

It provides the method calls in the views to get data to bind:

```
function derbyservice(){
  var baseServiceUrl =
  "http://derbynames.gravityworksdesign.com/DerbyNamesService.svc/";
  this.getAllNames = function (successFunction)
    {
    var serviceString = baseServiceUrl + "DerbyNames";
    odata.getData(serviceString, successFunction);
    }

  this.getTeamNames = function(successFunction)
  {
      var serviceString = baseServiceUrl + "Leagues";
      odata.getData(serviceString, successFunction);
  }

  this.getRoster = function (successFunction, leagueName)
  {
      var serviceString = baseServiceUrl +
```

```
     "DerbyNames?$filter=League eq '" + leagueName + "'";
     odata.getData(serviceString, successFunction);
   }
}
```

Now that you have a way to get data, this section discusses using location to pare down or request data.

GPS

As more and more people get smartphones with built-in GPS devices, the call for location-based content, information, games, social media integration, and driving directions is expected. Titanium does provide access to the metal for talking with the GPS. The methods to access GPS are available in the `Titanium.Geolocation` namespace within Titanium Mobile.

Depending on your usage, the geolocation API allows you to set the accuracy of the GPS data returned. You are afforded multiple options: Best, Nearest Ten Meters, Hundred Meters, Kilometer, and Three Kilometers. It is best practice to set your accuracy to one of these options prior to accessing the GPS:

```
     Titanium.Geolocation.accuracy = Titanium.Geolocation.ACCURACY_BEST;
```

The GPS also has an understanding of how far the device has moved, and triggers an update event when the threshold of the distance filter has been crossed. Distance Filter is a double, and it is in meters. Default, if nothing, is set to 0, which means GPS update events are continuously fired.

```
     Titanium.Geolocation.distanceFilter = 15.24; //50 Feet
```

To get the position as reported by the GPS, you must call the `Geolocation` function `getCurrentPosition`. It provides object location with the following properties: `latitude`, `longitude`, `altitude`, `accuracy`, `altitudeAccuracy`, `heading`, `speed`, and `timestamp`. The `location` property contains the following subproperties: `magneticHeading`, `trueHeading`, `accuracy`, `x`, `y`, `z`, and `timestamp`. The following code shows how to query the current position of the device and check with the web service to see what teams are close to your location:

```
     var cityToQueryBy = 'Lansing';

     Titanium.Geolocation.getCurrentPosition(function(e)
     {
         var latitude = e.coords.latitude;
         var longitude = e.coords.longitude;
         var altitude = e.coords.altitude;
         var accuracy = e.coords.accuracy;
         var altitudeAccuracy = e.coords.altitudeAccuracy;
         var heading = e.coords.heading;
         var speed = e.coords.speed;
         var timestamp = e.coords.timestamp;

         //This turns your location into a human readable object
         Titanium.Geolocation.reverseGeocoder(latitude, longitude, geolocationCallback);
```

```
});

function geolocationCallback(data)
{
    var places = data.places;
    if (places.length > 0)
    {
    cityToQueryBy = places[0].city;
    }

    derbyService.getTeamsByCity(cityToQueryBy, bindDataCallback);
}

function bindDataCallback(data)
{
  if (data.length > 0)
  {
    //There were teams based on your search criteria bind them to a UI element.
  }
}

//This would live in derbyservice.js
this.getAllNames = function (queryVal, successFunction)
{
    //OData Filter to look for Teams by City By Name
    var serviceString = baseServiceUrl +
    "DerbyNames?$filter=League like '%" + queryVal + "%'";
    odata.getData(serviceString, successFunction);
}
```

You can use a `headingfilter` as opposed to a `distancefilter` to track only where the user is going, versus information about where the user is. Difference in use cases would be a location-based application (foursquare), versus a heading-based app (compass).

Now that you understand location-based events, the next section discusses interactions with your device.

Accelerometer

Both the iPhone and Android devices have a built-in accelerometer and Titanium has an API for accessing it. The `Titanium.Accelerometer` namespace provides access for adding an event listener to read the coordinates of the accelerometer data, but the Appcelerator documentation recommends that you remove the event listener when not in use.

Common uses for accelerometer data include triggering aspect changes (portrait to landscape), triggering media (turn the ringer off when the phone headset is set down), and randomizing navigation (spin the wheel, or shake to refresh).

Here is a basic example of checking your accelerometer data on the x-axis:

```
var shakeCount = 5;
var xShakes = [];

Titanium.Accelerometer.addEventListener('update',function(e)
    {
    if (shakeCount > 0)
    {
        Ti.API.debug("accelerometer - x:"+e.x+",y:"+e.y+",z:"+e.z);
        xShakes.push(e.x);
        shakeCount--;
    }
    else
    {
        Ti.Accelerometer.removeEventListener('update');
        WhipItGood(xShakes[0], xShakes[3]);
    }
}
});

var shakeThreshold = 1.5;
function WhipItGood(int x1, int x2)
    {
    if((x1 - x2) >= Math.abs(shakeThreshold))
    {
        Ti.API.info("It can be said that on the x axis this device has been Whipped
        well.");
        GetRandomDerbyPlayer();
    }
}

function GetRandomDerbyPlayer()
{
    //Get a random Number (at last count our record count was around 25k
    var randomNumber=Math.floor(Math.random()*25001)
    derbyService.getDerbyPlayerById(randomNumber, randomDerbyCallback);
}

function randomDerbyCallback(data)
{
  if (data.length > 0)
  {
  //You received a random derby player.
  }
}

//This would live in derbyservice.js
this.getDerbyPlayerById = function (queryVal, successFunction)
{
    //OData Filter to look for Teams BY City BY Name
    var serviceString = baseServiceUrl +
    "DerbyNames?$filter=DerbyNameId eq '" + queryVal + "'";
    odata.getData(serviceString, successFunction);
}
```

SUMMARY

Titanium is not a magic bullet. It is a solid framework for developing a single codebase to deploy to multiple platforms. In addition, it allows developers to use a language they are more familiar with to create apps in a domain outside of their knowledge. Titanium is not an exact match to native languages. Not all features of the mobile platforms are exposed (or can necessarily be exposed) in its API. With the addition of Titanium Studio, developing in the framework has grown by leaps and bounds. The team at Appcelerator works to pack as much functionality into their framework as possible. Titanium is an excellent tool to learn mobile device programming, and for many projects can provide the necessary functionality to deliver a finished product.

11

Getting Started with PhoneGap

WHAT'S IN THIS CHAPTER?

➤ History of PhoneGap

➤ Differences between HTML5 and PhoneGap

➤ Getting a development environment set up

➤ Implementing the Derby App

PhoneGap is an open source set of tools created by Nitobi Solutions (now part of Adobe) that enables you to create mobile applications for multiple devices by utilizing the same code. PhoneGap is a hybrid mobile application framework that allows the use of HTML, CSS, and JavaScript to write applications that are based on the open standards of the web. These applications also have access to the native functionality of the device. PhoneGap has been downloaded more than 600,000 times, and more than 1,000 apps built with PhoneGap are available in the respective app stores, which makes PhoneGap a viable solution for creating cross-platform mobile apps.

HISTORY OF PHONEGAP

PhoneGap was started at the San Francisco iPhone Dev Camp in August 2008. iOS was shaping up to become a popular mobile platform, but the learning curve for Objective-C was more work than many developers wanted to take on. PhoneGap originally started as a headless browser implementation for the iPhone. Because of the popularity of HTML/CSS/JavaScript, it was a goal that this project use technologies with which many developers where already familiar.

Based on the growing popularity of the framework, in October 2008 Nitobi added support for Android and BlackBerry. PhoneGap was awarded the People's Choice award at the Web2.0 Expo Launch Pad in 2009, which was the start of developers recognizing PhoneGap as a valuable mobile development tool. PhoneGap version 0.7.2 was released in April 2009, and was the first version for which the Android and iPhone APIs were equivalent.

In September 2009 Apple approved the use of the PhoneGap platform to build apps for the iPhone store. Apple required that all PhoneGap apps be built using at least version 0.8.0 of the PhoneGap software. In July 2011, PhoneGap released version 1.0.0.

WHY USE PHONEGAP?

PhoneGap enables you to leverage your current HTML, CSS, and JavaScript skill sets to create a mobile application. This can greatly speed up development time. When you develop for multiple platforms using PhoneGap, you can reuse the majority of the code you have written for the mobile project, further reducing development costs. It isn't necessary to learn Java, C#, and Objective-C to create an application with PhoneGap that can target iPhone, Android, BlackBerry, and Windows Phone 7.

If you find native functionality missing from PhoneGap, you can extend the functionality of the PhoneGap platform using native code. With the PhoneGap add-in structure, you can create an add-in using the native language of the device and a JavaScript API that will call the native plug-in you created. Cross-platform development enables developers to maximize the amount of resources they are able to share. As the iOS and Android user base grows, this concept becomes more important.

WHO IS USING PHONEGAP?

Adopting a nonnative framework can be scary for a variety of reasons, such as stability and feature parity. Oftentimes, seeing other large projects created with the same framework will help alleviate some worries you may have. PhoneGap has recently released an updated showcase of applications built on its technology. Notable applications include an iOS application called METAR Reader, a cross-platform tool from Logitech for controlling its Squeezebox player on Android, iPad, or iPhone, and the official Android Wikipedia app.

METAR Reader

METAR Reader (`http://www.METARReader.com`) is a website for searching for and translating the Meteorological Terminal Aviation Routine Weather Report (METAR) weather data from airports and meteorological sites. The iOS app takes the branded interface of the METARReader.com website and ties into all the functionality the device can offer. Don't know your local airport's FAA identifier? Use your phone's GPS to find nearby airfields. You can then request their METAR information and convert it to human-readable format using this tool. The METAR Reader is currently available in the Apple iOS App Store. Figure 11-1 shows the clean UI that was created in PhoneGap for the METAR app.

FIGURE 11-1: METAR Reader PhoneGap app

Logitech Squeezebox Controller

Logitech Squeezebox is a network music player. The entire line of products can be controlled remotely from this multiplatform app. With a consistent look and feel between iOS and Andriod, this application leverages the quick deployment power of PhoneGap. The interfaces are nearly identical while still affording for the differences in screen resolution and platform idiosyncrasies. Figure 11-2 shows the interface for the Squeezebox controller.

Wikipedia

It really says something when a site like Wikipedia uses PhoneGap for its platform of choice for a mobile application. Because the appeal of Wikipedia has always been its use of hypertext, breaking that feel is no different than changing a brand. Simplicity expressed through text while still being a self-contained application is shown in Figure 11-3.

FIGURE 11-2: Logitech Squeezebox PhoneGap app

The next section discusses the differences between how PhoneGap works with the HTML5 standard and how HTML5 behaves on the web.

DIFFERENCES BETWEEN PHONEGAP AND HTML5

Because PhoneGap uses HTML5 as its base, it has access to any HTML5 features that are available in the web framework for the device that is running the application. One of the differences between PhoneGap and HTML5 is in the additional device interactions that are available in PhoneGap. These features can involve anything that talks to the bare metal of the device (sensors specifically), or more of a logical solution such as Push Notifications or In App Purchases. Another difference between PhoneGap and HTML5 is that PhoneGap implements the features the same way across the different devices, so that accessing the GPS function is handled with the same JavaScript for all PhoneGap devices. It doesn't matter if you are using the iPhone, Android, BlackBerry, or Windows Phone 7 GPS functions; the calls to get the data from the GPS are the same. The other difference between a PhoneGap app and HTML5 is that an application built with PhoneGap is compiled to a native app on the device, and can be used on the device without the Internet.

FIGURE 11-3: Wikipedia PhoneGap app

GETTING THE TOOLS YOU NEED

Even though PhoneGap applications are created using HTML, CSS, and JavaScript, you still need to have the native environments and SDKs installed for the platforms for which you want to develop. If you want your PhoneGap app to run on iOS, you need to have a Mac and have the xCode environment set up as well.

PhoneGap provides great "Get Started" pages for each platform. The documentation provided within the interface will be everything you need to get up and running with PhoneGap. The interface shown in Figure 11-4 makes it easy to find resources as you need them. To get started with PhoneGap, download the PhoneGap SDK at `http://phonegap.com/download`.

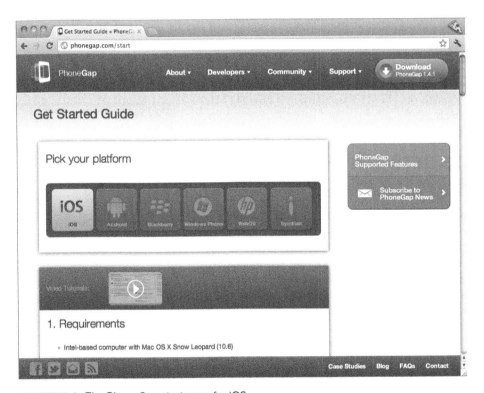

FIGURE 11-4: The PhoneGap start page for iOS

Installing PhoneGap for iOS

To develop PhoneGap apps for the iOS platform, you must install xCode and the iOS SDK. Chapter 7 discusses installing xCode and the iOS in depth.

Installing the PhoneGap Template

With PhoneGap downloaded and unarchived, navigate to the iOS directory of the extracted directories and run the PhoneGap `.pkg` installer shown in Figure 11-5.

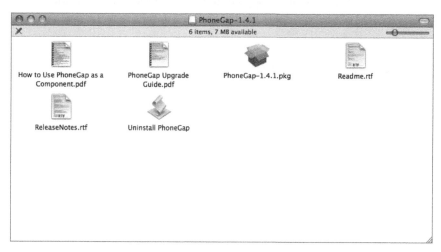

FIGURE 11-5: The PhoneGap iOS package

Creating Your First iOS PhoneGap Project

With the PhoneGap template installed, launch xCode and select Application from the iOS section, then select PhoneGap-based Application as shown in Figure 11-6.

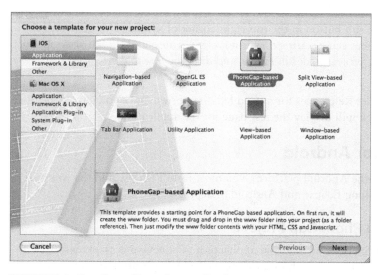

FIGURE 11-6: Creating a PhoneGap application

Fill out the project template as shown in Figure 11-7:

➤ **Product Name:** Name of your application.

➤ **Company Identifier:** This needs to be unique. Once you have distributed your application, you cannot change this because it will break your ability to upgrade the application.

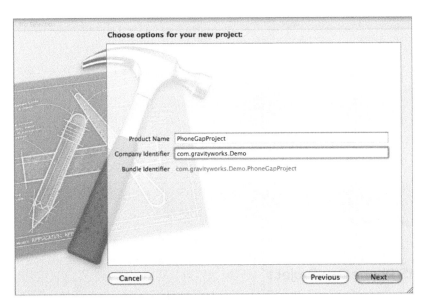

FIGURE 11-7: Selecting names for your PhoneGap project

Next, run the project. Click the run button in the top-right corner of xCode. This generates the www resources directory, but sometimes the www directory is not created automatically. If your application has thrown an error, open your project folder in Finder and drag the www folder to your target application project.

Make sure to select Create Folder References for any added directories. Once you have done this, run your application again and it will display the test page for the application.

Installing PhoneGap for Android

To develop PhoneGap apps for the Android platform, you must install Eclipse and the Android SDK. Chapter 6 discusses installing Eclipse and Android in depth.

Creating Your First Android PhoneGap Project

In Chapter 6 you learned how to create an Android application. PhoneGap is an extension of an Android app. To do this with Eclipse open, choose Create Android Application from the New Project wizard as shown in Figure 11-8.

Once you create the application you must copy some resources from the PhoneGap package into your application. In the root directory of the project, create two new directories named `libs` and `assets/www`.

After you create the directories, copy the following files:

➤ Copy `phonegap.js` from your PhoneGap zip file that was downloaded earlier to `assets/www`.

➤ Copy `phonegap.jar` from your earlier PhoneGap download to `/libs`.

➤ Copy the `xml` folder from your earlier PhoneGap download to `/res`.

The directory structure should look similar to Figure 11-9.

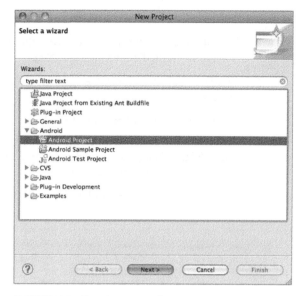

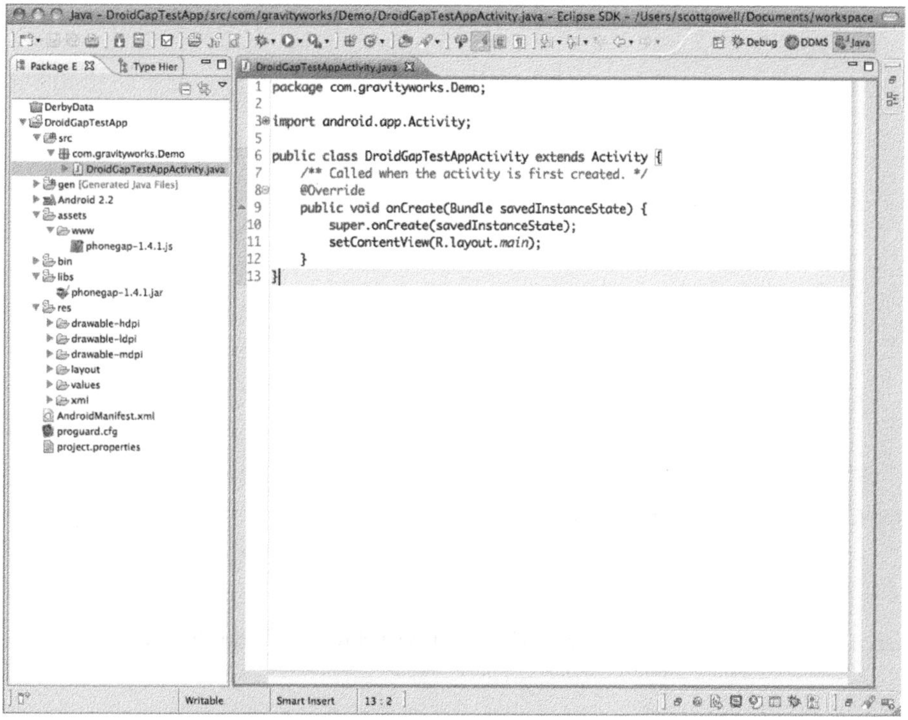

FIGURE 11-8: Creating a new Android project

FIGURE 11-9: Default application after adding resources

To get the PhoneGap framework to build correctly, you now need to make some code changes:

➤ Instead of extending your class from the Android `Activity` class, change your class to extend from the Phone Gap `DroidGap`.

➤ Replace the `setContentView()` line with `super.loadUrl("file:///android_asset/www/index.html");`.

➤ Add `import com.phonegap.*;`.

This may still result in an error. You will need to add the `phonegap.jar` file into your build path. Right-click `phonegap.jar` in your `libs` directory and select Build Path. Then remove `import android.app.Activity;`.

The Android PhoneGap app should look similar to Figure 11-10.

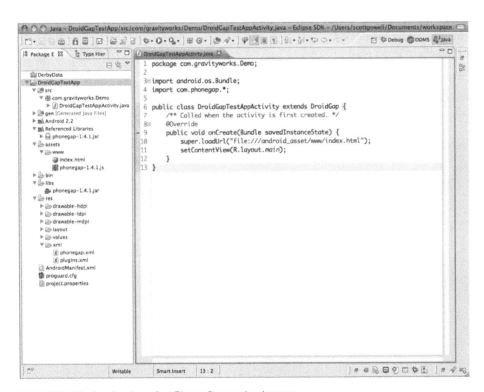

FIGURE 11-10: Application after PhoneGap code changes

Right-click `AndroidManifest.xml`, select Open With ➪ Text Editor, and add the following Android permissions:

```
<uses-permission android:name="android.permission.CAMERA" />
<uses-permission android:name="android.permission.VIBRATE" />
```

```
<uses-permission android:name="android.permission.ACCESS_COARSE_LOCATION" />
<uses-permission android:name="android.permission.ACCESS_FINE_LOCATION" />
<uses-permission android:name="android.permission.ACCESS_LOCATION_EXTRA_COMMANDS" />
<uses-permission android:name="android.permission.READ_PHONE_STATE" />
<uses-permission android:name="android.permission.INTERNET" />
<uses-permission android:name="android.permission.RECEIVE_SMS" />
<uses-permission android:name="android.permission.RECORD_AUDIO" />
<uses-permission android:name="android.permission.MODIFY_AUDIO_SETTINGS" />
<uses-permission android:name="android.permission.READ_CONTACTS" />
<uses-permission android:name="android.permission.WRITE_CONTACTS" />
<uses-permission android:name="android.permission.WRITE_EXTERNAL_STORAGE" />
<uses-permission android:name="android.permission.ACCESS_NETWORK_STATE" />
<uses-permission android:name="android.permission.GET_ACCOUNTS" />
<uses-permission android:name="android.permission.BROADCAST_STICKY" />
```

You are adding all of these permissions so that your application is afforded everything that PhoneGap supports in Android. Generally you would add only the permissions you need at the time you are creating the app, but PhoneGap wants to limit configuration to project start as opposed to as you go.

The last step in this process is to add an index.html file in your assets/www folder with the following content:

```
<!DOCTYPE HTML>
<html>
    <head>
        <title>PhoneGap</title>
        <script type="text/javascript" charset="utf-8" src="phonegap-1.4.1.js">
        </script>
    </head>
    <body>
        <h1>Hello World</h1>
    </body>
</html>
```

Installing PhoneGap for Windows Phone 7

To develop PhoneGap apps for Windows Phone 7, you must install Visual Studio and the Windows Phone SDK. Chapter 8 discusses installing Visual Studio and the Windows Phone SDK in depth.

With the Windows Phone SDK installed, navigate to the Windows Phone directory and copy the PhoneGapStarter.zip file to your templates folder located at C:\Users\username\Documents\ Visual Studio 2010\Templates\ProjectTemplates\Silverlight for Windows Phone as shown in Figure 11-11.

Open Visual Studio and create a new PhoneGapStarter project as shown in Figure 11-12.

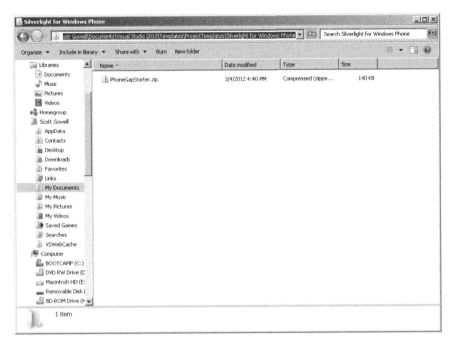

FIGURE 11-11: Visual Studio template directory

FIGURE 11-12: PhoneGapStarter project

Build the application by pressing F5 and the project should run in the emulator as shown in Figure 11-13.

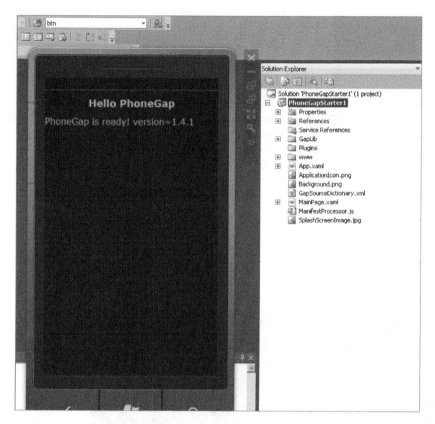

FIGURE 11-13: PhoneGap in Windows 7 emulator

PhoneGap Tools and IDE

Because PhoneGap apps are created using HTML, CSS, and JavaScript, developers are not restricted to the recommended mobile platform IDEs. Every developer and designer has their own set of tools they like to use when creating HTML, CSS, and JavaScript that will work well in the development cycle of PhoneGap apps.

TextMate and Notepad++

The most basic tools that you can use to create a PhoneGap app are text editors. TextMate is a text editor for the Mac, and Notepad++ is a text editor for a Windows computer. Because PhoneGap applications use HTML and JavaScript, a text editor is a tool that can be used across platforms. If you are creating an application for iPhone and Android you can create your code in TextMate.

If you are creating your application for BlackBerry, Windows Phone 7, or Android on Windows you can use Notepad++. Using the same editor for multiple platforms gives you consistency while editing. Both TextMate and Notepad++ offer syntax highlighting and code folding.

You can't build and compile using a text editor, but you can perform a great deal of the testing in a web browser or a tool such as Ripple.

Ripple

Working in an IDE that is not familiar can be very frustrating and a huge waste of time. In many situations it is not acceptable to ask a designer to use xCode or Eclipse, nor would you want to. Working with tools you are comfortable with is one of the great benefits of working with PhoneGap. Ripple might be one such tool. You can get the Ripple emulator from `http://ripple.tinyhippos .com/download`. From the download page, you click Install and then click the Add to Chrome button. Once you have Ripple installed, it will place an icon in your Chrome browser's menu bar, which will run the emulator when it is clicked.

Ripple is a mobile emulator that enables developers/designers to run HTML created for PhoneGap apps without having the platform SDKs installed. Figure 11-14 shows a PhoneGap app running in Ripple.

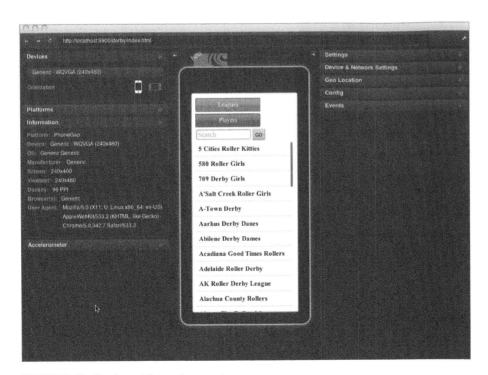

FIGURE 11-14: Ripple mobile environment

Firebug

Firebug is a plug-in for the Firefox browser. You can get Firebug from `https://addons.mozilla.org/en-US/firefox/addon/firebug/`. Because it is a Firefox extension, you just have to click on the Add to Firefox button. Firebug is useful for debugging HTML, JavaScript, and CSS. If you are writing a PhoneGap app, and none of your JavaScript is firing, it could be an indication that the JavaScript syntax is incorrect. If you load the `.html` page in Firefox, you can see the error in the Firebug console as shown in Figure 11-15.

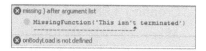

FIGURE 11-15: Firebug console showing syntax error

Another thing that Firebug is good for is inspecting HTML elements. It enables you to see which CSS styles are being applied to that element. The element inspector also enables you to test changes to the HTML and see the effect those changes will have. Firebug also has a layout inspector that shows what the CSS layout looks like and what the margins are, as well as the borders and padding.

Dreamweaver 5.5

The power of PhoneGap is that someone who knows HTML/CSS can get a mobile app running very quickly. Adobe caught on to this early on, and understood that the people who were using its tools, such as Adobe Fireworks, to create the designs for web applications were often the same people who were implementing the designs with HTML/CSS in Dreamweaver. Adobe knew there would be value in a tool that the Dreamweaver user demographic could use to create mobile applications easily. Dreamweaver is not just a WYSIWYG (what you see is what you get) editor as many believe it to be. Dreamweaver is a powerful tool that contains a great deal of features that enable HTML/CSS implementers to deliver great products.

Just before Adobe acquired Nitobi, it bundled PhoneGap tools to assist with mobile development within Dreamweaver 5.5. Because the target audience was users who may not even know what an SDK is, Adobe made it simple to get the emulators and SDKs for iOS (Mac only) and Android on the machine.

Setting up the Mobile Environment in Dreamweaver 5.5

You can find the paths to the SDKs in the Mobile Application feature found under the Site Menu settings. If you have a copy of Dreamweaver 5.5, and you have been working through this book chapter by chapter, you should have the SDKs downloaded and working, so just setting the paths to where the SDKs have been installed will do the trick.

If you are working with a machine that does not have the SDKs installed, the Easy Install button next to the Android path does exactly what the name implies: it downloads everything needed to run an Android application in the emulator. If you do not have the iOS SDK installed, there is a link with detailed instructions on how to do so in the Mobile Application setting. Figure 11-16 shows the SDKs configured and ready for use within Dreamweaver 5.5.

FIGURE 11-16: Dreamweaver 5.5 mobile framework configuration

Creating a PhoneGap Project in Dreamweaver 5.5

After you have set the paths to the mobile frameworks, it's just a matter of creating a new PhoneGap project within Dreamweaver 5.5. Choose Page from Sample ➪ Mobile Starters ➪ jQuery Mobile (PhoneGap) as shown in Figure 11-17 to create a new project.

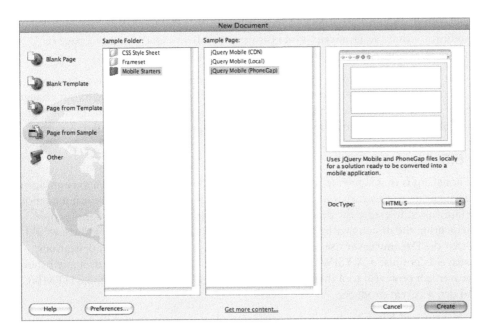

FIGURE 11-17: New PhoneGap project

After you select the project, Dreamweaver includes the JavaScript Library files for PhoneGap as well as jQuery and jQuery Mobile. At this point you can start adding logic to create the mobile PhoneGap application. When you are ready to see your application run in the emulator, simply select the framework under the Build and Emulate menu group under the Site Menu options as shown in Figure 11-18.

FIGURE 11-18: Running the project

Before your mobile application can be deployed to a device or the market, you need to set some other settings such as the provisioning file for iOS. Specific application framework settings such as the Application Icon, Startup Screen Image, and Target OS are located under the Site Menu ➪ Application option, as shown in Figure 11-19.

Dreamweaver is not the cheapest solution, but if you are used to the environment, or are looking for a rich HTML/CSS IDE, Dreamweaver is a powerful tool for creating PhoneGap applications.

With the understanding of the different development and testing environments that can be used to create PhoneGap mobile apps, you can dive PhoneGap code.

PHONEGAP PROJECT

With all of the setup out of the way, you can focus on working with the tools and examining code for mobile apps created with PhoneGap. This section assumes you have a fundamental understanding of HTML, CSS, JavaScript, and jQuery and have worked with these technologies on other platforms.

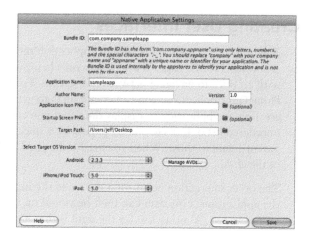

FIGURE 11-19: Application settings

Anatomy of a PhoneGap Application

PhoneGap applications have three components:

> **Native code:** This code isn't modified (with some small exceptions, like the initial setup of an Android application and setting up permissions for Android). Depending on which platform you are working with, your directory structure will match that of the platform. Figure 11-20 shows the directory structure in iOS and Android.

> **JavaScript:** Residing within the www folder of the PhoneGap project, the PhoneGap JavaScript gives your code access to the native functions of the device.

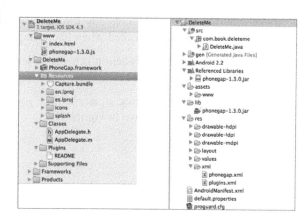

FIGURE 11-20: PhoneGap anatomy

> **HTML/CSS:** These files provide the UI layer of the application. The HTML, CSS, and JavaScript files live inside a www folder within the PhoneGap project.

Creating User Interfaces

The user interface for a PhoneGap application relies on inputs and links. Every screen in PhoneGap is another HTML page. With every screen being a different HTML page, you can use anchor tags with an `href` to navigate between the screens. From the index page, which is the main screen for the PhoneGap application, you can create links to get to the different sections of your app. When you are creating an application to display data that you can drill into, you can list the parent data in an unordered list of links to a child page with a query string parameter to know which individual parent's data to show. When you are on the child page, you can use the query string to drive the data of the child.

The other interaction point for a user is in the input fields. These fields allow the user to pass data to the application. This data can then be stored on the device, if it is user-specific data that isn't needed by the server. Another use for the data is that it can be sent up to a web service.

Many developers promote PhoneGap as a "write once, deploy to multiple platforms" environment without modifying any code. This can be true, but each platform should have a unique UI. Although possible, deploying an app to an Android device with an iOS UI would not provide the best UI experience. It's best to abstract business logic as much as possible from the UI, and plan for having separate UIs for the different platforms you plan to support.

Debugging

You can use a combination of Ripple and Firefox with Firebug platform simulators to debug applications in PhoneGap. The first thing to check when you are debugging a PhoneGap app is to make sure that your `onDeviceReady` JavaScript event is firing. The `onDeviceReady` event is the JavaScript function that is called when PhoneGap is working correctly with the device.

You can test to ensure the function is being called by adding an alert function in the `onDeviceReady` function `alert('onDeviceReady has fired');`.

If `onDeviceReady` is not firing, open the page you are working with in Firefox so that you can inspect it in Firebug as shown in Figure 11-21.

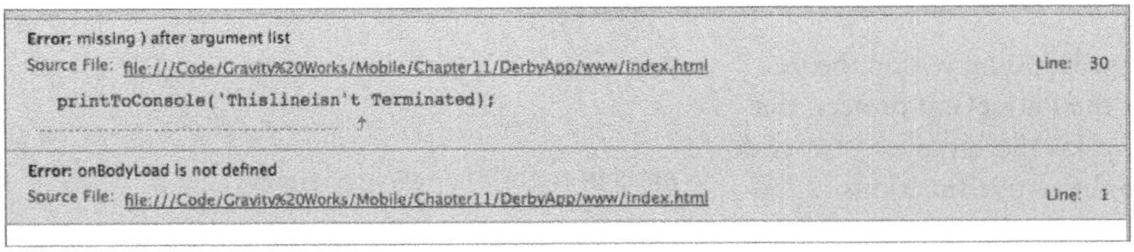

FIGURE 11-21: Firebug syntax error

The example illustrates a line has not been correctly terminated. If you fix that issue, you can check to make sure that no more syntax errors exist and try to run the program again. If `onDeviceReady` is still not firing, you need to make sure that you are including the PhoneGap JavaScript. Once that

is included you can try to run it again. If you are getting inside
`onDeviceReady`, but the function isn't running, you can wrap the call
in a try/catch block to ensure that the code isn't throwing an error.
Then when you run the code, you will see that you haven't declared
`printToConsole` as shown in Figure 11-22.

```
try{
    printToConsole('This line wasn\'t Terminated');
}
catch(err) {
    alert(err);
}
```

Now you can create the `printToConsole` function and run the project
again to see the code in action:

```
function printToConsole(stringToPrint){
    console.log(stringToPrint);
}
```

Figure 11-23 shows PhoneGap writing a log message to the console
screen of xCode.

FIGURE 11-22: Alert showing
caught JavaScript error

```
2012-02-04 13:39:53.588 DerbyApp[881:207] Device initialization: DeviceInfo = {"name":"iPhone Simulator","uuid":"50179
2F7-8217-5E2D-8E2A-1DD7CBA162EA","platform":"iPhone Simulator","gap":"1.3.0","version":"4.3.2","connection":{"type":"w
ifi"}};
[Switching to process 881 thread 0x207]
2012-02-04 13:39:55.722 DerbyApp[881:207] [INFO] This line wasn't Terminated
[Switching to process 881 thread 0x7407]
```

FIGURE 11-23: Console from successful run

With the log showing, you have seen the basic steps for debugging a PhoneGap application.
Start with checking the syntax of your page, then check to make sure you have included all
applicable libraries, wrap your code in try/catch blocks, and use alerts and the console log to ensure
that the code is producing the appropriate results.

Useful JavaScript Libraries

When we all started out as developers, "do not re-create the wheel" was driven into our heads. That
is a message that most developers take to heart, and they have amassed a great deal of useful tools
over the years. As a web developer, these tools could be simple JavaScript libraries that allow only
numbers to be entered into a text box or could be complex UI libraries that combine HTML/CSS
and JavaScript to create a slick interface to enter data.

PhoneGap embraces libraries, and the developer community has created a great deal of tools to help
mobile PhoneGap developers.

jQuery

jQuery is a JavaScript library that is used to make DOM selection, manipulation, event handling, and AJAX interactions easier for web development. Because PhoneGap is HTML5-based, the jQuery library is very useful. With jQuery you can select an individual element on the page so that you can manipulate it. jQuery is used in PhoneGap to bind events to buttons.

iScroll

One of the libraries used in most PhoneGap applications is the iScroll library. The iScroll library is useful for both iPhone and Android projects. This library enables you to set a scrolling area on part of the mobile screen, and have only that portion of the screen scroll. Without iScroll, PhoneGap apps scroll over the entire screen, and any headers or footers will scroll out of sight. When the header and footer scroll out of sight, it's a good sign that app was not created natively.

PhoneGap iPhone apps without iScroll have a rubber band effect (where the app bounced up and down like a stretched-out rubber band), which can be noticed any time the phone is scrolled. To set up iScroll you set a wrapper div and a scroller div. The scroller div is necessary because only the first element inside the wrapper div is actually scrolled. The iScroll library also enables you to add pinch to zoom (UI gestures where the thumb and index figure are "pinched" together on a screen to cause a zoom effect) support. This lets you set an area that can be zoomed, as well as setting a max zoom, a min zoom, a starting zoom, and an area that is prezoomed. Another feature of the iScroll library is a pull to refresh (UI gesture where the top of the app is pulled down, and the content on the page is refreshed). This enables you to set up calls that happen when the screen is pulled down, which can be a useful way to access more information in a list of information.

The HTML for a scroller is not very complicated. You need a wrapper div which will hold the scrolling area. Because iScroll scrolls only the first element inside the wrapper, you also need a div inside the wrapper that will be scrolled. The inner div is where the long list of elements will be held, which are inside the unordered list:

```
<body onload="onLoad()">
    <div id="wrapper">
    <div id="scroller">
        <ul></ul>
        </div>
    </div>
</body>
```

The JavaScript for the scroller requires two things. The first is that you need to stop the native scrolling events. You do this by adding an event listener to the touchmove event and calling preventDefault();. The second piece is to create the scrollView by calling iScroll and passing it the ID of the wrapper element:

```
<script type="text/javascript" charset="utf-8">
    var scrollView;

    function onLoad() {
        document.addEventListener('touchmove', function (e) { e.preventDefault(); }, false);
        document.addEventListener("deviceready", onDeviceReady, false);
    }
```

```
    function onDeviceReady() {
        setHeight();

        //Here we are adding a list of items which will require scrolling.
        var list = jQuery("#scroller").find('ul');
        for (var i = 0; i < 50; i++) {
singleItem = "<li title="+ i +" >Item" + i + "</li>";
            list.append(singleItem);
        }

        scrollView = new iScroll('wrapper', {desktopCompatibility:true});
    }
</script>
```

Use CSS to set the height of the wrapper. You can also use jQuery if you are using Android, where the devices do not have standard sizes.

```
var fullHeight = window.innerHeight;
var mainHeight = fullHeight - 60;
jQuery('#wrapper').css({height: mainHeight + 'px' });

/*---------Scroll area code----------*/

#wrapper {
    height:270px;       /* Of course you need to specify the object height */
    position:relative;
    z-index:1;          /* it seems that recent webkit is less picky and works anyway. */
    width:100%;
    overflow:hidden;
}
```

jQuery Mobile

jQuery mobile is library that you can use to provide a user interface that works seamlessly across all popular mobile platforms. jQuery mobile provides tools to make it easy to format controls and layout of a mobile page. Figure 11-24 is an example of a jQuery mobile page.

This page would look identical rendered on an Android device, so the drawback of using this library is that its controls look similar to iOS controls.

Pages are laid out very semantically in jQuery mobile. jQuery mobile takes advantage of the HTML5 data-role attribute to identify sections of the page, such as header, content, and footer:

```
<div data-role="page">

    <div data-role="header">
        <h1>Page Title</h1>
    </div><!-- /header -->

    <div data-role="content">
```

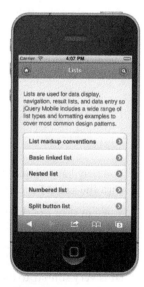

FIGURE 11-24: jQuery Mobile UI

```
            <p>Page content goes here.</p>
        </div><!-- /content -->

        <div data-role="footer">
            <h4>Page Footer</h4>
        </div><!-- /footer -->

    </div><!-- /page -->
```

With the data roles set, and the jQuery mobile JS file included, the app renders a header and footer with a scrollable content area without any more interaction required from the developer.

Sencha Touch

Sencha Touch is an MVC framework for creating HTML5 applications. It can be used with PhoneGap for iOS, Android, and BlackBerry apps. When Sencha Touch is combined with PhoneGap, it can be used to create native looking applications. To use Sencha Touch you need to get the free download from http://www.sencha.com/products/touch/. After that you can include the Sencha Touch SDK in a lib folder inside of the www folder of a PhoneGap project.

Convention for Sencha Touch projects is to have models, views, controllers, and lib folders inside the www folder of a PhoneGap project. The app folder contains the app.js file, which contains the launch events for Sencha Touch. Sencha projects need to wait for both the Sencha launch event and PhoneGap's device ready event before firing. You can check this by setting the launched property within the Sencha launch event. Then inside the mainLaunch function, you can check to make sure the framework is loaded by checking this property as shown in the following code.

```
    Ext.regApplication({
        name: 'app',
        launch: function() {
            this.launched = true;
            this.mainLaunch();
        },
        mainLaunch: function() {
            if (!device || !this.launched) {console.log('main Not Ready'); return;
        }

        console.log('mainLaunch');
        }
    });
```

You may have noticed this calls mainLaunch twice — once on ondeviceready and once on launch, with the mainLaunch function continuing on to the second call.

You can then use this with the MVC pattern to create the data layers, and use them to display the data back to the user. From the list example in the documentation you can see the differences between the Android and the iPhone versions of the Sencha Touch application. Figure 11-25 shows an example UI created with Sencha Touch rendered in both iOS and Android. Again, notice that the UI is very similar to an iOS interface.

XUI

XUI is an open source JavaScript library built specifically for mobile devices. It contains a subset of the functionality of jQuery, but with a much smaller footprint. Brian Leroux, who works for Nitobi on the PhoneGap project, started the XUI project in 2008. XUI provides selectors that use CSS3 style selectors. For example, to get an element in XUI you can use the following code to select the liTest item, and turn the text red:

FIGURE 11-25: iPhone Sencha list

```
x$("#liTest").css({'color':'red'});
```

XUI also gives you access to events. One of the events that you can access is the button click event, which takes a callback. You can select a button and assign a buttonPressed function to the click's callback. The buttonPressed function executes when the button is pressed:

```
<body>
    <button id="buttonTest" >Press For Alert</button>
</body>

function onDeviceReady(){
    x$("#buttonTest").click(buttonPressed);
}

function buttonPressed(){
    alert('Button Pressed');
}
```

XUI can also use transformations to make modifications to the CSS properties of elements on the DOM. It takes the new CSS style and applies the transformation based on the duration that is specified. It also has an optional callback that is called once the transformation is completed.

```
x$('#liTest').tween({ color:'blue', duration:1500 }, function() {
    alert('done!');
});
```

XUI also has an XmlHttpRequest (XHR) function to return objects from a call to a JSON service. These calls take a request string, a callback function for success, the headers to be passed, and a callback for errors:

```
x$().xhr(requestString, {
    callback: successFunction,
    headers: [{name:"Accept",
              value: "application/json"}],
              error: function(){alert('Error ');
```

```
    }
});
```

To make the call to an outside service for
iPhone, you need to add the service to the
external hosts in the `PhoneGap.plist` file.
The easiest way to enable the external service
for debugging is to add the * wildcard to the
external hosts, as shown in Figure 11-26.

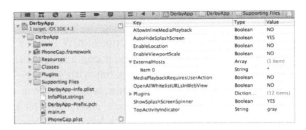

FIGURE 11-26: External hosts with Item 0 Set to *

The data from the request string is placed on
the `responseText` variable in the success callback. This can then be parsed with JavaScript's `eval`
function, which turns the XML into an array of items that can be used to get the items from the
JSON response:

```
function successFunction(){
    var dataItems = eval("("+this.responseText +")").d;

    for (var i = 0; i < dataItems.length; i++) {
        console.log(dataItems[i].Name);
    }
}
```

LawnChair

LawnChair is a JavaScript library that was built to allow persistent storage of data in a lightweight
application. The primary target for LawnChair is mobile HTML5 applications, due to LawnChair's
lightweight nature. To use LawnChair you need to set up a data store:

```
var store = new Lawnchair({name:'testing'}, function(store) {});
```

Once you have the store, you can create an object with a key, and then place that object in the store:

```
var me = {key:'adam', lastName:'Ryder'};
store.save(me);
```

Now that the object is stored, you can retrieve it from the store using the key:

```
store.get('adam', function(item) {
    alert(item.lastName);
});
```

This would get the object and alert the `lastName` item from the object. LawnChair is small; only 8 K in
size. This lends itself well to being packaged in PhoneGap, because it won't take much space on the device.

BUILDING THE DERBY APP IN PHONEGAP

The idea of the Derby App is to build the same app over all of the mobile platforms covered in this
book. The PhoneGap version is very similar to the other versions that you have built thus far or will
build in future chapters.

The requirements are to provide two pages: one that lists all the teams/leagues and one that lists all the players. When a league/team is selected, the application shows the roster for the team. When a player is selected, it shows which team the player belongs to and her number.

The first thing that you want to do in the Derby App is to create a placeholder which will hold the list of all the derby teams. You set this up on the index.html page:

```
<div id="wrapper">
    <div id="scroller">
        <ul>
        </ul>
    </div>
</div>
```

You have set up the wrapper with an unordered list inside of the scroller. You need to add the listener for PhoneGap's device ready event, and make a callback to the onDeviceReady function inside the onLoad function.

You also need to add a listener to the touchmove event to prevent the default touchmove behavior. Then you can use the iScroll library to control the movement of the screen:

```
function onLoad() {
    document.addEventListener('touchmove', function (e) { e.preventDefault(); }, false);
    document.addEventListener("deviceready", onDeviceReady, false);
}
```

With the ondevice events wired up you can now request data from the derby name service. To accomplish this, create a file named OData.js to handle all requests to the oData Derby Names web service. This OData.js file will need to be included in your index.html header. The OData.js file has a getData function that takes a request string and a successFunction callback. The actual request is made using XUI's XHR function, which calls the success function and passes the results from the request string to the function.

```
function OData() {
    this.getData = function (requestString, successFunction) {
        x$().xhr(requestString, { callback: successFunction,
                        headers: [{name:"Accept",
                        value: "application/json"}],
                        error: function(){alert('Error '); }});
    };
```

Next, set up a DerbyService function that contains all of the service calls and builds the request strings and sends them to the OData function. The calls in the DerbyService contain functions to get the leagues and take a callback.

```
function DerbyService() {

    this.HostName = 'http://derbynames.gravityworksdesign.com';
    this.BaseServiceUrl = this.HostName + '/DerbyNamesService.svc/';
    this.odataService = new oData();

    this.searchAllLeagues = function (successFunction) {
        var serviceString = this.BaseServiceUrl + "Leagues?$top=50";
```

```
            odataService = new oData();
            odataService.getData(serviceString, successFunction);
        };
    }
```

The onDeviceReady function calls setHeight, which is a function in your helper.js file and the searchAll function, which is a local function with a callback to an anonymous function that sets up the scrollView for your iScroll implementation:

```
    setHeight();
    searchAll(
            function(){
                setTimeout(function () {
                scrollView = new iScroll('wrapper', {desktopCompatibility:true});
                    }, 500);
                });
```

The searchAll function creates an instance of the DerbyService, and then calls the searchAllLeagues function of the derby service with an anonymous callback function. The anonymous callback will call another helper function to display the league data on the screen. The displayAllLeagueDataOnScreen function takes a parameter for the response from the OData service, the search string (currently empty string), and the ID of the div that will hold the results.

```
    function searchAll(callback){
            var service = new DerbyService();
            service.searchAllLeagues(function(){
                displayAllLeagueDataOnScreen(this.responseText, "", "scroller");
            }
        });

            callback();
        }
```

The displayAllLeagueDataOnScreen function uses jQuery to find the list name, and removes any list items that are currently in the list. It then calls the appendAllLeagueDataOnScreen function, passing it the data, search term, and the list name:

```
    function displayAllLeagueDataOnScreen(data, searchTerm, listName){
            jQuery("#" + listName).find('li').remove();
            appendAllLeagueDataOnScreen(data, searchTerm, listName);
        }
```

The appendAllLeagueDataOnScreen function calls the JavaScript eval function on the data to get an array of dataItems to work with. You also create a temporary singleItem to hold the league list item. You use jQuery again to find the unordered list inside of the listName that was passed in. For every dataItem, you create a link that will go to the leagues page, league.html, which shows all of the players for that league.

After the item is created you append those items to the list. If the data item's length is the same as the number of records you asked for, you also add a link to get more items when you scroll to the bottom of the list.

```
function appendAllLeagueDataOnScreen(data, searchTerm, listName){
    var dataItems = eval("("+ data +")").d;
    var singleItem = "";
    var list = jQuery("#" + listName).find('ul');

    for (var i = 0; i < dataItems.length; i++) {
singleItem = "<a href='league.html?League=" + dataItems[i].LeagueName + "'>
            <li title=";
        singleItem = singleItem + dataItems[i].LeagueName +" >";
        singleItem = singleItem + dataItems[i].LeagueName + "</li></a>";

        list.append(singleItem);
    }

    if(dataItems.length == 50){
        if(searchTerm == ""){
            singleItem = "<a href='#' id='btnGetMore' onclick='LoadMorePushed()'>"
            singleItem = singleItem + "<li id='liAddMore'>Load More</li></a>";
        }
        else{
            singleItem = "<a href='#' id='btnGetMore'
                onclick='LoadMoreSearchPushed(&quot;";
            singleItem = singleItem + searchTerm +
                "&quot;)'><li id='liAddMore'>Load More</li></a>";
        }

        list.append(singleItem);
    }
}
```

Figure 11-27 shows the index page rendering a list of roller derby teams.

Now that you have the leagues set up as a list of links to a league.html page, you can use CSS to change the links to look more like the native OS list items. You can set the list-style to none and the list-type to none, which will remove the bullets. When you set text-decorations to none for the anchor tabs, the links will no longer be underlined.

```
ul {
    list-style:none;
    padding:0;
    margin:0;
    width:100%;
    text-align:left;
}

li {
    margin:5px 0;
    padding:3px 7px 7px 7px;
    border-bottom:1px solid #ddd;
    list-style-type:none;
    font-size:15px;
    font-weight:bold;
    margin-right:5px;
}
```

FIGURE 11-27: List of derby teams rendered on an iPhone

```
a:link, a:visited {
    text-decoration:none;
    color:#000;
    font-weight:bold;
}
```

Figure 11-28 shows what the Derby app looks like after this small amount of CSS has been added.

With the scrolling working and the list looking like a list, you can add a header to the league page. The header consists of two links with classes, which will become image links through CSS. This header will also be used on the `individualList.html` page, just with different classes, so that the links look different.

```
<div class="header">
  <a id="btnLeague" href='index.html'
     class="btnTwoLeft">Leagues</a>
  <a id="btnIndividuals" href='individualList.html'
     class="btnTwoRightSelected" >Players</a>
</div>
```

FIGURE 11-28: Formatted league list displayed on an iPhone

Here is the CSS for the buttons; the images are stored inside the `images` directory within the www directory:

```
.btnTwoLeft {
    height:23px;
    width:150px;
    background:url(images/btn-two-left.png) no-repeat;
    float:left;
    text-align:center;
    font-size:14px;
    font-weight:200!important;
    color:#fff!important;
    font:Georgia, "Times New Roman", Times, serif;
    padding:7px 0 0 0;
    margin:2px 0;
}

.btnTwoLeftSelected {
    height:23px;
     width:150px;
    background:url(images/btn-two-left-selected.png) no-repeat;
    float:left;
    text-align:center;
    font-size:14px;
    font-weight:200!important;
    color:#fff!important;
    font:Georgia, "Times New Roman", Times, serif;
    padding:7px 0 0 0;
    margin:2px 0;
}
```

FIGURE 11-29: Derby App with header added

With the header added, the league screen is now starting to look like a mobile app. Figure 11-29 shows the header added to the league screen.

There is another useful option for a list this long, and that is the ability to search. To search, you need a text box for the search term, a button to search with, and another service call for searching:

```
<input id="txtSearch" type="search" placeholder="Search" class="searchbar">
<button id="btnSubmit" type="button" class="gobtn" label="Go" >GO</button>
```

Wire up the button click event in the onDeviceReady function. This click function gets the searchCriteria from the search text box and passes that to the searchLeagues function:

```
jQuery("#btnSubmit").click(function(){
    var searchCriteria = jQuery("#txtSearch").val();
    skipCount = 50;
    searchLeagues(searchCriteria);
});
```

The searchLeagues function creates a new instance of the DerbyService and calls the searchLeagues function in the service with a callback to displayAllLeagueDataOnScreen. This is the same function that you called when you displayed the unfiltered list.

```
function searchLeagues(searchCriteria){
    var service = new DerbyService();

    service.searchLeagues(searchCriteria, function(){
        displayAllLeagueDataOnScreen(this.responseText, searchCriteria, "scroller");
    });
}
```

The searchLeagues function in the service calls the OData object with a filter that looks for a substring of the searchString that is passed in the LeagueName property:

```
this.searchLeagues = function (searchString, successFunction) {
    var serviceString = this.BaseServiceUrl + "Leagues?$top=50&$filter=\
                        substringof('" + searchString +
        "',LeagueName)";

        this.odataService.getData(serviceString,
    successFunction);
    };
```

With the search in place, Figure 11-30 shows the completed UI for the Leagues screen in the Derby App.

With the Derby App completed, now you can take a look at some of the other useful functions in PhoneGap.

OTHER USEFUL PHONEGAP THINGS

Thus far, the examples in this chapter have provided the basics for creating a PhoneGap application. This application will go out to a web service and render the data on the screen. This does not cover every possible situation you will encounter as a PhoneGap mobile developer, so we will finish this

FIGURE 11-30: Derby App with league search added

chapter by providing a few short examples of other common tasks you may need to accomplish when working with PhoneGap.

Pickers

Pickers in PhoneGap come in two flavors. The first type of picker is a date-style picker. These pickers rely on plug-ins to function, because there isn't a uniform date picker available to the different platforms yet. iOS 5 does support the HTML date input type. You can get the code for the date picker from `https://github.com/phonegap/phonegap-plugins/tree/master/iPhone/DatePicker`. This will have the `.js`, `.h`, and `.m` files. The `.h` and `.m` files go into your `Plugins` directory. The `DatePicker.js` file belongs in your www directory. You also need to add a `DatePicker` key and value to the plugins section of your `phonegap.plist` file. You need to create a callback and a function that will be called during the `onclick` of a link.

```
var callbackFunction = function(date) {
    console.log(date.toString());
    document.getElementById("date").innerHTML = date.toString();
}

var showDatePicker = function(mode) {

    plugins.datePicker.show({
                        date: new Date(),
                        mode: mode, //date or time or blank for both
                        allowOldDates: false
                        }, callbackFunction);

}
```

The other way to create a picker, which is our recommended way, is to create a page that lists the items you want to pick from as links back to your selector. In your HTML you could have a link to a `pickList` page:

```
<a href='pickList.html'>Choose Your Favorite Color</a>
```

On the `pickList` page you can set up the list as a series of links back to the index with the choices differentiated by the query string parameter that is passed back:

```
<html>
    <ul>
        <li><a href='index.html?color=blue'>Blue</a>
        <li><a href='index.html?color=green'>Green</a>
        <li><a href='index.html?color=red'>Red</a>
    </ul>
</html>
```

Once back on the index page you can read the query string and take action based on what it contains. You can use regular expressions in JavaScript to decode the query string and return the value of the query string parameter. You could add another JavaScript library to handle this, but it is quicker and easier to just write the function yourself:

```
function getParameterByName( name ){
    name = name.replace(/[\[]/,"\\\[").replace(/[\]]/,"\\\]");
```

```
var regexS = "[\\?&]"+name+"=([^&#]*)";
var regex = new RegExp( regexS );
var results = regex.exec( window.location.href );

if( results == null )
    return "";
else
    return decodeURIComponent(results[1].replace(/\+/g, " "));
}
```

Once you make the call to getParameterByName you can use the information that you have in the query string:

```
var color = getParameterByName('color');
if (color != '')
{
    alert('You Chose: ' + color);
}
```

Figure 11-31 is an example of the color picker view.

Offline Storage

Sometimes you will need to store data on the device. This could be because the business rules for your app require offline usage, or it could be just a matter of saving a few settings such as username and password. This section shows you the different techniques you can use to store data offline so that it can be retrieved when the user is not connected to the web. Offline storage also allows you to store settings on the device for your user.

Web SQL

FIGURE 11-31: Color picker view

If you have a lot of data that needs to be stored, one of the better ways to store that data is in a database. PhoneGap provides a mechanism to create, maintain, and retrieve records from an internal database. The first thing you need to do to use the database is to open it. You must do this after PhoneGap's deviceready event has been fired. The following code creates or opens a database named PlayerDemo with a version of 1.0 and a display name of Player Demo. The 10000 is the size of the database in bytes.

```
function onDeviceReady() {
    var db = window.openDatabase("PlayerDemo", "1.0", "Player Demo", 10000);
}
```

Now that you have a database you can run transactions against it. You do that by calling the transaction function on the database, and passing in a callback function, an error callback, and a success callback. The callback function gets called with a transaction object. The first thing you do is populate the database:

```
db.transaction(populateDB, onDBError, onDBSuccess);
```

This calls the `populateDB` function and passes the function its transaction. This means that if any of the commands in the transaction fail, the entire transaction will be rolled back. The following function creates a players table:

```
function populateDB(tx){
    tx.executeSql('DROP TABLE IF EXISTS PLAYERS');
    tx.executeSql('CREATE TABLE IF NOT EXISTS PLAYERS (id unique, number, name)');
    tx.executeSql('INSERT INTO PLAYERS (id, number, name) VALUES (1, 6, "Adam")');
    tx.executeSql('INSERT INTO PLAYERS (id, number, name) VALUES (2, 1, "Jeff")');
    tx.executeSql('INSERT INTO PLAYERS (id, number, name) VALUES (3, 4, "Scott")');
    tx.executeSql('INSERT INTO PLAYERS (id, number, name) VALUES (4, 2, "Amelia")');
    tx.executeSql('INSERT INTO PLAYERS (id, number, name) VALUES (5, 5, "Dave")');
    tx.executeSql('INSERT INTO PLAYERS (id, number, name) VALUES (6, 3, "Lauren")');
    tx.executeSql('INSERT INTO PLAYERS (id, number, name) VALUES (7, 7, "Ashley")');
    tx.executeSql('INSERT INTO PLAYERS (id, number, name) VALUES (8, 9, "Nathan")');
    tx.executeSql('INSERT INTO PLAYERS (id, number, name) VALUES (9, 8, "Heather")');
}
```

Now that you have the database populated you can create another transaction that you can use to retrieve the data from the players table that you just created. To get the data back from a query, you call `executeSQL` and pass it the query, arguments, the success callback, and the error callback:

```
tx.executeSql('SELECT * FROM PLAYERS ORDER BY name',  [], onQuerySuccess, onDBError);
```

You can use the `onQuerySuccess` callback to iterate through the results and display them to the screen, as shown in Figure 11-32:

FIGURE 11-32: SQL
returned to screen

```
function onQuerySuccess(tx, results){

    try{
        var playerInfo = '<ul>';
        var len = results.rows.length;

        for (var i=0; i<len; i++){
            playerInfo += '<li><b>' + results.rows.item(i).name +
                '</b>(' + results.rows.item(i).number
                + ')</li>';
        }

        playerInfo += '</ul>';
        jQuery('#divPlayers').html(playerInfo);
    }
    catch(err){
        alert(err);
    }

}
```

Filesystem Storage

Local storage is also available. The local storage is available as key-value pairs. To store Lansing as a favorite, you would call setItem, passing in the key (favorite) and the value (Lansing):

```
window.localStorage.setItem("favorite", "Lansing");
```

This storage is persistent and will be available the next time the application is run. To retrieve the data you call getItem with the key that you are looking for. The following code retrieves the favorite item and then alerts that item, as shown in Figure 11-33:

```
var fav = window.localStorage.getItem("favorite");
alert(fav);
```

FIGURE 11-33: Local storage alert

GPS

You access the GPS through PhoneGap by calling the geolocation function with a callback:

```
function onDeviceReady() {
    navigator.geolocation.getCurrentPosition(gpsSuccess, gpsFailure);
}
```

As with all of the PhoneGap functions, the GPS functions cannot be called until the deviceready event has been fired. The success callback returns a position object, which has a coordinates object that contains properties for latitude, longitude, altitude, accuracy, heading, and speed:

```
function gpsSuccess(location){
    var gpsinfo = '<ul><li>Latitude: ' + location.coords.latitude + '</li>';
    gpsinfo += '<li>longitude: ' + location.coords.longitude + '</li>';
```

```
    gpsinfo += '<li>Altitude: ' + location.coords.altitude + '</li>';
    gpsinfo += '<li>Accuracy: ' + location.coords.accuracy + '</li>';
    gpsinfo += '<li>Speed: ' + location.coords.speed + '</li></ul>';

    jQuery('#GPSInfo').html(gpsinfo);
}
```

There is also a failure callback that returns a `positionError` object. The `positionError` object has a code and a message property:

```
function gpsFailure(PositionError){
    alert(PositionError.code);
    alert(PositionError.message);
}
```

Accelerometer

You can access the accelerometer using the accelerometer's `watchAcceleration` function with a callback for the success and for errors. `watchAcceleration` is set to a variable and fires on the frequency that is set in the options. The iPhone simulator does not transmit accelerometer data; however, the Android simulator does, so if you are testing without a device, the accelerometer needs to be tested on Android.

```
var options = { frequency: 3000 };
watch = navigator.accelerometer.watchAcceleration(successFunction,
                                        errorFunction, options);
//The success function takes an acceleration object.
//This object has the x, y and z change,
//as well as the timestamp from when the acceleration was gathered.
function successFunction(acceleration){
    try{
        x$("#spanX").html(acceleration.x);
        x$("#spanY").html(acceleration.y);
        x$("#spanZ").html(acceleration.z);
        x$("#spanTime").html(acceleration.timestamp);
    }
    catch(err) {
        alert(err);
    }
}
```

To stop the watch from firing constantly, you can call the `clearWatch` function and pass it the watch variable to stop the watch from firing:

```
x$('#btnStop').click(function(){
    navigator.accelerometer.clearWatch(watch);
});
```

Now that you have a working app you can connect the application to the markets.

CONNECTING PHONEGAP TO THE MARKETS

If you have been following through the book chapter by chapter, you have seen how to connect to the different markets. Because PhoneGap applications are compiled with their native frameworks, they are released to the markets in the same manner as their true native counterparts are released. Refer to the corresponding section of Chapters 6–9 for more information on connecting to the various markets.

SUMMARY

PhoneGap is an easy-to-learn framework for creating cross-platform mobile applications. Everything in PhoneGap derives from the `onDeviceReady` listener. Once `onDeviceReady` fires, you have access to the device's native components, like the GPS, camera, or accelerometer. Leveraging your current HTML, CSS, and JavaScript knowledge also enables you to create these applications with a lower learning curve.

Because PhoneGap is cross platform, you don't need to learn four different languages to be able to deploy your application across iPhone, Android, BlackBerry, and Windows Phone 7. Having the same codebase for all platforms can also give you a sense of parity through the different device platforms.

Now that you have created mobile applications with PhoneGap, the next chapter will show how to create Android and iPhone applications using .NET and the Mono framework.

12

Getting Started with MonoTouch and Mono for Android

Developing in the mobile space can be a daunting task for developers. You have to figure out which platforms you should support for your app, purchase the hardware, and join the developer programs for each platform, so the last thing you may want to do is to learn a new programming language.

In 2009 Miguel de Icaza, with a team of other developers, released version 1.0 of the MonoTouch framework. MonoTouch enabled .NET developers to create iOS applications in C# and then deploy to iOS hardware. After the initial launch of the MonoTouch framework, Apple modified the iTunes terms of service to allow only apps that were created using Objective-C into the market, a decision that was quickly reversed.

Although short lived, this edict from Apple is a fact that many developers keep in the back of their mind, knowing that Apple can change the terms of service again at any time. The bright side of this policy was that it was only for apps being deployed to the iOS store; if you created an app for internal company use that was deployed using an ad-hoc method, you were still free to use whatever non-Objective-C framework you liked.

THE MONO FRAMEWORK

MonoTouch and Mono for Android rely on the Mono Framework to function. Mono is a cross-platform open source implementation of the .NET Framework. The Mono project is led by Miguel de Icaza, with the sponsorship of his company Xamarin. The Mono project was started in 2001, with version 1.0 released in 2004. Throughout the years of development, a team of open source developers worked to keep parity with the C# and libraries within the .NET Framework. One of the most impressive development projects I have seen was when the Mono project released Moonlight, the Mono implementation of Silverlight, within 24 hours of Microsoft releasing Silverlight to the developer community at the Mix conference in 2007.

The Mono project focuses on providing:

➤ **An open source Common Language Infrastructure (CLI) implementation:** ECMA-335 is the open standard developed by Microsoft that describes the core of the .NET Framework. The Mono CLI provides a runtime environment for code that has been compiled to Common Intermediate Language (CIL).

➤ **A C# compiler:** ECMA-334 defines the open standard of the C# language. The Mono C# compiler is responsible for compiling C# code in the Common Intermediate Language that the CLI run time executes.

➤ **An open development stack:** The Mono project strives to provide tools that are both useful and easy for developers to use. At the forefront is the MonoDevelop IDE along with various other tools for linking, and other core libraries specific to UNIX environments such as the GTK# library used for GUIs.

The current Mono C# compiler provides a complete feature set for C# 1, 2, and 3, with partial support for C# 4.

MonoTouch

MonoTouch is a set of tools that enables a developer to build iOS applications using their existing knowledge of the .NET Framework. The MonoTouch tools provide a combination of the core .NET Framework features along with APIs provided in the iOS SDK. The MonoTouch team has spent a great deal of time trying to provide an interface with names that match the corresponding iOS feature, in an effort to make the MonoTouch API very similar to the iOS SDK without sacrificing conventions that .NET developers are accustomed to.

Although MonoTouch is based on the open source Mono project, MonoTouch is a commercial product, which is licensed on a developer basis. For up-to-date licensing info, visit the Xamarin store website at `https://store.xamarin.com/`.

The Microsoft .NET Framework languages (Visual Basic, C#, F#) are interpreted languages that compile to Common Intermediate Language (CIL), and then are just-in-time (JIT) compiled, meaning in the normal uses of the .NET Framework, your code isn't truly compiled until run time.

Interpreted code/JIT compilation is not supported within iOS and is blocked via the terms of service as well as functionality within the iOS kernel. This means that a different solution is needed for the Mono framework to work within iOS.

MonoTouch is delivered as a static compiler that turns .NET code into static byte code. MonoTouch apps are compiled using ahead-of-time (AOT) compilation (static compilation), which allows all code that is normally JITed to be generated from CIL to a single native binary that can then be signed, just like a C compiler would generate static byte code. This method loses some of the dynamic functionality of .NET, but features such as generics are still supported.

Linking

Because libraries cannot be reused in iOS, every time your app is installed on a device, the Mono Framework is bundled inside your app as well. When your MonoTouch app is compiled, a process runs that analyzes which portions of the Mono framework you are actually using, and creates a custom version of the Mono Framework ARM CPU architecture, with only the functionality your app is using, and then links this version into your app. What this means is that if you have five different MonoTouch apps installed on your iOS device, each app will have its own version of the Mono Framework. The fact that the Mono Framework needs to be installed increases the size of the app over a natively created app, but this is fully dependent on how much of the Mono Framework is being utilized. In most cases, the size increase of the app is trivial.

The linker is integrated into MonoTouch and the MonoDevelop IDE, so you do not need to worry about doing anything extra.

Performance

Both Objective-C and the Mono Framework's AOT compiler use the same low-level virtual machine (LLVM) for generating and optimizing the binary code, so there should be no performance difference using MonoTouch as opposed to Objective-C. Because portions of the Mono Framework are compiled into the final assembly, the apps may be larger.

Mono for Android

Mono for Android is the sibling product of MonoTouch. Mono for Android allows .NET developers to create apps for the Android operating system using a set of tools they are familiar with. With Mono for Android, developers can create Android applications within Visual Studio or the MonoDevelop IDE.

Mono for Android 1.0 was released in April 2011, and is much younger then the MonoTouch framework but is a viable alternative to native Android development.

The Android operating system is a Linux-based system where Android apps run on top of a virtual machine named Dalvik. Mono for Android apps do not run within Dalvik, but within Mono, which runs side-by-side with Dalvik. Mono for Android developers access features in the Android operating system by calling .NET APIs through Mono, or by classes exposed in the Android namespace provided for Mono for Android. This provides a bridge into the Java APIs that are exposed by Dalvik.

Both Mono and Dalvik run on top of the Linux kernel and expose API functionality to developers to access the operating system. Figure 12-1 shows the various components of a Mono for Android app and their interaction with the Mono framework and Dalvik.

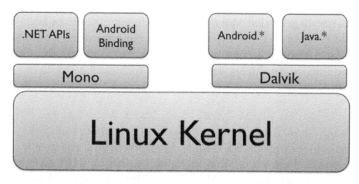

FIGURE 12-1: Mono for Android architecture

Linking

Very similar to how the linker in MonoTouch works, Mono for Android creates a custom static version of the Mono Framework that is distributed with your Mono for Android app. It's important to note that the default debug releases of your Mono for Android app will not use the linker and a shared runtime package will be installed. Although this makes repeated deploying much quicker, it's not a true test of your app, because turning on linking may have some unintended side effects. Figure 12-2 shows the build settings for a Mono for Android project in MonoDevelop. Notice the Linker Behavior setting for the Debug configuration. To enable linking, simply uncheck the Use Shared Mono Runtime setting and select Link All Assemblies.

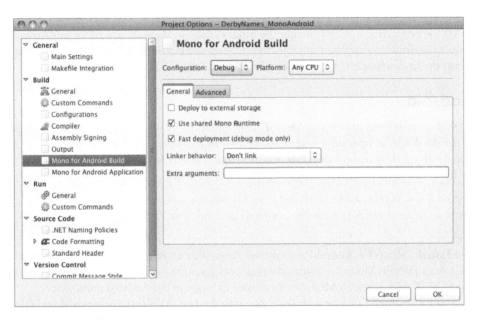

FIGURE 12-2: Linker settings

Performance

When it comes to performance, research suggests that Mono's JIT compiling is faster than Dalvik's (http://www.koushikdutta.com/2009/01/dalvik-vs-mono.html). In our experience with Mono for Android, both native and Mono for Android apps performed similarly. But to be fair, the apps we have created are not complex, and usually just display data retrieved from a web service.

Assemblies

Just as with Silverlight, MonoTouch and Mono for Android are subsets of assemblies included in the desktop .NET Framework, basically hybrids of .NET 4.0 and the Silverlight 2 API profile. MonoTouch/Mono for Android are extended subsets of Silverlight and the desktop .NET assemblies to aid in your iOS development. It's important to note that MonoTouch/Mono for Android are not

ABI compatible with assemblies compiled for a different profile, such as Silverlight or the desktop .NET Framework. Assemblies you want you use in your MonoTouch/Mono for Android app must be recompiled with the MonoTouch/Mono for Android profile, just as if you were using these assemblies in a Silverlight app.

Why MonoTouch/Mono for Android?

The true power of these frameworks comes with the ability to share code. As we have stressed in previous chapters of this book, UI is very important to the mobile app experience, and you should not try to plan on a single solution that works on both iOS and Android. However, a great deal of business logic can be abstracted and shared very easily between both your iOS implementation and your Android implementation.

As you become more experienced with a programming language, it becomes easier to follow patterns that have been identified as "good" programming practice. I know from firsthand experience that the first time I develop a project in a new language, it does not meet the quality I hold to other code bases with languages I have more experience with. With that being said, using MonoTouch and Mono for Android enable you to use a language where you already know the best practices, and let you focus on developing a great app.

Do not re-create the wheel and keep business logic outside of the UI. There is a set of rules that we as developers should follow, but if you are unfamiliar with a framework or programming language, following these rules is easier said than done. With MonoTouch and Mono for Android the expectation is that you are already familiar with .NET and C#, so you are able to take your existing knowledge and start developing platform-specific apps without leaning a new framework.

Downsides

As you may have noticed when it comes to mobile development, nothing is black and white. You can perform the exact same task in multiple ways, but many of them come with a downside. Developing with MonoTouch and Mono for Android is no different.

Waiting for Improvements

When Apple or Google have a press conference to promote the latest and greatest features contained in their respective mobile operating systems, in most situations, it is at that time you can update the SDKs and start working with the new great features if you are working with a native app. When you have selected MonoTouch or Mono for Android as your development platform, you must wait until Xamarin includes these new features in the MonoTouch/Mono for Android SDK.

Xamarin has a fraction of the developers on staff that Apple or Google have to perform development and testing of new features. Although Xamarian strives to keep feature parity complete, sometimes this process takes a bit longer than we as users of the framework would like. Because of the close interaction with xCode for the user interface development, when changes to xCode happen, it tends to take Xamarin a while to develop a product that works correctly. The release of xCode 4 left MonoTouch developers using an older version of the IDE for almost a year until a solution was delivered.

Licensing

Both MonoTouch and Mono for Android are commercial products and currently require developers to purchase a license for each. The evaluation version of both MonoTouch and Mono for Android enable developers to create apps and deploy to the simulator/emulator only; a fully licensed version is required to deploy to a device.

When a license is purchased, the key is entered within the IDE, and activation occurs over the Internet. The downside occurs if Xamarian goes out of business. What is the "escape" plan if you have to reinstall your machine, and activate the framework when the activation server no longer exists? You are putting the fate of a great deal of development resources in the hands of an external resource. Sure, you can argue the same fact about PhoneGap or Titanium, but because they are open source the projects can persist after corporation backing loses interest.

> *As a developer you may not initially think that this could be an issue. Before Xamarian obtained the rights for MonoTouch, the MonoTouch project was in this exact state of limbo, and we were burned on a project. With a newly installed machine, and no way to activate the MonoTouch license we had paid for, there was no way to make changes to an app that had been in the field for about a year. Luckily the app was small, and we were able to rewrite it natively for iOS. The client received their updates, but we lost time rewriting the app.*

Apple Confusion

With developer certificates and provisioning profiles, the hoops a developer has to jump through just to get an app installed on a device may make you start to lose your hair. Although the process of provisioning profiles and certificates can be a pain in the neck, xCode and other Apple tools have been created to help make this chore a bit easier—whereas the tools contained within MonoDevelop will make you lose even more hair. It's not that they don't function within MonoDevelop, but they are not very user-friendly, and to a new developer on the iOS platform it can be overwhelming.

Xamarin Mobile

With sharing code being one of the most appealing reasons to use MonoTouch and Mono for Android, the Xamarin team has taken the platform one step forward with the Xamarin Mobile library. This library provides tools to write device-specific functionality once. For example, MonoTouch requires a different set of APIs for getting a contact than Mono for Android does, because they both try to adhere to the native API naming conventions as much as possible. Xamarin Mobile provides a single API that allows you to return the contacts for either iOS or Android. The following code examples show how Xamarin Mobile can be useful.

To get a list of contacts in MonoTouch, you need to use the `ABAddress` object:

```
ABAddressBook addressBook = new ABAddressBook();
ABPerson[] contacts = iPhoneAddressBook.GetPeople();
```

```
foreach (ABPerson item in contacts) {
    // do something with the contact
}
```

In Mono for Android, you need to use the `ManagedQuery` object to get the contacts:

```
var contacts = ManagedQuery(ContactsContract.Contacts.ContentUri,
    null, null, null, null);

foreach (Contact contact in contacts)
{
    // do something with the contact
}
```

Xamarin Mobile uses a new `AddressBook` object that returns the contacts for either iOS or Android:

```
var book = new AddressBook ();


foreach (Contact contact in book)
{
    // do something with the contact
}
```

Xamarin Mobile is currently very early in development and is focusing only on the areas shown in Figure 12-3.

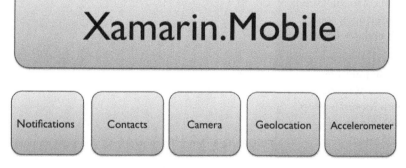

FIGURE 12-3: Xamarian Mobile features

With a fundamental understanding of how the Mono framework, MonoTouch, Mono for Android, and Xamarin Mobile interact with one another, you can move on to setting up a development environment.

GETTING THE TOOLS YOU NEED

The leadership for the Mono project is all open source advocates, and as such many of the tools required for creating mobile apps based on Mono are open source. Some companies, usually larger companies, may have strict policies about not allowing open source projects into production code. Often these polices stem from the licenses that some open source projects use, or management not willing to trust that a community-funded project will be able to succeed because if the company has issues with the product, oftentimes there is no one call to ask for support.

This chapter shows examples created within Mac OS X, and makes mention of when a particular tool can be installed within Windows as well

Mono Framework

Installing the Mono Framework is a relatively simple process. The Mono Framework is required for the remaining tools in this chapter to be installed. To find the latest version of Mono, navigate to `http://www.go-mono.com/mono-downloads/download.html` and install the latest stable version for your platform. The examples in this chapter are for Mac OS X because MonoTouch is supported only on Mac OS X, but if you are working on a Windows machine, you will be able to work with Mono for Android. After the Mono Framework is installed, you can check the version by executing `Mono --version` in a terminal session. The output of this command lists version information as shown in Figure 12-4.

MonoDevelop

MonoDevelop is an open source IDE supported under the Mono project. In 2003 developers forked another open source IDE named Sharp Develop into the MonoDevelop IDE. MonoDevelop has a large open source community following, with updates being published frequently.

MonoDevelop is supported on multiple platforms, with Mac OS X and Windows included. To get started with MonoDevelop, simply download the version for your platform from the download page (`http://monodevelop.com/Download`) and follow the install instructions. MonoDevelop is dependent on the Mono Framework, and if you have not already installed the Mono Framework, you will be prompted to do so.

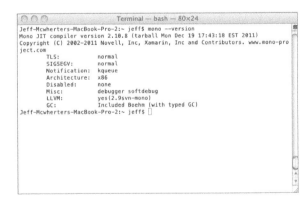

FIGURE 12-4: Mono Framework version from terminal

After MonoDevelop has been installed, you should be able to start the product and have a screen that looks similar to Figure 12-5.

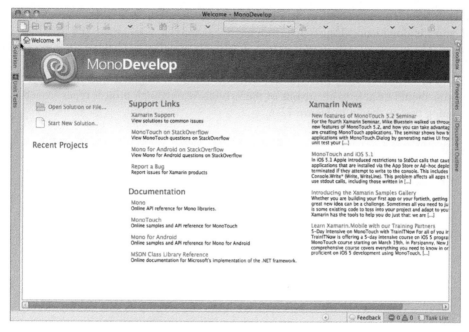

FIGURE 12-5: MonoDevelop start screen

Mono/MonoDevelop follow many of the same conventions that .NET and Visual Studio follow. Class files belong to project files and project files belong to solutions. If you have worked with Visual Studio in the past, you should feel right at home with this product.

The MonoDevelop IDE is used to create solutions written in various languages that can be run on the CLR. This means there is support for a great number of languages/frameworks ranging from ASP.NET MVC to Silverlight (Moonlight on Mono). MonoDevelop is the IDE that you use to create both Android and iOS applications with Mono for this chapter.

MonoTouch

The MonoTouch toolset has a very close relationship to xCode and the iOS SDK. Because of this close-knit relationship, MonoTouch can be run only on a Mac and cannot be installed on a Windows machine. This means that before you start to install MonoTouch, you should ensure that you have the iOS SDK and xCode installed. This was discussed in depth in Chapter 7.

MonoTouch is a commercial product offered through Xamarin and currently is licensed to developers, meaning that if you have a team of five developers working on a MonoTouch app, you will need to purchase five licenses from Xamarin. A full version of MonoTouch enables developers to deploy, build, and run MonoTouch apps on physical iOS devices. An unlicensed version enables developers to build and run MonoTouch apps on the iOS Simulator.

To get started with MonoTouch, you must install the MonoDevelop IDE. After MonoDevelop has been installed, you can download MonoTouch from `http://xamarin.com/trial` and install it using the installer. The installer is straightforward — it's simply a matter of clicking the Next button a few times. If for some reason a prerequisite for the install is missing, the MonoTouch installer will prompt you to install the missing prerequisite. After the install is complete and you restart MonoDevelop, you should be able to create one of the various MonoTouch project types from the New Solution dialog box as shown in Figure 12-6.

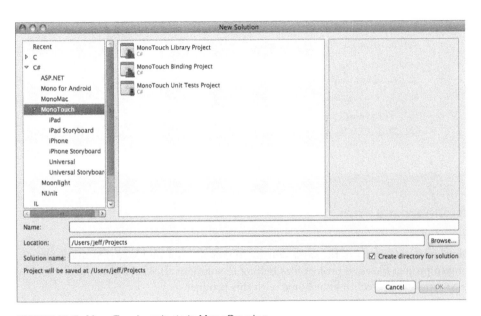

FIGURE 12-6: MonoTouch projects in MonoDevelop

Mono for Android

Mono for Android has a few options in regards to platforms and IDEs. Mono for Android can be run on either Mac OS X or Windows. If you decide on the Windows option you can use either MonoDevelop or Visual Studio to create Android apps. Whether you decide on Mac OS X or Windows, you can download Mono for Android from `http://xamarin.com/trial`. The prerequisites are similar to MonoTouch (Mono Framework, GTK+, MonoDevelop) with the addition of the Android SDK. Both the Mac OS X and Windows versions of Mono for Android check for the prerequisites and assist you with installing them if they are missing. After you have installed Mono for Android and started MonoDevelop, you should be able to create one of the various Mono for Android project types as shown in Figure 12-7.

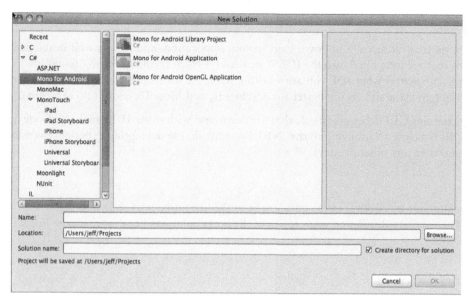

FIGURE 12-7: Mono for Android projects in MonoDevelop

Visual Studio Support

If you are familiar with Visual Studio, and plan to go down this development path, it's important to note that Visual Studio Express is not supported because of its lack of support for plug-ins. After you have installed Mono for Android, as mentioned previously, you will then need to install the Mono Tools for Visual Studio, which you can find at `http://mono-tools.com/download/`. This enables you to use Visual Studio to create solutions targeted at the Mono Framework, and in this case Mono for Android projects.

The examples in this chapter have been created using MonoDevelop on Mac OS X, but should function the same within Visual Studio in Windows.

GETTING TO KNOW MONODEVELOP

Xamarin is working to deliver a fully integrated solution for developers with knowledge of .NET to create apps for iOS and Android. It put a great deal of effort, along with other open source developers, to contribute to the IDE where MonoTouch and Mono for Android apps are created. The integration of MonoTouch and Mono for Android was very well thought out, and if you are already familiar with MonoDevelop it will be intuitive on how these products fit together.

MonoDevelop is not bloated full of features that most developers will never use. Its simple user interface enables developers to rapidly find tools they need when they are unfamiliar with the product.

Debugging

It can be extremely frustrating to hunt down bugs in your application, and having well-developed debugging tools that are integrated into the IDE is very useful when trying to resolve issues in your app quickly. No matter what IDE you are working with, the teams that develop the IDEs are constantly working to make debugging better for developers, and MonoDevelop is no exception.

MonoDevelop contains GUI debugging tools that are consistent with other IDEs such as xCode and Visual Studio. With a close relationship to the .NET Framework, the debugging experience is more like Visual Studio than any other product.

Breakpoints

You can set breakpoints by clicking in the gutter next to the line number as shown in Figure 12-8. When you are debugging your app, and the breakpoint has been reached, the line will be highlighted.

```
 8    namespace DerbyNames_MonoTouch
 9    {
10        public partial class LeaguesController : UIViewController
11        {
12            public LeaguesController () : base ("LeaguesController", null)
13            {
14                Title = NSBundle.MainBundle.LocalizedString ("Team Names", "Team Names");
15            }
16
17            public override void ViewDidLoad ()
18            {
19                base.ViewDidLoad ();
20                UITableView tableView;
21
22                List<League> fullLeagueData = Network.GetLeagueData();
23                List<string> data = new List<string>();
24                fullLeagueData.ForEach(leagueName => data.Add(leagueName.LeagueName));
25
26                tableView = new UITableView();
27                tableView.Delegate = new TableViewDelegate(data,this);
28                tableView.DataSource = new TableViewDataSource(data);
29                tableView.Frame = new RectangleF (0, 0, this.View.Frame.Width,this.View.Frame.
30
31                this.View.AddSubview(tableView);
32            }
33
34            public override void ViewDidUnload ()
35            {
```

FIGURE 12-8: Breakpoints within MonoDevelop

MonoDevelop provides tools to Step Over, Step Into, and Step Out on the Debug toolbar shown in Figure 12-9.

FIGURE 12-9: MonoDevelop Debug toolbar

Locals

The locals window shows you a list of all of the variables that are currently within scope of your current breakpoint, and enables you to view details about each variable. Figure 12-10 shows the locals window with an object named fullLeagueData that has a count of 908 items. If you wanted to see more information about the items in the `fullLeagueData` object, you could click the array next the variable name and drill into the data contained within.

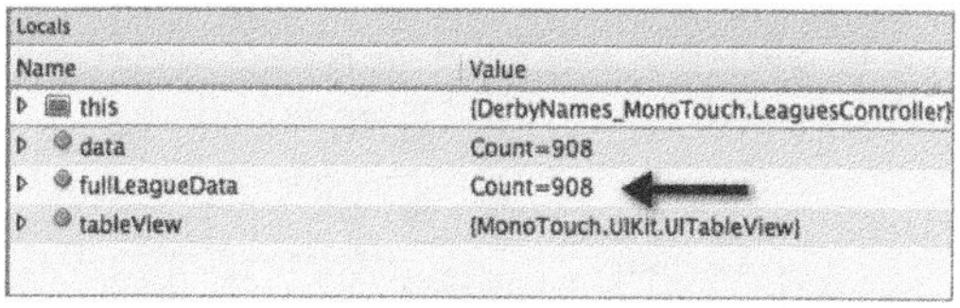

Call Stack

When hunting for bugs, it's useful to follow the execution path of a particular feature, in hopes of finding the issue. Figure 12-11 shows the Call Stack window within MonoDevelop.

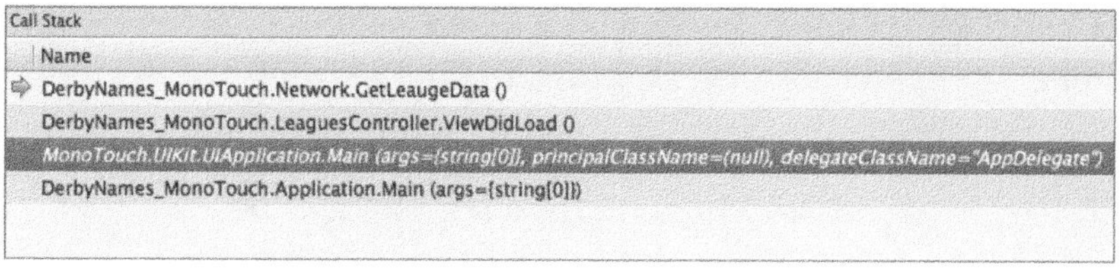

FIGURE 12-10: Locals window in MonoDevelop

FIGURE 12-11: Call Stack window in MonoDevelop

Output

The Application Output section provides important information about the execution of the app, as well as displays any log messages you may add in your code. Figure 12-12 shows the application output of an MonoTouch application that logged information received from a web service.

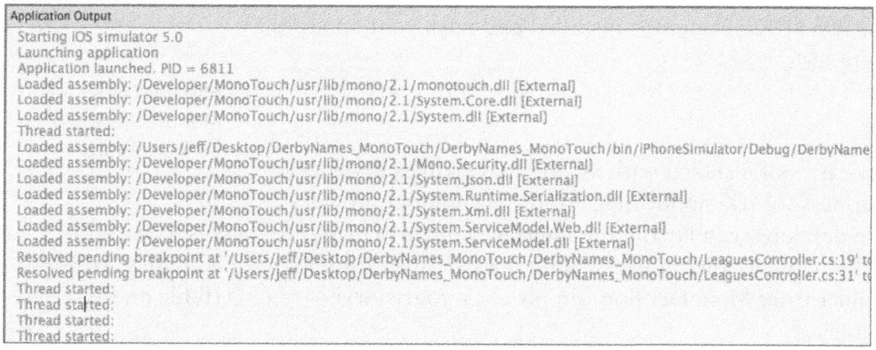

FIGURE 12-12: Application Output window in MonoDevelop

MonoTouch Specifics

When you install MonoTouch, new tools are added to the MonoDevelop IDE that will aid in your creation of iOS apps. These tools are specific to iOS apps and provide a range of functionality, such as creating a new iOS project type, as shown in Figure 12-13, to deploying your newly created app to a physical iOS device.

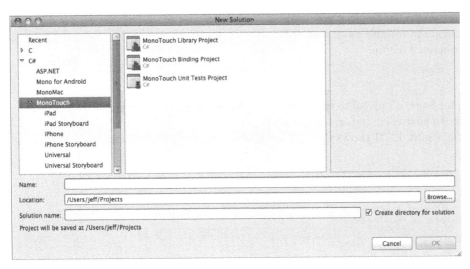

FIGURE 12-13: MonoTouch project types

iOS Simulator

Build configurations allow developers to create different build settings for different build scenarios. Every newly created MonoTouch app preconfigures four different build configurations, two for deploying to the iOS simulator and two for deploying to a physical device. Figure 12-14 shows the build configurations for a MonoTouch iPhone-only app.

When the iOS simulator is selected as an option in the build configuration, MonoDevelop/MonoTouch will launch the iOS simulator that was installed when the iOS SDK/xCode was installed and push your app to the simulator for you to test.

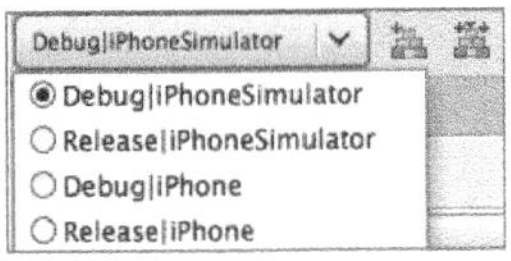

FIGURE 12-14: MonoTouch build configurations

Interface Builder

Interface Builder is the tool included with xCode that enables developers to create user interfaces for iOS applications. Interface Builder provides tools with which a developer can lay out the interface, and also map the controls to the events/functions that will be called. Interface Builder can open storyboard or XIB files. To work with Interface Builder from MonoDevelop, simply click your storyboard or XIB file and Interface Builder will be launched.

This interaction between MonoDevelop and xCode/Interface Builder can be somewhat fragile. Behind the scenes, MonoDevelop generates a temporary xCode project that contains stubbed-out Objective-C functions that match the C# classes, which allow the classes to be accessed from Interface Builder and synchronized back to MonoDevelop.

Mono for Android Specifics

When Mono for Android is installed, a set of tools specific to working with the Android platform is installed, and linked within the MonoDevelop IDE. The most notable of these tools are the tools pertaining to the Android emulator. MonoDevelop can deploy your newly created Mono for Android app to a physical Android device or an emulator.

The communication between MonoDevelop and the Android emulators is another one of those "fragile" areas. It's best to use the tools within MonoDevelop to start the emulators. By default the debug build configuration deploys your Mono for Android app to an emulator. The screen in Figure 12-15 is presented, which allows you select or create an AVD. If you are unfamiliar with the AVD concept, please see Chapter 6.

The list of AVDs enumerated in MonoDevelop is the same list of AVDs enumerated in the Eclipse AVD Manager as shown in Figure 12-16.

FIGURE 12-15: Android emulator selection

AVD Name	Target Name	Platform	API Level	CPU/ABI	
⌄ titanium_1_HVGA	Android 1.6	1.6	4	ARM (armeabi)	New...
⌄ titanium_2_HVGA	Android 1.6	1.6	4	ARM (armeabi)	Edit...
⌄ MonoForAndroid_A	Android 2.1	2.1	7	ARM (armeabi)	
⌄ Android-2.2	Android 2.2	2.2	8	ARM (armeabi)	Delete...
⌄ Android2_22	Android 2.2	2.2	8	ARM (armeabi)	Repair...
⌄ Archos_10i	Android 2.2	2.2	8	ARM (armeabi)	
⌄ MonoForAndroid_A	Android 2.2	2.2	8	ARM (armeabi)	Details...
⌄ titanium_4_HVGA	Android 2.2	2.2	8	ARM (armeabi)	Start...
⌄ titanium_5_HVGA	Google APIs (Google Inc.)	2.2	8	ARM (armeabi)	
⌄ Galaxy	GALAXY Tab Addon (Samsung Elec	2.2	8	ARM (armeabi)	
⌄ 2.3.3	Android 2.3.3	2.3.3	10	ARM (armeabi)	
⌄ DEMO	Android 2.3.3	2.3.3	10	ARM (armeabi)	
⌄ MonoForAndroid_A	Android 2.3.3	2.3.3	10	ARM (armeabi)	
⌄ MonoForAndroid_A	Android 3.1	3.1	12	ARM (armeabi)	
⬚ Android-4	Android 4.0	4.0	14	ARM (armeabi-v7a)	
⬚ MonoForAndroid_A	Android 4.0	4.0	14	ARM (armeabi-v7a)	
					Refresh

List of existing Android Virtual Devices located at /Users/jeff/.android/avd

⌄ A valid Android Virtual Device. ⬚ A repairable Android Virtual Device.
✗ An Android Virtual Device that failed to load. Click 'Details' to see the error.

FIGURE 12-16: Eclipse AVD Manager

It's important to note that the trial version of Mono for Android allows apps to be deployed only to the emulator. A full license is required if you want to deploy to a physical device.

With the development environments installed and the basics of debugging covered, you can now examine what exactly makes up a MonoTouch and Mono for Android project with regard to files and code.

MONO PROJECTS

The developers on both the MonoTouch and Mono for Android projects have spent a great deal of time making the development experience as similar to using the recommended native tools as possible. Core programming concepts from iOS will transfer to MonoTouch, as will concepts from

Android. Chapters 6 and 7 cover these core concepts and will be important for you to understand before jumping into learning MonoTouch and MonoDevelop. Understanding how to write apps using the "iOS way" and the "Android way" will help you interface with the MonoTouch and Mono for Android frameworks, as well as research issues when you encounter them.

Anatomy of a MonoTouch App

The MonoTouch structure shown in Figure 12-17 represents a newly created tabbed application type. If you have gone through Chapter 7, this structure should look very familiar. As with native iOS apps, MonoTouch apps use an MVC design pattern keeping UI and business logic separated. The following is a list of files and their function for a newly created MonoTouch tabbed application type.

➤ `Main.cs`: As with most other C programs, the execution of C# applications start from the `main()` function, which is located in the `main.cs` file.

➤ `AppDelegate.cs`: The `AppDelegate` receives messages from the application object during the lifetime of your application. The `AppDelegate` is called from the operating system, and contains events such as `didFinishLaunchingWithOptions`, which iOS would be interested in knowing about.

➤ `ViewController.cs`: The view controller classes contain the business logic that is passed to the UI views.

➤ `ViewController_iPhone.xib`: `ViewController` XIB files contain the user interface for the MonoTouch app.

➤ `ViewController_iPad.xib`: When a universal iOS app is created, `.xib` files are created for both iPhone and iPad. These files contain the UI specific to the iPad.

➤ `Info.plist`: This `plist` file contains configuration settings that are specific to the app.

The example MonoTouch project in Figure 12-17 shows the user interface created in XIB files. Chapter 7 discussed creating iOS user interfaces using the Storyboard concept. MonoTouch also provides project types to create Storyboards in addition to XIB files.

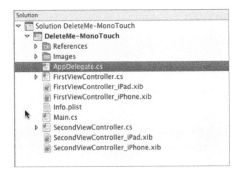

Project Options

To "polish" an iOS application and make it ready for deployment, numerous settings such as setting the provisioning profile and device orientation are extremely important in the deployment process, but seem to be hidden within MonoTouch and the MonoDevelop IDE. If you find yourself looking for a setting and can't seem to find it, it could be hidden under the project Options

FIGURE 12-17: MonoTouch project structure

setting, which you can find by right-clicking the project and selecting Options as shown in Figure 12-18.

Build Options

Figure 12-19 shows the build options for the iOS project. Options on this dialog box enable you to select which iOS SDK your app will run on. This dialog box also contains advanced features, such as the linker behavior. Earlier in this chapter we mentioned that all MonoTouch apps include a custom-built version of the Mono Framework, containing only features used in the related app. By default, debug versions running on the simulator do not link the assemblies, therefore the entire Mono Framework is included. This is because the time it takes to link the assemblies is greater than the time it takes to just include the entire framework with the app, which means making debugging much faster.

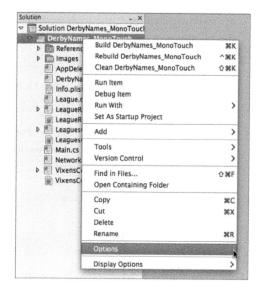

FIGURE 12-18: MonoTouch project options

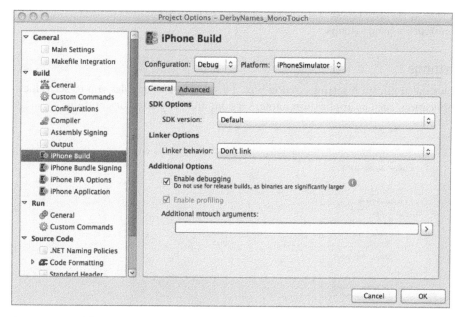

FIGURE 12-19: MonoTouch build settings

iOS Signing Options

In our opinion, one of most difficult concepts of iOS for new developers is the concept of certificates and provisioning profiles. Figure 12-20 shows the iOS signing options that enable you to relate both a certificate and a provisioning profile to your MonoTouch app. Certificates and provisioning profiles are still installed using the tools within xCode, and will show up automatically in this interface to use in your app.

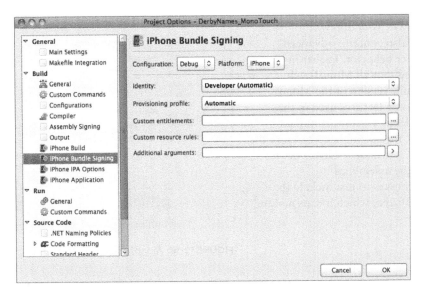

FIGURE 12-20: MonoTouch signing settings

Application Settings

Figure 12-21 shows the application settings dialog box. This dialog box enables you to set values specific to the application, such as application name, version, and supported orientations.

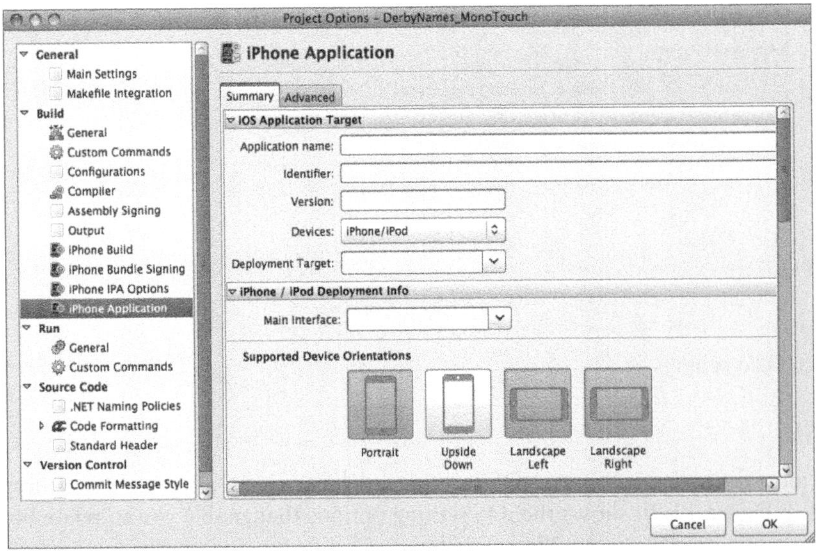

FIGURE 12-21: MonoTouch application settings

Anatomy of a Mono for Android App

The structure in Figure 12-22 represents a newly created Mono for Android application. If you have read through Chapter 6, this structure should look very familiar.

The following is a list of files and their function for a newly created Mono for Android application.

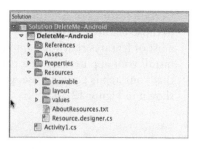

➤ **Assets:** The Assets directory contains assets such as sound files or other nonimage assets your Mono for Android app may use.

FIGURE 12-22: Mono for Android project structure

➤ **Drawable:** The Drawable directory contains images that will be used throughout your Mono for Android application.

➤ **Layout:** The Layout directory contains the user interface XML files that are used to render the UI on Mono for Android apps.

➤ **Values:** As with the convention that native Android apps use, the Mono for Android framework has a great deal of tools built in for localization of apps. The values for each localization schema are stored in the Values directory.

➤ **Activity:** The convention for an `Activity` is the same in Mono for Android as it is with native Android apps written in Java. The convention is that each activity should reside in its own class, which inherits from the Android `Activity` type. In the example in Figure 12-22, there is only one activity.

Project Options

Mono for Android behaves similarly to MonoTouch when it comes to linking development builds, with a few exceptions. By default debug builds do not link the Mono framework. The Mono Framework is installed as a separate library named Mono Shared Runtime for debug builds. Release builds link to a custom-built Mono Framework build containing only the features that your app uses. For debug builds, these settings can be changed using the build settings as shown in Figure 12-23.

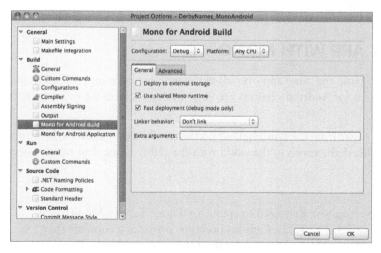

FIGURE 12-23: Mono for Android linker settings

Certain features of Android apps require permission from the user before the app can gain access to those features. Before users install your app on their mobile devices, they will be prompted with a list of features that your app will be using, providing the opportunity for the user to opt not to install your app because of a particular feature. In the Mono for Android app, to enable the features that your app is going to use, you must use the Mono for Android Project Options dialog box as shown in Figure 12-24.

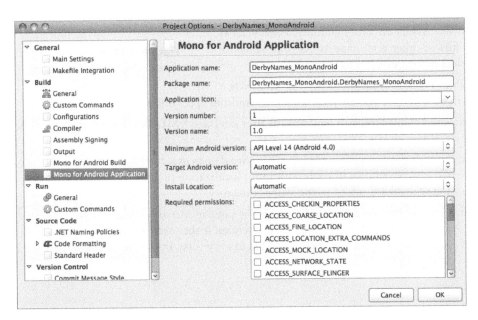

FIGURE 12-24: Mono for Android permissions

The intention of this section was to give you an idea of the project structure, and basic interaction between the UI and code. To build upon this, you will now tackle a more complex native MonoTouch and Mono for Android app.

BUILDING THE DERBY APP WITH MONO

The idea of the Derby App is to build the same app over all of the mobile platforms covered in this book. The MonoTouch and Mono for Android versions are very similar to the other versions that you have built thus far.

The requirements are to list the roster from the Lansing Derby Vixens roller derby team as the primary function, and then list all the roller derby teams in the world with the ability to see their team rosters.

MonoTouch

For the iOS version of the Derby App, you first need to create an iPhone Tabbed MonoTouch application as shown in Figure 12-25. The Tabbed application type provides a template that contains two views linked to a tab controller that you can use to start your project. The iPhone project type was selected because the only interface to the Derby App that has been shown has been a mobile phone interface, not a tablet interface. The Storyboard option was not selected, just to provide additional examples of how to work with user interfaces within iOS and Interface Builder.

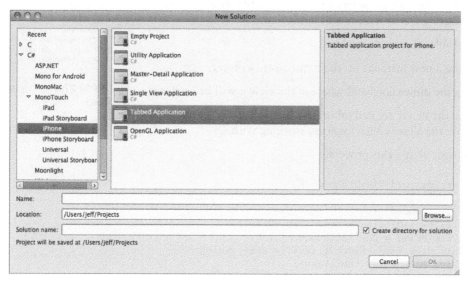

FIGURE 12-25: Tabbed MonoTouch iPhone app creation

User Interface

When it boils down to it, the Derby App does not contain a complex user interface. All of the screens are simply lists of data. When the user interface is simple, creating the controls within code is oftentimes an option. For the MonoTouch Derby App, the `UITableView` controls are created and added programmatically.

To get started, rename the first view code and XIB file from `FirstViewController` to `VixensController`. For the code files, it's best to right-click the class name and select the Rename option from the Refactor menu as shown in Figure 12-26. This ensures that all of the constructors and places that the class is initiated are changed as well.

With the first `ViewController` renamed, your project should look similar to the project shown in Figure 12-27.

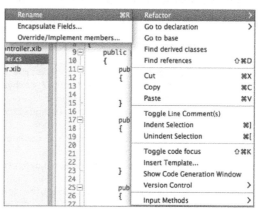

FIGURE 12-26: Rename refactor within MonoDevelop

Creating the Vixen Table View

Just as with a native iOS app created in Objective-C, the
`ViewDidLoad` event is fired right after the `View` has loaded. Within
the `VixensController`, this is where the table view that contains the
list of all the Lansing Derby Vixens will be created.

FIGURE 12-27: First view renamed

Creating a UI Table view is as simple as:

➤ Creating a new instance of the `UITableView` object.

➤ Setting the dimensions and where in the view it will be rendered.

➤ Adding the newly created table view as a subview to the view (in
this case the Vixens View) you are working with.

The following code shows this process.

```
public override void ViewDidLoad ()
{
    base.ViewDidLoad ();
    UITableView tableView = new UITableView();
    tableView.Frame = new RectangleF (0, 0,
        this.View.Frame.Width,this.View.Frame.Height);
    this.View.AddSubview(tableView);
}
```

Populating the Vixens Table View

After the table view has been created, the data that will populate the view needs to be received. To
do this, I have created a helper class named `Network` that contains static helper functions that will
retrieve the data needed to populate the table views throughout the Derby App.

To get the roster of a team, the `GetRoster` function is called with the team name of the data you are
looking for. You have a few different methods within .NET to choose when it comes to mapping a
JSON response to an object. The following example simply loops through each of the JSON items
returned and manually builds the `DerbyName` object:

```
public static List<DerbyName> GetRoster(string leagueName)
{
List<DerbyName> tmpRtn = new List<DerbyName>();
    String requestURL = "http://derbynames.gravityworksdesign.com
        /DerbyNamesService.svc
        /DerbyNames?$filter=League%20eq%20'" + leagueName + "'";

    HttpWebResponse response = GetServiceResponse(requestURL);
    JsonObject fullJsonObject =
        (JsonObject)JsonObject.Load(response.GetResponseStream());

    var rosterData = fullJsonObject["d"];

    foreach (JsonObject singleEntry in rosterData) {
        tmpRtn.Add(new DerbyName(singleEntry["DerbyNameId"],
```

```
                    singleEntry["Name"],singleEntry["Number"]
                    ,singleEntry["League"]));
        }

        return tmpRtn;
    }

    private static HttpWebResponse GetServiceResponse (string url)
    {
        HttpWebResponse tmpRtn;
        var request = (HttpWebRequest) WebRequest.Create (url);

        tmpRtn = (HttpWebResponse) request.GetResponse ();

        return tmpRtn;
    }
```

The data that is returned is a list of DerbyName name objects for the team name that was passed in; in this case, "Lansing Derby Vixens."

After the data has been retrieved, you need to set the DataSource property on the TableView that will display the data. In this case, set the DataSource to a new TableViewDataSource object (which you will create in the future), passing it a list of strings that contains the names of the Lansing Derby Vixens. You can do this by adding the following code to the ViewDidLoad event:

```
public override void ViewDidLoad ()
{
    base.ViewDidLoad ();
    UITableView tableView;
    string teamName = "Lansing Derby Vixens";
    List<DerbyName> fullRosterData = Network.GetRoster(teamName);
    List<string> data = new List<string>();
    fullRosterData.ForEach(derbyName => data.Add(derbyName.Name));

    tableView = new UITableView();
    tableView.DataSource = new TableViewDataSource(data);
    tableView.Frame = new RectangleF (0, 0,
        this.View.Frame.Width,this.View.Frame.Height);
    this.View.AddSubview(tableView);
}
```

To fully bind the data to the table view, you need to implement a few more functions. Create these functions in a new class named TableViewDataSource, which was bound to the data source of the table view.

The TableViewDataSource class contains a constructor that contains the data that will be bound to the TableView, in this case a list of strings:

```
public TableViewDataSource (List<string> list)
{
    this.list = list;
}
```

For the table view to know how many rows it needs to select, you must implement the
RowsInSection method. In this case, you just return the count of the number of items in the list
object, which is the list of strings that you populated when the view loaded:

```
public override int RowsInSection (UITableView tableview, int section)
{
    return list.Count;
}
```

The magic really happens in the GetCell method. This method is called for the number of times
that was returned in the RowsInSection. In your code, create a new cell, get the data for the correct
position in the list object, and then return the cell you created, which will be added to the table:

```
public override UITableViewCell GetCell (UITableView tableView, NSIndexPath indexPath)
{
    UITableViewCell cell = tableView.DequeueReusableCell (kCellIdentifier);

    if (cell == null)
    {
        cell = new UITableViewCell (UITableViewCellStyle.Default,kCellIdentifier);
    }

    cell.TextLabel.Text = list[indexPath.Row];
    return cell;
}
```

When complete, the TableViewDataSource class contains two methods and one constructor:

```
private class TableViewDataSource : UITableViewDataSource
{
    static NSString kCellIdentifier = new NSString ("DerbyName");
    private List<string> list;

    public TableViewDataSource (List<string> list)
    {
        this.list = list;
    }

    public override int RowsInSection (UITableView tableview, int section)
    {
        return list.Count;
    }

    public override UITableViewCell GetCell (UITableView tableView,
        NSIndexPath indexPath)
    {
        UITableViewCell cell = tableView.DequeueReusableCell (kCellIdentifier);

        if (cell == null)
        {
            cell = new UITableViewCell (
            UITableViewCellStyle.Default,
                kCellIdentifier);
```

```
        }

        cell.TextLabel.Text = list[indexPath.Row];
        return cell;
    }
}
```

With the table view data wired, you should be able to run the app, (by pressing the run button in the toolbar) and view the Derby Vixen roster as shown in Figure 12-28.

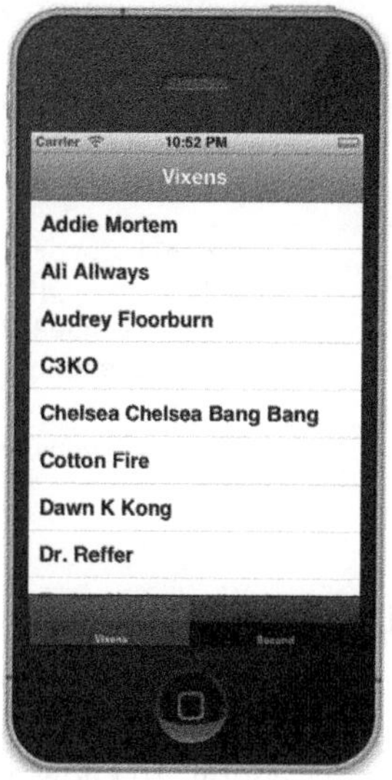

Leagues/Team Name

The Leagues tab lists all of the roller derby leagues in a `TableView`. The name of this controller is `LeagueController`. Creating the Leagues tab is very similar to the Vixens tab, with two exceptions. The first is the function that is called to obtain the data that is displayed in the list. Because this is a list of leagues, you will call the `GetLeagueData` function found in the network class. This function returns a list of `League` objects, returned from the `Derby` service.

FIGURE 12-28: Derby Vixens roster rendering in Table View

```
public static List<League> GetLeagueData()
{
    List<League> tmpRtn = new List<League>();
    string requestURL = "http://derbynames.gravityworksdesign.com
        /DerbyNamesService.svc/Leagues";

    HttpWebResponse response = GetServiceResponse(requestURL);
    JsonObject fullJsonObject =
        (JsonObject)JsonObject.Load(response.GetResponseStream());
    var leagueData = fullJsonObject["d"];

    foreach (JsonObject singleEntry in leagueData)
    {
        tmpRtn.Add(new League(singleEntry["LeagueId"],singleEntry["LeagueName"]));
    }

    return tmpRtn;
}
```

The second difference between the views is that the League Roster screen that lists the team members for the selected league should appear when a cell is touched on the leagues view. To accomplish this, within the `LeaguesController` code file, create a new delegate that derives from `UITableViewDelegate`. The `RowSelected` event is wired up inside this delegate, which simply creates a new `LeagueRoster` view (which you have not created yet), sets the team name you want to load, and then pushes the view to the iOS navigation stack to make the `LeagueRoster` view show.

```
private class TableViewDelegate : UITableViewDelegate
{
    LeaguesController leagueController;
    private List<string> list;
```

```
public TableViewDelegate(List<string> list, LeaguesController controller)
{
    this.leagueController = controller;
    this.list = list;
}

public override void RowSelected (UITableView tableView, NSIndexPath indexPath)
{
    LeagueRoster roster = new LeagueRoster();
    roster.TeamName = list[indexPath.Row];

    leagueController.NavigationController.PushViewController(roster,true);
}
}
```

League Roster

The `LeagueRoster` view is shown when a user selects a league/team from the team name page. The name of this view is `LeagueRoster`. This view is almost identical to the Vixens view with one exception. To know which league/team you are loading the roster for the name needs to be passed into this view. You can do this by adding a property named `TeamName` to the `LeagueRoster` class:

```
public string TeamName { get; set; }
```

The `GetRoster` function within the `ViewDidLoad` event uses the `TeamName` property instead of the hard-coded "Lansing Derby Vixens" value to retrieve the roster for the team name set in the `TeamName` property:

```
public override void ViewDidLoad ()
{
    base.ViewDidLoad ();
    UITableView tableView;

    List<DerbyName> fullRosterData = Network.GetRoster(this.TeamName);
    List<string> data = new List<string>();
    fullRosterData.ForEach(derbyName => data.Add(derbyName.Name));

    tableView = new UITableView();
    tableView.DataSource = new TableViewDataSource(data);
    tableView.Frame = new RectangleF (0, 0,this.View.Frame.Width,
        this.View.Frame.Height);

    this.View.AddSubview(tableView);
}
```

Figure 12-29 shows the roster view for a selected team.

Mono for Android

For the Android version of the Derby App, you first need to create a new Mono for Android application as shown in Figure 12-30. This will provide a simple Android app to which you will then be able to add your specific derby logic.

FIGURE 12-29: Roster View for team

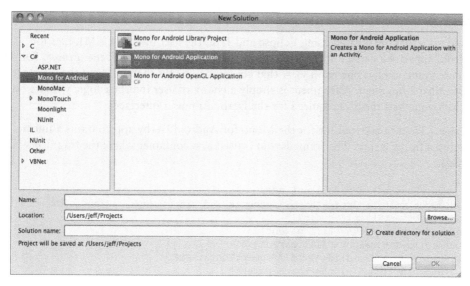

FIGURE 12-30: Creating a new Mono for Android project

This version of the Derby App is going to use a few Android features that were introduced with Android version 3.0, Gingerbread. To be on the safe side, for this project you will want to target the latest Android SDK. You will want to make sure that the Android project options have the minimum API level set to 14 for Android 4.0 as shown in Figure 12-31.

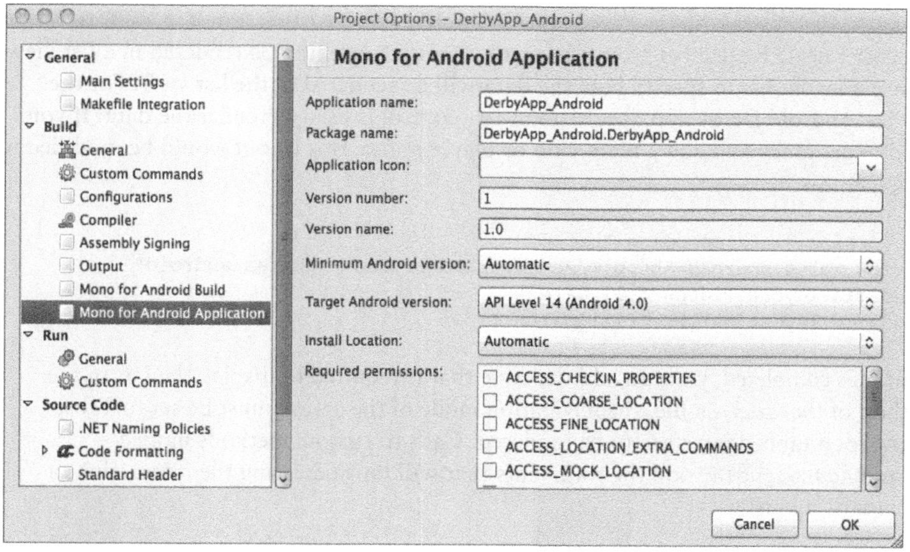

FIGURE 12-31: Setting the minimum SDK to the latest version

User Interface

As with Android apps that are created using Eclipse and Java, the user interface XML files for Mono for Android apps are located under the Resources ➪ Layouts directory of the project. For the Derby app you are going to have one main view that contains two tabs that will load the interface using a concept called a *fragment*. A fragment is simply a chunk of user interface logic with its own life cycle. The following lists the files required for the Derby App user interface:

➤ `Main.axml`: The Main layout file for the Mono for Android Derby app contains a linear layout and a frame layout. The frame layout is used as a container where the fragments will be loaded:

```
<?xml version="1.0" encoding="utf-8"?>
<LinearLayout xmlns:android="http://schemas.android.com/apk/res/android"
    android:orientation="vertical"
    android:layout_width="fill_parent"
    android:layout_height="fill_parent">
    <FrameLayout android:id="@+id/fragmentContainer"
        android:layout_width="match_parent"
        android:layout_height="0dip"
        android:layout_weight="1" />
</LinearLayout>
```

➤ `Tab.axml`: Each tab that is created for the Derby app will use `Tab.axml` for the interface. The tab's user interface is simply a list view that will render the data:

```
<ListView xmlns:android="http://schemas.android.com/apk/res/android"
    android:id="@+id/DerbyData"
    android:layout_width="wrap_content"
    android:layout_height="wrap_content" />
```

➤ `List_item.axml`: Remember from Chapter 6 that each item that is rendered in a list view will have a layout file to specify how the data will be rendered in the list view. For the Mono for Android Derby app, just a `TextView` control is used to render the data. If you wanted to get fancy and add a team icon or player photo, this layout would be modified to accomplish this:

```
<?xml version="1.0" encoding="utf-8"?>
<TextView xmlns:android="http://schemas.android.com/apk/res/android"
    android:layout_width="fill_parent"
    android:layout_height="fill_parent" />
```

With the layout files completed, you can add the code that is required to display the UI. In the `OnCreate` method of the `Main.cs` file, the navigation mode of the action must be set to Tabs, which will allow for a tabbed interface to be rendered. Calls to custom methods named `AddVixenTab` and `AddLeagueTab` add the fragments that will finish creating the interaction of the tab and the main layout:

```
protected override void OnCreate (Bundle bundle)
{
    base.OnCreate (bundle);

    SetContentView (Resource.Layout.Main);

    this.ActionBar.NavigationMode = ActionBarNavigationMode.Tabs;

    AddVixenTab ("Vixens");
    AddLeagueTab ("Teams");
}
```

To add the tabs to the Action Bar, first create an `ActionBar.New` tab with the text that will be rendered on the screen:

```
var tab = this.ActionBar.NewTab ();
tab.SetText (tabText);
```

After the tab has been created, you need to wire the `TabSelected` event to load the user interface of the tab that was selected. In this case the Vixen Tab was selected, therefore you should remove the `LeagueTab` from focus and display a new Vixen Tab to the user using fragments.

```
tab.TabSelected += delegate(object sender, ActionBar.TabEventArgs e) {
    m_vixenTab = new VixenTab();
    e.FragmentTransaction.Add (Resource.Id.fragmentContainer, m_vixenTab);
    e.FragmentTransaction.Remove(m_leagueTab);
};
```

After the `TabSelected` event has been wired, you simply need to add the newly created `ActionBar.Tab` to the `ActionBar` of the Derby App:

```
this.ActionBar.AddTab (tab);
```

Creating the tabs for both the Vixens and the Leagues/Teams names is similar, with the only exception of what is rendered in the tab (`VixenTab` or `LeagueTab`). The following code shows the completed logic for adding both the Vixens and Leagues tabs:

```
private void AddVixenTab (string tabText)
{
    var tab = this.ActionBar.NewTab ();
    tab.SetText (tabText);

    tab.TabSelected += delegate(object sender, ActionBar.TabEventArgs e) {
        m_vixenTab = new VixenTab();
        e.FragmentTransaction.Add (Resource.Id.fragmentContainer, m_vixenTab);

        e.FragmentTransaction.Remove(m_leagueTab);
    };

    this.ActionBar.AddTab (tab);
}
```

```
private void AddLeagueTab (string tabText)
{
    var tab = this.ActionBar.NewTab ();
    tab.SetText (tabText);

    tab.TabSelected += delegate(object sender, ActionBar.TabEventArgs e) {
        m_leagueTab = new LeagueTab();
        e.FragmentTransaction.Add (Resource.Id.fragmentContainer, m_leagueTab);

        e.FragmentTransaction.Remove(m_vixenTab);
    };

    this.ActionBar.AddTab (tab);
}
```

Getting The Vixens Roster

With the user interface complete, you can now complete the logic to render the data on the screen for the Vixens tab. The user interface that will be inflated for the Vixens tab is the Tab.axml. If you remember, this layout file contains only a ListView control:

```
var view = inflater.Inflate (Resource.Layout.tab, container, false);
```

To get the roster for the Lansing Derby Vixens, you call the static GetRoster function found within the Network class. This code is identical to the logic that was created for the MonoTouch app:

```
List<DerbyName> fullDerbyNameData = Network.GetRoster(teamName);
```

After the user interface has been inflated and the data has been received, you can bind the data to the ListView:

```
derbyData.Adapter = new ArrayAdapter<string> (container.Context,
    Resource.Layout.list_item, data.ToArray());
```

The following code shows the entire OnCreateView function for the Vixens tab:

```
public override View OnCreateView (LayoutInflater inflater, ViewGroup container,
    Bundle savedInstanceState)
{
    base.OnCreateView (inflater, container, savedInstanceState);

    var view = inflater.Inflate (Resource.Layout.tab, container, false);
    var derbyData = view.FindViewById<ListView> (Resource.Id.DerbyData);
    string teamName = "Lansing Derby Vixens";

    List<DerbyName> fullDerbyNameData = Network.GetRoster(teamName);
    List<string> data = new List<string>();
    fullDerbyNameData.ForEach(derbyName => data.Add(derbyName.Name));

    derbyData.Adapter = new ArrayAdapter<string> (container.Context,
        Resource.Layout.list_item, data.ToArray());

    return view;
}
```

Getting the Leagues and TeamName

The logic for creating the Leagues tab is similar to the logic used for creating the Vixens tab. First you call the static function `GetLeagues` found within the `Network` class to retrieve a list of leagues. Again this code is identical to the logic used in the MonoTouch Derby App to retrieve the leagues.

Also, the `ItemClick` event on the `derbyData` list view has been wired so that when it is clicked, a new activity is started that will display the roster for the team that was selected. To accomplish this, you create a new `Intent`, and save the `TeamName` as an extra that is pushed to the newly created activity:

```
derbyData.ItemClick += delegate (object sender, ItemEventArgs args) {
    string teamName = ((TextView)args.View).Text;
    Intent rosterList = new Intent(container.Context, typeof(LeagueRoster));

    rosterList.PutExtra("TeamName", teamName);
    this.StartActivity(rosterList);
};
```

The entire `OnCreateView` function for the Leagues tab is shown here:

```
public override View OnCreateView (LayoutInflater inflater, ViewGroup container,
    Bundle savedInstanceState)
{
    base.OnCreateView (inflater, container, savedInstanceState);

    var view = inflater.Inflate (Resource.Layout.tab, container, false);
    var derbyData = view.FindViewById<ListView> (Resource.Id.DerbyData);

    List<League> fullLeagueData = Network.GetLeagueData();
    List<string> data = new List<string>();
    fullLeagueData.ForEach(league => data.Add(league.LeagueName));

    derbyData.Adapter = new ArrayAdapter<string> (container.Context,
        Resource.Layout.list_item, data.ToArray());

    derbyData.ItemClick += delegate (object sender, ItemEventArgs args) {
        string teamName = ((TextView)args.View).Text;
        Intent rosterList = new Intent(container.Context, typeof(LeagueRoster));

        rosterList.PutExtra("TeamName", teamName);
        this.StartActivity(rosterList);
    };

    return view;
}
```

Getting The Team Roster

The pattern of pushing data to a list view should be starting to look very familiar to you by now. The team roster view again is the same concept. The `LeagueRoster` class inherits from `ListActivity` so there is no need to inflate the user interface that contains the `ListView` control.

Also, to load the team roster, you need to get the `TeamName` that was passed into the `Activity`. You can do this by calling the `GetStringExtra` method found within the `Intent`. In this case, if one is not passed in, you default to "Lansing Derby Vixens":

```
string teamName = Intent.GetStringExtra("TeamName") ?? "Lansing Derby Vixens";
```

The entire `onCreate` method for the `LeagueRoster` class is as follows:

```
protected override void OnCreate (Bundle bundle)
{
    base.OnCreate (bundle);

    string teamName = Intent.GetStringExtra("TeamName") ??
        "Lansing Derby Vixens";
    List<DerbyName> fullRosterData = Network.GetRoster(teamName);
    List<string> data = new List<string>();
    fullRosterData.ForEach(derbyName => data.Add(derbyName.Name));

    ListAdapter = new ArrayAdapter<string> (this, Resource.Layout.list_item,
        data.ToArray());
}
```

With all of the code in place, the Mono for Android Derby app should look similar to Figure 12-32.

OTHER USEFUL MONOTOUCH/MONO FEATURES

In the two example projects up to this point we have provided the basics for creating MonoTouch and Mono for Android applications that will go out to a web service and render the collected data on the screen. By no means do we feel that we have covered every possible situation you may need to develop a solution for, so we wanted to finish this chapter by providing a few more short examples that will help you out when discovering how MonoTouch and Mono for Android work.

Local Storage

Even if your application is using a web service for retrieving information, at some point you may need to save information on the device.

MonoTouch plist

For apps written in MonoTouch, property lists (plists) are the simplest way to store information on the device. In the Mac world, many applications use the plist format to store

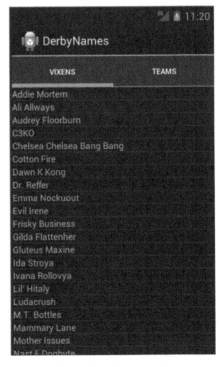

FIGURE 12-32: Mono for Android Derby App

application settings, information about the application, and even serialized objects. It's best to keep the data contained in these files simple, though.

Different variable types require different functions to retrieve and get the plist setting. The following example illustrates the different ways to retrieve and then save plist settings within MonoTouch:

```
var plist = NSUserDefaults.StandardUserDefaults;

// get plist item
string stringSetting = plist.StringForKey("StringSetting");
int intSetting = plist.IntForKey("myIntKey");
bool boolSetting = plist.BoolForKey("myBoolKey");

// save plist item
plist.SetString("string", "StringSetting");
plist.SetInt(1, "IntSetting");
plist.SetBool(true, "BoolSetting");

plist.Synchronize();
```

Mono for Android Shared Preferences

For apps written in Mono for Android, shared preferences are the simplest way to store information on the device. The Android framework enables shared preferences to be restricted to a single app, or even shared as world-readable/writable, allowing all apps to access these settings if you choose.

The following code illustrates saving and retrieving shared preferences:

```
// save shared preference item
ISharedPreferences saveSharedPreference = GetPreferences (FileCreationMode.Append);
ISharedPreferencesEditor editor = saveSharedPreference.Edit ();
editor.PutString ("StringSetting", "string");
editor.PutInt ("IntSetting", 1);
editor.PutBoolean ("BoolSetting", false);

editor.Commit ();

// get shared preference item
ISharedPreferences getSharedPreference = GetPreferences (FileCreationMode.Append);
string stringSetting = getSharedPreference.GetString ("StringSetting",
    "Default Value");

int intSetting = getSharedPreference.GetInt ("IntSetting", 1);
bool boolSetting = getSharedPreference.GetBoolean ("BoolSetting", true);
```

GPS

One of the great benefits of mobile devices is GPS functionality. Once you are able to get over the hurdles of learning the basic functions within MonoTouch and Mono for Android, working with the GPS functions can be a great deal of fun.

MonoTouch GPS

For MonoTouch, you can find the GPS functionality in the `MonoTouch.CoreLocation` namespace.
The `CLLocationManager` is the class you will be using to obtain the GPS information. Keeping
with the pattern on MonoTouch trying to match the Objective-C way of doing things, MonoTouch
uses the delegate design pattern to handle the location updates. Simply put, GPS in MonoTouch is
just a matter of:

> ➤ Instantiating a `CLLocationManager` object.

> ➤ Configuring settings on the `CLLocation` manager such as accuracy.

> ➤ Assigning a delegate that will handle the location updates.

The following code creates the `CLLocationManager` object, and tells it to start tracking
your location. You assign the delegate of the location manager object to an object named
`LocationDelegate`, which is a custom-created class.

```
CLLocationManager locationManager = new CLLocationManager ();

locationManager.Delegate = new LocationDelegate ();
locationManager.StartUpdatingLocation ();
```

The custom-created `LocationDelegate` object derives from `CLLocationManagerDelegate` and will
handle location updates when they occur. In this example, you simply write the new location to the
console:

```
public class LocationDelegate : CLLocationManagerDelegate
{
    public LocationDelegate () : base()
    {
    }

    public override void UpdatedLocation (CLLocationManager manager, CLLocation
        newLocation, CLLocation oldLocation)
    {
        Console.WriteLine(newLocation.Speed.ToString () + "meters/s");
        Console.WriteLine(newLocation.Coordinate.Longitude.ToString () + "°");
        Console.WriteLine(newLocation.Coordinate.Latitude.ToString () + "°");
        Console.WriteLine(newLocation.Altitude.ToString () + "meters");
    }
}
```

Mono for Android GPS

Mono for Android provides an interface named `ILocationListener` located in the `Android`
`.Locations` namespace that will allow GPS information to be collected from the device:

```
public class MonoForAndroidOther : Activity,ILocationListener
```

Before looking at the code, it's important to note that you must ensure that your app has permission
to obtain the level of GPS information you are looking to retrieve. Figure 12-33 shows a Mono for
Android app with both `ACCESS_COARSE_LOCATION` and `ACCESS_FINE_LOCATION` permissions set.

With the correct permissions set, you need to create a new `LocationManager` object when the activity first starts. This object manages the aspects of the location data that is being sent to your app from the operating system. You can set a `Criteria` object, which contains settings such as `Accuracy`, on the `LocationManager` to give you fine

FIGURE 12-33: Android location permission

control of the data that is being sent from the operating system. The `RequestLocationUpdates` function enables a developer to set how often the GPS data is being sent to your app, which is useful to help conserve battery life.

The following code example creates a new `LocationManager` with no `Accuracy` requirements. The last location is also retrieved and written to the console if it exists.

```
LocationManager locationManager =
    (LocationManager)GetSystemService(LocationService);

var criteria = new Criteria() { Accuracy = Accuracy.NoRequirement };
string bestProvider = locationManager.GetBestProvider(criteria, true);

Location lastLocation = locationManager.GetLastKnownLocation(bestProvider);

if (lastLocation != null)
{
    Console.WriteLine("Last location, lat: {0}, long: {1}", lastLocation.Latitude,
        lastLocation.Longitude);
}

locationManager.RequestLocationUpdates(bestProvider, 5000, 2, this);
```

When implementing the `ILocationListener`, the `OnLocationChanged` event is required. This event is fired when the location has changed. In the following example, the `Latitude` and `Longitude` are written to the console:

```
void ILocationListener.OnLocationChanged (Location location)
{
    Console.WriteLine("Location updated, lat: {0}, long: {1}",
        location.Latitude, location.Longitude);
}
```

SUMMARY

This chapter spent a great deal of time describing the MonoTouch and Mono for Android platform. After reading this chapter, you should be comfortable installing the development tools and getting started developing and debugging your first MonoTouch and Mono for Android app. Every development platform has trade-offs. As discussed in this chapter, the major downside to creating mobile apps with MonoTouch and Mono for Android is that they are third-party commercial products, which can leave you waiting for updates to the standard device SDKs and out of luck if the company goes out of business.

If you have a good working understanding of .NET and C#, creating mobile apps in MonoTouch and Mono for Android may be a viable option. If you or your team already has this understanding, you may be able to roll out your mobile app faster and cheaper. However, just understanding .NET is not enough. To develop MonoTouch and Mono for Android apps, a good working knowledge of the key components of an iOS and Android app are required to be successful.

INDEX

Q

R

S

U

Printed and bound by CPI Group (UK) Ltd, Croydon, CR0 4YY

09/06/2025

14685923-0005